Elementary Physics
COMPLETE EDITION

NOTE

This book is also
available in two
separate volumes

Volume 1—Chapters 1–15
Volume 2—Chapters 16–31

Elementary Physics
COMPLETE EDITION

A. F. ABBOTT, B.Sc.
Formerly Head of the Science Department
Latymer Upper School, London

AND

M. NELKON, M.Sc., A.Inst.P., A.K.C.
Formerly Head of the Science Department
William Ellis School, London

Second Edition in SI Units
revised by
MICHAEL SAYER, B.Sc.Tech., M.Inst.P.
Lecturer in Education
University of Keele

HEINEMANN EDUCATIONAL BOOKS
LONDON

Heinemann Educational Books Ltd
LONDON EDINBURGH MELBOURNE AUCKLAND TORONTO
SINGAPORE HONG KONG KUALA LUMPUR
IBADAN NAIROBI JOHANNESBURG
NEW DELHI

ISBN 0 435 67656 3

© A. F. Abbott and M. Nelkon 1971
First published in two volumes 1957
Reprinted 1957
Reprinted with additional exercises 1958
Reprinted 1959, 1960, 1962, 1963
Complete Edition
First published 1964
Reprinted 1966, 1969
Second Edition in SI Units 1971
Reprinted 1972, 1973

Published by
Heinemann Educational Books Ltd
48 Charles Street, London W1X 8AH
Printed and bound in Great Britain by
Butler & Tanner Ltd, Frome and London

Preface to Second Edition

This new edition of *Elementary Physics* retains most of the text of the first edition but with major revisions in certain areas which reflect present thinking in teaching methods.

It provides an introduction to physics for the first two or three years of a secondary school course leading to C.S.E. or to G.C.E. 'O' level.

The text and exercises have been completely revised so that SI units are used exclusively and the original order of chapters has been re-arranged to allow development of the subject in terms of energy relations, and to present in the early chapters material relevant to pupils' ordinary experience. Experiments derived from the Nuffield syllabus have been introduced, particularly wave-tank and oil-film observations, and experiments retained from the first edition have been re-written in the form of 'testing' or 'discovering' a principle in preference of 'verifying' it.

All the diagrams have been re-drawn and over fifty new photographs introduced with the object of illustrating the relevance and application of Physics to common situations.

M.S.
1971

Acknowledgements

We thank the following firms for permission to include the photographs which appear in this book.

Ever Ready Co. Ltd. (Plates 1 and 9); Marine Instruments Ltd. (Plate 3); Hallowes and Johnston Ltd. (Plate 4); Rapid Magnetting Co. Ltd. (Plate 5); Vactric Control Equipment Ltd. (Plate 6); Salisbury Photo Press (Plate 7); The Chloride Electric Storage Co. Ltd. (Plates 10 and 11); General Electric Company (Plates 12 and 13); Joseph Lucas Ltd. (Plate 14); Griffin & George Ltd. (Plates 15, 24 and 43); Mullard Ltd. (Plates 16 and 17); Cossor & Co. Ltd. (Plate 18); United Kingdom Atomic Energy Authority (Plates 19 and 47); Elsam, Mann & Cooper Ltd. (Plate 21); Associated Press Ltd. (Plates 22 and 23); M. Wiseman & Co. (Plate 25); J. J. Silber Ltd. (Plate 26); Mount Wilson and Palomar Observatories (Plate 27); B.I.P.S. (Plate 28); H. G. Zeal Ltd. (Plate 29); Hodgson, Northallerton (Plate 30); British Railways (Plates 31, 33, 37, 38, 41 and 45); Picture Post (Plates 32 and 52); National Physical Laboratory, Teddington (Crown copyright reserved) (Plates 34, 35 and 54); Radio Times Hulton Picture Library (Plates 36, 48, 49 and 53); London Transport Board (Plate 34); British Leyland Motor Corporation Ltd. (Plates 40 and 46); The Science Museum (Plate 42); Ferranti Ltd. (Plate 44); Merryweather and Sons Ltd. (Plate 50); Alcan Castings and Forgings Ltd. (Plate 51).

To the Pupil

A person may read and digest all the books he can get on the practical subject of say swimming, but he will never learn to swim until he enters the water to practise it. In like manner, people only become good scientists by spending time in a laboratory carrying out experiments. Seeing experiments performed or, better still, being able to do them yourself is of the greatest importance in understanding the methods and principles of science.

Faraday, one of the greatest scientists of the nineteenth century, performed many experiments over a period of years in his search for a way of making electricity from magnetism. As everyone knows, his labours eventually resulted in the invention of the dynamo. Faraday's original laboratory notebooks are now among the treasures of the Royal Institution. They show that he wrote a concise account of each experiment performed, illustrated, where necessary, by sketches and diagrams, together with the results and conclusion. The particular piece of research mentioned above was only one of the many problems on which Faraday was engaged, and he knew full well how important it was to be able to refer to the results of his earlier experiments to provide data for planning new ones.

Right from the start, therefore, you should accustom yourself to writing careful accounts of the experiments you have performed or seen demonstrated. Your teacher will explain the details of writing up a notebook usually observed in your particular laboratory. Generally speaking, it will be found useful to do this under the following headings:

1. TITLE AND DATE

2. DIAGRAM
    Draw neat sketches, using a ruler and a pencil with a sharp point. Label or letter the diagram.

3. ACCOUNT OR METHOD
    Carefully go over the experiment again in your mind, look at the measurements taken and write your account in the order in which they were done. Mention particularly any precautions taken to get an accurate result, and any obvious sources of error. Refer also to the diagram in your account, especially in a demonstration, so that your teacher can follow your description.

4. MEASUREMENTS
    Write down your measurements one below the other. Arrange all equal signs, decimal points and figures so that they are in line in a vertical column and give the units, e.g. gm, $°C$, or cm, beside each figure.

TO THE PUPIL

5. RESULT OR CONCLUSION

(a) Always give the units of your final result. e.g. the density of copper = 8·9 gm per c.c.

(b) Be especially careful to refrain from giving absurd results. For example, a boy once gave his final result for the density of copper as 8·92357 gm per c.c. It turned out that there were more figures after the 7 in his final division sum, but fortunately he was too tired to go on. In his experiment, the boy was only able to make the necessary measurements of mass and volume to two significant figures. Consequently he was wasting his time in working out the result to more than two significant figures, and the last "2357" in the above result is both inaccurate and meaningless.

Cover Photographs

Front Eruption in Hekla, Iceland, May 1970. (*Picture point Ltd*)

Back The Forth road and rail bridges, West Lothian, Scotland.
(*British Tourist Authority*)

Contents

1. Electric Current   1
The Electric Cell—Current—Potential Difference—Electric circuit; conductors and insulators—Connecting and Resistance Wire—The Rheostat—Carbon Microphone

2. Magnets   9
Early Magnets—The Compass—Modern Magnets—Properties of Magnets—Magnetic and Non-magnetic Substances—Ancient and Modern Methods of Making Magnets—Demagnetising a Magnet—Magnetic Differences between Iron and Steel—Magnetic Fields and Lines of Flux—Plotting Lines of Flux—Induced Magnetism with Mumetal—Magnetic Induction—Magnetic Separators

3. Magnetic Fields   21
Neutral Points with Bar-magnet—Effect of Soft Iron—Field between Parallel Bar-magnets—Theory of Magnetism—Molecular Theory of Magnetism—Experiments which support the Molecular Theory of Magnetism—Magnetic Keepers—The Earth's Magnetism—Angle of Dip (inclination)—Angle of Declination (variation)

4. Electromagnets   31
Magnetic Field round Straight Wire—Direction of Magnetic Field—Conventional Current—Circular Coil—Magnetic Field round Circular Coil—Solenoid—Magnetic Field round a Solenoid—Permanent Magnets—Electromagnets—Electric Bell Circuit—Magnetic Relay

5. Electrical Energy   41
Heating Effect—Applications—Cables and Fuses—Electric Filament Lamps—Electric Fluorescent Lamp—Chemical Effect of a Current—Uses of Electrolysis

6. Batteries, Motors and Generators   49
Simple Cell—Daniell and Leclanché Cells—Dry Battery—The Accumulator—Nife Cell—Moving-iron Instruments—

Moving-coil Ammeter and Voltmeter—Principle of Electric Motor—Induced Currents—Generators

7. Electric Charges 62
Early Discoveries—Positive and Negative Charges—Fundamental Law—Conductors and Insulators—Electric Charge in Atoms—Gold-leaf Electroscope—Testing the Sign (or Polarity) of Charges—Induced Charges—Charging an Electroscope by Induction—Franklin's experiment—The Lightning Conductor—Van de Graaff Generator

8. Electrons and Particles 71
The Electron—The Radio Valve—The Cathode-ray Tube—Photo-electric Cell—Atomic Particles—Nuclear Energy—Larger Particles—Moleculars

9. Acoustics 78
Sound and Vibration—Sound and The Medium—Sound Waves—Wave Tank Observations—Pressure variation in Sound Wave—Wavelength—Frequency—Pitch and Frequency—Seebeck's Disc—Amplitude and Loudness—Quality or Timbre—Echoes—Depth Sounding—Vibrations in Strings—Variation of Frequency with Length—Vibrations in Pipes—Resonance and Resonance-tube Experiment—Stationary Waves—Frequency of Vibrating Strings—Violin and Piano—Organ-pipe Frequency

10. Luminous Energy 95
Light Travels in Straight Lines—Rays of Light—The Ray Box—The Pinhole Camera—Shadows—Eclipses—The Nature of Light

11. Plane Mirrors 102
Reflection of Light—Laws of Reflection—Pin Method for Locating Images—Wave Tank Observations—Diffuse Reflection—Parallax—Locating Images by no Parallax—Study of the Image formed in a Plane Mirror—Looking into a Plane Mirror—How the Eye sees an Image in a Plane Mirror—Images formed in Two Mirrors inclined at 90°—The Kaleidoscope—Parallel Mirrors—The Periscope—Seeing Through a Brick—Pepper's Ghost

12. Curved Mirrors 115
Principal Focus—Wave Tank Observations—Difference between Large and Small Mirrors of Same Radius—Special Rays for Locating Images—Images formed by a Concave

CONTENTS

Mirror—Reflecting Telescope—Images Formed by a Convex Mirror—Accurate Construction of Ray Diagrams—Determination of the Focal Length of a Concave Mirror—Optical Formulae—Sign Convention—Magnification Formula

13. Refraction of Light   131
Wave Tank Observations—Some Effects of Refraction—Apparent Depth—Experiments on Refraction—The Laws of Refraction—Refractive Index—The Principle of Reversibility of Light—Total Internal Reflection—Critical Angle—Relation between Critical Angle and Refractive Index—Two Methods of Measuring Critical Angle and Refractive Index of Glass—Multiple Images Formed by a Silvered Glass Mirror—Total Internal Reflection in Prisms—The Mirage—Deviation of Light by a Triangular Prism

14. Lenses   144
Principal Focus of a Lens—Lenses compared with Prisms—Optical Centre of a Lens—Focal Length—A Lens has Two Principal Foci—Special Rays for Locating Images—The Magnifying Glass. Images formed by Converging Lens—Image formed by Diverging Lens—Accurate Construction of Ray Diagrams—Magnification—Determination of Focal Length of Convex Lens, using Plane Mirror—The Camera—The Eye—The Compound Microscope—Telescopes—Lens Formula and Calculations

15. Dispersion and Colour   161
Newton's Experiment with Prism—Production of a Pure Spectrum—Recombination of the Colours of the Spectrum—Colour of Objects in White Light—Light Filters—Appearance of Coloured Objects in Coloured Light—Primary and Secondary Colours—Mixture of Coloured Lights—Mixing Coloured Pigments

16. Radiation   168
Detecting Thermal Radiation: Thermocouples—Comparing the Radiation from Different Surfaces—Absorption of Radiant Heat by a Surface—Practical Uses of Thermal Radiation—The Vacuum Flask

17. Measurement of Temperature   173
Measurement of Temperature—Making a Mercury Thermometer—The Fixed Temperature Points—The Celsius Scale—Testing the Upper Fixed Point—Lower Fixed Point—Using a Thermometer to measure Temperature—The

Clinical Thermometer—Six's Maximum and Minimum Thermometer—The Choice between Mercury and Alcohol

18. Thermal Expansion 181
Gas Expansion—Comparison of the Thermal Expansion of Different Liquids—The Cubic Expansivity of a Liquid or Gas—Measuring the Apparent Expansivity—Expansion of Solids—Large Forces in Expansion—Disadvantages of Thermal Expansion—Uses of Thermal Expansion—Bimetal Strips—Compensation for Expansion in Clocks and Watches—Thermal Expansion in the Kitchen—The Gas Thermostat—Measuring Expansion in Solids

19. Convection 199
Convection in Liquids—Explanation of Convection Currents—Convection in Air—Land and Sea Breezes—The Domestic Hot Water Supply System—The Hot Water Central Heating System

20. Thermal Conduction 206
Good and Bad Conductors of Heat—Lagging—Handling Good and Bad Conductors—Ignition Point of a Gas—The Miner's Safety Lamp—Variation in Conductivity—Conduction of Heat through Liquid

21. Measurement of Length, Volume and Mass 213
Measurement in Physics—Measuring the larger distances—Dimensions of a Solid Body—The Vernier—Vernier Calipers—Measuring Shorter Distances—Volume of Liquids—Mass and Weight—The Common (Chemical) Balance—The Spring Balance

22. Stationary Forces 225
Forces—Types of Forces—How Forces are Represented—Turning Moments, or Torque—How Moments are Calculated—Clockwise and Anticlockwise Moments—Experiment to Demonstrate Definition of Torque—Other Examples of Torque—Principles of Levers—Further Example on Moments and Torque—Equilibrium of Parallel Forces—Position of Centre of Gravity—Locating Centre of Gravity—Stable, Unstable, Neutral Equilibrium—Practical Applications

23. Moving Forces: Work, Energy, Power 240
Work and Energy—Energy and its Sources—Mechanical Energy—The Conservation of Energy and Mass—Trans-

formation of Energy from One Kind to Another—Measurement of Work and Energy—Power

24. Thermal Energy Measurement 246
Calorimeters: Prevention of Thermal Losses—Thermal Capacity—Specific Heat Capacity—An Experiment to Find the Thermal Capacity of a Calorimeter—Measuring the Power of a Gas Burner—Calculation of Heat Energy Lost or Gained—Experiment to Find the Specific Heat Capacity of Copper—Calculation of Thermal Capacity of Calorimeter—To find Specific Heat Capacity of a Metal other than Copper—To find the Specific Heat Capacity of a Liquid

25. Latent Heat 257
Latent Heat of Vaporisation—Latent Heat of Fusion—Cooling Curve and Melting-point of Naphthalene—Cooling produced by Evaporation—Making Ice by the Evaporation of Ether—The Refrigerator—Latent Heat Calculations—Experiment to Determine the Specific Latent Heat of Ice: of Steam

26. Machines 268
The Lever—Mechanical Advantage—Mechanical Advantage of a Lever—Pulleys—The Single Fixed Pulley—The Single Moving Pulley—Direction of a Tension in a String—The First System of Pulleys—The Second System of Pulleys—Velocity Ratio (or Speed Ratio)—Work Done by a Machine—Efficiency—Experiment to show how the Practical Mechanical Advantage and Efficiency of a Pulley System vary with the Load—The Inclined Plane—Velocity Ratio and Mechanical Advantage of Inclined Plane—The Screw—The Wheel and Axle

27. Density and Relative Density 283
Density—Applications of Density—An Experiment to Determine the Density of Alcohol—To Find the Density of a Solid—Relative Density—To Find the Relative Density of a Liquid—The Relative Density of a Solid

28. Hydrostatics: Pressure 289
Atmospheric Pressure—Crushing Can Experiment—Meaning of Pressure—Pressure of Air—The Magdeburg Hemispheres—The Vacuum Pump—Pressure in a Liquid—Calculation of Pressure—A Liquid Finds its Own Level—Measurement of Gas Pressure by the Manometer—Torricelli's Experiment—Simple Barometer—Calculation of

ELEMENTARY PHYSICS

Atmospheric Pressure from Barometric Height—Pascal's Experiments with Barometers—The Fortin Barometer—The Aneroid Barometer and Altimeter—The Water Barometer—Deep Water Diving and High Flying—Boyle's Law—Verifying Boyle's Law by Plotting a Graph

29. Applications of Atmospheric and Liquid Pressure   307
The Suction Pad—The Common Pump—The Force Pump—Early Fire Pumps—The Preserving Jar—The Transmission of Pressure in Fluids—Hydraulic Pressure—Hare's Apparatus

30. The Principle of Archimedes   317
Upthrust of Liquid—Apparent Loss in Weight—Archimedes' Principle—Experiment to verify Archimedes' Principle for a Body in Liquid—Relative Density of a Solid using Archimedes' Principle—Relative Density of a Liquid using Archimedes' Principle—Relative Density of a Solid which Floats—Corks and Balloons—Ships, Cartesian Diver, Submarines—The Law of Flotation—An Experiment to Verify the Law of Flotation—Hydrometers

31. Parallelogram and Triangle Forces   327
Forces and their Resultant—Parallelogram of Forces—Experiment to verify Parallelogram of Forces Principle—Three Forces in Equilibrium—Triangle of Forces

Answers   335

Tables   339

Index   344

Part One

CHAPTER ONE

Electric Current

Physics is concerned with energy and the properties of materials, and the uses to which these can be put in ordinary life. Electrical energy is now the most commonly used source of energy for all purposes, since it can easily and efficiently be transferred into, for example, thermal energy in heaters, luminous energy in lamps, mechanical energy in motors, and acoustic energy in loudspeakers.

Nowadays electric current and its uses are so familiar that we are apt to forget the many useful items which would be missing from our everyday lives had we lived in 1850, for example. In those days there was no electric lighting of any kind, no radio, no television, no telephone, no electric trains, and none of the thousands of machines, such as vacuum cleaners and electric irons, which depend on electrical energy for their working.

The Electric Cell

The applications of electric current can be said to have begun about 1800 with the invention of the electric *cell* by Volta, a famous Italian scientist. Some years before, his friend Galvani had noticed that a dead frog's leg twitched when the nerve was touched by two unlike metals. Volta thought that the movement had something to do with the solution or liquid in the nerve and with the two metals used. Eventually, after years of experiments, he placed cloth soaked in brine between a number of copper and zinc plates, and found that a wire became warm when it was connected between the *poles,* or *terminals,* P, N, of the "pile", as it was called (Fig. 1 (i)). Nowadays we call one unit of the pile, that is, one copper and one zinc plate with brine between them, a *cell*; the whole arrangement of cells, that is, the pile, is called a *battery*.

The familiar *torch cell* is also made of two different substances, carbon and zinc, with chemicals inside the zinc container (Fig. 1 (ii)). *Accumulators* also contain two metallic substances, lead peroxide, and lead in sulphuric acid solution (Fig. 1 (iii)). One battery terminal or pole is called "positive", the other is called "negative"; sometimes the positive ($+$) terminal is painted red, or with a plus sign, and the other is painted blue or black, or with a negative sign. When representing cells

Plate 1. A torch cell, the modern form of dry Leclanché cell, gives 1·5 volt at up to 300 mA.

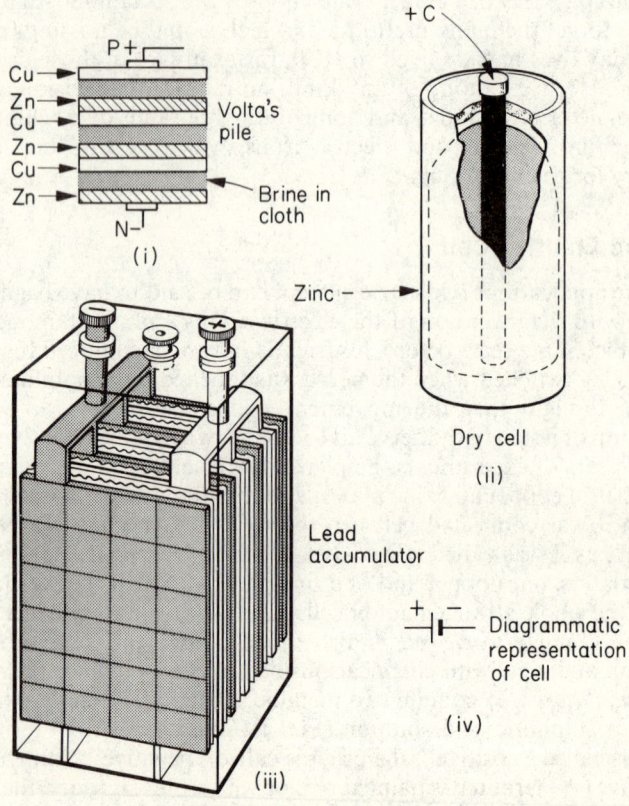

Fig. 1. Types of cells

(i) Volta's pile — Brine in cloth
(ii) Dry cell
(iii) Lead accumulator
(iv) Diagrammatic representation of cell

Plate 2. The coiled-coil filament of a lamp

in circuit diagrams, the positive pole is indicated by a thin line and the negative pole by a thicker, shorter line, as shown in Fig. 1 (iv). Details of batteries are discussed later.

Current

When a torch is switched on, the terminals of the battery are joined to the ends of a small tungsten wire in the bulb, the *filament,* which then glows brightly. We now say that an "electric current" flows in the wire. If the battery is run down, and a feeble glow is obtained, a smaller electric current then flows in the wire. The electric current is due to a flow along the wire of tiny particles called **electrons,** which are present in the atoms of the metal (see Chapter 8). The electrons flow out of the negative pole of the battery and return to the battery at its positive pole; that is, electrons are subtracted from the − terminal of the battery and added again at the + terminal. The total number of electrons in a battery is therefore always the same although the electrons flow through the battery when it is switched on.

The current in a wire or circuit is measured in **ampere,** abbreviated as A, after Ampère, a famous French scientist who made notable discoveries in electricity in 1821. Powerful electric motors, such as those used in electric trains or trolley buses may carry large currents of 200 A or more; smaller motors may carry currents of a few ampere; the current in an electric lamp filament may perhaps be $\frac{1}{2}$ amp.; the current in a radio receiver may be a few thousandths of an ampere. One thousandth of an ampere is called a *milliampere* (mA). A current of 1 A represents about 6 000 000 000 000 000 000 (or 6×10^{18}) electrons per second passing any point in the wire.

Potential Difference

A water-pump produces a difference of pressure, so that water in a pipe begins to flow when the pump is joined to the ends of the pipe. In the same way, we can look upon an electric battery as an "electric pump", which produces a difference of electrical pressure at its terminals or poles. When the poles of the battery are joined to a wire, the electrons in the metal are pushed along at a certain rate. If a more powerful battery is joined to the wire, the electrons flow at a faster rate. The electric current is greater in this case, and the wire would become hotter.

"Electrical pressure" is more properly called *potential*; "electrical pressure difference" is thus *potential difference* (*p.d.*). Potential difference is measured in **volt,** after Volta. The potential difference across the filaments (wires) in the electric lamps in buildings and houses is the potential difference at the mains terminals, about 240 volt. Batteries, used in transistor radios, have a p.d. of 6 or 9 volt between their terminals. An accumulator has a p.d. of 2 volt between its terminals; a torch battery is made up of units each having a p.d. of about $1\frac{1}{2}$ volt. Very high (and dangerous) p.d.s, about 11 000 volt, are produced by the dynamos at power stations. 1000 volt is called 1 kilovolt (kV).

Electric Circuit: Conductors and Insulators

A simple electric circuit is shown in Fig. 2 (i). The battery is represented by PN; it is connected to the filament F of a bulb D and to two separated metal terminals, A, B. A switch, represented by S, is also in the circuit.

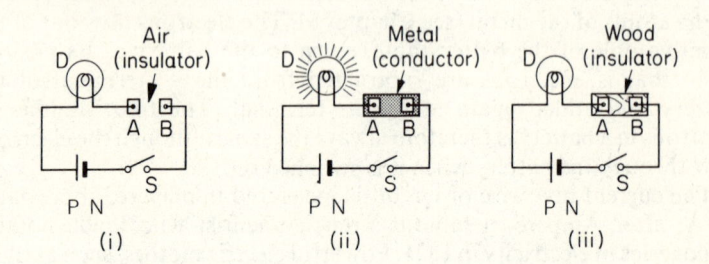

Fig. 2. Conductors and insulators in a simple circuit

Since the bulb in Fig. 2 (i) does not light up, we deduce that air does not normally conduct electric current. Air is called an *insulator*. It is fortunate that air is an insulator, otherwise the electric current along telegraph wires and high voltage cables above the ground would leak away into the air. When the blade of a pen-knife, or a coin or copper wire, is placed across A, B, the bulb lights up (Fig. 2 (ii)). All metals are electric *conductors*. The bulb also lights up when wires from A, B dip into acid and salt solutions, so these are also conductors. Glass, paper, wood, porcelain, cotton, rubber and all plastic materials do not make the bulb light up, and hence these substances are insulators (Fig. 2 (iii)). Flex has plastic or rubber and thread as insulators covering the copper wire inside it which conducts the current; telephone cables below the ground are similarly covered; submarine cables are surrounded by layers of insulating material, as well as by gutta-percha and other hard materials which prevent water entering and fishes biting their way through to the cable. Electric light switches have bakelite or plastic coverings for insulation.

Connecting and Resistance Wire

Silver is the best conductor; copper is the next best conductor and is much cheaper. Consequently connecting wire for all electrical circuits is made of pure copper, called "electrolytic copper" from the way in which it is manufactured; a slight impurity in copper makes it conduct much less, that is, its electrical *resistance* increases.

Pure metals generally have low resistance, but alloys have much higher resistance. *Resistance wire* is made of alloys with a high percentage of copper. *Nichrome* is widely used for heating coils in electric fires and cookers, and alloys called *eureka* and *manganin* are used for making resistance coils of various values.

In circuit diagrams, connecting wire is represented by a straight line, and resistance wire by a zig-zag line (Fig. 3 (i), (ii)). A resistance which can be altered, called a "variable resistance" or **rheostat,** is represented by a zig-zag line with an arrow through or touching it (Fig. 3 (iii)).

Electrical resistance is measured in **ohm,** after Ohm, a German scientist who investigated resistance in 1827. Radio and television receivers contain resistances of the order of millions of ohms and others of the order of thousands of ohms. An electric lamp filament, which is made of tungsten, may have a resistance of several hundred ohms. A small torch-bulb filament may have a resistance of a few ohms. The copper wire in the cable from a mains plug to a radio receiver in a room may have only a resistance of less than one-tenth of an ohm, as copper is a very good conductor.

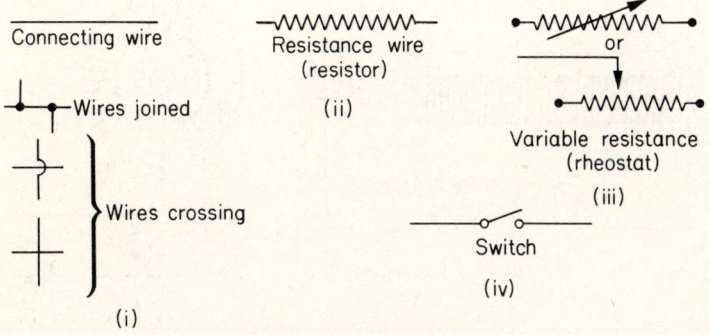

Fig. 3. Diagram symbols

The Rheostat

The rheostat, a variable resistance device, is used in theatres to dim the lights gradually. As we shall soon show, it controls smoothly the amount of electric current in the circuit.

In one form of rheostat, widely used in laboratories, a coil of eureka (resistance) wire is wound on a cylindrical porcelain frame between two terminals C, B (Fig. 4 (i)). The wire is insulated by its own coating of oxide, so that although the turns may actually touch they are separated electrically. A metal clip below S, which makes contact with the wire, can be moved along a brass bar by the holder S, called the "slider". Fig. 4 (i) shows a battery joined to the rheostat at C, A, with a bulb in the circuit. A current flows through *that part of the resistance wire between C and S* and through the part SA of the bar. The latter has negligible resistance, as brass is a good conductor like copper. When S is moved towards the terminal A the amount of resistance wire in the circuit increases; the current hence becomes smaller, and the bulb light becomes dimmer. When S is moved towards C the resistance decreases, and the bulb burns more brightly. There is no resistance wire in the circuit when S is moved to the end at C.

To economise in space, the resistance wire is sometimes wound between C, B on a circular frame, and the length of resistance wire is varied by turning a knob S (Fig. 4 (ii)). This is called a *rotary rheostat*. Rotary rheostats are used to control the sound volume in radio or television receivers, and to control the brightness of the picture in television sets.

Carbon Microphone

A *microphone* is a device which changes sound pulses to electric current variations. The earliest practical microphone was invented by Hughes in 1872, and basically the same kind of instrument is used today throughout the country in the telephone system. It contains two

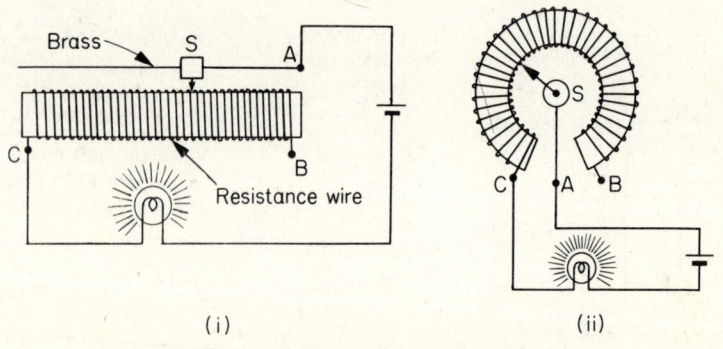

Fig. 4. Variable resistors (rheostats)

ELECTRIC CURRENT · 7

carbon blocks, CC, with carbon particles (A) between them in a container (Fig. 5). Large accumulators at the Post Office telephone exchanges represented by B, maintain a steady current which flows through the carbon particles.

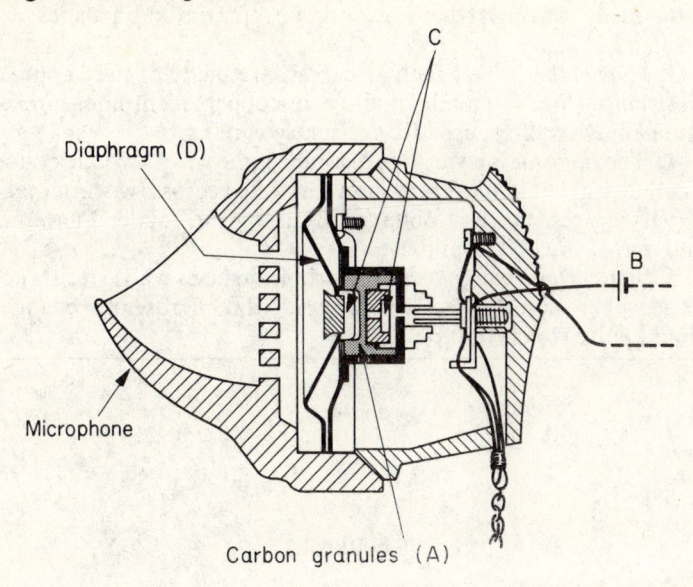

Fig. 5. Carbon microphone

When a person speaks into the mouthpiece, sound waves strike a diaphragm or cone D attached to one block C, and the carbon particles are alternately compressed and released in accordance with the varying pressure of the sound wave. When the particles are compressed together they have less electrical resistance, and a larger current then flows. When the particles are released they have greater electrical resistance: a smaller current then flows. In this way a varying electric current flows along the telephone wires to the distant listener, where it is changed back to sound by the telephone earpiece (p. 36). As the varying electric current is a "copy" of the varying pressure in the sound pulses, the sound is reproduced faithfully in the earpiece.

Summary

1. *Electric current* is a flow of electrons; it is measured in *ampere*. *Potential difference* is difference of electrical pressure; it is measured in *volt*. An electric current flows in a wire when a potential difference is applied across it. *Resistance* is measured in ohm. A current of about 6 000 000 000 000 000 000 electrons per second is called 1 ampere.

2. *Conductors* are substances which allow electric current to flow easily through them; metals and salt and acid solutions are conductors but pure water is a very poor conductor.

Insulators are substances which do not allow electric current to flow easily through them; wood, air, paper and plastics are insulators.

3. *Connecting wires,* such as cables, are made of pure copper. *Resistance wires* are made of alloys of copper; nichrome, eureka, manganin are alloys used for resistance wire.

4. The *rheostat* is a variable resistance; the wire is wound round a cylindrical or circular frame and connected across two terminals. A varying resistance is obtained by using the "slider" terminal and one of the coil terminals.

5. The *carbon microphone* has carbon particles whose resistance varies when sound pulses are received; the microphone changes sound pulses to current pulses.

EXERCISES

1. Draw neat sketches of the *symbols* used to represent the following in electrical circuits, and write down what it represents beneath your sketch: (i) resistance wire, (ii) battery, (iii) connecting wire, (iv) switch, (v) rheostat.

2. What are the units in which *potential difference (p.d.)* and *current* are measured? Write down the p.d. obtained with (i) the mains, (ii) a small torch battery, (iii) an accumulator. What, approximately, is the current obtained in a 60-watt electric lamp filament, and in a small electric fire when connected to the mains supply?

3. Write down a list of four conducting materials and four insulating materials. Name some of the materials used in a piece of *flex* and a *submarine cable;* draw neat labelled sketches showing a cross-section of each.

4. Draw a labelled circuit sketch showing how you would obtain a varying current through a lamp. How would you obtain the maximum current, and then the minimum current, through the lamp?

5. What is a *rheostat?* Describe, with suitable diagrams, a rheostat, and explain how it works.

6. Describe the *carbon microphone,* and explain how it works.

7. Draw a labelled sketch of a *rotary rheostat.* Name as many materials as you can which are used in making the rheostat.

8. Draw a sketch showing an accumulator joined by connecting wire to the terminals T_1 and T_2 of an electric motor X, with a rheostat and key in the circuit. Label each of these items.

CHAPTER TWO

Magnets

For many years scientists had suspected that there might be a connection between electricity and magnetism, but nobody could bring experimental evidence in support of this idea. In 1820, however, Oersted, a Danish professor, was lecturing to students on the electric current when he noticed a slight movement of a suspended magnetic needle as a nearby wire was connected to a battery. On further inves-

Plate 3. A magnetic compass for marine use. The iron spheres are adjusted to correct the compass for the magnetic effect of the ship itself

tigation Oersted found that an electric current causes a magnet to move. *An electric current has therefore a magnetic effect.*

As soon as the discovery was announced, scientists all over the world began experiments on the magnetic effect of a current. The importance of Oersted's discovery can be judged from the fact that it has led to the invention of instruments such as the electric motor, the moving-coil loudspeaker, the telephone earpiece and the electromagnet.

Early Magnets.   The Compass

Magnets have been known to exist from early times. More than two thousand years ago, for example, the Chinese steered on long journeys with the aid of a special piece of rock or mineral suspended in the stern of the ship. The mineral was a natural magnet, and it was called *loadstone,* or "leading stone", by early navigators because it always came to rest pointing roughly north–south when suspended. Since it gave an approximate north–south direction, the magnet was used as a compass or direction finder in ships all over the world. It still serves the same purpose in many ships, being housed on deck at the top of a tall container called a *binnacle.*

Fig. 6 shows the card, graduated in degrees, of a ship's compass. Several small magnets (not shown) are attached beneath the card, which is pivoted inside a non-magnetic bowl filled with alcohol and water. This buoys up the card and damps its vibrations; the alcohol prevents the water freezing at low temperatures. A special type of mounting in two concentric rings R, called a *gimbal,* keeps the card horizontal whether the ship is tilting about axis A or axis B.

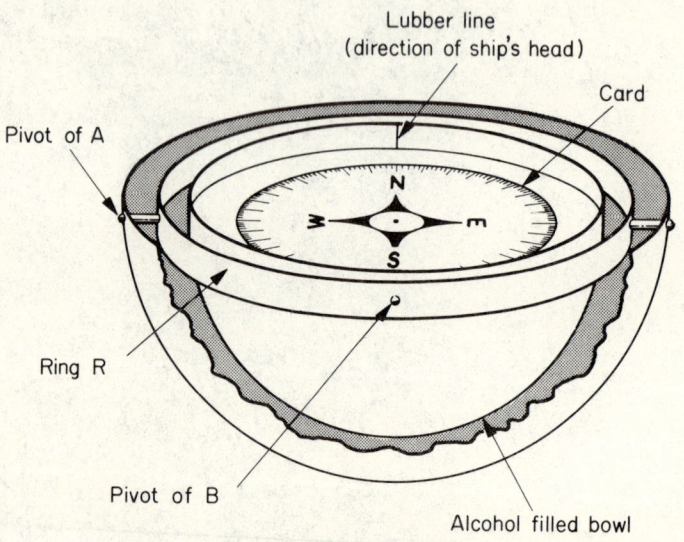

Fig. 6. A ship's compass

A magnet was soon found to attract iron and steel, but for many hundreds of years little further was discovered. About 1580, however, Dr. Gilbert, later physician to Queen Elizabeth, became interested in magnetism. Like every true scientist he began to perform experiments, and he made important discoveries about magnets. Eventually he published a work on magnetism called *De Magnete,* and he is regarded as the "father of magnetism".

Modern Magnets

As other scientists took up the study of magnetism, more discoveries were made. In comparatively recent times, for example, research work has shown how very powerful magnets can be made. Powerful magnets are needed in many intruments. The loudspeaker in a radio or television set has one; so has the microphone into which a studio announcer speaks; a bicycle dynamo has a strong magnet; a telephone earpiece has a strong magnet. Fig. 7 shows some of the different shapes of magnets used today.

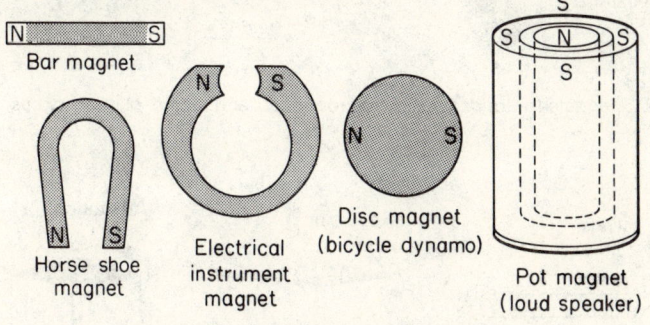

Fig. 7. Common types of magnet

Properties of Magnets

We now deal with some of the main properties of magnets. If a magnet is dipped into iron filings and then raised clear, the filings are observed to cling mainly round the ends or *poles* of the magnet Fig. 8 (i). The poles are therefore the places where the attracting power of the magnet is greatest.

If a pivoted magnet is turned so that it points in any direction and then released, the magnet swings round and eventually comes to rest with the same end always pointing approximately northwards. This end is therefore called the north-seeking or *north pole,* N, of the magnet. The other end, which always points south, is called the *south pole,* S.

When the N-pole of another magnet B is moved towards the N-pole of a pivoted magnet A, the latter moves away or is repelled (Fig. 8 (ii)). When the S-pole of B is brought near to the S-pole of A, repulsion occurs again. Thus two similar or like poles repel each other. The

Plate 4. Magnets for loudspeakers, microphones, and record-player pickups

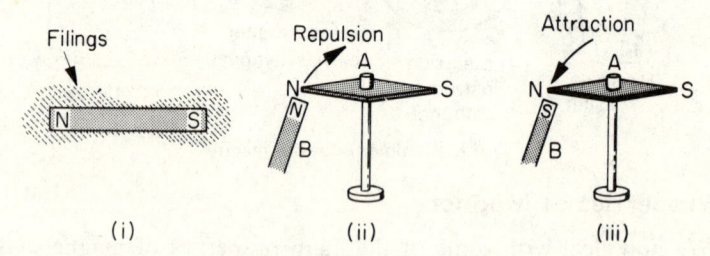

Fig. 8. Forces between magnets

S-pole of B, however, attracts the N-pole of A (Fig. 8 (iii)). The N-pole of B attracts the S-pole of A. Every case of attraction or repulsion can be remembered by the following rule:

Like poles repel.   Unlike poles attract.

This is a fundamental law of magnetism, and must be memorised.

Magnetic and Non-magnetic Substances

If a magnet is placed in a mixture of iron nails, steel pins, copper turnings and pieces of zinc, wood and paper, the nails and pins stick to the magnet when it is lifted clear but the other substances remain unaffected. Thus iron and steel are attracted by magnets; we therefore call them *magnetic* substances. Copper, zinc, wood and paper are examples of *non-magnetic* substances.

Steel is a much harder substance physically than iron. It is an alloy of iron, made by adding a small percentage of carbon to pure iron. Nickel and cobalt are also magnetic substances. These elements were neglected in favour of iron and steel for many years, but powerful magnets in use in industry are now made with alloys of nickel and cobalt. Alcomax, Alnico and Ticonal are modern magnet alloys made from these elements, these alloys also containing aluminium.

Ancient and Modern Methods of Making Magnets

In the days of Dr. Gilbert, about 1600, magnets were made by heating iron until it was red-hot, placing it in a north-south direction, and then hammering the iron repeatedly while it cooled. Fig. 9 illustrates how a bar of iron or steel can be made into a magnet by hammering while holding it. On testing with a compass-needle, the lower end will be found to be a north pole. The best position to hold the bar in England is at 70° to the horizontal.

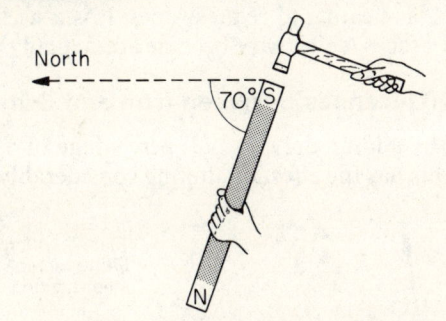

Fig. 9. Magnetising by hammering

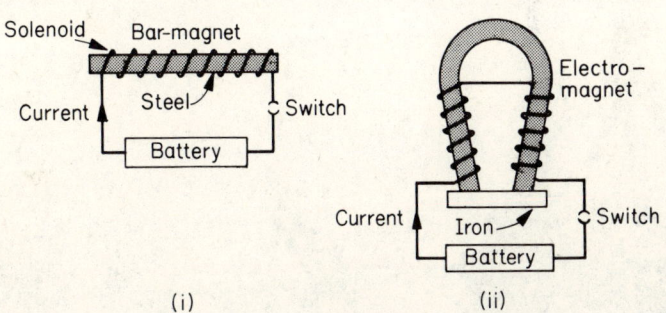

Fig. 10. Magnetising by electric current

Magnets made in this way are very weak. Powerful magnets are made by using electric current. If a bar-magnet is required, for example, a steel bar is placed inside a long coil of insulated copper wire, called a *solenoid,* to which is connected a battery and a switch (Fig. 10 (i)). When the current is switched on for a few moments, and then switched off, the steel will be found to have become a magnet. If a horse-shoe type of magnet is required, a coil of insulated copper wire is wound round the steel and its ends are connected to a battery and switch (Fig. 10 (ii)). The current is switched on, then switched off, and the coil is removed. A current of fairly high value should be used.

Demagnetising a Magnet

Years ago magnets were demagnetised by heating them strongly, or by hammering them strongly. Much of the magnetism disappeared by these methods, but there was always some left. Nowadays, the best method of demagnetising a magnet is to place it in a solenoid with its axis pointing east-west, and then pass an alternating current (a.c.) into the solenoid from a 12-volt or 24-volt a.c. supply. After a short time it is slowly withdrawn from the solenoid, with the current still flowing, to a distance of about a metre, and it is then found to be demagnetised. This method possesses the merit of not altering the physical characteristics of the steel, as heating to redness does. It is a useful method for demagnetising watches which have become accidentally magnetised.

Magnetic Differences between Iron and Steel

Steel is made by adding only a small percentage of carbon to pure (soft) iron, but this has the effect of altering considerably the magnetic properties.

Plate 5. A large electromagnet lifting scrap iron for use in steel-making

MAGNETS · 15

To illustrate the difference, place an unmagnetised iron bar in the solenoid shown in Fig. 10(i). When the current is switched on the bar will pick up pins and iron filings, showing that it has become a magnet. When the current is switched off, however, the pins and most of the filings drop off the bar, showing it has lost most of its magnetism. We therefore conclude that *iron loses its magnetism rapidly*. When the experiment is repeated with a steel bar, pins and iron filings are again picked up when the current is switched on. When the current is switched off, however, the pins and filings remain sticking to the steel, showing that, unlike iron, *steel retains its magnetism*.

We now deduce that if a permanent magnet is wanted, for example for a loudspeaker, steel must be used. If a temporary magnet is required, for example for an electromagnet, iron must be used.

When iron is placed inside a solenoid carrying a small electric current, it becomes a magnet and is capable of picking up a fair number of nails. When the experiment is repeated with a steel bar of similar dimensions, fewer nails are raised. This shows that *iron is more strongly magnetised than steel* by the same magnetising force.

Magnetic Fields and Lines of Flux

When iron filings are sprinkled round a *bar-magnet* on a sheet of paper, and the paper is lightly tapped, the filings settle in a definite pattern. They form curves beginning and ending at the north and south poles of the magnet (Fig. 11 (i)). Similar curves are formed between the poles of a *horse-shoe magnet*, but there are some straight lines directly between the poles (Fig. 11 (ii)). If a magnet is placed vertically with one pole on the table, the filings form straight lines radiating from the pole (Fig. 11 (iii)).

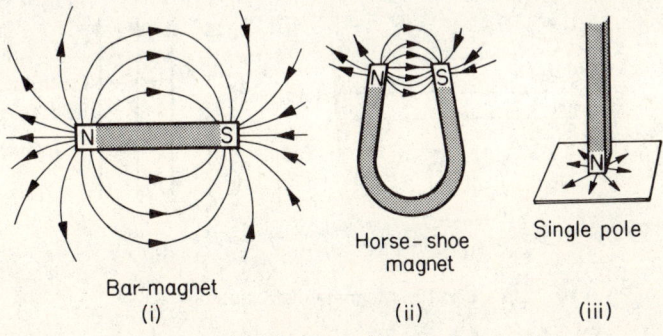

Bar-magnet (i)   Horse-shoe magnet (ii)   Single pole (iii)

Fig. 11. Lines of flux

We can account for the patterns if we remember that iron becomes magnestised, by induction, in the neighbourhood of a magnet (see p. 17). The iron filings thus become tiny magnets, and when the paper is tapped they move slightly and settle along the direction of the magnetic force due to the magnet. The direction of the magnetic force differs at different places round the magnet. Consequently the filings point in various directions, and together they lie along lines having the appearance shown in Fig. 11. The region round a magnet is called a *magnetic field,* because a magnetic force can be detected there. The lines in the field showing the magnetic force directions are called magnetic *lines of flux.*

Plotting Lines of Flux

A compass-needle is more sensitive than iron filings to magnetic force because it can turn more easily. To map out the field round a magnet for example, the compass is placed near one end N, and after the needle has settled down the positions of the two ends A, B, are marked with a pencil (Fig. 12(i)). The compass is now moved so that its south pole is at B, and the new position C of its north pole is marked. By moving the compass along, a series of dots is obtained on the paper and a smooth curve is then drawn through them. This gives one line of flux. Other lines are drawn in a similar way, beginning near a pole of the magnet each time. By general agreement, arrows are placed on all lines of flux to show the direction in which the *north* pole of a compass needle would point if placed on that line.

Unlike the field round a bar-magnet, the magnetic field of the earth at any point not near the poles is a series of straight parallel lines, because the compass-needle always points in the same direction (magnetic north) in the earth's field (Fig. 12(ii)).

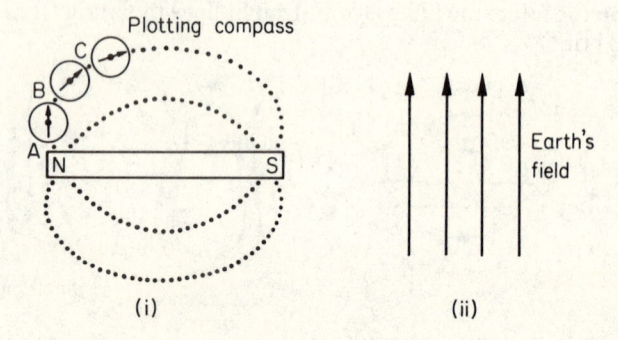

Fig. 12. Magnetic field plotting

Induced Magnetism with Mumetal

Mumetal is a magnetic alloy which has been developed for use in electrical instruments. It contains about 76 per cent of nickel, 17 per cent of iron, some copper and chromium, and is very easily magnetised, as we shall now show.

MAGNETS · 17

A rod of mumetal AB, pointing downward at about an angle of 70° to the horizontal, is placed in a north–south direction (Fig. 13(i)). When the end A approaches the north pole of a pivoted compass-needle, the latter is repelled. This shows that A has become a north pole, and the rod is thus magnetised. The rod is now placed horizontally in the east–west direction, where-upon the north pole of the needle is attracted to A (Fig. 13(ii)). On bringing A to the south pole attraction again occurs. This shows that A is *not* a magnetic pole, and hence AB is now not magnetised. On raising the end B and placing AB north–south, as in Fig. 13(i), A again repels the north pole N, showing the bar has become magnetised once more.

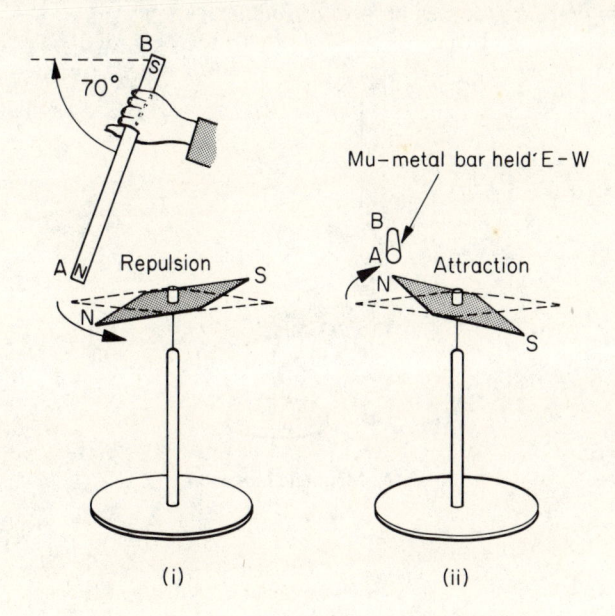

Fig. 13. Magnetic induction in the earth's field

These surprising results are explained as follows. When AB is at 70° the earth's field magnetises the rod, the lower end becoming a north pole. An ordinary iron (or steel) bar would require to be hammered considerably to assist the earth's magnetic action (see p. 13). Mumetal, however, is very easily magnetised, and no hammering is required. When the rod is held east–west the earth's field has no effect, and the rod then becomes demagnetised, as we have shown.

Magnetic Induction

In the experiment just described, the mumetal rod became magnetised by the earth's magnetic field, without being touched. This is known as *magnetic induction,* and the rod is said to have induced *magnetism.* When three iron nails P, Q, R are raised by a magnet A, the end of the lowest nail R repels the north pole N of a pivoted magnetic needle, showing that R has become magnetised by induction (Fig. 14). The nails P, Q are also magnetised, as shown.

We can now explain why iron or steel is attracted to a magnet. Suppose the north pole N of a magnet A is moved towards an iron nail X (Fig. 15 (i)). When A is close to X it magnetises the nail by induction, with an opposite pole *s* near A (Fig. 15 (ii)). Since unlike poles attract, and *s* is nearer to N than the induced north pole *n*, the nail moves towards A (Fig. 15 (iii)). It can be said, therefore, that *induction precedes* (comes before) *attraction.*

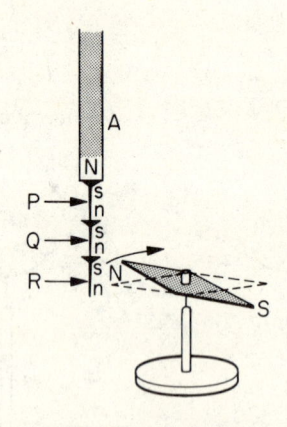

Fig. 14. Magnetic induction

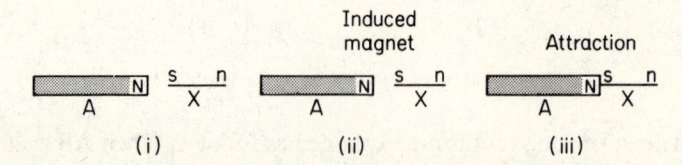

Fig. 15. Induction precedes attraction

Magnetic Separators

Industry makes use of powerful magnets to separate magnetic (ferrous) materials, such as iron, steel, nickel, cobalt or their alloys, from non-magnetic (non-ferrous) materials, such as brass, copper, tin for example. In large metal works, the metallic dust is swept up and poured into a large funnel F suspended over a revolving drum (Fig. 16). The drum W has a powerful magnet M inside it, and the ferrous

MAGNETS · 19

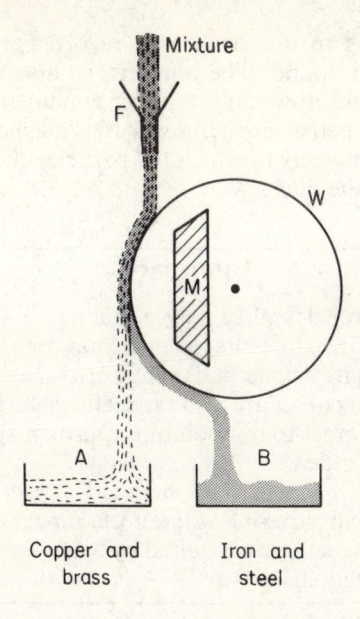

Fig. 16. Magnetic separation of metals

Plate *6*. Magnetic separation of steel particles in oil. The magnet on the left has removed from the lubricating oil of a machine particles of steel which had flaked off the ball-bearing on the right. The particles, if left in the oil, would have caused further damage to the machine

materials thus cling to the drum as it revolves and drop off into a container B further round. The non-ferrous materials on the drum, however, fall straight down into another container A. Iron and steel particles in oil or petrol are removed by "magnetic filters". These contain powerful magnets to which the particles cling when the liquid is poured through the filter.

Summary

1. Like poles repel; unlike poles attract.
2. Soft (pure) iron loses its magnetism more readily than steel, and is more strongly magnetised than steel by the same magnetising force. Nickel and cobalt are also magnetic materials.
3. A magnet comes to rest pointing approximately north–south when freely suspended.
4. Permanent magnets may be made from steel by these methods: electrical, stroking with another magnet.
5. Induced magnetism is acquired by a magnetic material when placed in a magnetic field.

EXERCISES

1. Name two properties of a magnet. Which of the following substances are magnetic: copper, nickel, iron, platinum, lead, cobalt, steel?

2. Write down the differences between the magnetic properties of iron and steel. Which material would you use for making (i) a permanent magnet, (ii) an electromagnet?

3. The south pole of a magnet is brought near to (i) the south pole of a compass, (ii) the north pole, (iii) a piece of iron, (iv) a piece of copper. What happens in each case? State the general law of force between magnetic poles.

4. Three metals A, B, C are each painted white. One is a magnet, another is magnetic, the third is non-magnetic. Describe experiments you would make to determine the nature of A, B, C respectively.

5. Describe fully how a magnet is made by an electrical method. Give a complete circuit diagram and label it.

6. Draw a sketch of a magnet with "consequent" poles. Describe how you would make a magnet with consequent poles. How would you show it was different from an ordinary magnet?

7. Describe a *magnetic separator* of metals, and explain how it works.

8. *"Soft iron loses its magnetism more easily than steel."* Describe an experiment which demonstrates this statement. What other difference between iron and steel do you know?

9. Describe two methods of demagnetising a magnet.

10. What is *magnetic induction?* Describe and explain an experiment to illustrate magnetic induction.

CHAPTER THREE

Magnetic Fields

In Chapter 2 we saw that the magnetic field round a magnet caused iron filings to settle in a pattern when they were sprinkled there. It was also pointed out that a small magnetic compass-needle enabled the lines of flux, which show the directions of the magnetic forces in the field, to be plotted accurately. Arrows on the lines show the conventional direction of the flux lines (see page 16).

When the field between the north poles N of two magnets is plotted, it is found that the lines of flux turn away from a certain point P (Fig. 17). Consequently there is no magnetic force at P, and a compass-needle does not therefore settle in any particular direction. P is called a *neutral point* in the field. Its existence is explained by the fact that if a north pole is imagined to be at P, it is repelled by one N-pole with a force exactly equal and opposite to that exerted by the other N-pole. As the two forces cancel each other, the resultant force is zero. A neutral point can thus be defined as a point were the resultant magnetic field is zero.

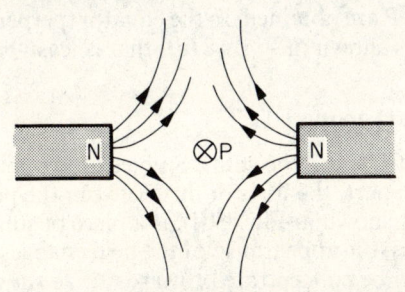

Fig. 17. Neutral point between similar poles

Neutral Points with Bar-magnet

We know that the earth's field makes the north pole of a compass-needle move or point northwards. If we wish to neutralise completely the effect of the earth's field with a bar-magnet, the magnet must be positioned to have an exactly opposite effect. The bar-magnet is therefore placed with its south pole pointing northwards (Fig. 18(i)).

22 · ELEMENTARY PHYSICS

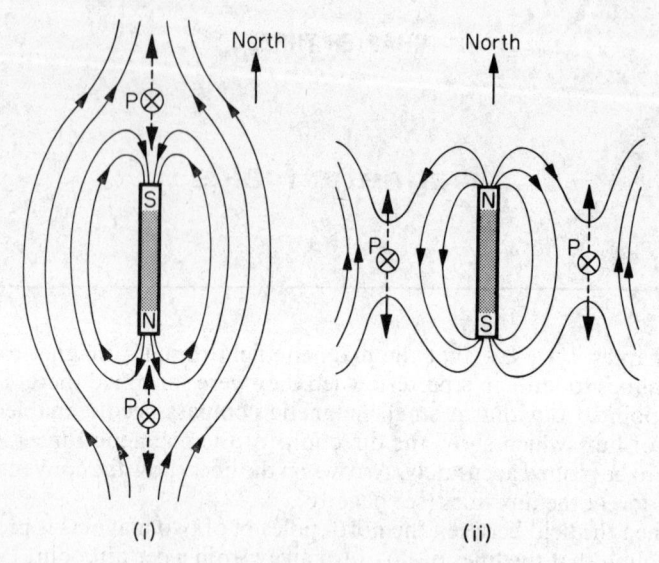

(i)   (ii)

Fig. 18. Neutral points with bar-magnets

The field round the magnet now has two neutral points P, P along its axis. At either point the earth's force would make a north pole move northwards, but the magnet would make it move southwards with an equal and opposite force; and hence the total force at P is zero.

If the magnet is placed with its north pole pointing northwards, neutral points P, P are obtained on the equator (perpendicular bisector) of the magnet, as shown in Fig. 18 (ii), that is, east–west.

Effect of Soft Iron

When the north N and the south S poles of two magnets are placed a short distance apart, the lines of flux between the poles are found to be similar to that shown in Fig. 19 (i). If a piece of soft iron A is placed between the poles, the appearance of the field changes; the lines of flux are now found to be concentrated towards A, as shown in Fig. 19 (ii). This is due to the magnetism induced in the iron, which now has south, s, and north, n, poles as shown. The magnetic field between N & S at A is now much stronger than previously, and this property of soft iron is used in many instruments to increase the density of the magnetic flux. Motors and dynamos, for example, contain coils of wire wound on soft iron.

When a bar of soft iron is placed pointing north–south in the earth's field, the field is concentrated in the iron, which acquires induced magnetism (see Fig. 19 (iii)).

MAGNETIC FIELDS · 23

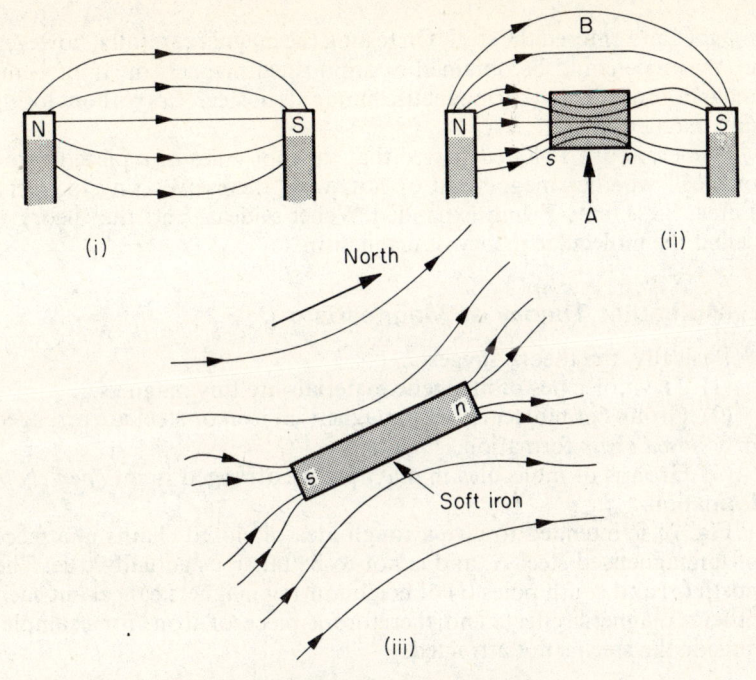

Fig. 19. Effect of soft iron in fields

Field between Parallel Bar-magnets

The appearance of the field between two similar parallel bar-magnets directly opposite each other is shown in Fig. 20. In Fig. 20(i) like poles face each other; no lines are obtained at points marked with a cross between the poles, showing the existence of neutral points. In Fig. 20(ii), unlike poles face each other; a neutral point, marked with a cross, is obtained midway between the two magnets.

Theory of Magnetism

From the year 1600, scientists suggested theories about magnetism. Having observed that a steel bar can be magnetised by stroking it with a magnet, people at first thought that some magnetism had left the

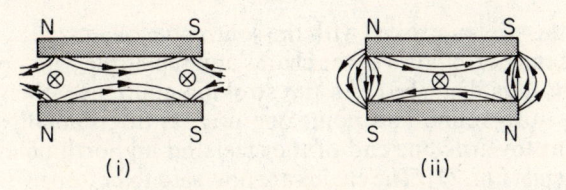

Fig. 20. Fields between parallel magnets

magnet and entered the steel. On testing the magnet carefully, however, no evidence could be obtained of diminished magnetism. In fact, the magnet could be used to magnetise hundreds of steel bars without losing any magnetism.

Weber, about 1840, suggested that the molecules of a piece of iron or steel, whether magnetised or not, were themselves tiny magnets. Later, Sir James Ewing expanded Weber's ideas, and the theory is called the molecular theory of magnetism.

Molecular Theory of Magnestism

Basically, the theory suggests:
(1) The molecules of magnetic materials are tiny magnets.
(2) Groups of molecules in unmagnetised iron or steel are arranged in a *closed chain* formation.
(3) Groups of molecules in magnets are arranged in an *open chain* formation.

Fig. 21 is intended to give a rough idea of closed chains in a piece of unmagnetised steel A, and is not to be taken as actually true. The north (n) and south poles (s) of neighbouring magnets cancel out each other's magnetic effect, and therefore a piece of iron, for example, outside the steel is not attracted.

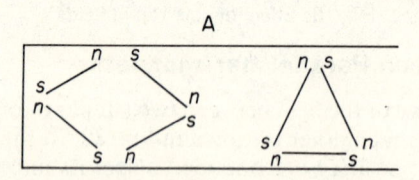

Fig. 21. Closed chains of molecular magnets

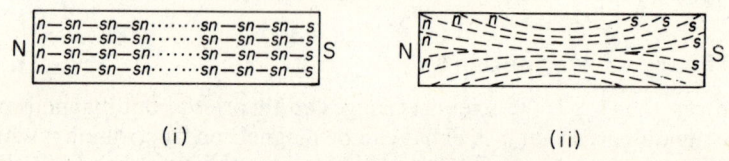

Fig. 22. Open chains of molecular magnets

When the steel is stroked with the south pole of a magnet, however, it attracts the north poles in the chains and repels the south poles. The chains are thus disturbed. As the stroking continues, the groups of molecules turn round and point one way, until eventually all south poles point towards one end of the steel and all north poles towards the other end (Fig. 22). The chains are now said to be "open", and since there are no opposite poles to cancel out the poles at the very ends, one

MAGNETIC FIELDS

end of the steel is a south pole S, and the other is a north pole N. Fig. 22(i) shows the "open chains" in an ideal magnet, Fig. 22(ii) in an actual magnet. In the latter case the poles at the end repel each other, and hence in practice iron filings are attracted round the sides of the magnet as well as at the ends.

Experiments which Support the Molecular Theory of Magnetism

If five compass-needles are arranged near each other, they will form a closed chain, as in Fig. 23(i). When the south pole S of a magnet is brought near (Fig. 23(ii)), the magnets all swing round and point towards S, forming an open chain. When S is taken away, the magnets fall back to their closed chain position. This experiment shows that closed chains become open chains when a magnet is brought near.

When a steel magnetised needle is broken in two parts, each part becomes a magnet, as shown by testing them with a compass-needle (Fig. 24). When the two parts are each broken, the new parts also become magnets. This experiment suggests that, if we go on breaking the magnet into smaller and smaller parts, no matter how tiny they may be, each part is a magnet.

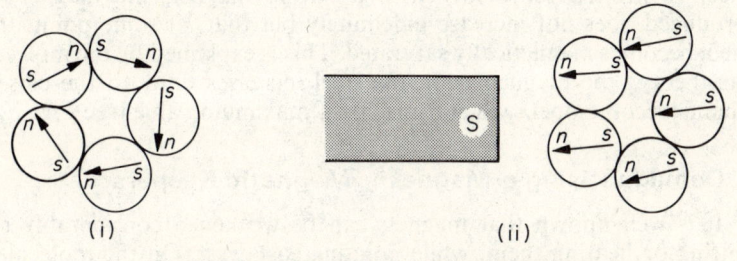

Fig. 23. Chain formations of compass needles

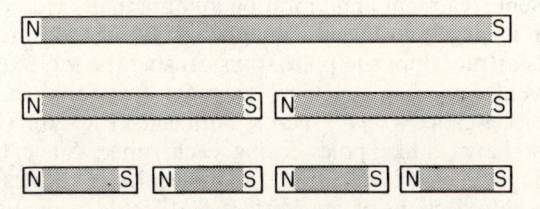

Fig. 24. Effect of breaking a magnet

When the closed end of a test-tube of iron filings T is brought near to either pole of a pivoted magnetic needle, the needle is attracted in each case, showing that the end of the iron filings is not magnetised. The test-tube is now stroked repeatedly with one pole of a powerful magnet, as shown in Fig. 25 (or placed inside a solenoid carrying a high current and withdrawn) and its end A again tested with the compass-needle. One pole of the needle is repelled, showing that A has now become a magnetic pole. The iron particles have now become magnetised, and are lined up in an "open chain" formation. On shaking the test-tube vigorously and testing again, polarity at A will be found to have disappeared.

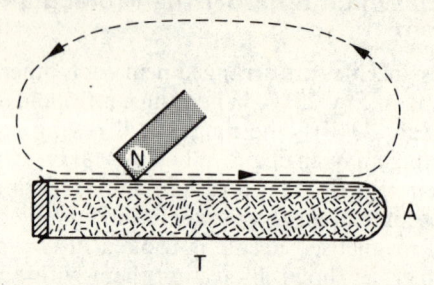

Fig. 25. Magnetizing iron filings in a test-tube

Finally, there is one other piece of evidence in support of the molecular theory of magnetism. Experiment shows that if a piece of steel is stroked repeatedly with a strong magnet, the magnetism produced does not increase indefinitely but that, at some point, the steel becomes magnetically saturated. This is explained by the molecular theory; the magnetism in the steel increases until all the closed chains become open, when it reaches a maximum value (see Fig. 22).

Demagnetising a Magnet. Magnetic Keepers

It is well known that magnets can be weakened considerably by hitting or heating them, while pointing east–west. On the molecular theory, it is thought that the groups of open chains become disturbed by the violent treatment and vibration and gradually close, so that the magnetism is largely lost. Self-demagnetisation also occurs; the poles at the ends attract opposite poles, thus causing the molecules to turn.

To prevent loss of magnetism, magnets are stored in pairs with soft-iron pieces called *keepers,* across both ends (Fig. 26). The magnets A, B must have unlike poles facing each other. Since the keepers become magnetised by induction, the molecules in them and in A, B all form a closed chain of magnets. It is difficult to disturb a closed chain; hence the molecules in A and B retain their position, and thus the magnetism in A, B is preserved.

The Earth's Magnetism

Since a pivoted magnetic needle always comes to rest pointing approximately north–south, it follows that the earth acts like a magnet

MAGNETIC FIELDS · 27

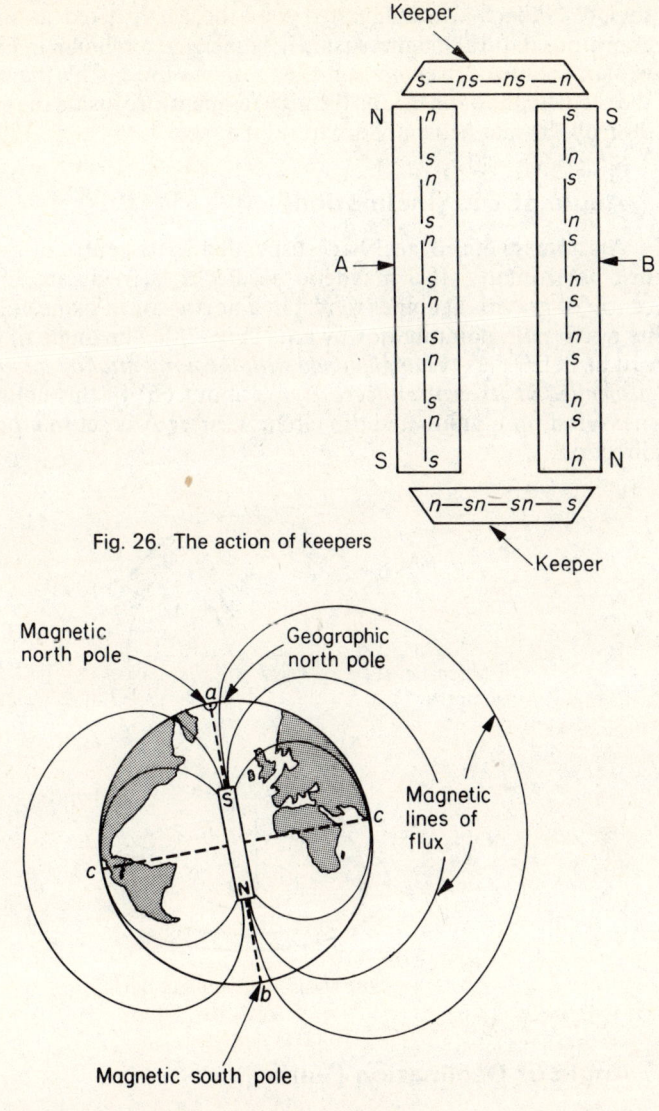

Fig. 26. The action of keepers

Fig. 27. The earth as a magnet

with one pole in the north direction and the other pole in the south direction. As unlike poles attract, the pole near the north geographic pole must be of south polarity; the pole near the south geographic pole must be of north polarity.

The origin of the earth's magnetism is at present not clear; it remains one of the unsolved mysteries of science. The earliest theory was due to Dr. Gilbert, who suggested that the earth acted as if it had an enormous natural magnet inside it, somewhat as shown in Fig. 27. This explains some of the common effects due to the earth's magnetism, but the theory cannot be true as the high temperature inside the earth would destroy the magnetism of a natural magnet.

Angle of Dip (Inclination)

An unmagnetised steel bar, suspended at its centre of gravity, may rest horizontally. If a magnetic needle M is freely suspended at its centre of gravity, it comes to rest in a north–south plane and dips with its north pole pointing downwards (Fig. 28). The angle of dip, which can be defined as *the angle made with the horizontal by a magnet freely suspended at its centre of gravity,* is about 66° in this country and is measured on a graduated dip circle A, after A is set in a north–south direction.

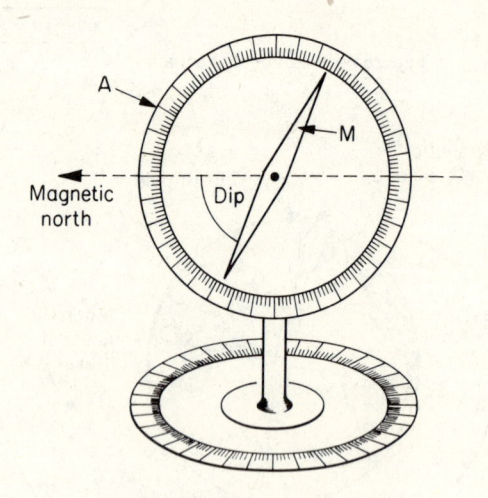

Fig. 28. Measuring angle of dip

Angle of Declination (Variation)

The angle of dip varies all over the world. At the magnetic poles of the earth a freely-suspended magnet points vertically downwards, i.e. the angle of dip is 90°. At the magnetic equator, which is near the geographic equator, the angle of dip is zero. In Australia, on the other side of the globe to Great Britain, a magnetic needle dips with its *south* pole pointing downwards. The lines of flux due to the imaginary magnet in the earth are shown in Fig. 27; a dip needle lies along the direction of the tangent to the earth's line of flux where it is situated.

The angle between the geographic or true north direction at a place on the earth and the magnetic north direction at that place is called the *angle of declination* or *variation*. The variation varies all over the world. Since ships, and other craft, navigate by reference to maps based on the true or geographic north, ships which steer by a magnetic compass are provided by the Admiralty with charts which show variation values at various parts of the world, so that a correction can be made to the compass reading. In 1970, the variation in London was about 7° westerly, that is, the magnetic north was then 7° west of the true (geographic) north, and decreasing at the rate of about 1° in 12 years.

Summary

1. A *magnetic field* is a region where a magnetic force can be detected. The field is mapped out by *lines of flux*, whose direction is that along which a north pole would tend to move if placed in the field.

2. *Soft iron* concentrates the lines of flux when it is placed in a magnetic field.

3. A *neutral point* is a point where there is no resultant magnetic field. Neutral points are obtained along the axis of a bar-magnet placed with its south pole pointing northwards; they are obtained along the equator of a bar-magnet placed with its north pole pointing northwards.

4. The *molecular theory of magnetism* states that the molecules of iron or steel are tiny magnets. When the iron or steel is unmagnetised, the molecules are arranged in "closed chains"; when it is magnetised, the molecules are arranged in "open chains".

5. *Evidence in support of the molecular theory:* (i) A magnet can be broken into small pieces each of which is a magnet. (ii) A closed "chain" of compass-needles can be made into an "open" chain. (iii) A test-tube of iron filings can be made into a "magnet".

6. *Keepers of soft iron* are used in storing bar-magnets, which have opposite poles facing each other. A closed and stable chain of molecular magnets is then formed.

7. The *angle of dip* is the angle which a magnet freely suspended at its centre of gravity makes with the horizontal; the *angle of declination* (or variation) is the angle between the magnetic north and geographic (true) north.

EXERCISES

1. Draw neat sketches of the lines of flux in the magnetic fields of (i) a bar-magnet, (ii) a single south pole, (iii) the earth, (iv) between two similar parallel bar-magnets with unlike poles facing each other. What do the arrows on lines indicate?

2. Describe how you would plot the field round a bar-magnet with a compass-needle. Draw a diagram in illustration. What is the behaviour of a compass-needle at a neutral point?

3. Draw a sketch of the lines of flux in air between the north and south poles of a horse-shoe magnet. Draw another sketch showing the appearance of the field when a piece of soft iron is placed between the poles.

4. What is the general effect of soft iron in a magnetic field? A bar of soft iron is placed in the north–south direction in the earth's magnetic field. Draw a sketch of the field round the iron, and explain its appearance.

5. What is a *neutral point*? A bar-magnet is placed with its south pole pointing northwards. Draw the field round the magnet and mark the neutral points.

6. The south pole of a vertical magnet is placed on a horizontal table. Draw the field round the pole, marking any special features.

7. How does the molecular theory of magnetism explain an unmagnetised steel bar? Explain, on the molecular theory, what happens when the bar is magnetised.

8. A bar-magnet is placed near a steel pin. Using the molecular theory, explain what happens.

9. Describe three experiments in favour of the molecular theory of magnetism, stating the conclusion you draw from each experiment.

10. Describe how you would store bar-magnets in a box. Explain the reason for the arrangement you choose.

11. A pair of steel pliers are often found to be magnetised. Explain how this occurs. How would you demagnetise the pliers?

12. Describe what happens to a freely suspended magnetic needle when it is taken all over the world. How can this be explained?

13. What is meant by (i) *angle of dip,* (ii) *angle of declination?* Describe how you would attempt to measure the angle of dip. Why is a knowledge of declination important?

CHAPTER FOUR

Electromagnets

The magnetic effect of a current can easily be demonstrated by joining a long piece of connecting wire to an accumulator and rheostat (Fig. 29 (i)). When the wire is held close and parallel to a suspended needle NS, the latter is deflected. As the current is increased by means of the rheostat the deflection increases, showing that the magnetic effect increases as the current increases.

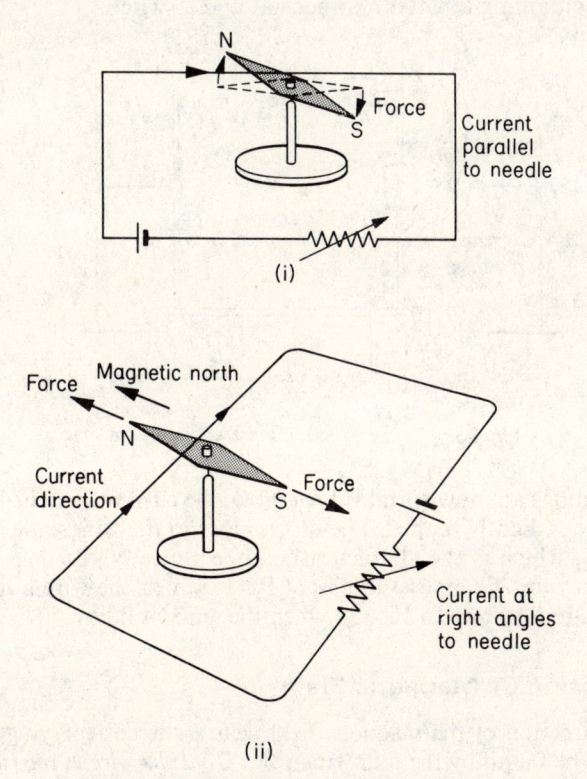

Fig. 29. Magnetic fields near a straight wire

Since NS turns when the wire is parallel to it, the forces on the poles of the needle must be perpendicular to the wire, as shown (Fig. 29 (i)). When the wire is turned so that the current flows perpendicularly to NS, no movement of the needle is observed (Fig. 29 (ii)). The magnetic force, which is still perpendicular to the wire, now acts along the needle as shown, and the forces on the poles now do not turn the needle. It is a general rule that *the magnetic flux resulting from an electric current at a point is always perpendicular to the current direction at a given point.*

Magnetic Field round Straight Wire

In order to investigate the appearance of the flux lines round a straight conductor, one side AD of a large rectangle of wire ABCD is placed vertically (Fig. 30). A piece of cardboard, X, held horizontally in a wooden clamp, is placed so that the wire AD passes through the middle, O, of the board. The rectangle has many turns of wire to intensify the magnetic flux round O, and the terminals are joined to a circuit containing a battery, a rheostat and a switch.

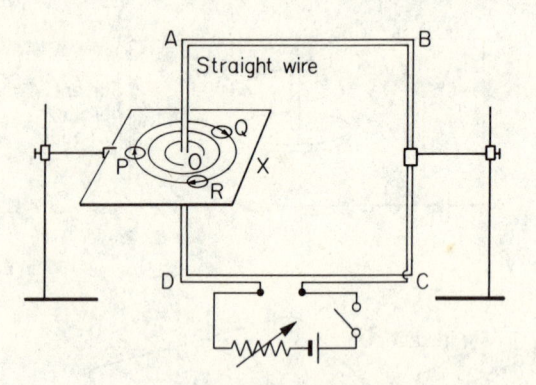

Fig. 30. Magnetic field round a straight wire

Iron filings are now sprinkled round O, the current switched on, and the board X lightly tapped. The filings close to the wire settle in *circles* round O, which is the characteristic appearance of the lines of force round the wire. Compass-needles at P, Q, R near the wire point along the directions shown in Fig. 30 when the current flows.

Direction of Magnetic Field

The direction of the magnetic field near a current-carrying straight wire can be found by the following rule: *Hold the wire in the right hand so that the thumb points along the direction of the conventional current. The fingers then point in the direction of the magnetic field.*

ELECTROMAGNETS

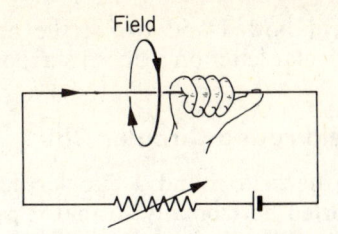

Fig. 31. Direction of field round a current

Conventional Current

Before the electron nature of a current was discovered, it was thought that an electric current might be a flow of particles in the opposite direction. This is called conventional flow and diagrams should make clear when electron direction is being used, otherwise conventional flow is understood.

Circular Coil

A length of connecting wire can be made into a small *short coil* by winding it round a finger or a pencil. If the coil is joined to a battery and rheostat, and one end X of the coil is brought near to the south pole S of a pivoted magnetic needle, the latter is repelled (Fig. 32). If X is now brought near to the north pole N of the needle the latter is attracted. This shows that X acts like a south pole.

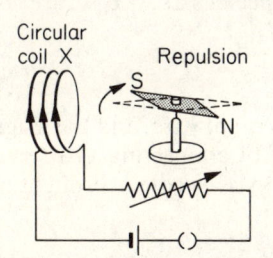

Fig. 32. Field of a circular coil

At this stage, it is interesting to note that the earliest current-measuring instruments consisted basically of circular coils with a light magnet in the centre. They were called *moving-magnet galvanometers*. When the current was switched on, the magnet was deflected through an angle depending on the magnitude of the current. The earliest *telegraph system* in Great Britain, invented in 1837 by Wheatstone and Cooke, had five magnetic needles with small coils round them. When operated, a current flowed and two of the needles were deflected, pointing to a particular letter on a board surrounding the needles.

Magnetic Field round Circular Coil

To investigate the field round a circular current-carrying coil, a board X is supported horizontally so that it passes through the coil (Fig. 33). The coil is placed vertically, and its terminals are joined to

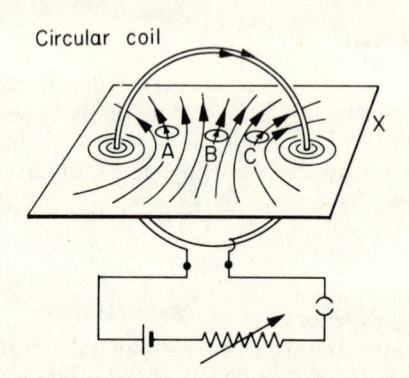

Fig. 33. Field inside a circular coil

a circuit containing a battery and a rheostat. Iron filings are sprinkled on X, and when the board is tapped the filings settle in circles round the coil. In the middle of the coil, at B, the lines of flux are straight. The directions of compass-needles at A, B, C are shown in Fig. 33.

Solenoid

A solenoid is a long coil of wire, and the magnetic effect of a current in it can be investigated by connecting a battery, rheostat and switch to it (Fig. 34(i)). If a compass-needle is brought near to the end B when

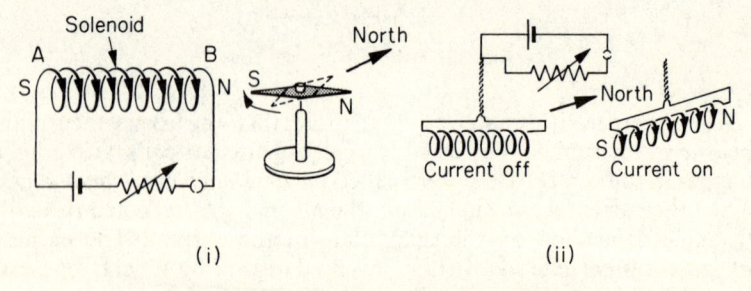

Fig. 34. Field of a cylindrical coil (solenoid)

the current is switched on, the south pole swings round towards B, as shown. Thus B acts like the north pole of a magnet. If the experiment is repeated with the compass at the other end A, the north pole is attracted, showing that A acts like a south pole.

Since the solenoid has one end a south pole and the other end a north pole when carrying a current, the coil should behave like a bar-magnet. This can be verified by suspending the coil by thin flex (Fig. 34(ii)). When the current is switched on the coil begins to turn round, and eventually it settles pointing north–south, like a suspended bar-magnet. When the current is switched off the coil returns to its original position due to twist in the flex.

Magnetic Field round a Solenoid

The flux pattern round a solenoid can be obtained by sprinkling iron filings on a horizontal board C passing through the middle of the coil AB, which is placed with its turns vertical (Fig. 35). A rheostat is a suitable solenoid. When a large current is passed through the solenoid, and C is lightly tapped, the filings arrange themselves in curves round the coil, as shown in Fig. 35. The lines of flux pass through the middle of the coil, and have a similar appearance to the field round a bar-magnet (see Fig. 11(i)).

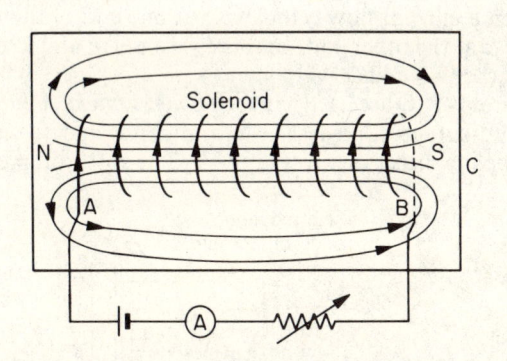

Fig. 35. Field round a solenoid

Permanent Magnets

The magnetic effect of a current is used commercially for making magnets. If a bar-magnet is required, the steel bar CB is placed inside a solenoid, and a heavy current is switched on for an instant and then switched off (Fig. 36(i)). If a horse-shoe magnet is required a large number of turns of wire could be wound round steel made into that shape, a battery connected to the wire, and the current switched on and then off (Fig. 36(ii)). An ammeter A, which measures the current, is placed in the circuit to check that the current is strong enough.

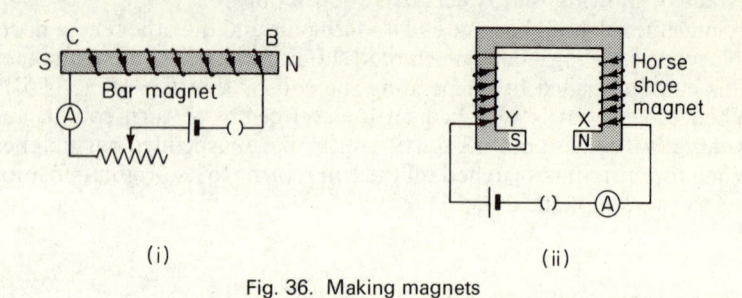

Fig. 36. Making magnets

Electromagnets

If a temporary magnet (a magnet required for a short time only) is required, soft iron must be used, not steel. A large and powerful *electromagnet*, as the temporary magnet is called, is used to raise massive steel girders or iron scrap at goods yards. An electric bell circuit also contains an electromagnet.

An electromagnet for raising small loads is shown in Fig. 36(ii). Coils of wire are *oppositely* wound on the two limbs of the soft iron, so that when a current flows clockwise at one end of the iron, it flows anticlockwise at the other end. In this case a north and a south pole are obtained at the two ends.

Two solenoids P, Q are used in a *telephone earpiece* (Fig. 37). They are wound round soft iron pieces X, Y and connected so that a current flows in opposite directions round them. The soft iron pieces are fixed

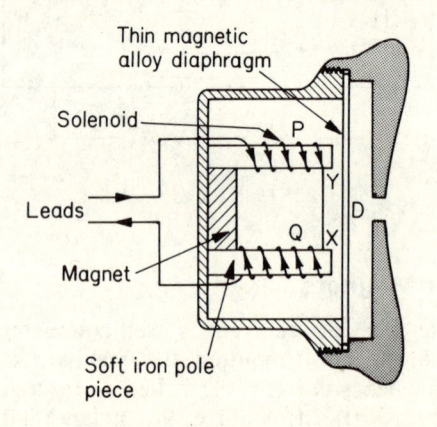

Fig. 37. Telephone earpiece

at the opposite ends of a short powerful magnet, so that X becomes a S-pole and Y a N-pole. When a person talks into a microphone at the other end of the line a varying current flows in the solenoids P, Q, thus producing a variation in the strength of the magnetism in X and Y. This causes X, Y to exert a varying pull on the springy iron diaphragm D. D thus vibrates and reproduces a copy of the original sound pulses which entered the microphone.

Electric Bell Circuit

The electric bell contains an electromagnet consisting of two solenoids wound in opposite directions on two parallel soft iron cores joined by a soft iron yoke (Fig. 38). Adjoining the cores is a soft armature mounted on a short flat spring. Attached to the armature by a light

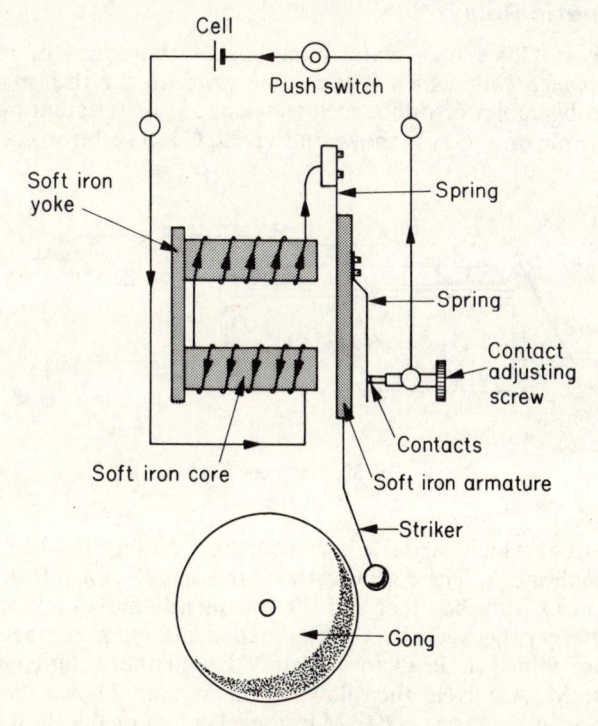

Fig. 38. Bell circuit

spring is a silver contact which bears against a silver-tipped contact adjusting screw. The various components of the bell are connected by insulated wire as shown in the diagram, and the circuit is completed through a cell and push switch.

38 · ELEMENTARY PHYSICS

When the push is pressed, current flows from the cell, through the two solenoids, down the armature, across the contacts and thence back to the cell. This causes the cores to become magnetised with opposite polarity and the armature is attracted towards them. As a result the striker hits the gong and, at the same time, the circuit is broken at the contacts. Magnetism disappears from the cores and the armature is pulled back by the spring so as to restore contact. The action just described begins all over again, with the result that the armature moves to- and fro, and the gong is struck repeatedly. If a bell circuit does not work we may suspect, among other causes, that (i) the contact breaker needs adjustment, or (ii) a new battery is needed, or (iii) the bell-push is faulty, or (iv) the coil is broken.

Magnetic Relay

The Post Office uses many hundreds of thousands of relays in *telecommunications,* which is the name given to the transmission of messages by cables or radio, such as telephone or telegram messages. The principle of a relay is shown in Fig. 39. C is a soft iron core inside

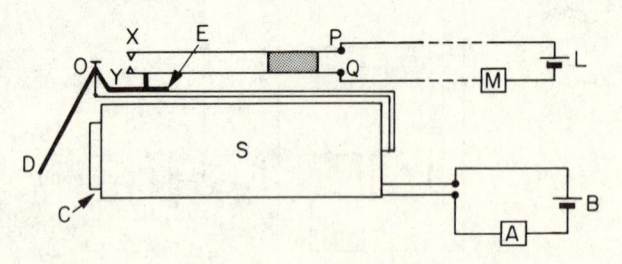

Fig. 39. Magnetic relay

a solenoid S, which carries a current from a battery B when dialling from telephone A. The core C attracts the end D of a soft iron lever pivoted at O, and the other end E consequently moves upward. This closes the gap between two spring-loaded platinum contacts X, Y, which are joined at P, Q to a battery L and the distant telephone exchange M. A current then flows in this circuit. Thus a "message" sent by operating A is passed to M by the relay. In practice the telephone and telegraph systems use many thousands of relays to pass messages over long distances.

Electric lift circuits have relays. On pressing the button, a relay closes a circuit carrying a large current, which operates a powerful motor. It would be unsatisfactory and dangerous to close the heavy-current circuit by a hand-operated switch, and the relay solves the problem.

ELECTROMAGNETS

> **Summary**
>
> **1.** An electric current has a magnetic effect in the region round it, that is, the electric current produces a magnetic field.
>
> **2.** The magnetic field round a *straight wire* consists of circular lines of flux concentric with the wire. For a *circular coil,* it consists of circles round the wires of the coil and straight lines in the middle of the coil. For a *solenoid,* the field is similar to that of a bar-magnet.
>
> **3.** For a *straight current-carrying wire,* the direction of the magnetic field (direction of movement of a north pole) can be found as follows: Hold the wire in the right hand, with the thumb pointing in the conventional current direction; the fingers then point in the direction of the magnetic field.
>
> **4.** For a circular coil carrying an electric current, one face acts like a south pole whilst the other face acts like a north magnetic pole.
>
> **5.** A permanent magnet is made by placing *steel* inside a solenoid carrying a current; an electromagnet is made by using *soft iron* in a solenoid. Electromagnets are used in electric bells, magnetic relays and the telephone earpiece.

EXERCISES

1. With neat diagrams, describe how you would make an electro-magnet from a straight piece of suitable metal, and also from a horse-shoe shaped piece of the metal. On your diagram show clearly the poles obtained in each case.

2. Describe how you would determine the relation between the magnetic poles of a circular coil and the direction of electric current in the coil.

3. Draw the circuit of an experiment to show how the magnetic fields due to a solenoid and a current-carrying straight wire can be obtained. Draw the lines of flux in each case, and mark their direction and that of the current.

4. A light solenoid carries a current, and is suspended by a thread from a point in the middle. If the solenoid is free to turn, in what direction will it eventually settle and why? Explain what happens if the south pole of a magnet is brought near to one end of the solenoid when carrying a current, and draw a diagram in illustration.

5. Describe an *electric bell circuit,* and explain how it works.

6. Railway points are operated with the aid of the magnetic effect of a current. Draw a circuit diagram of an arrangement you consider would be suitable, and explain its action.

7. Draw a diagram of the inside of a *telephone earpiece*. Explain briefly how it converts electrical current variations to sound.

8. The Post Office uses many "magnetic relays". What is the purpose of a magnetic relay? Describe a relay, and explain how it works.

40 · ELEMENTARY PHYSICS

9. If you were given a circular coil of wire and a small light magnet, explain how you would design a simple current-measuring instrument. Draw a sketch of the arrangement.

10. Describe how you would obtain the magnetic field pattern round a short circular coil, labelling the complete circuit used. Sketch the appearance of the lines of flux marking their direction and that of the electron current in the coil.

CHAPTER FIVE

Electrical Energy

Heating Effect

As we have already seen, a small electric lamp lights up when a battery B is joined to it with a rheostat R in the circuit (Fig. 40(i)). Thus an electric current has a heating effect—since the source of light is a white-hot filament. When the resistance is decreased by the rheostat R, the filament glows brighter, showing that the temperature is increased when the electric current is increased. This fact can also be demonstrated by immersing a resistance coil inside water in a vessel, and joining it to a battery and a rheostat S (Fig. 40(ii)). The current is switched on, measured by the instrument A, and the temperature rise in 2 minutes is observed by a thermometer in the water. Suppose it is 4 degrees. The resistance in the circuit is then diminished by S so that the current now increases, and the temperature rise in 2 minutes is again observed. This time it is greater than 4 degrees, showing that the heat energy produced in a wire in a given time increases when the current increases.

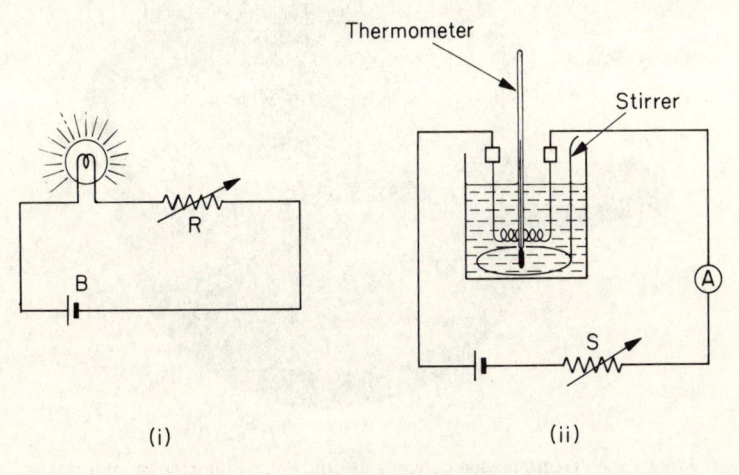

Fig. 40. Thermal energy from electric energy

By experiments with a longer length of coiled wire, and with a stop-clock, it can also be shown that the heat energy produced per minute by a given current increases when the resistance of the coil increases. The heat also increases when the time increases; in twice the time, the heat produced in a given wire is also doubled.

Applications of the Heating Effect

The heating effect of an electric current has many useful applications in the home. Electric fires, for example, contain nichrome (high resistance) wire between their terminals, and the heat produced when the wire is connected to the mains is sufficient to make the wire glow and give out considerable heat. The power consumed by the electric fire is expressed in *watt* or *kilowatt*. A fire of 1 kilowatt will give out twice as much heat energy per second as one of $\frac{1}{2}$ kilowatt. The power of any electrical device can be found from the simple relation = watts = volts × amperes. Thus a heater using 4 A from a 250 V supply has a power input of $250 \times 4 = 1000$ watt = 1 kilowatt.

Electric cookers and electric irons also contain nichrome wire.

Plate 7. An electric kettle converts electric energy directly into thermal energy by means of a heater fully immersed in the water

heated by the electric current which flows through them. In the electric cooker, the wire is wound on fireclay formers attached to the oven walls; in the electric iron, the wire is situated in the base.

Cables and Fuses

The heating effect of the electric current is used to supply lighting in the home and buildings generally. The current is carried from the mains electric supply by cables beneath the floor. The electric current required for lighting is much smaller than that required for heating, and consequently the cables for the lighting circuit are thinner than those used in a heating circuit. The maximum safe current in lighting circuits is about 5 ampere; larger currents would make the copper cables become too hot, thus damaging the insulation and giving rise to the possibility of fire. Electric heaters, which may take more than 5 ampere, must therefore never be used in a lighting circuit. They are used in the circuits which can carry currents up to 10 or 15 ampere and which have relatively thick cables.

Fuses are used for safeguarding lighting and heating circuits in buildings. They are also used for safeguarding against excessive currents in instruments such as television sets, for example. Fuse wire has a low melting-point; it is made of an alloy of tin and lead, the former having a low melting-point. Thin fuse wire may be graded as "5 A" wire, and is used in the lighting circuit; thicker fuse wire may be graded as "10 A" or "15 A" wire, and is used in the heating circuit. If a current greater than 5 A flows in the lighting circuit, for example when the wires from the mains accidentally touch each other, the high current causes the fuse to melt and break. The fuse can easily be renewed after the circuit fault is found.

Electric Filament Lamps

The electric filament lamp was invented in America by Edison in 1879 and in England by Swan about the same time. The early electric lamp contained a thin carbon wire or filament, but this tended to oxidise owing to the air in the lamp. It also tended to vaporise at high temperatures, with deposit of carbon on the glass bulb, so that the "life" of the filament was short.

To overcome these difficulties metals with high melting-points were used, and the air was pumped out of the bulb before it was sealed. The metals osmium and tantalum were used in 1903, and tungsten about 1910. In 1913 Langmuir introduced the coiled filament, and in 1937 the filament was wound on itself, making a "coiled-coil" filament, thereby increasing the amount of light given out (Fig. 41).

Nowadays, the air is pumped out of lamps greater than 40 watt in

44 · ELEMENTARY PHYSICS

power, and replaced by traces of the inactive gas argon. The "atmosphere" round the filament reduces evaporation from the tungsten. This type of lamp is called a "gas-filled" lamp. In lamps of smaller power than 40 watt the space round the filament is left as a vacuum, as excessive evaporation does not occur.

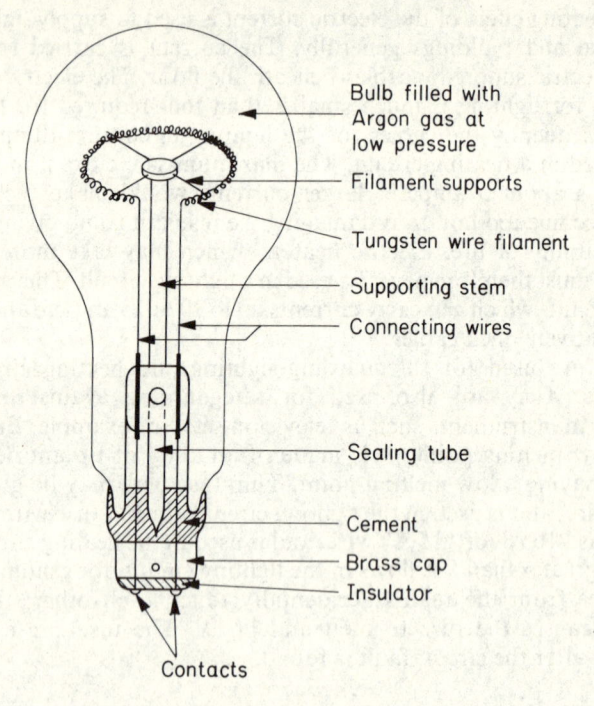

Fig. 41. Filament lamp

Plate 8. Magnified photograph of a coiled-coil filament

Electric Fluorescent Lamp

The brightly coloured signs outside shops in busy thoroughfares are due to glowing gases inside glass tubes, and they are produced when a high voltage, originating from the mains, is connected across metal electrodes at each end of the tube containing the gas. Mercury vapour has a greenish glow; neon gas has a red glow; sodium vapour has an orange glow. The glowing gas is called generally a "discharge".

Fluorescent lamps are now widely used in buildings and roads. They contain powders called "phosphors" along the sides of the tube, which glow when exposed to ultra-violet light. When the lamp is switched on a discharge is started. Ultra-violet light is also produced, and by a suitable mixture of powders light approximating to daylight can be obtained. The fluorescent lamps give as much light as the filament lamp with far less consumption of energy, and are therefore much cheaper to run.

Chemical Effect of a Current

Electrolysis of water. The flow of electric current through liquids was studied by Faraday and other scientists from the early 19th century. It was soon discovered that water, for example, was decomposed by a current. To demonstrate this effect, some water is placed in a beaker, together with a little dilute acid to make it conduct better, and the ends A, C of two wires joined to an accumulator B are dipped into the water (Fig. 42). Gases are then observed to rise from A and C.

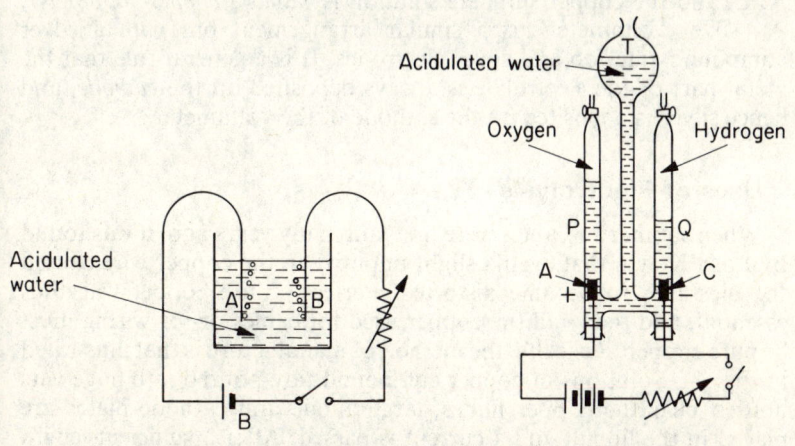

Fig. 42. Electrolysis of water in a beaker

Fig. 43. Electrolysis of water in a Hoffmann voltameter

In order to collect and measure the gases a special apparatus called a *Hoffmann voltameter* or *water voltameter* is used. This consists essentially of two inverted burettes P, Q, joined to a central tube T into which acidulated water is poured (Fig. 43). Two wires A, C, with small pieces of platinum foil attached, dip into the liquid at the bottom of each burette. These are called *electrodes*. The electrode A joined to the positive side of the battery is called the *anode* of the voltameter; the electrode C joined to the negative side of the battery is called the *cathode*. When the burettes are completely filled, and a battery or the mains is connected to A, C, and switched on, gases begin to rise from A, C and collect at the top of P and Q. When the current is switched off, twice as much volume of gas is found in Q as in P. By means of a glowing splint, which bursts into flame when placed in it, the gas in P is found to be oxygen. When a lighted taper is placed in a test-tube of the gas collected from Q, a slight explosion is heard; the gas in Q is hydrogen. These gases come from water (H_2O), some of which has therefore been decomposed by the electric current. The acidulated water is said to be "electrolysed" by the current, and a study of the subject is called *electrolysis*. Liquids which conduct electricity and are decomposed at the electrodes are called *electrolytes*.

Electrolysis of copper sulphate solution. The electrolysis of a solution of a metallic salt such as copper sulphate solution can be studied by placing two copper plates A, C inside a beaker containing the liquid (Fig. 44). A battery is connected to A & C, the current is switched on, and about 20 minutes later it is switched off. When the cathode plate C is removed from the liquid, a fresh deposit of copper is observed on the plate. No deposit is obtained on A. The beaker, the copper electrodes A, C, and the copper sulphate solution is called a *copper voltameter*. A "silver voltameter" is a similar arrangement but with a silver compound solution and silver electrodes. It is a general rule that the metal part of the electrolyte is always deposited on the *cathode*, and hence silver is deposited on the cathode of the voltameter.

Uses of Electrolysis

When submarine cables were first laid many years ago, it was found by Lord Kelvin that even a slight impurity in the copper wire caused the messages to become distorted. Perfectly pure copper was thus essential, and today all the copper used for cables or for wiring must be pure copper. Basically, the method of manufacture is that illustrated in Fig. 44. Solutions of copper compounds are poured into huge vats housed near the copper mines, large anode and cathode plates are placed in the liquid, and a current is passed. After a sufficient length of time a thick deposit of pure copper is formed on the cathode plate, and the metal is then stripped off. As it is manufactured by electrolysis, this is known as "electrolytic copper". Aluminium is manufactured by an electrolytic method in Scotland; the metals sodium and potassium are also manufactured by electrolysis.

Silverplating of all descriptions is done by electrolysis. The articles concerned, perhaps spoons, forks or knives, are suspended in a silver compound solution, and a current is passed for a suitable time. The articles to be plated are made the cathode, as the metal is always deposited on the cathode.

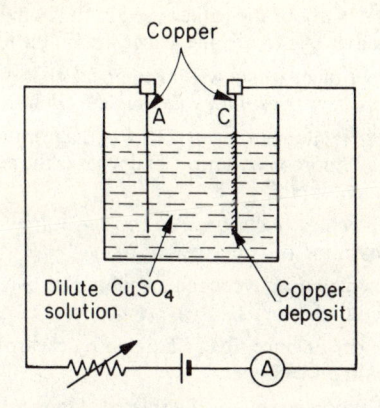

Fig. 44. Electrolysis of copper sulphate solution

Summary

1. The heat energy produced by an electric current depends on the current, resistance and time.
2. Cables which carry electric current for heating in buildings or the home are thicker than those carrying current for lighting.
3. A fuse is made of a tin alloy of low melting-point; when the maximum safe current is exceeded the fuse melts and breaks the circuit.
4. An electric lamp filament is made of tungsten coiled on itself; a gas-filled lamp contains a small amount of argon.
5. Fluorescent lamps contain powders which fluoresce when they are exposed to ultra-violet rays.
6. *Electrolysis* is the name given to the chemical effects produced by an electric current. An *electrolyte* is a liquid which conducts an electric current and is decomposed at the electrodes. A *voltameter* is a vessel used in electrolysis.
7. The *anode* of a voltameter is the electrode which is joined to the positive side of the battery: the *cathode* is the electrode which is joined to the negative side of the battery. In electrolysis of solutions of metallic compounds, the metal is always deposited on the cathode.

EXERCISES

1. Name three uses of the heating effect of the current in the home. What type of wire is used in these appliances?

2. Describe a *fuse*. Explain its purpose in a circuit.

3. What do you know about the cables used in the home for lighting and for heating? Why is it inadvisable to use an electric fire on the light mains?

4. Describe an experiment to show that the heat energy produced in a wire increases as the current increases. Draw a complete circuit.

5. Describe an electric filament lamp. Draw a diagram in illustration. What produces the light in a "fluorescent lamp", and what is the advantage of this type of lamp over the filament lamp?

6. What are the following: *electrolysis, electrolyte, voltameter, anode, cathode?* Draw a sketch in illustration of your answers.

7. Describe how oxygen and hydrogen are obtained by electrolysis of water. Draw a complete circuit.

8. How is pure copper or pure silver obtained by electrolysis? Describe fully an experiment to obtain pure copper.

9. Describe how a spoon could be silverplated. Draw a fully labelled circuit.

CHAPTER SIX

Batteries, Motors & Generators

Simple Cell

About 1790, an Italian scientist called Galvani noticed the twitching of a dead frog's leg when the nerve was touched by two unlike metals in contact. He told his friend Volta about it, and after many experiments Volta concluded that an electric current had been generated in the muscle by the presence of the two metals and the chemical solutions in the nerve. About 1800 Volta made a great discovery and invention. He placed a number of copper and zinc discs together, with cloth or cardboard soaked in brine between them, and found that an electric current was generated when the terminals were joined (Fig. 45(i)). One pair of copper and zinc plates with brine between them, such as A, B, forms a unit or *cell*; the whole arrangement was called "Volta's pile" and a number of such cells joined together to assist each other is called a "battery".

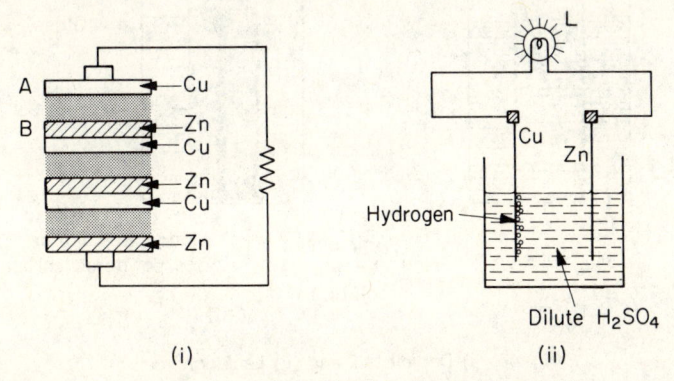

Fig. 45. Volta's pile (i), and a simple cell (ii)

Nowadays, a simple cell can be made by dipping a copper plate and a zinc rod inside dilute sulphuric acid in a beaker; the acid takes the place of the brine (Fig. 45(ii)). This cell has an *electromotive force (e.m.f.)*, which can be thought of as "electron-moving force", of about 1 volt. When a small torch bulb is joined to the terminals of the copper and zinc the bulb lights up for a time, but it soon becomes dim and goes out. The cell is now said to be "polarised". The main cause of the polarisation is hydrogen gas, which is produced at the copper plate when the cell is working. This sets up what is called a "back" e.m.f., which opposes the main e.m.f. Further, the gas has a high electrical resistance, thus tending to diminish the current flowing.

Daniell and Leclanché Cells

Many different kinds of cells were invented in the nineteenth century. All of them aimed at eliminating polarisation so that the cell kept on working, and most of them used chemicals which were abundant and relatively cheap.

One typical cell, rarely used now, was invented in 1836 by John Daniell, a professor of chemistry at London University. It has a copper vessel B as the positive pole, a zinc rod as the negative pole, dilute sulphuric acid in a porous pot A as the main liquid or electrolyte, and copper sulpate solution in the vessel to eliminate the hydrogen (Fig. 46 (i)). The copper sulphate solution is called the *depolariser*. The porous pot allows the two liquids to be brought into contact with each other but prevents them from mixing. The electromotive force of the Daniell cell is just over one volt; this cell can maintain a small current for a long time.

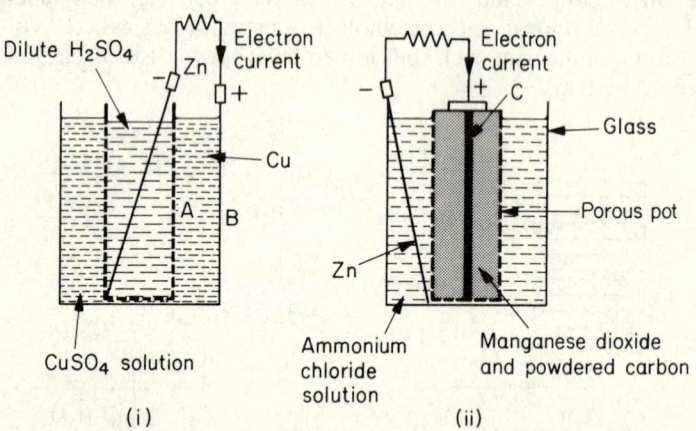

Fig. 46. (i) Daniell cell, and (ii) Leclanché cell.

Leclanché invented a cell which used a zinc rod as the negative pole, a carbon rod as the positive pole, ammonium chloride solution as the electrolyte and manganese dioxide as the depolariser. The oxide is a powder packed round the carbon rod, and to make it more conducting it is mixed with carbon powder. The Leclanché cell has an e.m.f. of about $1\frac{1}{2}$ volt, but it polarises after a time. The cell recovers from polarisation when it is allowed to rest.

Dry Battery

The Leclanché type of cell is used nowadays in torch batteries and in radio batteries. The ammonium chloride is made in the form of a paste because liquids are impracticable when a battery is carried about, so the cell becomes relatively "dry", and the container is made of zinc (Fig. 46(iii)). The manganese dioxide and powdered carbon are in a muslin container round the carbon rod, and a layer of cardboard at the bottom insulates the carbon rod from the zinc container.

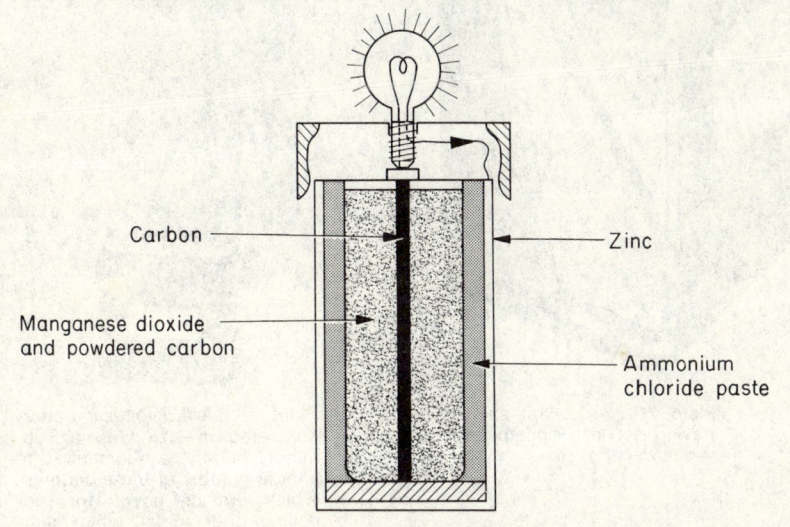

Fig. 46. (iii) Dry cell

Plate 9. The structure of a dry cell

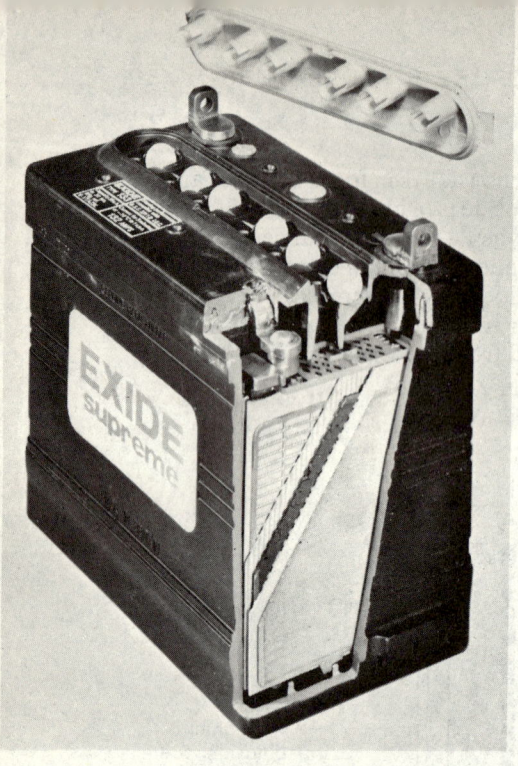

Plate *10*. A 12-volt car battery having six lead accumulators in series

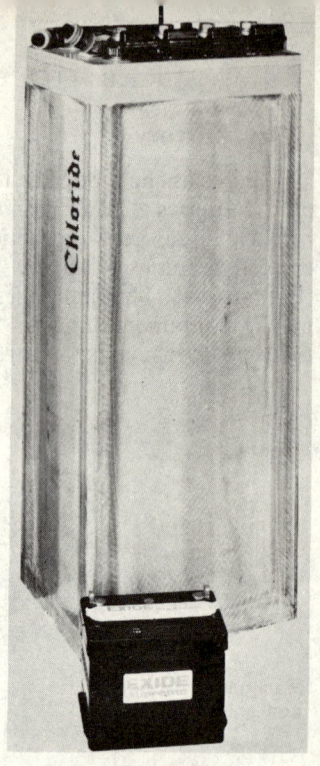

Plate *11*. A 12-volt car battery compared in size with a submarine battery. A submarine has a large number of these batteries, which provide power for propelling the vessel when submerged. They are then recharged when the vessel surfaces.

Torch batteries may contain several "dry" cells, as they are known, and a 120-volt battery contains eighty such cells. When a torch battery switch is pressed, the case makes contact with one end of the lamp filament through the outer casing of the bulb. The other end of the filament is connected to the bottom of the bulb, which presses on the terminal joined to the carbon rod in the middle of the battery. As the zinc base of the cell is in contact with the torch case a complete electric circuit is made, and a current now flows through the filament.

The Accumulator

The cells previously discussed are known as *primary cells,* and are only capable of supplying a small current for a relatively short time. If a large current is required for several hours for example, an *accumulator* or *secondary cell* is used. The most common form is the lead–acid accumulator, which has a plate containing lead peroxide (chocolate-brown in colour) and a plate containing lead (slate-grey in colour), both

BATTERIES, MOTORS & GENERATORS · 53

plates being immersed in sulphuric acid (Fig. 47 (i)). The lead peroxide is the positive pole; the lead is the negative pole. No depolariser is necessary. Further, the accumulator can easily be recharged when run-down, whereas the primary cells are then of little value.

After the accumulator has been used for many hours chemical changes occur, the density of the acid drops and the e.m.f. falls from about 2·0 to 1·9 volt. In this condition the accumulator will be damaged if it is used further. The cell is therefore "re-charged" by passing an electric current through it in the *opposite direction* to the way in which it supplied current when it was used. This is achieved by connecting the positive terminal of a direct voltage supply to the positive pole of the accumulator, and the negative terminal to the negative pole (Fig. 47 (i)). A rheostat R is essential in the circuit to control the amount of current passing through the accumulator, which is registered by an ammeter A. The current value recommended by the manufacturers should be used. After a time, as determined by testing the relative

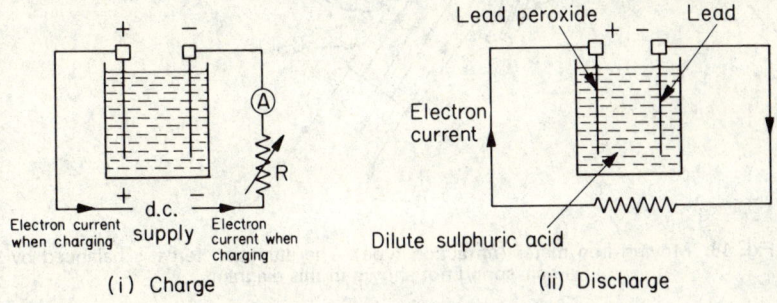

Fig. 47. A lead accumulator in use

density (see chapter 27) of the acid with a bulb hydrometer, the accumulator is re-charged and is again ready for use.

Accumulators are used at telephone exchanges by the Post Office; they maintain the steady current required in telegraph and telephone lines. They are also used in cars to operate the starter motor and for operating the lights, for supplying current to the electric motors in light trucks, and for providing emergency lighting in ships.

Nife Cell

In addition to the lead–acid accumulator just described, the Nife accumulator is now widely used. This has a positive pole of nickel hydroxide, a negative pole mainly of iron and an electrolyte of caustic potash solution. The Nife cell is not affected by mechanical vibration or by being left in an uncharged condition, both of which spoil the lead–acid accumulator. It has a long life, and does not require skilled attention as it is not easily damaged.

Moving-iron Instruments

We now turn to consider the principles of electrical measuring instruments which utilise the magnetic effect of a current. We shall describe an *ammeter*, an instrument which measures electric current; in fact, an ammeter is an "ampere-meter", the ampere being the unit

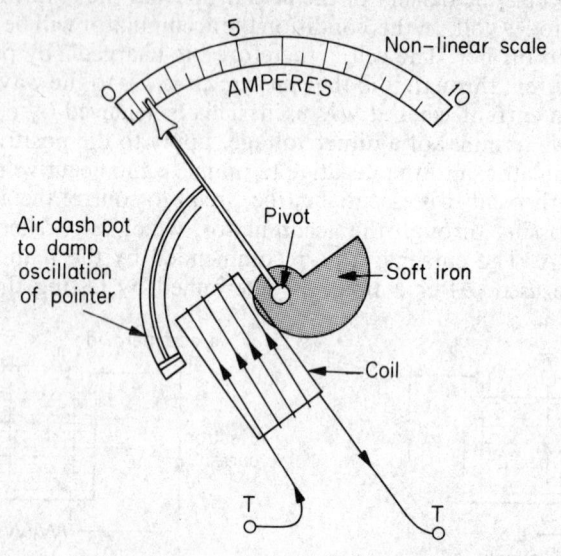

Fig. 48. Moving-iron meter (attraction type). The attraction force is balanced by a hair-spring not shown in this diagram

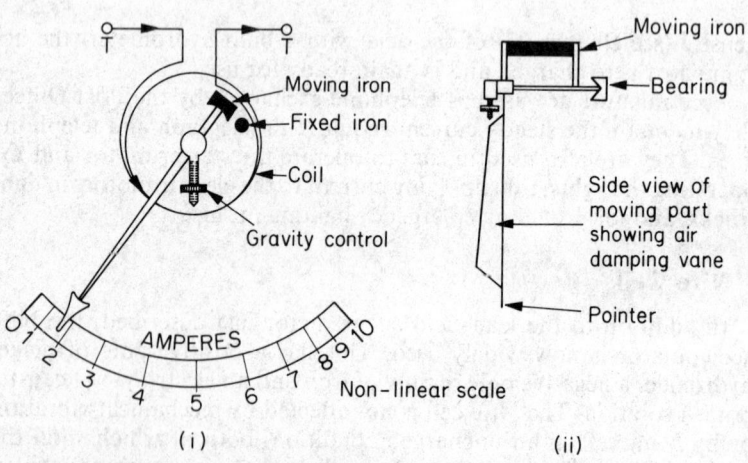

Fig. 49. Moving-iron meter (repulsion type). If the instrument is to be used horizontally, the gravity control is replaced by a hair-spring

BATTERIES, MOTORS & GENERATORS

of current. A *voltmeter* is an instrument with a similar construction which measures potential difference (p.d.); the volt is the unit of p.d. It should not be confused with the unfortunate term "voltameter" encountered in chapter 5.

The moving-iron ammeter is a robust one, and is used for measuring large currents. In the *attraction type* (Fig. 48), the current flows through a solenoid. A piece of soft iron near one end of the coil is then attracted, and a pointer is then deflected over a scale. Since the force of attraction increases when the current increases, the deflection provides a measure of the current.

In the *repulsion type* (Fig. 49), the solenoid contains two soft-iron rods. One is fixed, the other can move. When a current flows, each rod becomes magnestised with like poles facing each other. The rods then repel each other, and a pointer, operated by the movable rod, is then deflected. As the rods become more powerfully magnetised when the current is increased, the deflection provides a measure of the current.

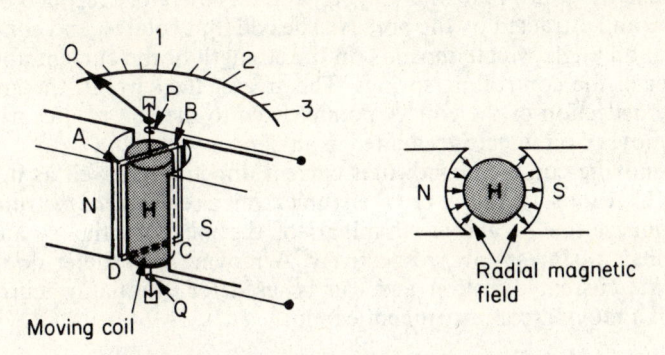

Fig. 50. Construction of a moving-coil meter

Moving-coil Ammeter and Voltmeter

The most reliable and widely-used ammeter or voltmeter has basically a *moving-coil system,* Fig. 50. This consists of
(1) A permanent magnet with curved poles N, S,
(2) a soft-iron cylindrical core H,
(3) a rectangular coil of insulated wire ABCD moving in the space between the poles N, S and the core H,
(4) springs P, Q, which control the deflection of ABCD and also convey the current to and from the coil.

The core H creates a powerful radial magnetic field in the region of the coil ABCD, which can move about a vertical spindle in a narrow air-gap between H and the poles N, S.

When the ammeter or voltmeter is connected in a circuit, the current

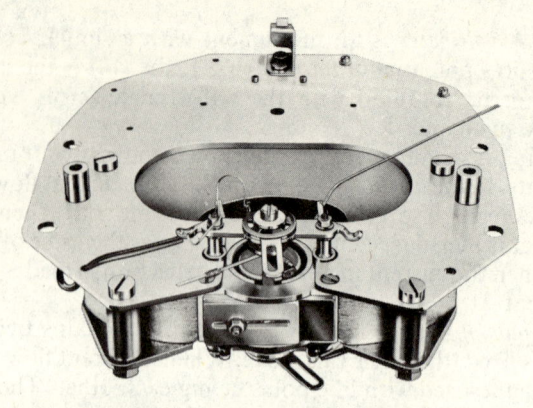

Plate *12*. A moving-coil meter. (*Courtesy of Saugamo Weston Ltd.*)

to be measured flows through the coil ABCD. One face of the coil then acts like the south pole of a magnet, and it is therefore repelled by the pole S and attracted by the pole N. The coil thus rotates, and comes to rest at an angle which depends on the strength of the current and the power of the controlling springs. The greater the current, the greater is the deflection of the coil. A pointer fixed to the coil rotates with it, and moves over a scale graduated in ampere or volt.

A moving-coil meter indicates current direction, as well as magnitude. Care must therefore be taken (unless it is a centre-zero instrument) to connect the + and − terminals of the meter to the + and − terminals of the supply, respectively. A moving-iron meter does not indicate current direction and can be used for alternating currents, which a moving-coil instrument cannot.

Principle of Electric Motor

The moving-coil meter is the simplest form of electric motor, but the existence of the springs prevents the coil moving more than a fraction of a complete revolution.

Electric motors are used to pull electric trains and trolley-buses, to move escalators and lifts and to operate vacuum cleaners. All electric motors contain two fundamental parts: (*a*) a coil of wire wound on a soft-iron core which spins round, often called the *armature*, (*b*) a permanent magnet or electro-magnet, which is called the *field magnet*.

A simple electric motor is shown in Fig. 51 (i). A coil of wire *abcd* is situated between the poles N, S of a magnet, and is capable of turning about an axis A. In the position shown, a current from a battery flows round the coil. The upper face then acts like a north pole. Since unlike poles attract and like poles repel, the coil turns round to face the south pole of the magnet. If the current continued to flow in the same direction, the coil would come to rest with its plane vertical. *As the coil passes the vertical, however, the current is made to reverse* (Fig. 51 (ii)). The face of the coil now changes to a south pole, repulsion occurs, and the coil hence rotates further. Every time the coil reaches the vertical, the current is made to reverse, and so the coil keeps spinning round.

The device which automatically changes the direction of the current in the coil is called a *commutator*. As shown in Fig. 51, a simple type

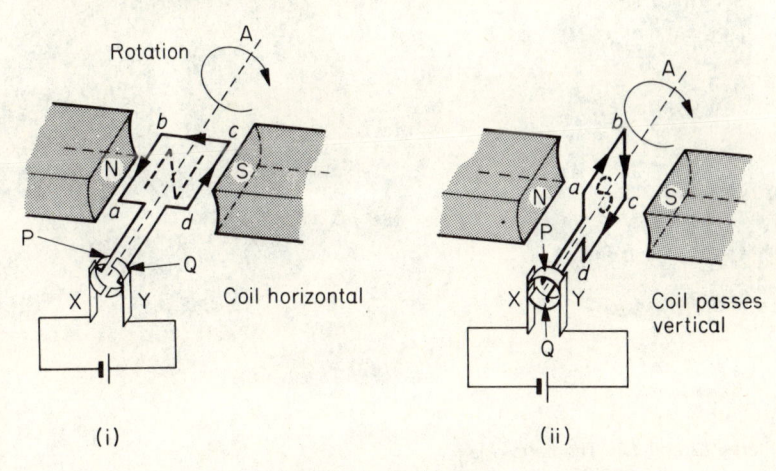

Fig. 51. A simple motor

consists of two insulated halves P, Q of a copper ring, to which the ends of the coil are permanently connected. The commutator rotates with the coil, and while so doing P, Q press against brushes X, Y, to which the battery poles are connected. When the coil passes the vertical, P moves from brush X to brush Y, and Q from Y to X (see Fig. 51 (i), (ii)). The connections to the battery poles are thus automatically reversed, and hence the current flows through the coil in the opposite direction.

Induced Currents

In 1831, after many years of experiment, Michael Faraday made a great discovery. He found that an electric current was produced when a magnet was moved to or from a coil of wire. A prominent Cabinet minister of the day visited Faraday soon after, and looking somewhat disdainfully at the simple apparatus, he enquired "What use can this discovery be?" "Sir," replied Faraday, "of what use is a new-born child?" And, indeed, this discovery led to the invention of dynamos and generators, which produce electricity for lighting and power today in homes and factories.

Faraday's discovery can be demonstrated by connecting a solenoid

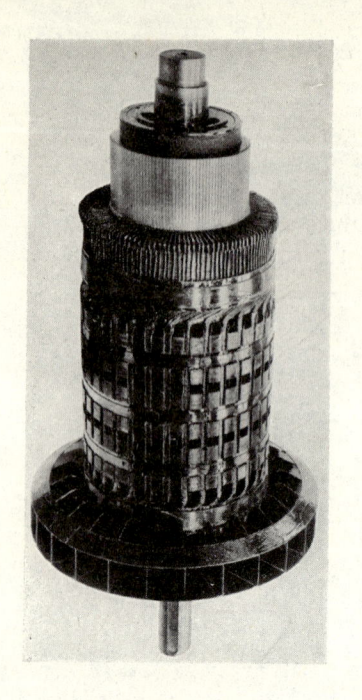

Plates *12* and *13*. The parts of a
d.c. motor

Plate *14*. A motor vehicle starting motor. On the left can be seen the commutator with many segments to which current is supplied through carbon "brushes" pressed against the commutator by thick springs. The coils consist of thick copper strips to carry the very large current required

C to a milliammeter A, i.e. an ammeter reading to one-thousandth of an ampere (Fig. 52(i)). When a magnet M is pushed into C, the needle in A is deflected, showing that an electric current flows. The current ceases as soon as the magnet stops. When the coil is moved but M stays still, a current is again obtained. Faraday pictured lines of flux passing from M through C, as illustrated in Fig. 52(i), and he said that an induced current is obtained in a coil when there is a *change* in the number of lines which pass through or link the coil. This occurs when the magnet, or the coil, is moved.

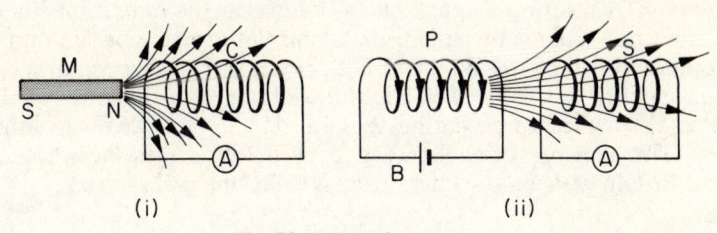

Fig. 52. Induced current

Faraday also used a coil P connected to a battery B instead of a magnet (Fig. 52(ii)). P then acted like a magnet owing to the magnetic effect of the current, and an induced current flowed momentarily in a neighbouring coil S joined to the milliammeter A.

Generators

A simple generator consists of a coil of wire *abcd* rotating steadily between the poles N, S of a magnet (Fig. 53(i)). As the coil rotates, it cuts the flux between the poles continuously. An induced current thus flows continuously in *abcd*. It is known as an *alternating current* (*a.c.*), as the current keeps reversing every half-revolution as it passes the

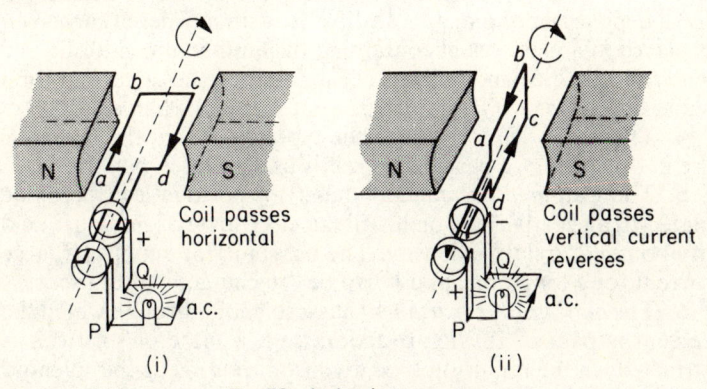

Fig. 53. A simple generator

vertical (Fig. 53(ii)). The current is led from the coil by two rings, which press against brushes P, Q to which a lamp, for example, may be connected. Higher induced voltages are obtained if the strength of the magnet is increased, if the coil is wound on a soft-iron core, if the coil is rotated faster and if the number of turns and area of the coil are increased.

Alternators, used at power-stations, are basically as above but with a somewhat different construction. Long parallel wires are connected together and contained in slots in a huge stationary iron ring known as the *stator*. A rotating magnetic field, known as the *rotor*, consists of magnetic poles, made by passing direct current from a separate supply through coils wound round them. The rotor is turned at constant speed by an engine, and induced voltages are obtained in the wires in the stator. From the power station the electric energy is "fed" to other areas. This network of cables carried by pylons serves the whole of Great Britain with electric energy and is called the **grid system.**

Summary

1. A *simple cell* contains (i) a positive copper pole, (ii) a negative zinc pole, (iii) a sulphuric acid electrolyte. The hydrogen, at the positive pole, causes polarisation in a short time.

2. A *Daniell cell* contains (i) a positive copper pole, (ii) a negative zinc pole, (iii) a sulphuric acid electrolyte, (iv) a depolariser; the porous pot is placed in copper sulphate solution in a copper can. The Daniell cell gives a small current for a fairly long time.

3. A *Leclanché cell* contains (i) a positive carbon pole, (ii) a negative zinc pole, (iii) ammonium chloride solution electrolyte, (iv) a depolariser of manganese dioxide, with powdered carbon; it is placed in a glass vessel containing the ammonium chloride and zinc rod. The Leclanché cell is cheap, and supplies a current for a short time, after which it polarises but recovers when rested.

4. The *"dry" cell* is a Leclanché type of cell, but the materials are in the form of a paste. This cell is used in torch batteries.

5. The *lead-acid accumulator* has (i) a positive lead peroxide plate, (ii) a negative lead plate, (iii) an electrolyte of sulphuric acid of about 1·25 relative density. The accumulator supplies a large current for a long time, and it can be "re-charged" after use.

6. The *moving-iron instrument* has a solenoid through which the current is passed. In the attraction type, a piece of soft iron is attracted; in the repulsion type, two iron rods inside the solenoid repel each other.

BATTERIES, MOTORS & GENERATORS · 61

7. The *moving-coil instrument* has a rectangular coil which rotates in the narrow space between a soft-iron cylinder and curved pole-pieces of a horse-shoe magnet. Springs control the deflection.

8. The *electric motor* has a coil wound on an armature between the poles of a magnet, and is similar in principle to a moving-coil meter. The ends of the coil are joined to the halves of a split-ring commutator. The commutator rotates with the coil, and presses continuously against fixed brushes, to which a battery is connected.

9. The generator has a coil which is driven round at constant speed between the poles of a magnet. An induced voltage is then set up at the terminals, so that the generator acts like a battery.

EXERCISES

1. Write down the contents of a "simple cell". Which is the negative pole and which is the positive pole? What are the disadvantages of the simple cell?

2. Draw a sketch of a *Daniell cell*. Write down its contents under the headings of: (i) Positive pole, (ii) negative pole, (iii) electrolyte. What is the purpose of the depolariser?

3. Draw a sketch of a *Leclanché cell*. What are (i) the positive pole, (ii) the negative pole, (iii) depolariser, (iv) electrolyte of the Leclanché cell?

4. Describe a *dry cell*. Draw a diagram of the dry cell. Why are dry cells preferred to "wet" Leclanché cells?

5. What are the approximate values of the e.m.f. at the terminals of (i) a Daniell cell, (ii) a Leclanché cell, (iii) a "simple cell", (iv) a dry cell?

6. What are the disadvantages of a Leclanché and a Daniell cell? Draw a labelled diagram of a Leclanché cell and a Daniell cell.

7. What are the advantages of an *accumulator?* Name the positive pole, negative pole and electrolyte of the lead-acid accumulator. Describe how the accumulator is restored to its original condition.

8. Describe fully the *moving-coil ammeter*. Explain how it works, and state its advantages.

9. How would you obtain an electric current in a coil without using a battery? How would you increase the current obtained? Draw diagrams to illustrate your answer.

10. Describe a generator and explain how it works. How can the voltage at the terminals be increased?

11. Describe one type of *moving-iron instrument*. Draw a diagram of it, and explain how it works.

CHAPTER SEVEN

Electric Charges

Early Discoveries

More than 2000 years ago, about 300 B.C., the Greeks knew that particles of chaff were attracted to amber necklaces which peasants wore in the fields. They called the phenomenon "electricity", after the Greek word for amber. Subsequently, many substances were found to possess the power, after they were rubbed, of attracting light particles, and they were then said to be "electrified" or *charged*. Today, the power of attraction can easily be shown by rubbing a plastic pen, ruler or a rubber balloon, on one's sleeve and bringing it near to small pieces of paper, which then fly up and cling to the pen or balloon. Thus stationary or electrostatic charges of electricity were first known about 300 B.C., whereas the electric current from a battery was not discovered until A.D. 1800.

Positive and Negative Charges

A small ebonite rod, charged by rubbing with fur and suspended by thread in a wire stirrup, can be used to test electric charges on substances. When another ebonite rod, charged by rubbing with fur, is

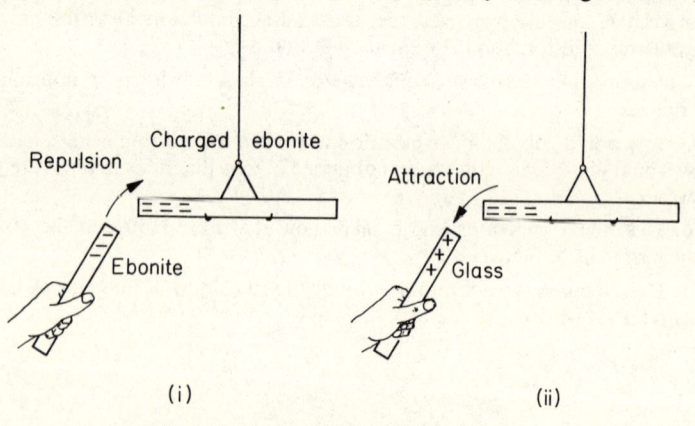

Fig. 54. Positive and negative charges

brought near to it, the former is repelled (Fig. 54(i)). When a glass rod, charged by rubbing with silk, is now brought near, the ebonite rod is attracted (Fig. 54(ii)). From these experiments, we conclude that the charge on ebonite is different from that on glass; and to distinguish between them, Benjamin Franklin, a noted American scientist of the eighteenth century, called the charge on an ebonite rod rubbed with fur *negative* and that on a glass rod rubbed with silk *positive*. Experiments show that *all rubbed substances have either negative charges or positive.*

Fundamental Law

From the experiments just described it follows that two negative electric charges repel each other, and that a positive electric charge attracts a negative charge. This is summarised by the rule
    Like (similar) charges repel, unlike (opposite) charges attract
and this is a fundamental law. It is similar to the fundamental law of magnetism, which says that like poles repel, unlike poles attract. Two positive charges thus repel each other, as can be shown with two charged glass rods.

Conductors and Insulators

It was discovered by Gray in 1729 that charged conductors lose their charge when suspended by wire but retain it when suspended by silk thread. He came to the conclusion that wire conducts electric charge but silk does not. He also found that the charge was lost when the thread was covered with dew, so that water is a conductor.

Substances can be divided into electric *conductors*, and non-conductors, or *insulators*. All metals, the human body and the earth are conductors; plastics, glass, sulphur, ebonite, bakelite, paper are normally insulators. A metal rod held in the hand cannot be charged permanently by rubbing, because the charge leaks away along the metal through the body to earth. If an ebonite handle is attached to the metal rod, however, and the ebonite is held in the hand, the metal rod becomes charged negatively when rubbed with fur. This is shown by bringing the metal near to a suspended piece of charged ebonite which is then repelled.

Electric Charge in Atoms

At this stage we should ask ourselves where the electric charges come from. The answer is simply that *the atoms of all substances contain electric charge*. This was discovered between 1897 and 1911 (see p. 71). Inside atoms there are particles which carry negative charge, called

electrons, and particles which carry positive charge called **protons** concentrated in a small central part of the atom called its *nucleus*. The electrons are very light particles which move round the nucleus. In the atoms of metals some of the electrons are relatively "free"; they can move about from one part of the metal to another. In the atoms of insulators, however, the electrons are firmly "bound" to their particular nucleus and are thus normally unable to move.

When an ebonite rod is rubbed with fur, some of the electrons in the atoms of the fur, however, do move to the ebonite. Since electrons carry negative charge, the ebonite rod now has a negative charge and it then attracts light particles as already stated. Having lost some negative charge, the fur has a surplus of *positive* charge. Consequently the rubbing material has a charge, as well as the substance rubbed. It should be carefully noted that rubbing causes electrons to be transferred from one substance to another; the process of rubbing does not create electric charge.

Gold-leaf Electroscope

The gold-leaf electroscope, invented in 1787, is a simple instrument which has been extensively used to detect electric charges. It consists of a vertical metal rod B with a gold-leaf L attached at the lower end and a metal disc or cap A at the upper end (Fig. 55(i)). The leaf and most of B are encased in a metal box C with glass windows, and insulated from C by a suitable plug. The box is usually placed on the table, and as wood contains some moisture, which is a conductor of electric charges the metal box is really connected to the earth.

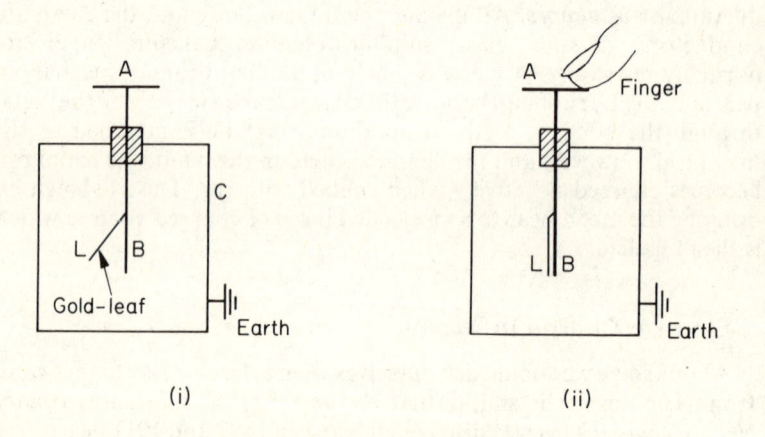

Fig. 55. A gold-leaf electroscope

ELECTRIC CHARGES · 65

When a charged rod is brought in contact with the cap A some of the charge passes to B and to L, and since like charges repel, the leaf L diverges from B, as shown in Fig. 55(i). The electroscope is now said to be "charged". When a finger is placed on A the charge leaks away through the body to the earth, and the leaf collapses (Fig. 55(ii)). The electroscope is now said to be "discharged".

Testing the Sign (or Polarity) of Charges

The gold-leaf electroscope can be used to find whether a charge is a positive or a negative one. The leaf L is given a negative charge, so that it diverges, and the unknown charge on a rod X is brought near to the cap (Fig. 56(i)). If the leaf diverges further, to L′, for example, the charge on X is negative.

Leaf diverges further
(i)

Leaf diverges further
(ii)

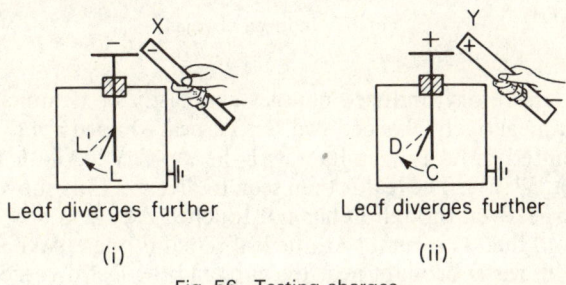

Fig. 56. Testing charges

When an uncharged object is brought near to the cap, the divergence of the leaf diminishes. The same effect is produced when a positively-charged rod is brought near to the cap. The sure way of testing a positive charge Y, therefore, is to bring it near to a positively-charged electroscope (Fig. 56(ii)). The divergence of the leaf then increases, from C to D, for example.

Induced Charges

About 1730 Gray amused his scientific friends one day by suspending his boy servant horizontally from two insulating ropes, and bringing a large charged rod D near his feet *without touching them*. Light particles such as pieces of paper were then attracted to the boy's nose! It thus appears that the nose had acquired a charge without being touched. To explain this, suppose that a negatively-charged rod D is brought near to the feet F (Fig. 57(i)). Since like charges repel, the electrons (which carry negative charges) in the body are repelled by D to the head, which thus has a negative charge. The nose is therefore now able to attract light particles. It should also be noted that the movement

D

of negative charge from the feet to the head leaves the feet with an excess positive charge. The charges at each end are called *induced charges* as they are not obtained by contact with a charged body. The "inducing charge" is D.

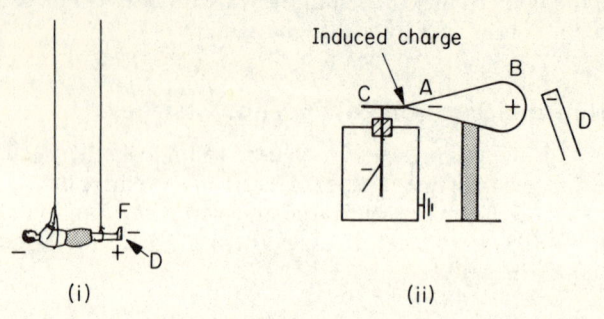

Fig. 57. Induced charges

In the laboratory, induced charges can easily be demonstrated by bringing a negatively-charged rod D to a pear-shaped conductor AB, whose pointed end A is in contact with the cap C of a gold-leaf electroscope (Fig. 57 (ii)). The leaf is then seen to diverge, thus showing it has some charge, even though D has not touched AB. A is now removed from C, and then D is removed; the leaf remains open. An ebonite rod rubbed with fur is brought near the cap, and the leaf diverges further, showing that the induced charge on C is negative. This is explained in the same way as the negative induced charge in Fig. 57 (i).

Charging an Electroscope by Induction

A gold-leaf electroscope can be charged by induction in four stages, illustrated in Fig. 58. A negatively-charged rod E is brought near to the cap A, whereupon the leaf L diverges (Fig. 58 (i)). The finger is now placed on the cap A, when the leaf closes (Fig. 58 (ii), then the finger is taken away, the leaf still remaining closed (Fig. 58 (iii), and

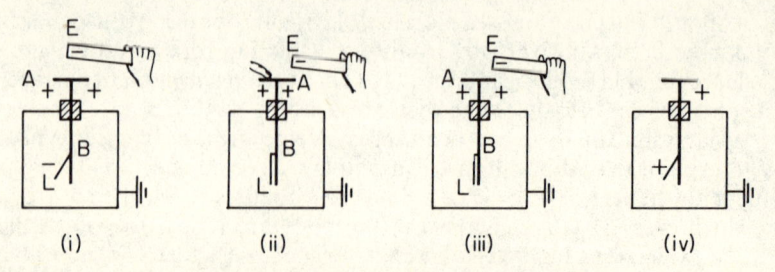

Fig. 58. Charging on electroscope by induction

finally the rod E is removed, when the leaf opens (Fig. 58 (iv)). The leaf thus has an induced charge, and on testing it is found to be a *positive* charge.

When the negatively-charged rod is brought near to the cap A, electrons (negative charges) are repelled to the leaf L, leaving the cap A with an equal positive charge (Fig. 58 (i)). When the finger is placed on A, the electrons on L now find an "escape path" through the body to earth and the leaf now closes (Fig. 58 (ii)). The leaf remains closed when the finger is taken away, *the rod E still being present* (Fig. 58 (iii)), but when the rod is taken away, the positive charge spreads over the cap and leaf, and the leaf therefore opens (Fig. 58 (iv)).

Franklin's Experiment

Franklin (see p. 63) was particularly interested in electrical phenomena, and he was the first person to demonstrate that lightning was due to electricity and not to an explosion of gases in the air, as had previously been thought. He attached a kite by silk thread to a key near the ground, and then flew the kite in a thunderstorm. Franklin had previously obtained sparks when presenting a knuckle to a charged rod, and he hoped to obtain sparks from the key. Nothing happened for a time. He was about to give up in despair when the rain came, and sparks were then obtained from the key. The rain had made the kite and silk thread conducting, and the charges in the air had then reached the key.

The Lightning Conductor

Franklin invented the lightning conductor, a long vertical rod with a sharp point at the top, placed near buildings to safeguard them. The lower end of the rod is buried with a metal plate in the earth (Fig. 59). When a thundercloud carrying negative charge is in the neighbourhood of a lightning conductor, a positive charge is induced at the point. *Now a pointed conductor loses its charge through the point to the surrounding air very easily,* that is, a pointed conductor discharges at the point. A positive charge is thus carried upward from the point of the lightning conductor, and this makes the thundercloud discharge silently. In the absence of the lightning conductor the thundercloud would discharge violently to the tops of buildings in the neighbourhood.

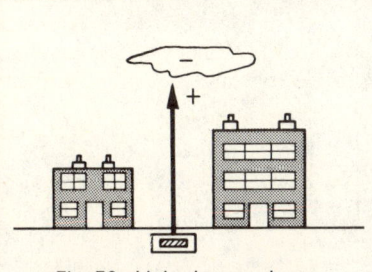

Fig. 59. Lightning conductor

Van de Graaff Generator

On p. 62 it was pointed out that electrostatics had been studied long before the invention of the cell or battery by Volta, which produces moving charges, known as electric current. In the nineteenth century many eminent scientists designed generators which produced high e.m.f. with static charges; these were therefore electrostatic generators. In the *Wimshurst machine,* first made in 1882, two circular plates carrying strips of metal were rotated, and an increasing electric charge was built up at two terminals. *Lord Kelvin* invented a number of electrostatic generators in the mid-nineteenth century. About 1860, however, dynamos, or generators of an electric current of moving charges, were invented, and as these machines produced high voltages more efficiently than electrostatic machines, the latter were to remain only as scientific curiosities.

About 1930, an American scientist, Robert Van de Graaff, read an account of Lord Kelvin's work on electrostatic machines, and was inspired to design a modern *electrostatic generator*. An early model about a foot high made his hair stand on end when he gripped the terminal of the instrument, showing that a very high voltage had been reached. The principle of the Van de Graaff generator, as it is now known, is illustrated in Fig. 60. A rubber (insulating) belt S revolves continuously round insulating rollers X, Y. The upper roller X is inside a large metal hemisphere R at the top of an insulating perspex column C, and a conductor Q, consisting of the pointed ends at the edge of a

Plate 15. A Van de Graaff generator for laboratory use

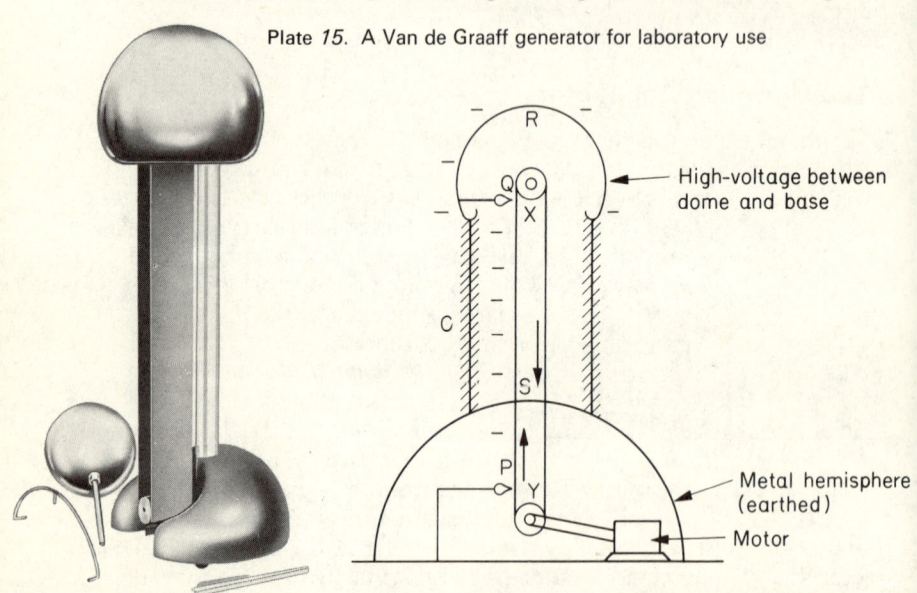

Fig. 60. Van de Graaff generator

wire gauze is placed opposite the belt near X and joined to R. P may be a similar piece of gauze in contact with the earthed base of the machine.

The belt is charged by friction with the roller Y; this charge is carried by belt to the top. When it comes opposite the pointed conductor Q, a positive charge is induced on Q and a negative charge on R. The positive charge is then sprayed from the pointed conductor Q to the belt in front of it, which neutralises the negative charge on the belt, and leaves it uncharged as it passes round X. When the belt comes round to P again the action is repeated. The net result is that R gains an increasing electron charge, and hence an increasing high voltage. High voltages can be roughly measured by the length of spark in air; 3000 V will spark across about 1 mm of air, 30 000 V across about 10 mm, and so on. Van de Graaff generators can produce several million volts, and they are used in Universities and nuclear-physics laboratories for atomic research.

Summary

1. *Negative* charge is formed on an ebonite rod rubbed with fur; *positive* charge is that on a glass rod rubbed with silk.

2. Electrons carry negative electric charge; protons carry positive charge.

3. Like charges repel; unlike charges attract.

4. The *gold-leaf electroscope* has a leaf attached near the end of a metal rod, which is insulated from the surrounding metal case. When the leaf is given a charge, the electroscope can be used to test other charges.

5. An *induced charge* is one obtained without any contact being made with another charge. To obtain an induced charge on an object A, (i) bring a charge X near to A, (ii) touch A, (iii) remove the finger from A, (iv) finally remove X.

6. *Pointed conductors* lose their charge easily. They are used in the lightning conductor and in the Van de Graaff high voltage generator.

EXERCISES

1. What is meant by a *positive charge* and by a *negative charge?* Describe how you would show that like charges repel, unlike charges attract.

2. Describe a *gold-leaf electroscope;* draw a diagram in illustration. How would you use the electroscope to test for a positive charge?

3. An ebonite rod X is rubbed with fur, and another ebonite rod Y is rubbed with flannel. Describe fully how you would test whether the charge on X is the same as on Y (i) without using an electroscope, (ii) using an electroscope.

4. A negatively-charged metal sphere A, on an insulating stand, is used to charge a metal sphere B also on an insulating stand. Describe fully how this is done, and explain what happens.

5. Describe a *lightning conductor*, and explain how it works.

6. What is an induced charge? Describe how you would obtain an induced positive charge on a gold-leaf electroscope.

7. Draw a diagram of a Van de Graaff generator. Describe how it works.

CHAPTER EIGHT

Electrons and Particles

The Electron

In 1897 Sir J. J. Thomson carried out experiments at Cambridge which revealed the existence of a particle much smaller than the hydrogen atom. Scientists had thought hitherto that the hydrogen atom was the smallest particle, but the new particle was about $\frac{1}{2000}$th of its weight. As it also carried a quantity of negative electricity the particle was called an *electron*.

As time passed, scientists made more discoveries about electrons. They found, for example, that electrons were present in every atom, from the lightest to the heaviest. Hydrogen has one electron, copper has 29 electrons; uranium, one of the heaviest elements, has 92 electrons. Also present in each atom is a small massive central core or *nucleus,* containing a quantity of positive electricity numerically equal to that on all the electrons. The electrons are moving round the nucleus, and are normally kept in their paths by a force of attraction; just as the planets, for example, are kept in their path round the sun by a force of attraction. In metals, however, some of the electrons are relatively "free", and when a battery is connected the electric force makes these electrons drift along the wire with a definite velocity. This movement is an "electric current". When the speed of the drift increases, the electric current increases; this is brought about by using a more powerful battery.

The Radio Valve

In 1902 Sir O. W. Richardson showed that some electrons escape from a metal such as tungsten when its temperature is very high. The process is similar to the evaporation of water when it is brought to its boiling-point; at this stage some of the molecules have received so much energy that they escape through the water surface and exist outside as vapour or "steam". In the same way, electrons can break through the "skin" of a metal and exist outside it if the metal is brought to a high temperature. This can be achieved simply by using a fine tungsten wire, and joining an accumulator to the ends. The wire

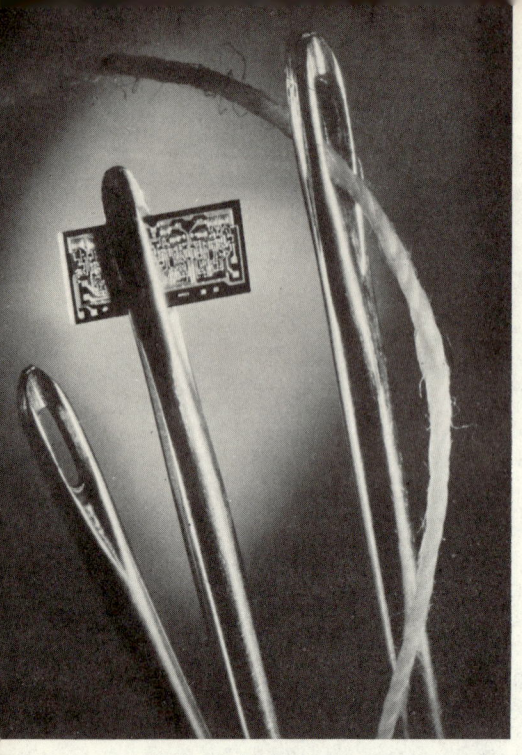

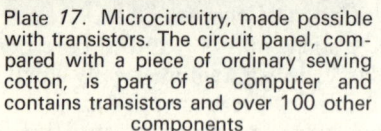

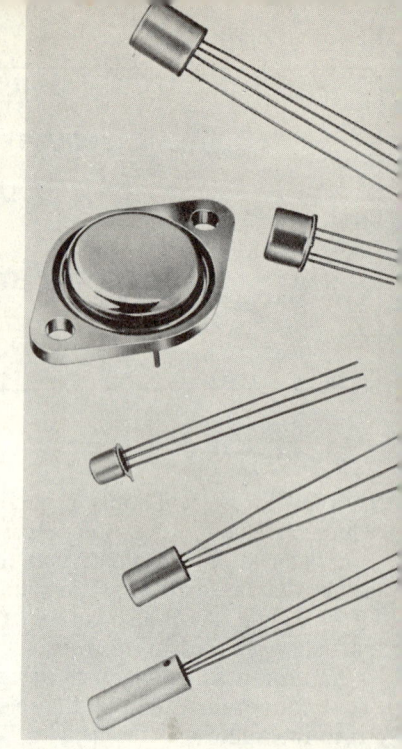

Plate *17*. Microcircuitry, made possible with transistors. The circuit panel, compared with a piece of ordinary sewing cotton, is part of a computer and contains transistors and over 100 other components

Plate *16*. Various types of transistors

becomes white-hot, and then emits electrons. This is called *thermionic emission*.

In 1904 Sir J. A. Fleming invented the *radio valve*; his original valve can be seen at the Science Museum, London. Without this invention, it is true to say that radio reception and transmission, including television, could never have advanced as far as it has today. Fleming's valve has a metal *filament* or *cathode* C, which emits electrons when heated as explained before, and an *anode* A, which collects the electrons (Fig. 61 (i)). When the valve is made, all the air is pumped out, leaving

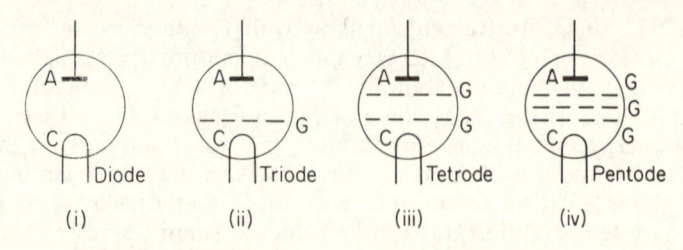

| (i) Diode | (ii) Triode | (iii) Tetrode | (iv) Pentode |

Fig. 61. Common types of radio valves

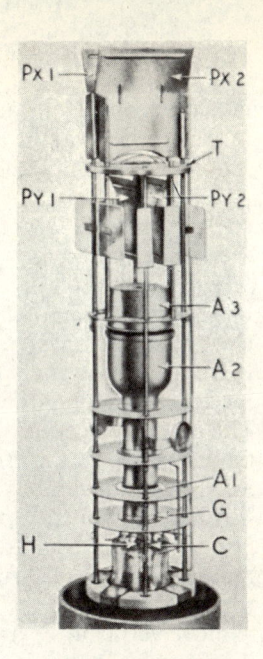

Plate *18*. A commercial oscilloscope tube; compare with Fig. 62

a vacuum. This type of valve is called a *diode,* a two-electrode valve, and it is used today in radio receivers. Other valves used today are the *triode,* the *tetrode* and the *pentode.* Besides its cathode and anode, the triode has a wire surrounding the cathode in the form of a grid G, Fig. 61 (ii). The tetrode has two grids G, G (Fig. 61 (iii)), and the pentode has three grids (Fig. 61 (iv)).

The **transistor** is a solid state device which performs the same function as a triode valve, but is much smaller, more reliable, and requires a lower voltage supply.

The Cathode-ray Tube

In television, or radar, a picture is obtained on a screen at the end of a glass tube called a cathode-ray tube. This tube, like the radio valve,

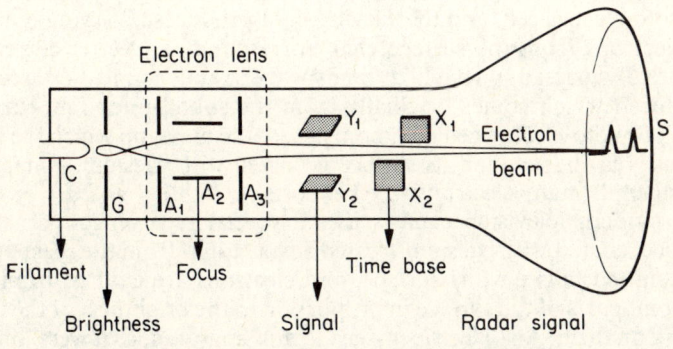

Fig. 62. The components of an oscilloscope tube

uses electrons which are emitted from a heated filament or cathode C at the other end of the tube (Fig. 62). The electron beam passes through a hole in a plate G, then through a number of plates or cylinders A_1, A_2, A_3, and passes between two pairs of plates $X_1 X_2$, $Y_1 Y_2$ before striking the end S, which is coated with zinc sulphide or other fluorescent material.

The plates and cylinder G, A_1, A_2, A_3 are kept at various potentials or voltages. The potential of G relative to C controls the number of electrons which pass on to the screen S; and since the *brightness* of the light increases when the number of electrons striking the screen increases, the brightness is controlled by altering the potential of G. The path of the electrons through A_1, A_2, A_3 depends on their potentials, which is of the order of several thousand volts relative to C. The electron beam can be *focused* on to S by altering the potential of A_2.

A varying voltage applied to the X plates X_1, X_2, deflects the beam horizontally at a uniform speed. This is called the fine time-base. A radio signal reflected from an aircraft, for example produces a voltage which is applied to the Y plates, Y_1 Y_2. This causes the electron beam to move vertically up and down the screen and indicates the presence of the aircraft. The position of the vertical trace along the horizontal line also enables the distance of the aircraft from the observer to be determined.

Photo-electric Cell

About 1880 it was discovered that light caused some electrons to break through a metal surface. Fundamentally, this is due to the fact that light is a form of energy, and some of the electrons near the surface gain sufficient extra energy to break through the surface. This phenomenon has led to the invention of the *photo-electric cell,* which used in cinema cameras to obtain the sound from a film strip called a "sound track". This runs alongside the film picture, and has a variation in density to light exactly similar to the sound waves required. A beam of light is shone through the moving film-track on to a metal surface in a photo-electric cell, and the varying light produces a varying number of electrons from the surface. The corresponding electric current is eventually passed through a loudspeaker, and sound is therefore produced which comes originally from the sound-track film. In one type of photo-electric cell commonly used, the metal on which the light shines is U-shaped, and its surface is coated with caesium, a material which emits many electrons when exposed to light.

A modern television camera uses a special type of light-sensitive surface, coated with caesium-treated silver. Light from the scene to be transmitted falls on this surface, and electrons are emitted from the different parts of the surface in proportion to the brightness of the light falling on them. An "electric image" is thus engraved, as it were, on the surface. The electric current so produced is amplified, sent out as radio waves from the transmitting station, and then received at the aerial of the television receiver. Here the "electric image" is extracted by radio circuits and then connected to the plates of a cathode-ray tube, producing a light image on the screen.

Atomic Particles.   Nuclear energy

Since the beginning of the twentieth century, many scientists have tried to find out whether particles other than electrons are contained in the atom. In the hydrogen atom, the lightest or simplest atom, the name *proton* was given to the hydrogen core or nucleus. The proton carries a positive charge equal numerically to the charge on an electron, because the hydrogen atom as a whole is electrically neutral, but the proton is about 1800 times as heavy as the electron and contains practically the whole mass of the hydrogen atom. The nucleus of a heavier atom is built up partly of protons.

In 1932 Sir James Chadwick discovered the existence of another particle in an atomic nucleus. It is called a *neutron* because it has no charge, but it is as heavy as a proton. A nucleus is built up of protons, neutrons and other particles not yet clearly defined. In 1939 Otto Hahn of Germany used neutrons as "bullets" which he fired at the nucleus of elements, because neutrons could penetrate deeply into the nucleus. He studied the resulting particles from the nuclear "explosion" or *fission* which resulted, and found in the case of uranium that a relatively large amount of energy was released and that more neutrons were released. It was then suggested that these neutrons can produce fission in turn in other uranium nuclei, so that a rapid *chain reaction* occurs in a mass of uranium. In this way there is a large release of nuclear energy.

Plate *19*. The nuclear power station at Dounreay, Scotland. The fuel is radioactive uranium, which produces plutonium as well as heat. The heat generates steam to drive turbines coupled to the electric generators

In 1955, Sir John Cockcroft stated that if used efficiently, 1 ton of uranium could produce as much energy as 1 million tons of coal, and many countries are now engaged in developing nuclear energy. In Britain, for example, the atomic energy centre at Harwell contains an atomic pile or nuclear reactor, a large "breeding" house for atomic energy materials such as uranium or plutonium. The reactor has blocks of uranium, with graphite rods dispersed among them to modify the velocity of the neutrons bombarding the uranium. The Central Electricity Generating Board has built several stations to assist the national grid; in these, nuclear energy replaces the energy obtained from burning coal in the older-type power stations. The nuclear energy, however, is still used to generate the steam which drives the turbines, and these, in turn drive generators as in a coal-fired power station.

Larger Particles—Molecules

The particles which determine the characteristics of materials are combinations of atoms, called *molecules*. The molecules of some oils are large enough to be measured, approximately, by a very simple method.

A metal tray is filled to overflowing with water; some melted wax, painted round the edge, will, on solidifying allow the water to reach a depth slightly greater than the depth of the tray, when level. Any dust on the water surface can now be scraped away by a clean rod or ruler resting across the edges of the tray. Some fine powder (lycopodium) is now sprinkled on the surface and a tiny drop of olive oil placed in the middle of the powdered surface. The oil will immediately spread out, pushing the powder before it, until it can spread no further; this can only occur when the layer of oil (which does not mix with water) can become no thinner. The thickness of the oil film must therefore be the length of one molecule.

If the initial oil-drop is held on a wire loop and compared with a millimetre scale, it will be found to be about 0·5 mm in diameter. The volume of this spherical drop ($\frac{4}{3}\pi r^3$) must be equal to the volume of the circular film which it forms ($\pi R^2 L$), where L is the thickness of the film, or the approximate length of a molecule. If r (radius of oil-drop) and R (radius of oil film) are measured, then L can be found from $\frac{4}{3}\pi r^3 = \pi R^2 L$.

Summary

1. The *atom* has a central core or nucleus carrying a positive charge, surrounded by moving electrons which carry an equal total negative charge. The mass of the atom is concentrated mainly in the nucleus; the electrons are extremely light.

2. The *radio valve* has a filament or cathode which emits electrons when it is heated, and an anode which collects the electrons.

The *transistor* is a solid state device which has replaced the valves in domestic radios and in computers.

3. The *cathode-ray tube* has a cathode which emits electrons towards a screen coated with a fluorescent paint, and a light is observed on the screen. There are controls for brightness, focus and a time-base. The signal is connected to the Y-plates, which deflects the electron beam up and down.

4. The *photo-electric cell* has a metal surface such as caesium which emits electrons when it is illuminated. The electrons are attracted to the anode, and an electric current flows whose strength is proportional to the intensity of the light.

5. *Nuclear (atomic) energy* is the energy released from the nucleus of a heavy atom, such as uranium, when it breaks up into several parts. The *neutron* is used to disrupt the nucleus.

EXERCISES

1. Describe a *diode valve*. Explain briefly how electrons are produced in the valve.

2. Draw a diagram of a *cathode-ray tube*. Describe the electrodes and interior of the tube, and explain briefly their various purposes.

3. Draw a diagram of a *photo-electric cell*. Describe how it works.

4. Describe the particles inside (i) a hydrogen atom, (ii) any other atom. What do you know about the electrons inside the atom of a metal, compared with those in the atom of an insulator like glass?

5. Describe how you could estimate the length of a molecule of olive oil.

CHAPTER NINE

Acoustics

One of the many uses of the cathode-ray tube described in chapter 8 is in the oscilloscope, an instrument used for making measurements on waves and the vibrations of particles—in particular the vibrations which carry acoustic energy (or sound).

Sound and Vibration

If you place your fingers lightly on a ringing bicycle bell, you will feel that the metal is *vibrating,* that is, moving to-and-fro. Vibrations can also be felt by touching a person's larynx while he or she is talking. If one end of a strip S of metal is clamped, and the other is pulled aside and released, a low hum can be heard and the strip can be seen vibrating (Fig. 63(i)). These and other observations lead to the conclusion that *sounding objects are vibrating.*

Vibrating metal strip

(i)

Vibrating tuning fork

(ii)

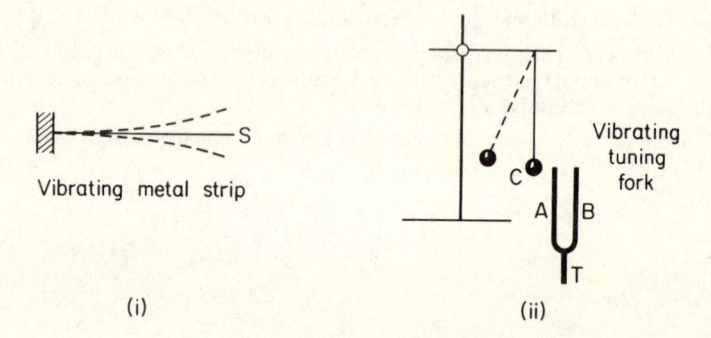

Fig. 63. Audible vibrations

A **tuning-fork** T has two prongs A, B which vibrate when the tuning-fork is struck (Fig. 63(ii)). The to-and-fro movement of each prong is very small, so that only close observation shows they are in rapid motion. The energy in the vibrating prong can be demonstrated, however, by bringing it near to a suspended piece of cork C, which flies away as the prong touches it (Fig. 63(ii)).

Sound and The Medium

Light, we know, reaches us from the sun after passing through many miles of largely empty space or a vacuum. In 1660 Boyle demonstrated, however, that sound requires a medium, or matter, for its transmission, and his experiment can be repeated in the school laboratory by suspending an electric bell B inside a glass jar A, taking care that the bell does not touch the sides of the jar (Fig. 64).

The jar is placed on a platform P with an opening through which the air can be pumped out. When the bell is connected to a battery C, ringing can be heard. As the air is pumped out, however, the ringing dies down, and after a time only a very faint sound can be heard, even though the clapper can be seen to strike the gong repeatedly. When the pump is stopped, and air is allowed to enter the jar again, the sound increases in loudness.

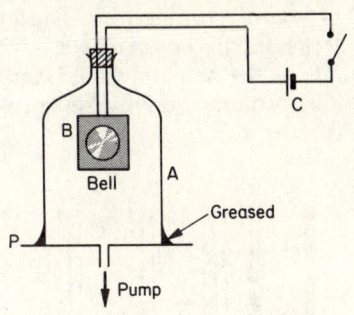

Fig. 64. The bell is inaudible in a vacuum

This experiment shows that sound does not pass through a vacuum. It passes through liquids such as water, and solids such as metals, in addition to passing through gases. As we shall now see, the medium plays an active part in transmitting sound pulses, or waves.

Sound Waves

If a number of stones are dropped one after the other into a pool of water, waves can be seen spreading out along the surface from the point where the stones strike the water. A floating object such as a piece of straw or a light twig will then be seen to move up and down as the waves reach it, but the object keeps its position approximately as the waves travel along the water. A snapshot of the water wave shows that it consists of a series of crests and troughs.

Wave Tank Observations

The observations outlined in the previous paragraph, and many more, can be made with the aid of a shallow wave tank. If water at one end of the tank is disturbed, for example by touching with a finger, a circular wave is seen to spread out from the point of disturbance. If now the finger is replaced by a vibrating point, driven by a small motor, the circular waves are now seen to be continuous; these are analogous to the pulses which carry sound in air. It can easily be seen that the water itself does not move, except slightly in a vertical direction as a wave passes a point on the surface; similarly any given particle of air is moved only slightly by a sound pulse—just enough, in fact, to transfer its energy of motion to the adjacent particles. The wave tank also shows that, if the vibrator has a fixed *frequency* (that is, a constant number of pulses per second), then the distance between corresponding points on successive waves is always the same. That is, there is a constant *wavelength* if the waves always move at the same speed. The relation between velocity, frequency, and wavelength is given on page 81.

Sound waves have an exactly analogous action. They are produced by a regular disturbance, for example by the movement of the vibrating prongs of a tuning-fork. The layer of air A immediately next to a prong P presses on the next layer B when the prong moves to R, and B in turn affects the neighbouring layer C (Fig. 65) In this way the layers pass energy along, and in a short time the disturbance, or pulse, reaches the listener at E.

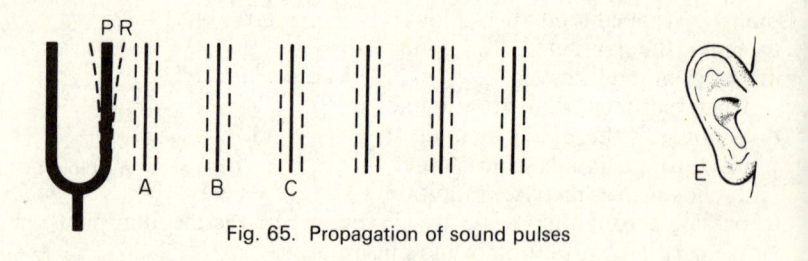

Fig. 65. Propagation of sound pulses

The movement of the air at a particular place such as C can be seen by sounding a tuning-fork near a microphone connected to an oscilloscope tube (Fig. 66). A wavy trace then appears on the screen. Thus the air at C vibrates (moves to-and-fro) while the sound travels. This is not surprising, as the movement of the air layers follow the movement of the source of disturbance, which is the vibrating tuning-fork.

An explosion, or loud bang, would not create a wave of this type in the air because it is not a regular disturbance, and it is called a *noise* in distinction from the "note" we are discussing.

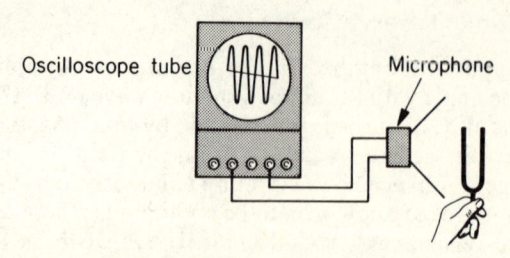

Fig. 66. Detection of sound pulses

ACOUSTICS · 81

Pressure Variation in Sound Wave

As the disturbance, or sound pulse, takes a small but definite time to travel from place to place in the air, the layers at different places in the medium are not vibrating "in step" with each other. Thus if a "snapshot" of all the layers is taken at some instant, we find that at some places such as *a, d, e* layers are crowded together, that is the pressure is a little above normal; at other places such as *b* the layers are relatively far apart, that is the pressure is a little below normal; and at other places the pressure is normal (Fig. 67(i)). As the pulse or disturbance travels along, the pressure at different points changes (Fig. 67(ii)). At each point in the air the pressure varies continously as the pulse travels along.

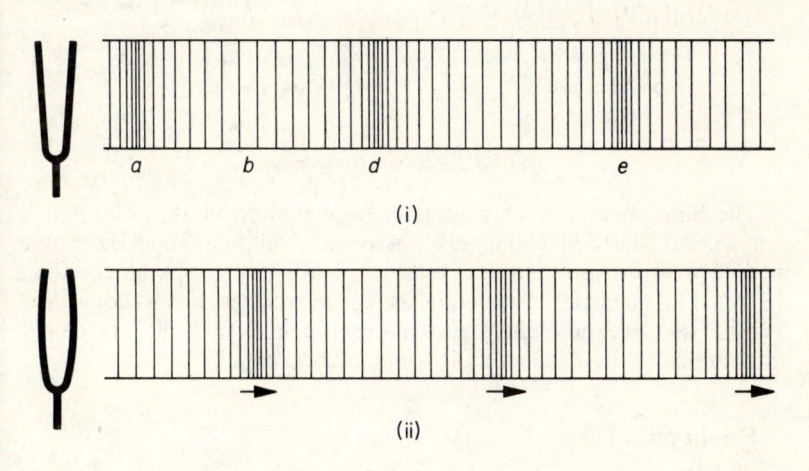

Fig. 67. Sound consists of pressure pulses

Wavelength.   Frequency

The distance between successive crests of a wave is called its *wavelength*, λ. The number of pulses per second of the layers, which is the same as that of the source of sound, is known as the *frequency*, f, of the vibration. The *velocity* of the wave, V, is given by
$$V = f\lambda,$$
as f waves, each of wavelength λ, spread out from the source in one second.

The speed of sound in air (or other gases) depends on its temperature. At normal temperatures the speed is about 330 m per second. The speed of light is about 3×10^8 m per second, and this explains why we can see a football kicked some distance away before the sound of the kick is heard. For the same reason, lightning is seen before the thunder is heard, although both phenomena occur almost simultaneously. If the time interval between the arrival of the flash and thunder is one second, the centre of the storm is roughly 330 m or $\frac{1}{3}$ km away.

Pitch and Frequency

If a person whistles into a microphone connected to an oscilloscope waves such as those shown in Fig. 68 (i) may be seen on the screen. If the pitch of the whistle is lowered, fewer waves are now observed on the screen, as illustrated in Fig. 68 (ii). We therefore conclude that *the greater the frequency of vibration of a note, the higher is the pitch.*

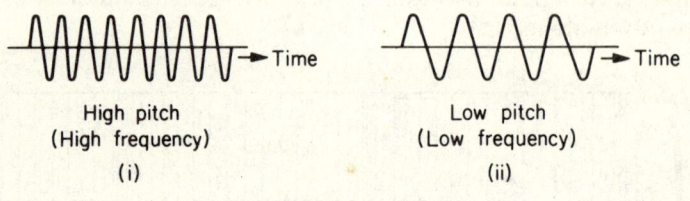

High pitch
(High frequency)
(i)

Low pitch
(Low frequency)
(ii)

Fig. 68. Pitch and frequency

The human ear can hear notes of frequency from about 20 pulses per second (hertz or Hz), a very low note, to about 15 000 Hz. Some people with exceptionally acute hearing can hear notes higher than 15 000. The "whistle" detected in television receivers in this country is 10 000 Hz. Cats and dogs can hear notes higher than 20 000 Hz, called ultrasonics, which are inaudible to the human ear.

Seebeck's Disc

The connection between pitch and frequency can also be shown with the aid of a Seebeck siren or disc (Fig. 69). This consists of a disc W with a number of equally-spaced holes in circles A, B round the centre C. The number of holes in the outer circle A is more than in B.

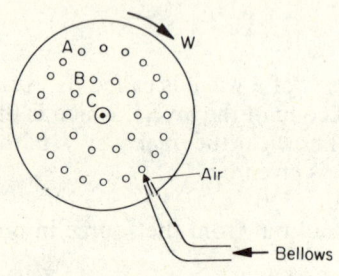

Fig. 69. Seebeck's disc, or siren

By means of a tube connected to a bellows, a constant stream of air can be made to pass through the holes in A or B. The disc is set up vertically, and rotated about C at a steady speed by means of a motor. A note is then heard whose frequency is equal to the number of "puffs" made per second by the air through the holes. If the number of holes is 20, and the disc makes 25 revolutions per second, the frequency is 20×25 or 500 pulses per second. When the air passes through the holes in B, which are fewer than in A, a note of lower pitch is heard. If W is rotated twice as fast, a note one octave higher in pitch is heard. This experiment shows that *the higher the frequency, the higher is the pitch of the note.*

Amplitude and Loudness. Quality or Timbre

When a tuning-fork is struck and quickly held in front of the microphone, large waves are first obtained on the screen (Fig. 70 (i)), but as the note dies down, smaller waves are obtained (Fig. 70 (ii)). The waves have the same frequency in each case, but they differ in *amplitude*. This is the name given to the maximum distance moved on one side of the time-axis; the amplitudes of the two waves are represented by a, b in

Loud sound
(Large amplitude – a)
(i)

Soft sound
(Small amplitude – b)
(ii)

Fig. 70. Loudness and amplitude

Tuning-fork
(i)

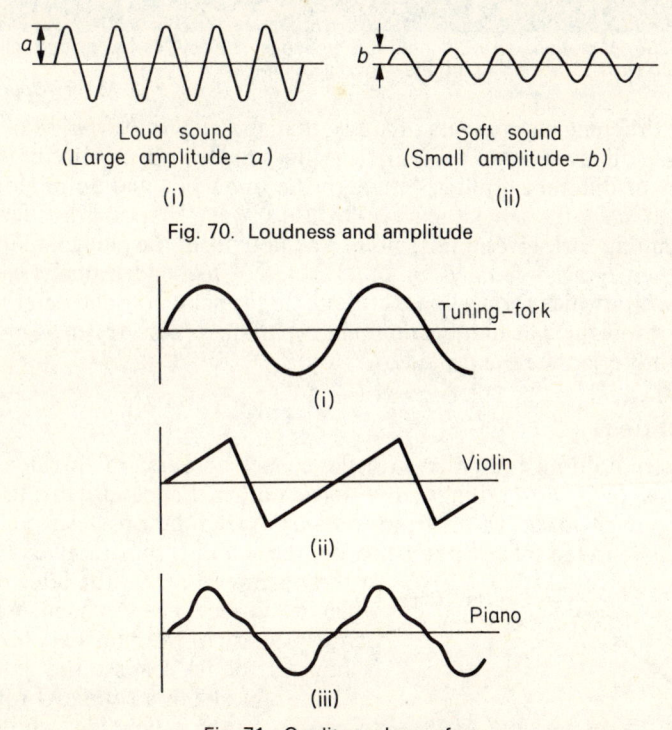

Violin
(ii)

Piano
(iii)

Fig. 71. Quality and waveform

Fig. 70 (i), (ii) respectively. We therefore conclude from this measurement that *the greater the amplitude of a wave, the greater is the loudness.* Thus further away from a speaker, where the sound is softer, the layers of air are vibrating through a smaller amplitude.

When two notes of the same pitch and loudness are played on the piano and violin respectively, one recognises by ear that the notes come

84 · ELEMENTARY PHYSICS

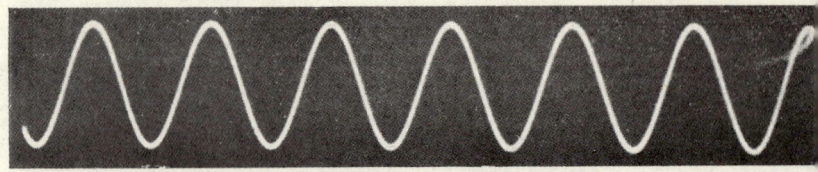

Plate 20a. Vibrations of a Tuning-fork note, frequency 391 cycles per second, photographed from a trace on a cathode-ray oscillograph.
(*From F. G. Mee's "Sound".*)

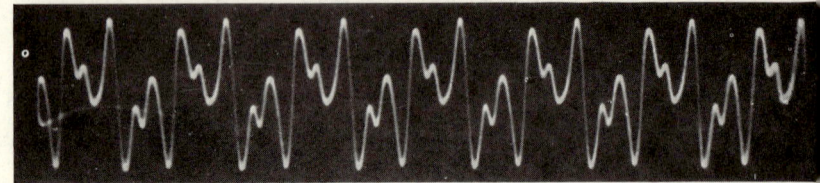

Plate 20b. Vibrations of a Clarinet note, frequency 196 cycles per second, photographed from a trace on a cathode-ray oscillograph.
(*From F. G. Mee's "Sound".*)

from different instruments. We say that the *quality* or *timbre* of the notes is different. Fig. 71 (i), (ii), (iii) illustrate the appearance of three waves of different timbre. Although the frequency and amplitude of the waves are the same, the wave-forms (or wave-shapes) are different. The tuning-fork gives a pure note. The note from the piano or violin, however, is accompanied by other notes of higher frequency called *harmonics*, which form a "background" to the main note and determine the wave-form. The number and relative loudness of the overtones give the timbre to the note produced.

Echoes

You are no doubt familiar with the echoes obtained in corridors or caverns, or by iron railings close to each other. Echoes are due to the reflection of sound waves from walls or other solid obstacles, just as light is reflected from a plane mirror; the sound is thus received back at the observer's ear a little later than when it started. The rounded Whispering Gallery of St. Paul's Cathedral is famous for its echoes; the gallery reflects sound from a source O round to people on the other side, who can then hear clearly what is being whispered (Fig. 72).

Echoes from ship's sirens have been used to find how close large icebergs are to ships at night in the Arctic. As an illustration, suppose the siren of a ship is sounded and an echo is received

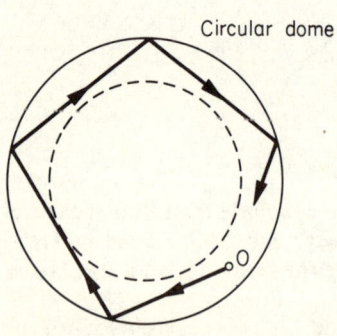

Fig. 72. Whispering gallery

ACOUSTICS · 85

4 seconds later. Since the speed of sound in air is about 330 m/s (p. 81), the distance from the ship to the iceberg *and back* is 4×330 or 1320 m. Thus the distance from the ship to the iceberg is 660 m or about $\frac{2}{3}$ km.

Depth Sounding

Nowadays many large trawlers are equipped with instruments which automatically record the depth of the sea-bed or of large shoals of fish. These instruments contain high-frequency transmitters T which send sound waves repeatedly vertically downwards through the water (Fig. 73). When a large solid obstacle on the sea-bed is encountered the waves are reflected, and the echo is received back in the instrument. The speed

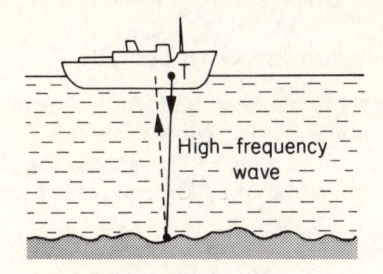

Fig. 73. Depth sounding

of sound waves in water is about 1440 m/s, and the depth of the sea-bed or shoal of fish can thus be calculated from the time taken by the sound waves to return. In the *echo-sounder*, as the instrument is called, a pen is made to move when the waves are received back, and an outline of the sea-bed is automatically recorded on a moving strip of paper.

Vibrations in Strings

In musical stringed instruments, strings are stretched tightly between two fixed points. The violinist or cellist places one finger on a string, and bows between that finger and the bridge, where the string also cannot move. In this way, a definite length of the string vibrates. By altering the position of the finger, longer or shorter lengths of strings are obtained, and this gives rise to different notes.

The laws relating to the vibrations of strings were first given by the French scientist Mersenne about 1636. He used a *sonometer*, a hollow box Q with a thin horizontal wire AP stretched across it, to investigate how the frequency of the note depended on the length bowed or plucked, on the tautness or tension in the wire, and on the material of the wire itself (Fig. 74). The wire passed over bridges at B and C, and the length of the wire plucked could be varied by altering the position of the bridge C. The tension in the wire was kept fixed by attaching a weight M at the end of the wire, as shown.

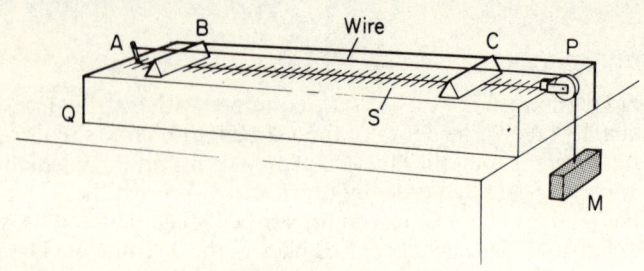

Fig. 74. A sonometer

Variation of Frequency with Length

To investigate how the frequency f of a note depends on the vibrating length l, a set of tuning-forks of known frequencies is used. The wire is gradually tuned in turn to each fork by plucking the string between B, C and altering the position of C. The following results were obtained in an experiment:

Frequency (f)	Length of BC (l)	$f \times l$
256 Hz	77·0 cm	19 710
320	61·7	19 740
384	51·3	19 700
427	45·9	19 600
512	38·4	19 660

From the results, it is at once apparent that the shorter the vibrating length of string, the higher is the frequency of the note. A closer examination shows that if the vibrating length l is halved a note of twice the frequency is obtained; thus the length decreases from 77·0 to 38·4 cm when the frequency increases from 256 to 512 pulses per second. If the length is decreased to one-third of its original value, a note of three times the frequency is produced. When we multiply the frequency f by the length l a constant number is obtained, as shown in the above table. The frequency is thus said to be inversely proportional to the length of the string.

Vibrations in Pipes

Unlike the case of stringed instruments, the notes in wind instruments such as the trumpet or organ-pipe are due to vibrations of *air* inside them.

ACOUSTICS · 87

A number of test-tubes A, B, C, D, E, filled with water to different levels, provides a useful indication of how the note from different pipes varies in frequency or pitch (Fig. 75(i)). On blowing gently in turn across the top of each tube, the notes are observed to increase in frequency in the order A, B, C, D, E. Thus *a short vibrating column of air produces a note of high frequency*. This is analogous to the case of a

Plate *21*. The organ in Liverpool Metropolitan Cathedral. The longest pipe in the centre is over 10 m long and produces a note 4 octaves below middle C; clustered round its foot are tiny pipes giving a brilliant high-pitch sound. At the bottom left and right are square wooden pipes; the bell-ends of horizontal trumpet pipes may also be seen. Tone-quality is determined by the shape and material of the various sets of pipes

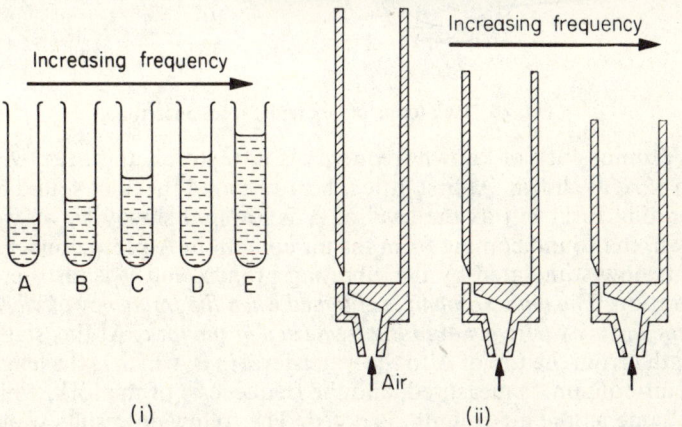

Fig. 75. Frequency of vibration depends on the length of tube containing air

vibrating string, which also produces a note of higher frequency the shorter the string. Fig. 75 (ii) illustrates three open organ-pipes. When a flow of air is introduced at the bottom, notes are obtained; they are due to the vibrations of the air particles inside the pipes. As we have just seen, the shortest pipe produces a note of higher frequency than the others.

Resonance and Resonance-tube Experiment

If we wish to find out more exactly how the frequency of the note from a vibrating air column depends on its length, a "resonance tube" is employed. This consists of a glass tube A of constant diameter, connected by rubber tubing to a wider glass tube B (Fig. 76 (i)). Water is poured into the apparatus, and the level in A can be altered by raising or lowering B, thus altering the length l of the air column in A. A tube T, which can move up and down a column of water in a jar J, can also be used to vary the length of the air column (Fig. 76 (ii)).

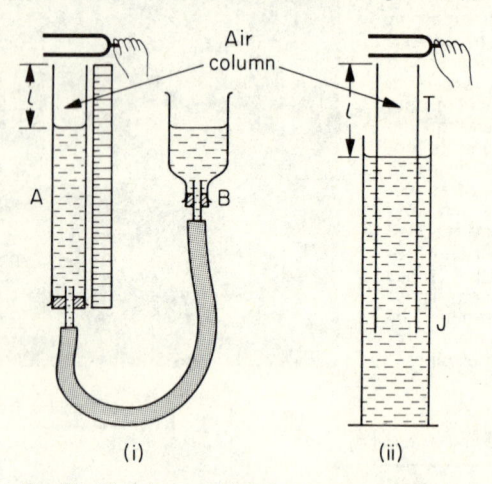

Fig. 76. Two forms of laboratory resonance tube

A tuning-fork of known frequency is now struck and held over the top of A, as shown. At first little is heard beyond the faint sound of the vibrating fork, but as the level of A is lowered slowly by moving B down, the sound coming from the air column in A grows louder. The air is now stimulated by the vibrating prongs, and it is also set into vibration. *The loudest sound is obtained when the frequency of vibration of the air is exactly equal to the frequency of the fork.* At this stage the length l from the top of A to the water-level in it, which is the length of the air-column, is measured, and the frequency f of the fork, which is the same as the air-column, is noted. The following results were obtained:

ACOUSTICS · 89

Frequency (f)	Length (l)	f × l
512 Hz	16·4 cm	83 790
384	21·9	84 090
320	26·2	83 830
256	32·9	84 220

Conclusion. These results, which show that the product $f \times l$ is practically constant, are similar to those obtained with a vibrating string (see p. 86). Thus the frequency of a vibrating air-column is doubled when its length is halved, and the frequency is trebled when the length is reduced to one-third. Short organ pipes thus give notes of higher frequency than long ones.

Stationary Waves

The type of wave obtained in a vibrating violin string or a vibrating air-column in an organ-pipe is completely different from the sound wave in air when a person is talking, which was discussed on p. 80. When the violin string is bowed or plucked, a wave travels along the string and is *reflected* at the fixed end. The vibration of the string is thus due, in effect, to two waves travelling in opposite directions along it. Similarly, a wave travelling along the air in an organ-pipe is reflected at one end; thus the vibrations of the air in the pipe are due to two waves travelling in opposite directions. In contrast, when a sound wave spreads through the air, for example when a person talks, only one wave is travelling outwards.

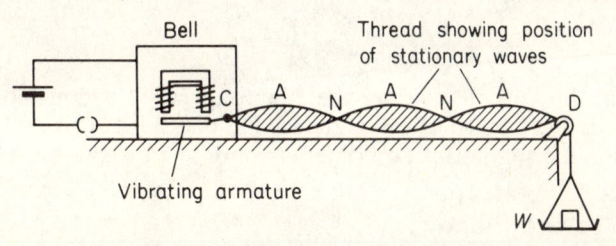

Fig. 77. Stationary waves on a string

A simple experiment to demonstrate the effect of two waves travelling in opposite directions can be performed with the aid of an electric bell B (Fig. 77). A length of thread is connected to the end C of the clapper, the gong having been removed, and passes over a grooved wheel D. A scale-pan with weight W is connected to this end of the thread to provide a tension in the thread. When a battery is connected to the bell the clapper vibrates to and fro, and sends waves along the thread which are reflected at D. By altering the weight W, the thread can be made to vibrate in a definite number of loops and then appears stationary (see Fig. 77). This type of wave in the string is called a *stationary wave*, and the points N on it, where no movement occurs, are called the *nodes* of the stationary wave. The points A, exactly midway between the nodes, where the amplitude of vibration is greatest, are called the *antinodes* of the wave. A *node* is thus a point of *no-displacement*.

Frequency of Vibrating Strings

From the stationary wave shown in Fig. 77, it can be seen that

$$\text{the distance NN between successive nodes} = \frac{\lambda}{2} \quad . \quad (1)$$

where λ is the wavelength. Also,

$$\text{the distance AA between successive antinodes} = \frac{\lambda}{2} \quad . \quad (2)$$

and

$$\text{the distance NA} = \frac{\lambda}{4} \quad . \quad (3)$$

where N is a node and A is a neighbouring antinode.

When a violin string is plucked lightly in the middle, a stationary wave is produced in the string, as explained on p. 85. The ends are nodes of the wave because the string is permanently at rest at the ends, and the centre, where the string moves most, is an antinode. From (1) above, it follows that the length l of the string $= \lambda/2$.

$$\therefore \lambda = 2l$$

Now $V = f\lambda$, where V is the velocity of the wave and f is the frequency of vibration (see p. 81).

$$\therefore f = \frac{V}{\lambda} = \frac{V}{2l}$$

From this formula, we see that the frequency f is doubled when l is halved, and trebled when l is reduced to one-third. This explains the results in the sonometer experiment (p. 86).

Violin and Piano

The *violin* is an instrument in which strings are kept taut, as in the sonometer, and bowed to produce the required note. The strings are of different material, such as gut, or wire-covered gut, or wire alone. For strings of the same length and tension, the lightest string produces the highest note and the heaviest produces the lowest note. Thus gut produces the highest note for the case of the three strings mentioned above. When a violinist moves his finger up a given string, thus effectively shortening the string, higher notes are produced. Also, the harder the bowing, the greater is the amplitude of vibration and hence the loudness increases. Fig. 78 illustrates roughly violin strings and some notes which can be obtained.

In the *pianoforte,* a string is struck with a hammer covered with soft felt when the key is pressed (Fig. 79). When the finger is removed, another felt, known as the "damper", presses against the string and stops the vibration. The dampers are lifted from the strings by pressing the loud pedal, and this allows the vibrations to die away more slowly.

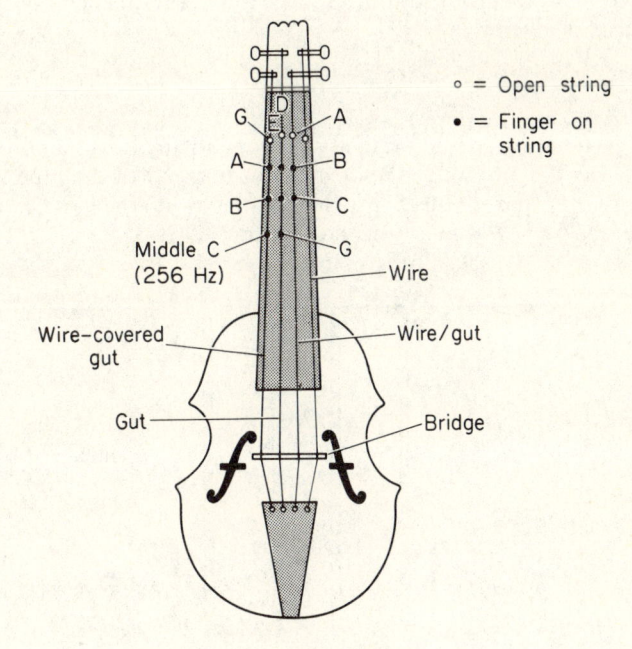

Fig. 78. Violin strings

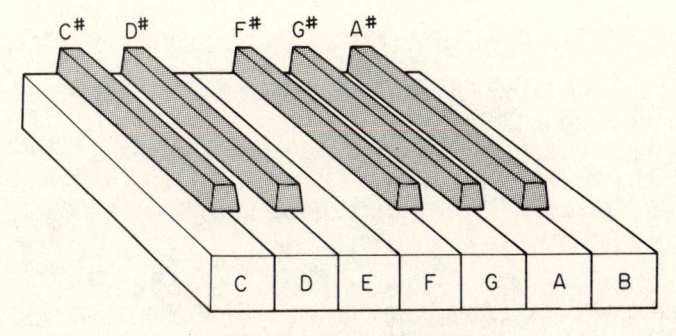

Fig. 79. One octave of a keyboard

Organ-pipe Frequency

When air is blown into an organ-pipe *closed at one end* X, a stationary wave is set up in the air inside the pipe (Fig 80(i)) (see p. 89). The end X where the air cannot move is a node N of the stationary wave; the other end, where the air is free to vibrate, is an antinode A. Now the distance NA between the node and antinode = $\lambda/4$, where λ is the wavelength, as stated on p. 90). Thus the length l of the pipe = $\lambda/4$, and hence $\lambda = 4l$. From $V = f\lambda$, it follows that the frequency f of the note produced is given by

$$f = \frac{V}{\lambda} = \frac{V}{4l}$$

In this formula, V is the velocity of sound in air; it is an approximate formula as the antinode is not exactly at one end of the pipe. Thus if $V = 340$ m/s and $l = 0.25$ m, the frequency of the note = $V/4l$ = $340/(4 \times 0.25)$ = 340 pulses per second (or 340 Hz).

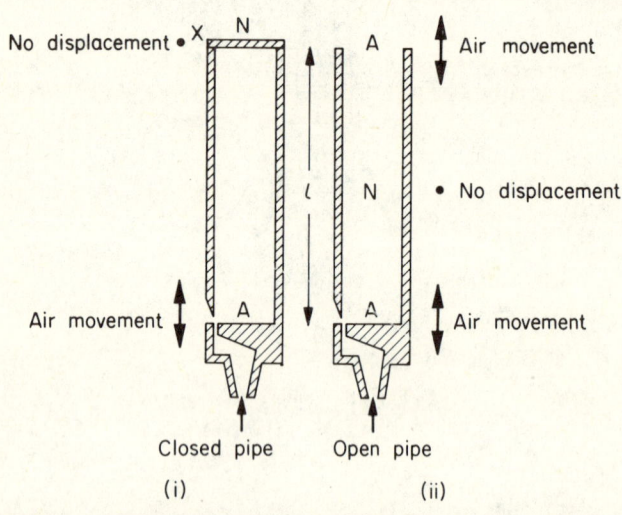

Fig. 80. Vibrations in organ pipes

An *open* organ-pipe has both ends open, and a stationary wave is again produced in the pipe when air is blown in at one end (Fig. 80(ii)). This time, however, both ends of the pipe, where the air is free, are antinodes A, A. Now AA = $\lambda/2$, or $\lambda = 2AA = 2l$, where l is the length of the pipe. The frequency of the note obtained is thus given, from $V = f\lambda$, by

$$f = \frac{V}{\lambda} = \frac{V}{2l}$$

If $V = 340$ m/s and $l = 0.25$ m, then $f = V/2l = 340/(2 \times 0.25)$ = 680 pulses per second (Hz). If the length is doubled to 0·50 m, then

$f = 340$ pulses per second (Hz) by calculation. A longer pipe always gives a lower note, and, conversely, a shorter pipe gives a higher note. The law relating the frequency of the note from a pipe to its length is the same, in fact, as that between the frequency and length of a vibrating string (see p. 90).

Summary

1. Sound is due to vibrations. Sound requires a medium; it cannot pass through a vacuum.

2. Sound pulses cause regular variations of pressure at places in the air and also vibrations of the layers of air. The *wavelength*, λ, is the distance between successive crests (or troughs) of the wave, and $V = f\lambda$.

3. The *frequency, f,* of a vibration is the number of pulses per second; the pitch increases when the frequency increases. The *amplitude* of vibration is the maximum displacement from the original position; the loudness increases when the amplitude of vibration increases. The *timbre* or *quality* of a note depends on the wave-form.

4. The speed of sound in air is about 330 metre per second (the actual value depends on the temperature). The velocity in water is about 1440 metre per second. *Echoes* are due to the reflection of sound. Echo-sounding is used to measure the depth of the sea-bed.

5. The frequency of the note from a *violin string* depends on the length, the tension and the material of the string. The frequency increases as the length decreases; this is shown by the *sonometer* experiment.

6. The frequency of the note from an *organ-pipe* depends on the length of the pipe. The frequency increases as the length decreases; this is shown by the *resonance-tube* experiment.

7. *Stationary waves* are produced in musical instruments. Points which are permanently at rest in the wave called "nodes"; points which are vibrating with the maximum amplitude are called "antinodes". The distance between two antinodes or two nodes is $\lambda/2$, where λ is the wavelength; the distance between a node and the nearest antinode is $\lambda/4$.

EXERCISES

1. Describe an experiment to show that the prongs of a sounding tuning-fork are moving very rapidly. What, briefly, do you know about the way in which the prongs move? Draw diagrams.

2. Describe fully an experiment to show that sound cannot pass through a vacuum.

3. Describe how a sound wave passes through air when a tuning-fork is sounding. In your answer, mention how the various layers of air are moving, how the sound is passed on, and illustrate your answer by diagrams.

4. Define *wavelength, frequency* and *amplitude*. On what factors do the pitch and loudness of a note depend? Draw suitable sketches illustrating (*a*) a high and low note, (*b*) a loud and soft sound.

5. What is the *timbre* or *quality* of a note? On what does the timbre depend? Draw suitable sketches to illustrate that a note may have the same pitch but different quality.

6. What is an *echo*? Describe and explain, using imaginary figures, how echoes are used in (i) depth-sounding, (ii) detecting the closeness of icebergs to ships.

7. How does the pitch of a note from a given violin string depend on (i) its length, (ii) its thickness, (iii) its tension? Describe how a sonometer can be used to show that the length of a given taut string is halved when a note of double the frequency is obtained.

8. Describe the *Whispering Gallery* of St. Paul's. What is the explanation of the phenomenon?

9. Draw a sketch of closed organ-pipes, giving respectively a low and a high note when they are sounded. On what does the frequency of the note depend? Describe a simple experiment with four test-tubes which illustrates your answer.

10. Describe the sonometer, drawing a neat diagram. Describe fully an experiment to show how the frequency of the note from a plucked length of string varies with the length. In your answer, state the measurements taken and the conclusion.

11. Describe the *resonance-tube* experiment. In your answer, state the measurements taken and the conclusion.

CHAPTER TEN

Luminous Energy

Acoustic energy, studied in chapter 9, is transmitted by pulses in air or some other medium. Other forms of energy are radiated without the need for a meterial medium but, like acoustic pulses, this radiation is also pulse-like, having speed, frequency and wavelength.

The sun is a great natural source of light, and electric lamps of all kinds produce artificial light. In this chapter we shall study how light travels and explain some of the effects of light.

Light Travels in Straight Lines

A simple experiment which reveals how light travels can be performed with three cardboard or metal screens having small holes in their centres. These are adjusted so that the holes are in a straight line by threading string through the holes and pulling it taut (Fig. 81). The light from a candle flame placed at A can then be seen through the holes by an eye at B. If, however, one of the screens is moved so that the holes are no longer in a straight line, the light is cut off. We therefore conclude that light travels in straight lines.

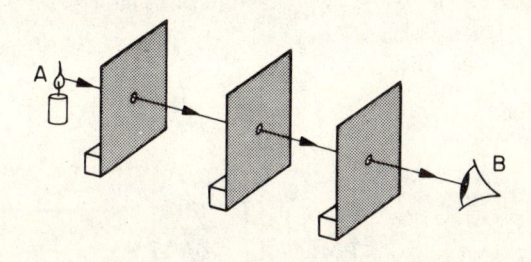

Fig. 81. Light travels in straight lines

Rays of Light

A *ray* of light is the name given to the direction of the path taken by light, and is represented in diagrams by a pencilled line with an arrow on it.

A *beam* of light is a collection of rays. An electric torch may give a diverging beam, a lens can provide a converging beam, and a searchlight sends out a parallel beam (Fig. 82).

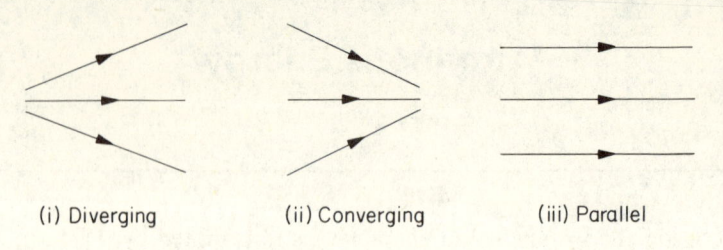

(i) Diverging (ii) Converging (iii) Parallel

Fig. 82. Light beams and rays

The Ray Box

Although the word ray strictly means the direction of the light it is nevertheless customary to describe a very thin parallel beam also as a ray of light. For producing such rays we use a ray box, which consists of a straight filament electric lamp on a sliding support, a cylindrical lens, and a screen with a slit cut in it (Fig. 83). To adjust the box it is placed on a sheet of white material on a flat table, and a metal comb is placed in front of the lens. On switching on the lamp a series of bright rays, either convergent or divergent, will be seen on the paper. The distance of the lamp from the lens can be altered until the rays become parallel. A single ray may now be obtained by replacing the comb by a screen having one slit only.

The various uses of the ray box will be described in due course.

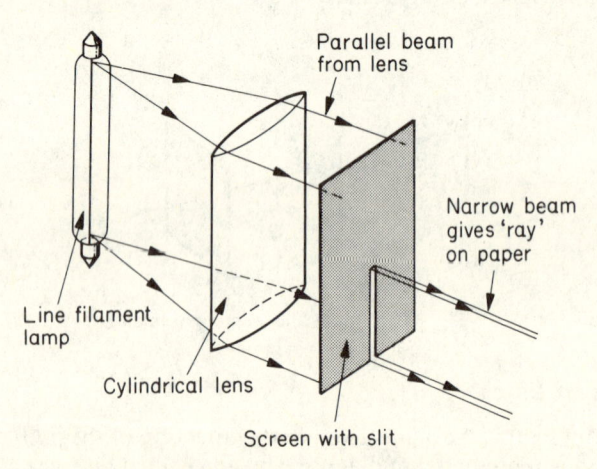

Fig. 83. Forming a "ray" on the laboratory bench

The Pinhole Camera

This interesting device was known and used in the sixteenth century. It consists of a box with a pinhole in the centre of one end and a screen of tracing paper or frosted glass at the opposite end. Since light travels in straight lines, it follows that a given point on the screen will be illuminated solely by light coming in a straight line through the pinhole from a certain point on an object outside (Fig. 84). Rays of light from the various parts of an object outside will thus travel in straight lines through the pinhole, and form a multitude of tiny patches on the screen. These tiny patches combine to form an image of the object.

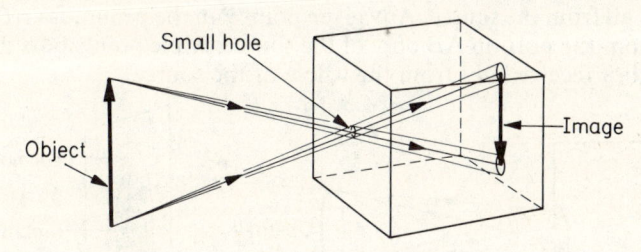

Fig. 84. A pinhole camera

A blurred image results if the hole is made much larger than a pinhole. This may be explained if we think of the larger hole as being equivalent to a group of small holes close together, each of which produces its own image on the screen. These images overlap, and the resultant effect is an image which is brighter but very blurred.

If the screen is replaced by a photographic plate or film, very satisfactory pictures of still subjects may be taken with this camera using suitable time exposures. Snapshots, of course, can only be taken with a lens camera since the wider aperture of the lens admits more light energy in a given time than a pinhole.

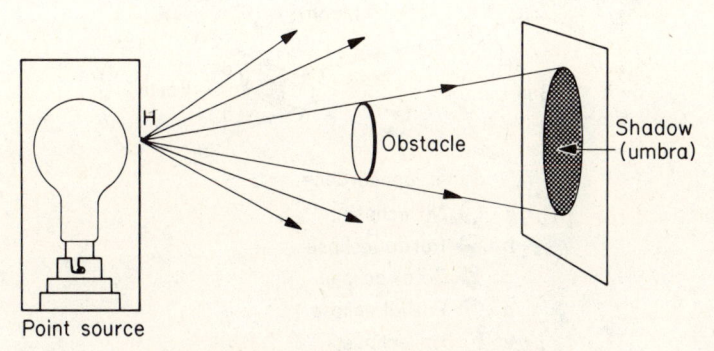

Fig. 85. Sharp shadow from a point of light

Shadows

The formation of sharp-edged shadows results directly from the straight line propagation of light. With a point source of light, e.g. a small hole H in a screen illuminated by a lamp, the shadow of an obstacle, such as a wooden ball, formed on a screen is uniformly dark (see Fig. 85).

If the point source is replaced by an extended source such as part of the surface of a pearl electric lamp, the shadow is seen to be edged with a border of partial shadow (Fig. 86). This partial shadow is called a *penumbra* to distinguish it from the complete shadow or *umbra*. Examination of Fig. 86 shows that points within the umbra receive no light at all from the source. Any given point P in the penumbra receives light from the portion AB only of the source, while points outside the penumbra receive light from the whole of the source.

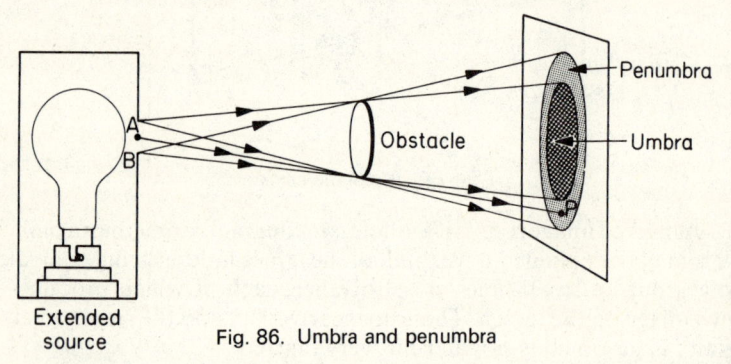

Fig. 86. Umbra and penumbra

Eclipses

An eclipse of the sun by the moon occurs when the moon passes between the sun and the earth and all three are in a straight line. Fig. 87 shows how the umbra and penumbra are produced, and the ap-

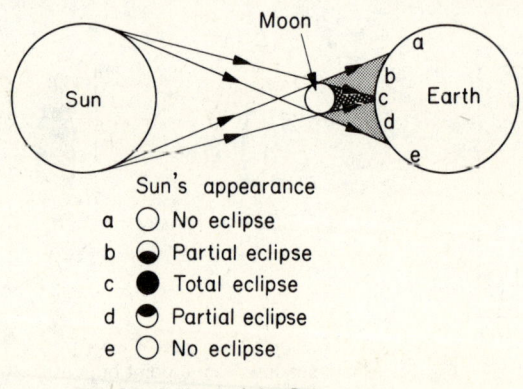

Sun's appearance
a ○ No eclipse
b ◐ Partial eclipse
c ● Total eclipse
d ◐ Partial eclipse
e ○ No eclipse

Fig. 87. Eclipse of the Sun

LUMINOUS ENERGY · 99

pearance of the sun as seen from various positions on the earth's surface. Plate 22 shows the progress of an eclipse of the sun at intervals of five minutes. The eclipse of the moon is also shown in Plate 23.

On occasions when the distance of the moon from the earth is such that the tip of the umbra fails to reach the earth's surface, an *annular eclipse* occurs and from one place on the earth the sun presents the appearance of a ring of light (Fig. 88).

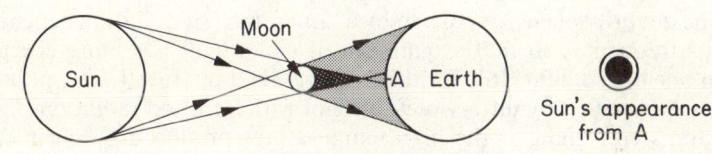

Fig. 88. Annular eclipse

The Nature of Light

Scientists have always been puzzled by the nature of light. In the seventeenth century there were two schools of thought concerning it. Sir Isaac Newton regarded light as a stream of corpuscles or tiny particles travelling in straight lines, whilst the Dutch physicist Huygens

Plate 22. Eclipse of the Sun: a gradual covering of the Sun by the Moon. The photographs were taken at 5-minute intervals from an island in mid-Pacific

Plate 23. Eclipse of the Moon: a shadow of the Earth crosses the face of the Moon. Photographed from Iowa City, USA

held that light consisted of waves in a substance called the 'ether'. which he supposed filled the whole of space including that between the atoms of matter and which could not be removed even from a vacuum.

As time went on and more became known about the behaviour of light, Huygens' wave theory came to be accepted as the better one. At present day, however, we have evidence to suppose that light consists of streams of tiny wave-like packets of energy called "quanta", which travel at a speed of 300 000 km per second.

The quantity of energy carried by a "quantum" of radiation depends on its frequency, so that a quantum of violet light has more energy than one of red light. It is for this reason that a photocell will operate when illuminated by ultra-violet, but not with infra-red radiation.

Atoms emit light at the high temperatures produced by chemical reaction in a flame, by the electrical heating of thin tungsten wire in the ordinary electric lamp or by the bombardment of gas molecules by electrons in a discharge lamp tube.

Summary

1. Light travels in straight lines; it is a form of radiated energy.
2. A ray of light is the direction of the path along which light travels.
3. A beam of light is a collection of rays. Beams are usually converging, diverging or parallel.
4. A *penumbra* is a region of partial shadow; an *umbra* is a region of full or total shadow.
5. Eclipses are explained by the formation of shadows due to light travelling in straight lines from the sun, and stopped by the earth or by the moon.

EXERCISES

1. Describe a simple experiment to show that light travels in straight lines.

2. What is meant by (*a*) a ray, (*b*) a beam of light? Draw sketches of a diverging and parallel beam.

3. What is a *shadow*? Describe an experiment which produces an umbra and penumbra, and explain with diagrams the formation of these shadows.

4. Describe a pinhole camera and explain how the image is formed. What is the effect of enlarging the pinhole? Explain the effect you describe.

5. An image 100 mm long of a man 2 m tall is formed on the screen of a pinhole camera. Find the distance of the pinhole from the screen, if the man is standing 6 m from the pinhole.

6. Explain, with the aid of diagrams, the formation of (*a*) a partial, (*b*) a total, (*c*) an annular eclipse of the sun.

7. The shadow of a vertical pole due to the sun becomes shorter as mid-day is reached and then lengthens. Explain this phenomenon, and draw diagrams to illustrate it.

CHAPTER ELEVEN

Plane Mirrors

Bodies like the sun and other sources of light with which we are familiar are said to be "self-luminous" since they emit light of their own accord. On the other hand, the common objects around us are not self-luminous. Nevertheless, these bodies are visible as they reflect in all directions the light which falls on them from the sun. Mirrors and highly polished surfaces reflect light strongly in a particular direction, and we will now examine the laws governing this reflection.

Reflection of Light

Fig. 89 illustrates the terms we use in the study of reflected light. MM' represents the surface of a plane mirror. AO, called the *incident ray,* is the direction in which light falls on to the reflecting surface. O is the point of incidence and OB the *reflected ray*. The angles *i* and *r* which the incident and reflected rays make with ON, the normal or perpendicular to the reflecting surface at the point of incidence, are called the *angles of incidence and reflection* respectively.

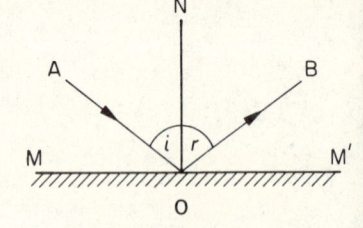

Fig. 89. Reflection of light

Experiment

A straight line MM', together with a normal ON, are drawn on a sheet of paper placed on a drawing board, and a strip of plane mirror is stood vertically with its silvered surface over the line MM' (Fig. 90). A ray box is then placed so that an incident ray AO falls on the mirror. This gives rise to a reflected ray OB and the positions of both are marked by two fine pencil crosses on each. The experiment having been repeated for several different angles of incidence, the mirror and ray box are removed and the rays drawn in by joining the crosses with pencil and ruler. The angles of incidence and reflection are then measured with a protractor and the values tabulated.

PLANE MIRRORS

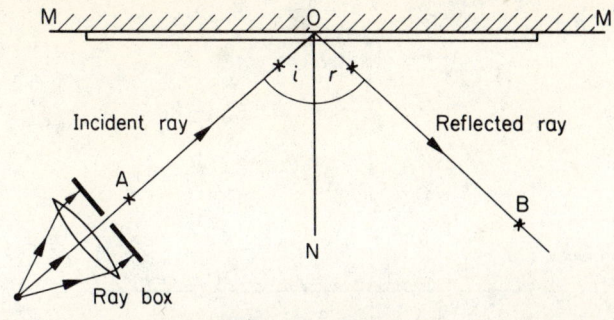

Fig. 90. Laws of reflection

The table shows that the angle of incidence is practically equal to the corresponding angle of reflection in every case, this is a law of reflection.

Angle of incidence (i)	Angle of reflection (r)

The fact that this experiment is performed with a mirror standing vertically on a flat sheet of paper, this being the common plane of the rays and the normal, is evidence for a further first law of reflection. If the mirror is tilted so that the normal at the point of incidence no longer lies in the place of the paper, the reflected ray cannot be seen as it is now reflected either upwards or downwards according to the direction in which the mirror is tilted.

Laws of Reflection

I. The incident ray, the reflected ray and the normal at the point of incidence all lie in the same plane.

II. The angle of incidence is equal to the angle of reflection.

Pin Method for Locating Images

A strip of plane mirror is set up vertically, with its silvered surface on a line MM' drawn on a sheet of white paper on a drawing board (Fig. 91). A pin O, to serve as an object, is stuck into the paper about 7 or 8 cm from MM'.

With the eye in some convenient position E_1, two pins P_1 and P_2 are stuck into the paper so as to be in a straight line with the image I of the pin O seen in the mirror. The two sighting pins are next removed, and their positions marked by small pencil crosses and lettered P_1 and P_2. The same procedure is carried out with the eye in several other positions

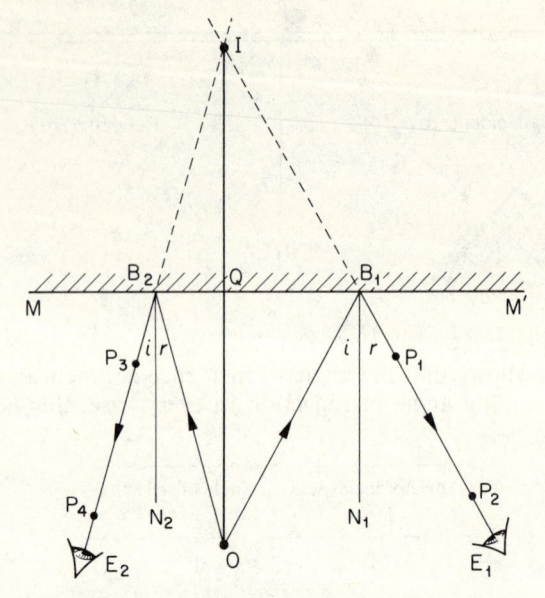

Fig. 91. Locating image in a plane mirror

such as E_2, at least two positions on either side of the object O being taken. When this has been completed, the mirror is removed.

The points P_1 and P_2, etc., are then joined by pencil lines to cut MM′ at B_1, etc., and at the same time are produced backwards behind the mirror. Here they ought all to intersect at I. OI is joined, cutting MM′ in Q. The object and image distances from the mirror, OQ and IQ, are measured and also the angle which OI makes with MM′.

The results show that
 (i) OQ = IQ,
 (ii) OI is at right angles to MM′.

Clearly, the lines $B_1P_1P_2$, $B_2P_3P_4$, etc., represent reflected rays for which the corresponding incident rays are OB_1, OB_2, etc. Normals B_1N_1, B_2N_2, etc., to the mirror MM′ are constructed at the points of incidence B_1, B_2, etc., and the angles of incidence and reflection measured. These should be found approximately equal for each pair of rays.

Wave Tank Observations

The wave tank has already been referred to in chapter 9 as a method of observing the behaviour of waves. Reflection can be simply investigated in the tank. If a straight, vertical metal strip is placed in the tank, then any wave striking it is reflected; a circular wave, after

PLANE MIRRORS · 105

reflection, appears to have its point of origin behind the reflector at the place where a mirror-image of the vibrator would be. Parallel waves are reflected as if originating from a distant object behind the reflector.

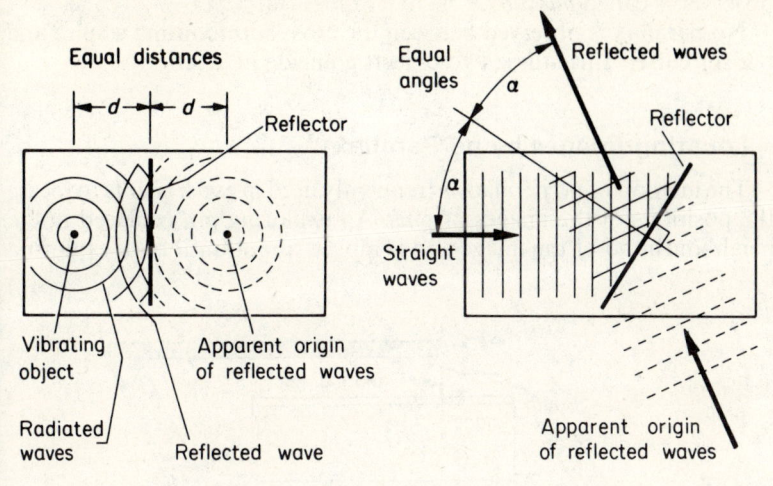

Fig. 92. Reflection in a wave tank

Diffuse Reflection

Mirrors and sheets of glass are highly polished surfaces. The surfaces of most objects, however, are found to have tiny irregularities when they are examined under a microscope. Paper is an example. Thus when a parallel beam of light falls on such a surface, the individual rays strike

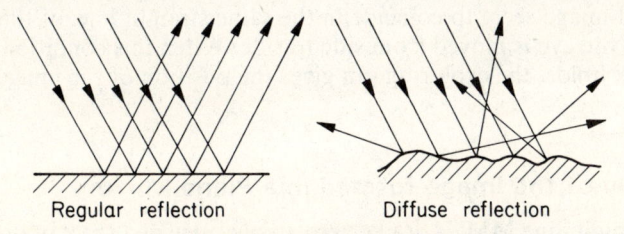

Fig. 93. Regular and diffuse reflection

the surface at different angles of incidence. The rays are therefore reflected in different directions from the surface (Fig. 93). We say that the light is *diffusely reflected* from the surface.

Parallax

When we look out of the window of a moving train, trees, chimneys, towers and other objects in the landscape appear to be moving relatively to each other. Thus at one moment a tree may appear to be to the right of a church spire and a few seconds later to the left of it. Their actual positions in space have, of course, remained fixed. This apparent relative movement of two objects due to a movement on the part of the observer is called *parallax*.

No parallax is observed between the cross surmounting a spire and the spire itself since these two objects coincide in position.

Locating Images by no Parallax

The method of no parallax is frequently used in experiments to locate the positions of the images of pins. An exploring pin is placed in the neighbourhood of the image and is moved about until both exploring

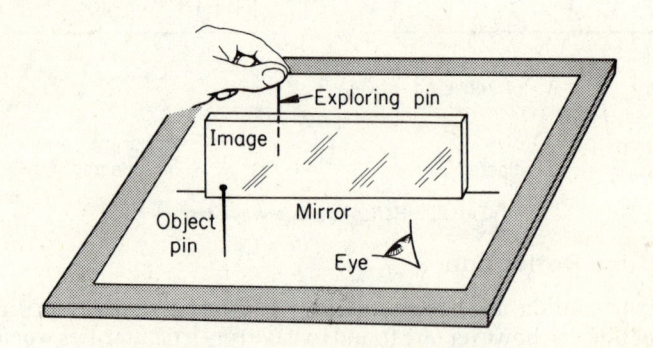

Fig. 94. Image location by no-parallax

pin and image seem to coincide in the same straight line, at the same time as the eye is moved from side to side. When this condition of no parallax holds, the exploring pin gives the position of the image (Fig. 94).

Study of the Image formed in a Plane Mirror

A straight line MM' is drawn across the centre of a sheet of drawing paper to represent a reflecting surface and a large letter E to serve as an object (Fig. 95). A strip of plane mirror is then stood vertically with its silvered surface over MM' and the image of the object letter E seen in the mirror is found in the following manner. An object pin is stuck into the paper at the various points O_1, O_2, etc., in turn on the object letter, and each time the images I_1, I_2, etc., are located by the method of no parallax, using an exploring pin as described in the last section. When adjusting the exploring pin to coincidence with the image it is useful to keep in mind that, of the two, *the further one moves with the eye*.

Suitable measurements should now be taken on the diagram;

observations recorded in the notebook should establish that the image in a plane mirror is:

1. The same size as the object.
2. The same distance behind the mirror as the object is in front.
3. Laterally inverted.
4. Virtual (it cannot be formed on a screen).

Finally we see from this experiment that the line joining any point on the object to its corresponding point on the image cuts the mirror at right angles. It is most important to remember this, as we shall use it when making graphical constructions of images in plane mirrors. See also p. 104.

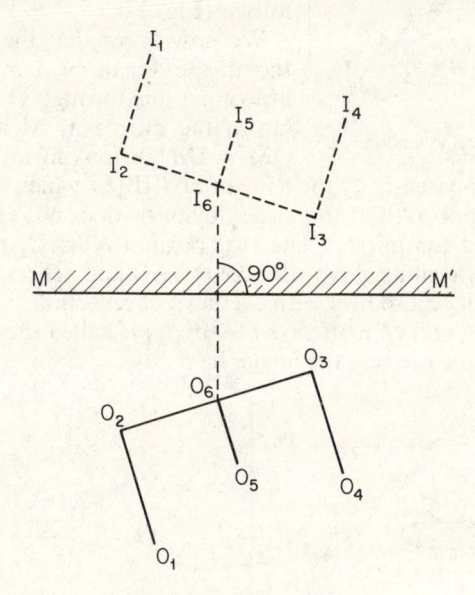

Fig. 95. Images in a plane mirror

Looking into a Plane Mirror

We were, of course, already familiar with some of the above facts from our everyday experience with mirrors. Looking into a mirror we see an image of the face situated apparently behind the mirror. It we now move backwards, the image will recede so that it is always the same distance behind the mirror as the object is in front. Unlike the images we see on the cinema screen, which are said to be *real* in the sense that they are formed by the actual projection of real rays, the image we see in the mirror cannot be formed on a screen. It is said to be *virtual* and is produced at the place where the reflected rays appear to intersect when their directions are produced backwards behind the mirror. This is further explained in the next paragraph and Fig. 99. It is also to be noticed that the left ear of the image is formed from our own right ear as object. This effect is called *lateral inversion*: it is even more strikingly demonstrated when we look at the image of a printed page in a mirror (Fig. 96).

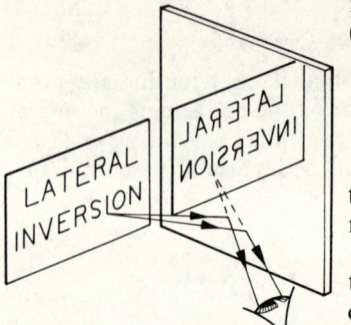

Fig. 96. Lateral inversion

How the Eye sees an Image in a Plane Mirror

Let us consider how the eye sees the tip of the image of a lamp in a plane mirror (Fig. 97).

We now know that the position of the image I can be constructed by drawing a line through O perpendicular to the mirror at M and making OM = IM. On looking into the mirror the eye sees I apparently by the cone of rays IE_1E_2 which enter the eye pupil. The portion IAB of this cone obviously does not exist: there is no light behind the mirror. The real portion ABE_1E_2 results from light from O travelling down the cone OAB and reflected from the mirror at AB in accordance with the laws of reflection.

The complete real cone of rays $OABE_1E_2$ is called the "pencil" of light by which the eye sees the image I.

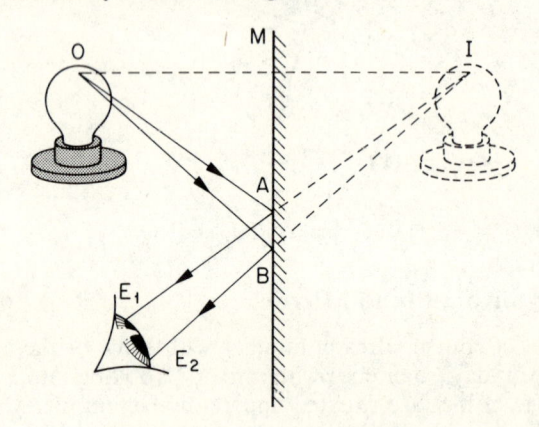

Fig. 97. How the eye sees an image

Images formed in Two Mirrors inclined at 90°

When two mirrors are inclined at right angles, we have not only the images I_1 and I_2 formed by a single reflection, but in addition two extra produced by *two* reflections. The pencil of light by which the eye sees

PLANE MIRRORS · 109

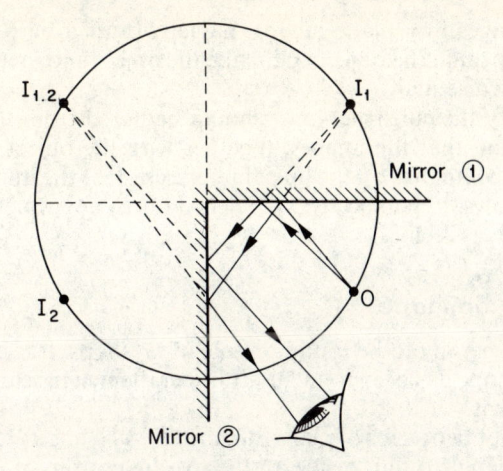

Fig. 98. Images in two inclined mirrors

one of these $I_{1.2}$, is shown in Fig. 98. The subscript 1.2 in the symbol $I_{1.2}$ signifies the order in which the reflections take place from the mirrors 1 and 2.

The other image $I_{2.1}$ may be seen by looking into mirror 1. See Fig. 99.

Images $I_{1.2}$ and $I_{2.1}$ are constructed by treating the images I_1 and I_2 as their respective objects and applying the ordinary rule for con-

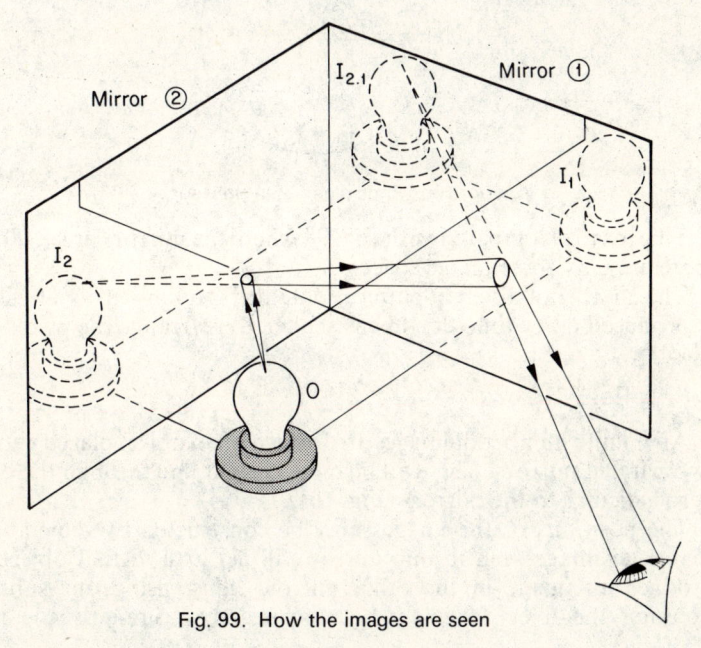

Fig. 99. How the images are seen

structing images in a plane mirror, namely, draw a perpendicular to the mirror through the object and make the object and image distances from the mirror equal.

To simplify the construction it should be noted from the geometry of the diagram that the images, together with the object, all lie on a circle whose centre lies on the line of intersection of the mirrors.

Fig. 99 shows, in perspective, the pencil of rays by which a point on the image $I_{2.1}$ is seen.

The Kaleidoscope

Though generally to be found on sale in toyshops, it is claimed that the kaleidoscope has been found useful by craftsmen in search of varied colour patterns.

It consists of two strips of plane mirror, M_1, M_2, about 150 mm long, placed at an angle of 60° inside a tube. At the bottom of the tube is a ground-glass plate to admit light, on which is scattered small pieces of brightly coloured glass. These pieces of coloured glass act as objects and on looking down the tube five images are seen, which together with the object form a symmetrical pattern in six sectors (Fig. 100).

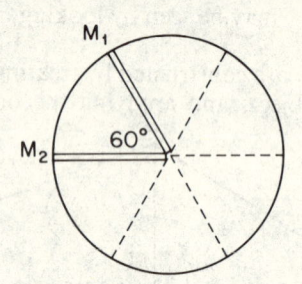

Fig. 100. Principle of a kaleidoscope

This may be compared with Fig. 98 where the mirrors are at 90° and there are only three image spaces.

The number of different patterns obtained is unlimited as a fresh one is produced every time the tube is shaken to rearrange the pieces.

Parallel Mirrors

An infinite number of images are formed of an object placed between two parallel mirrors. These all lie on a straight line through the object perpendicular to the mirrors (Fig. 101).

The positions of the images may be constructed by remembering that each image seen in one mirror will act as a virtual object and produce an image in the other mirror. Thus, using our subscript notation, the object for image $I_{2.1.2}$ is image $I_{2.1}$. Similarly, the object

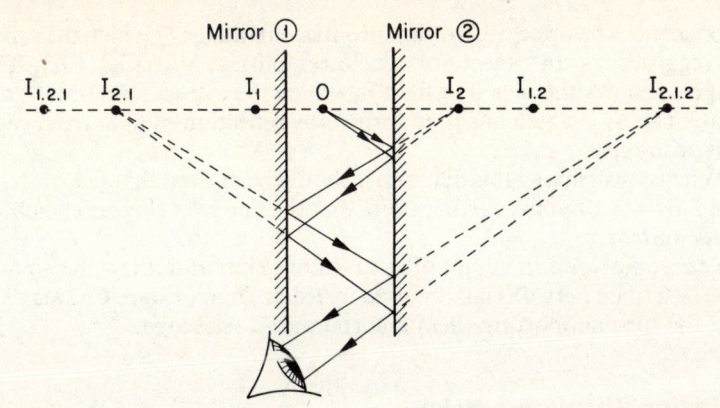

Fig. 101. Images in parallel mirrors

for $I_{2.1}$ is I_2, while I_2 was produced by a single reflection in the mirror 2 by light from the object O.

It is well to notice that $I_{1.2}$, which is the image of I_1 in the mirror 2, is not concerned in constructing the pencil of light by which the eye sees $I_{2.1.2}$.

Two parallel plane mirrors should be set up to examine the images of a candle or other object placed between them. The more remote the images the fainter they become, since some of the light energy is absorbed by the mirrors at each successive reflection.

The Periscope

The simple periscope consists of two plane mirrors, fixed facing one another at an angle of 45° to the line joining them. The user is enabled to see over the heads of a crowd or over the surface of the sea from a

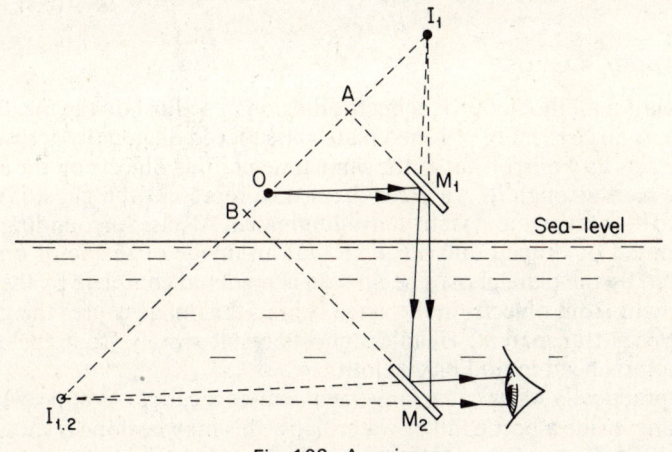

Fig. 102. A periscope

submarine. The upper mirror M_1 produces an image I_1 which may then be regarded as an object for the lower mirror M_2 (Fig. 102). The diagram shows the pencil of light by which the eye sees a point on the final image $I_{1.2}$ which has been formed by reflection of light from each mirror in turn.

When constructing this diagram it should be noticed that $OA = I_1A$, and $I_1B = I_{1.2}B$, and, furthermore, that the line $I_1 I_{1.2}$ is perpendicular to the mirrors.

Periscopes used in submarines are more elaborate than the simple type described here. Prisms are used instead of mirrors (see Chapter 13) and the tube supporting them incorporates a telescope.

Seeing Through a Brick

The illusion of seeing through a brick may be produced by a double periscope arrangement of mirrors as shown in Fig. 103. By looking into the tube B, the lamp is seen by light which has undergone four reflections, one at each of the mirrors in turn.

The lamp, of course, is still visible even when a brick is placed between the tubes A and B.

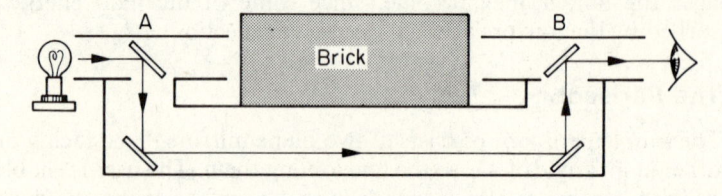

Fig. 103. Seeing through a brick

Pepper's Ghost

This is a method of producing the illusion of a ghost on the theatrical stage. A large sheet of polished plate glass placed diagonally across the stage acts as a mirror but at the same time permits objects on the stage to be seen through it. An actor dressed to represent the ghost is concealed in the wings and is strongly illuminated. All else surrounding him is painted or draped dull black so that an image of the actor only is formed by the plate glass. The illusion is rendered complete by the fact that light from objects on the stage behind the image causes the ghost to appear transparent. Headless ghosts result simply from enclosing the actor's head in dull black cloth.

A practically identical arrangement causes a candle to appear to be burning inside a bottle full of water. How this may be done is shown in Fig. 104.

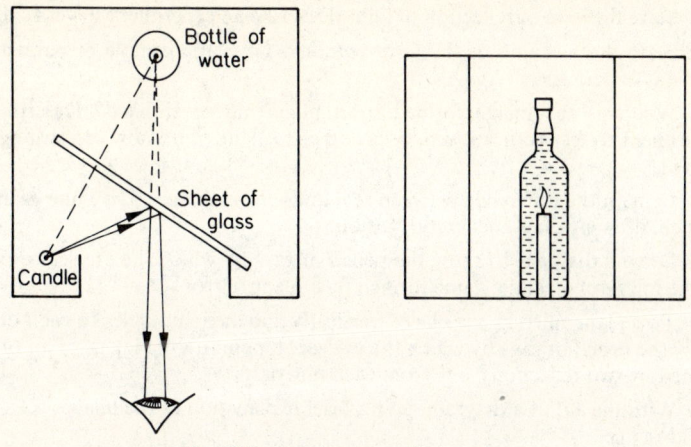

Fig. 104. Burning a candle in water

Summary

1. *The Laws of Reflection.*
Law I. The incident ray, the reflected ray and the normal at the point of incidence all lie in the same plane.
Law II. The angle which the incident ray makes with the normal is equal to the angle which the reflected ray makes with the normal.

2. *Parallax* is the name given to the apparent relative displacement of two objects due to a movement on the part of the observer.

3. The *image formed by a plane mirror* is
  (i) The same size as the object.
  (ii) The same distance behind the mirror as the object is in front, and lies on a line through the object perpendicular to the mirror.
  (iii) Laterally inverted.
  (iv) Virtual (it cannot be formed on a screen).

EXERCISES

1. What do you understand by the *normal* to a surface? Draw a sketch showing an incident and reflected ray, and the normal, for light incident on a plane mirror at an angle less than 45°.

2. What is meant by (*a*) angle of incidence and (*b*) angle of reflection of a ray of light? Draw accurate diagrams for reflection of light from a plane mirror when the angles of incidence is first 30° and then 45°. Measure the angle between the incident and reflected rays in each case.

3. State the laws of reflection of light. Describe an experiment to verify them.

4. State the meaning of the term *parallax*. Give an example of parallax in everyday experience.

5. Where is the image formed by a plane mirror situated? Describe an experiment to test your answer. What other facts do you know concerning the image?

6. Explain the difference between real and virtual images. Give one example of each, drawing diagrams in illustration.

7. Draw a diagram to show the pencil of rays by which the eye sees a point on the image of a candle flame formed by a plane mirror.

8. Two plane mirrors are placed vertically and at right angles to each other. Draw the pencil of rays by which the eye sees a point on the image of an object formed by two reflections, one from each mirror.

9. With the aid of a diagram, give a brief explanation of the images seen in a kaleidoscope.

10. Two mirrors are placed vertically and parallel to each other on a drawing board. A pin is stuck in the board between the mirrors. Show by a diagram the pencil of rays by which the eye sees a point on the third image of the pin in one of the mirrors.

11. A man wears a hat which brings his total height to 2·0 m. His eye level is 0·2 m below the top of his hat. Find by means of a ray diagram the minimum length of a mirror fixed to a vertical wall, in which he can see the whole of himself. At what height must the lower edge of this mirror be placed above the floor?

12. What is the purpose of a periscope? Explain the principle of a periscope with the aid of a ray diagram.

13. Give a concise description of any optical illusion which may be produced by means of light reflected from a plane sheet of plate glass.

14. Two objects, one represented by the letter P and the other by the letter S, are placed in front of a plane mirror. Draw an accurate diagram showing the image formed in each case.

15. State the laws of reflection of light.

A ray of light is reflected from two mirrors in succession, and the initial and final paths are parallel to each other. Draw a ray diagram to illustrate this, and state the size of the angle of incidence on each mirror.

(*Hint.*—In answers to questions involving accurate ray diagrams, better results will be obtained if the vertical scale used is larger than the horizontal scale. The mirror should be represented by a straight line, p. 104.)

CHAPTER TWELVE

Curved Mirrors

At some time or another most people have caught a glimpse of themselves by reflection from the polished convex surface of a car body or brass door handle. The image formed is small and usually so grotesque that few stay to admire it. By contrast, a concave reflecting surface will, under certain conditions, give a magnified image. For this reason, some men prefer a concave mirror for use while shaving.

In this chapter we shall study the way in which images are formed by spherical mirrors. Such mirrors are generally made by silvering a piece of glass which would form part of the shell of a hollow sphere. Silvering the glass on the outside gives a concave or converging mirror, while silvering on the inside gives a convex or diverging mirror.

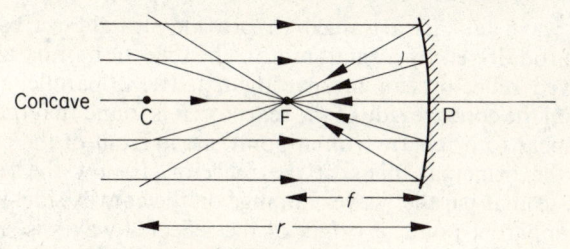

Fig. 105. Concave mirror

Every spherical mirror has a *principal axis* CFP (Fig. 105). This is the line joining the *pole* P, or centre of the mirror, to its *centre of curvature* C, or centre of the sphere of which the mirror forms a part. The distance CP is the *radius of curvature, r,* of the mirror. In the case of a concave mirror the centre of curvature is in front of the mirror; in a convex mirror it is behind the mirror, or virtual.

Principal Focus

When a parallel beam of light falls on a plane mirror, it is reflected as a parallel beam, but in the case of a concave mirror the rays in a parallel beam are all reflected so as to converge to a point called a focus.

If the incident rays are parallel to the principal axis, the point through which all the reflected rays pass is on the principal axis just midway between the pole and the centre of curvature and is called the *principal focus*. This is shown in Fig. 105.

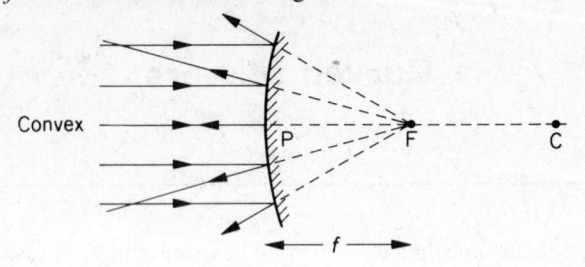

Fig. 106. Convex mirror

Fig. 106 shows what happens when a beam of light parallel to the principal axis falls on a convex mirror. In this case the rays are reflected so that they diverge and appear to be coming from a principal focus midway between the pole and centre of curvature, but this time behind the mirror.

A concave (converging) mirror therefore has a real principal focus, while a convex (diverging) mirror has a virtual one.

Wave Tank Observations

If the wave tank is arranged to provide straight waves, using a vibrating rod driven by a small motor, the reflection of parallel waves at a curved reflector can be investigated. If the parallel waves are incident on the concave side of the reflector, it is found that the reflected waves appear to originate from a point just in front of the curve; this point is the principal focus of the reflector. If now the reflector is reversed, so that parallel waves impinge on the convex side, it is found that the apparent point of origin of the reflected waves is still on the concave side, and at the same principal focus as before.

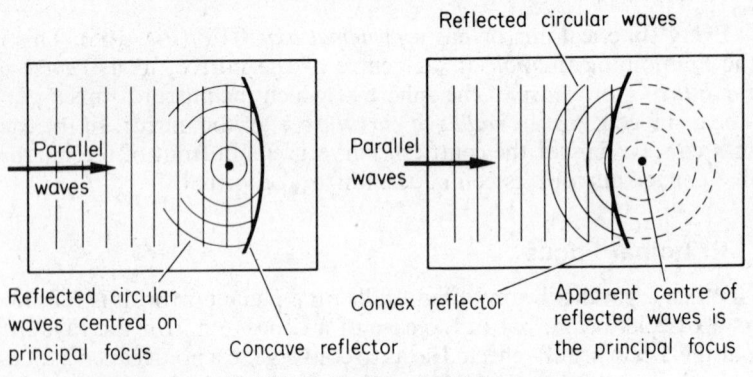

Fig. 107. Reflection of straight waves

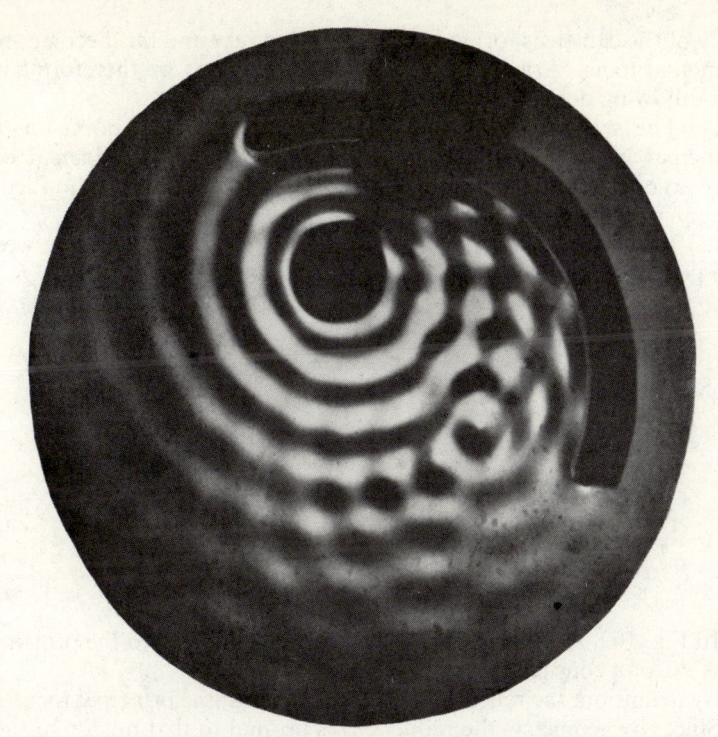

CURVED MIRRORS · 117

Plate *24*. Reflection of circular waves in a wave tank: waves produced by the vibrator (the large black spot) are reflected to form an image, object and image being located symmetrically in front of the reflector

Difference between Large and Small Mirrors of Same Radius

Before proceeding any further it must be stated that the remarks in the foregoing paragraph apply only to mirrors which are small in size compared with their radii of curvature. If this is not the case, as for example with a hemispherical mirror, then instead of getting a point focus from a parallel beam, the reflected rays intersect to form a bright curve called a caustic. This is illustrated in Fig. 108.

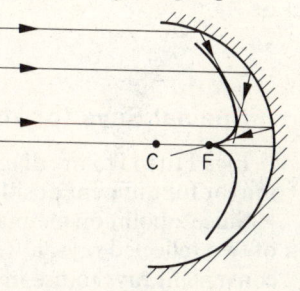

Doubtless the reader will have noticed a bright caustic curve on the surface of tea in a cup. This is formed when light from a distant lamp is reflected from the inside of the cup, which acts as a large curved mirror.

If the mirror is small, or what amounts to the same thing, if only rays close to the principal axis are employed, then the apex

Fig. 108. Formation of a caustic curve by a wide beam of light

only of the caustic is formed by the reflected rays and this becomes the principal focus. Arising from these considerations we therefore have the following definitions:

(1) The *principal focus* of a spherical mirror is that point on the principal axis to which all rays parallel and close to the principal axis converge, or from which they appear to diverge after reflection from the mirror.

(2) The *focal length, f,* of a spherical mirror is the distance between the pole of the mirror and the principal focus.

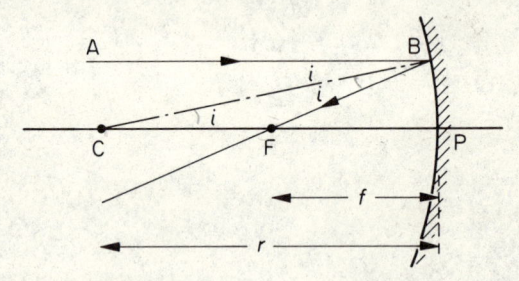

Fig. 109. $r = 2f$ in a curved mirror.

In Fig. 109, AB is an incident ray parallel and close to the principal axis PC of a concave mirror.

By definition, the reflected ray passes through the principal focus F.

Since, by geometry, the radius CB is normal to that mirror surface at B, it follows from the laws of reflection that,

$$A\hat{B}C = C\hat{B}F$$

But $\quad A\hat{B}C = B\hat{C}F$ (alternate angles)

$\therefore C\hat{B}F = B\hat{C}F$

$\quad BF = FC$ (sides of isos. $\triangle$)

Now B is very close to P.

$\therefore BF = PF$ very nearly

$\therefore PF = FC$

or $$f = \frac{r}{2}$$

Special Rays for Locating Images

Figs 110 to 115 are diagrams showing the image formed by a concave mirror for different positions of an object along the principal axis.

Since a point on an image can be located by the point of intersection of two reflected rays, it will be well to consider now which are the most convenient rays to use in the construction of these ray diagrams.

Remembering that, by geometry, the normal to a curved surface at any point is the radius of curvature at that point, one very useful ray to draw will be one which is incident along a radius of curvature. Since this is incident normally on the mirror, it will be reflected back along its own path.

A second useful ray is one which is incident parallel to the principal axis. By definition, this will be reflected through the principal focus. Furthermore, since the angles of incidence and reflection are equal, any ray when reversed must necessarily retrace its own path and be reflected back the way it came. It follows that a third useful construction ray is one which passes through the principal focus. This will be reflected parallel to the principal axis.

These considerations also apply to convex mirrors; so we may sum them up briefly into a set of simple rules for constructing images formed by a spherical mirror:

1. Rays passing through the centre of curvature are reflected back along their own paths.
2. Rays parallel to the principal axis are reflected through the principal focus.
3. Rays through the principal focus are reflected parallel to the principal axis.

Images formed by a Concave Mirror

In Fig. 110 the object is represented as a vertical arrow OA standing on the principal axis between the pole of the mirror and the principal focus. Rules 1 and 2 are used in the construction of the image of the point A on the object. When the two reflected rays have been drawn,

OBJECT BETWEEN F and P the image is,

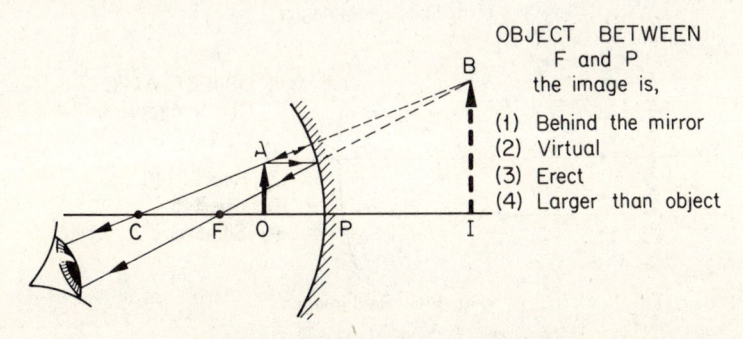

(1) Behind the mirror
(2) Virtual
(3) Erect
(4) Larger than object

Fig. 110. Object between pole and focus

they appear to be diverging from a point B behind the mirror. B is thus a *virtual image* of A. If the same construction is carried out for a series of other points along the object OA a corresponding set of image points will be formed along a vertical line IB. The image formed in this case is thus larger than the object—virtual, erect and behind the mirror.

This is the case of the shaving mirror which we mentioned earlier, and also that of the small mirror used by the dentist for examining teeth.

In Fig. 111 the object has been moved so as to be at the principal focus. Rays from any point on the object are reflected parallel to one

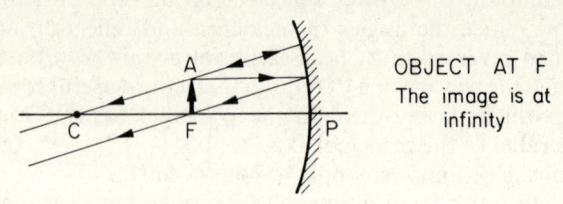

OBJECT AT F
The image is at infinity

Fig. 111. Object at the principal focus

another. It is usual, in such cases, to regard the rays as intersecting to form an image at infinity.

Fig. 112 to 115 are of particular interest since in these cases *real images* are formed. If a white screen is placed at the image position the image will be formed on it and thus rendered visible from all directions. It is important to be able to distinguish clearly between real and virtual

OBJECT BETWEEN
F and C
the image is,

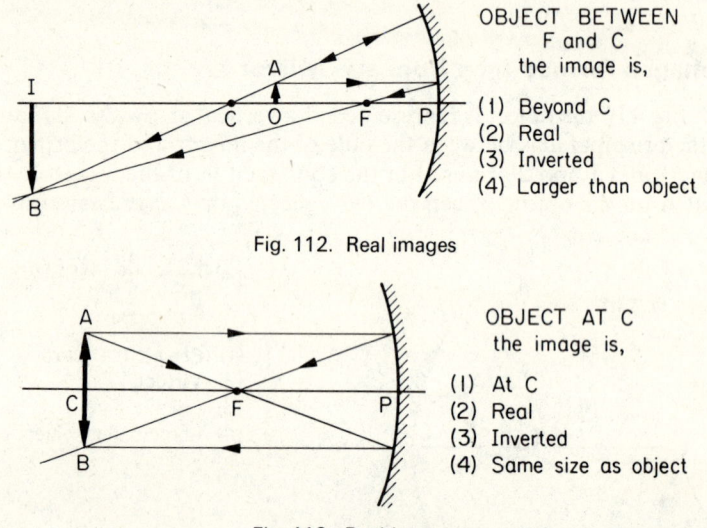

(1) Beyond C
(2) Real
(3) Inverted
(4) Larger than object

Fig. 112. Real images

OBJECT AT C
the image is,

(1) At C
(2) Real
(3) Inverted
(4) Same size as object

Fig. 113. Real images

images. A real image is formed by the actual intersection of rays, whereas a virtual image is one formed by the apparent intersection of rays when their directions have been produced backwards. The practical distinction is that a **real image can be formed on a screen while a virtual image cannot.**

At this stage we would remind the reader that the use of full and dotted lines in ray diagrams is not a matter of personal preference but of convention. Full lines are used to indicate real rays, objects and real images, while dotted lines are reserved for virtual rays and images. If this convention is duly observed, together with the labelling of rays with arrows to show the direction of the light, the diagrams will be made more informative and confusion is less likely to arise.

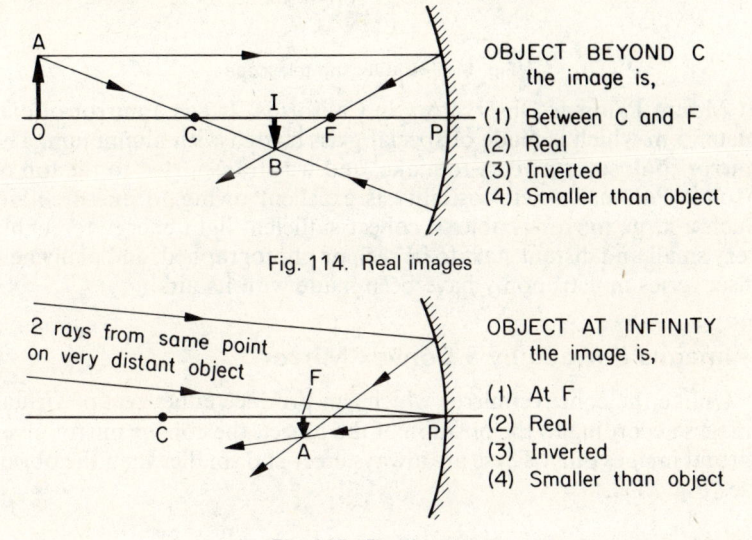

OBJECT BEYOND C
the image is,
(1) Between C and F
(2) Real
(3) Inverted
(4) Smaller than object

Fig. 114. Real images

OBJECT AT INFINITY
the image is,
(1) At F
(2) Real
(3) Inverted
(4) Smaller than object

Fig. 115. Real images

In Figs. 112 and 113 the object and image positions are examples of *conjugate foci*. Conjugate foci are any pair of points such that an object placed at one of them gives rise to a real image at the other. The fact that an object and its real image can be interchanged is an application of the principle of reversibility of light mentioned on p. 135.

Reflecting Telescope

The final case which is shown in Fig. 115 illustrates the principle of the reflecting telescope. When the object is a very long distance away from the mirror, the rays from any particular point on it are practically parallel when they reach the mirror. Consequently an image is formed at the principal focus.

The first telescope of this type was made by Sir Isaac Newton in the seventeenth century (Fig. 116). In order to see the image conveniently a small plane mirror M is placed at 45° to the axis of the mirror and between the principal focus and the mirror. This reflects the rays to one side and the image may now be viewed through a lens.

Newton's first telescope had a mirror of diameter 25 mm. The largest reflecting telescope in use today, called the *Hale Telescope*, is

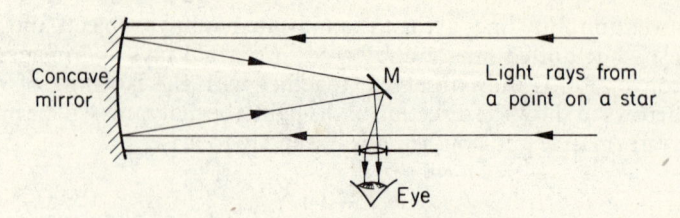

Fig. 116. A reflecting telescope

at Mount Palomar Observatory in California. It has a mirror of diameter 5 m which is made of special glass coated with aluminium. The mirror took several years to make, and was transported to the top of Mount Palomar where visibility is excellent owing to dust-free air. Such a large mirror is able to collect sufficient light energy to enable very small and distant stars to be seen or photographed, and many new discoveries in astronomy have been made with its aid.

Images Formed by a Convex Mirror

Unlike the concave mirror which can produce either real or virtual images according to the position of the object, the convex mirror gives virtual images only. These are always erect and smaller than the object (see Fig. 117).

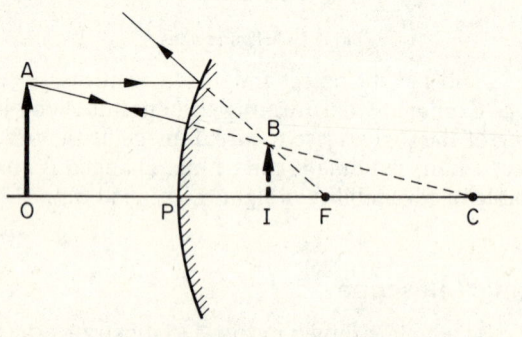

Fig. 117. Image in a convex mirror

Convex mirrors are very convenient for use as car-driving mirrors since they always give an erect image and a wide field of view. Fig. 118 shows why a convex mirror has a wider field of view than a plane mirror of the same size.

Accurate Construction of Ray Diagrams

Earlier in this chapter we mentioned that only rays parallel and *close* to the principal axis are brought to a true point focus. If we are to have an undistorted image, the same condition of closeness to the axis

CURVED MIRRORS · 123

applies to all rays forming the image. Nevertheless, we can locate an image accurately, using rays drawn well away from the axis, provided we represent that spherical mirror by a straight line instead of a curved one.

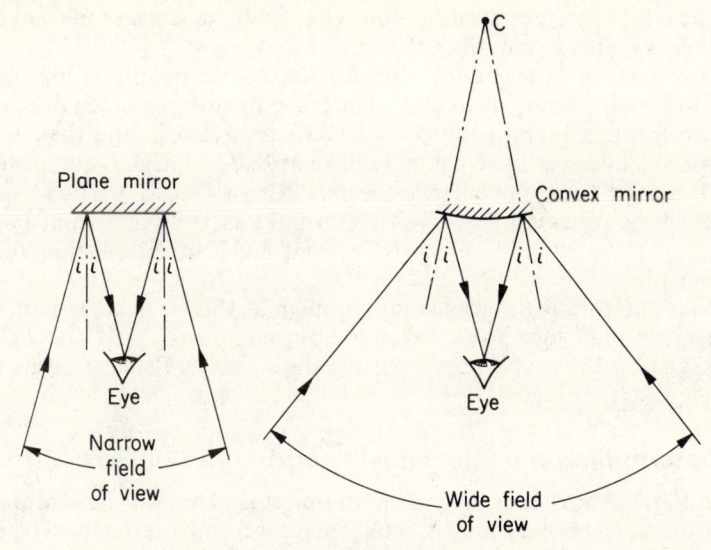

Fig. 118. Fields of view

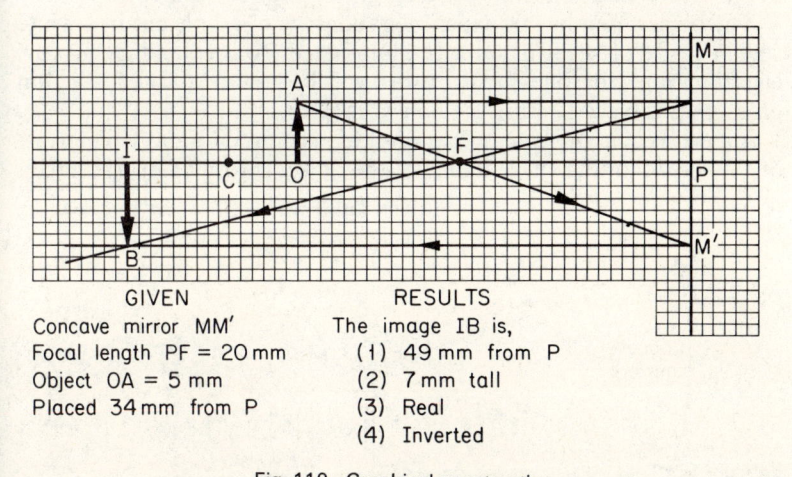

GIVEN
Concave mirror MM'
Focal length PF = 20 mm
Object OA = 5 mm
Placed 34 mm from P

RESULTS
The image IB is,
(1) 49 mm from P
(2) 7 mm tall
(3) Real
(4) Inverted

Fig. 119. Graphical construction

Example. By means of an accurate graphical construction, determine the position, size and nature of the image of an object 5 mm tall, standing on the principal axis of a concave mirror of focal length 20 mm and 34 mm from the mirror.

The construction is best performed using graph paper with squares. A straight line CP is drawn to represent the principal axis with a line MPM' at right angles to it to represent the concave mirror (Fig. 119).

The principal focus F is marked 20 mm from P.

The object is represented by a line OA, 5 mm long, perpendicular to the axis PC and 34 mm from P.

Two incident rays are now drawn from A, one parallel to the axis and the other passing through F. The corresponding reflected rays are drawn through F and parallel to the axis respectively, and these will be seen to intersect to give a real image at B. The image is completed by drawing IB perpendicular to the axis PC.

It will be observed that IB is 7 mm tall and is 49 mm from P. It therefore follows that the image is 7 mm tall and is situated 49 mm from the mirror.

When performing constructions similar to this, it is important to remember that your work has not been completed until you have recorded on the graph paper, (*a*) the data given, (*b*) the scale used, (*c*) the results obtained.

Determination of the Focal Length of a Concave Mirror

In Fig. 113 it is seen that when an object is placed at the centre of curvature of a concave mirror, a real image is formed at the same place as the object. This fact is used in a simple method for finding the radius of curvature, and hence the focal length of a cancave mirror.

The object used in this experiment consists of a hole cut in a white screen made of sheet metal and illuminated from behind by a pearl electric lamp. Sharpness of focusing will be greatly assisted if a thin cross-wire is placed across the hole (Fig. 120).

A concave mirror, mounted in a holder, is moved to-and-fro in front of the screen until a sharp image of the object is formed on the screen

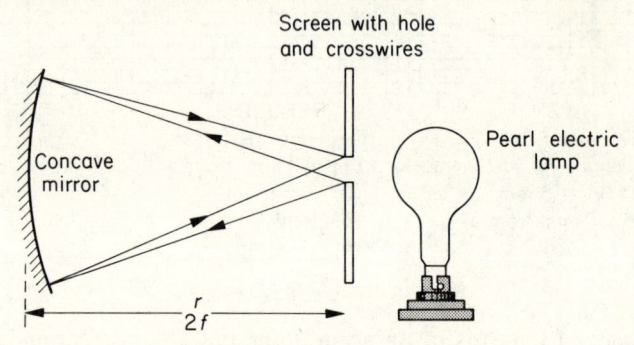

Fig. 120. Measuring radius of curvature

adjacent to the object. When this has been done both object and image are at the same distance from the mirror, and hence both must be

CURVED MIRRORS · 125

situated in a plane passing through the centre of curvature and at right angles to the axis. The distance between mirror and screen is measured. Half this distance is the focal length of the mirror.

Optical Formulae. Sign Convention

It can be shown by methods outside the scope of this book that, for both concave and convex mirrors,

$$\frac{1}{v} + \frac{1}{u} = \frac{1}{f} \qquad . \qquad . \qquad . \qquad . \qquad \text{(i)}$$

where u is the object distance from the mirror, v is the image distance and f is the focal length. This is called the *optical formula*. When the formula is used, the object and image distances are written as positive (+) or negative (−) according to a sign rule or convention stated shortly. The formula then fits every possible case of image and object position, whether real or virtual.

"Real is Positive" Convention

When an object or image is real, the distance is given a + sign; when the object or image is virtual, the distance is given a − sign.

Thus a concave mirror has a + focal length (real focus), but a convex mirror has a − focal length (virtual focus). A concave mirror of 10 cm focal length has thus $f = +10$ cm; a convex mirror of 12 cm focal length has $f = -12$ cm.

Examples 1. An object is placed (i) 18 cm, (ii) 6 cm in front of a concave mirror of focal length 15 cm. Find the image distance in each case.

(i) We have

$u = +18$ (real object)
$f = +15$ (concave mirror)

Substituting in

$$\frac{1}{v} + \frac{1}{u} = \frac{1}{f}$$

$$\therefore \frac{1}{v} + \frac{1}{(+18)} = \frac{1}{(+15)}$$

$$\therefore \frac{1}{v} + \frac{1}{18} = \frac{1}{15}$$

$$\therefore \frac{1}{v} = \frac{1}{15} - \frac{1}{18} = \frac{1}{90}$$

$$\therefore \frac{v}{1} = \frac{90}{1} \text{ or } v = 90$$

New Cartesian Convention

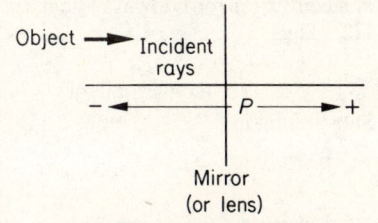

Fig. 121. Sign convention

Distances are measured from the mirror (or lens) position P (Fig. 121). Distances to the right of P are given a + sign; distances to the left are given a − sign. The object is always placed on the left of P.

Thus a concave mirror has a − focal length, since the focus is on the left of P, but a convex mirror has a + focal length since the focus is behind or to the right of P. A mirror of $f = -15$ cm is therefore a concave mirror.

Examples 1. An object is placed (i) 18 cm, (ii) 6 cm in front of a concave mirror of focal length 15 cm. Find the image distance in each case.

(i) We have

$u = -18$ (object on left of mirror)
$f = -15$ (concave mirror)

Thus the image distance is 90 cm
  (ii) In this case
$$u = +6 \text{ (real object)},$$
$$f = +15.$$
$$\therefore \frac{1}{v} + \frac{1}{(+6)} = \frac{1}{(+15)}$$
$$\therefore \frac{1}{v} + \frac{1}{6} = \frac{1}{15}$$
$$\therefore \frac{1}{v} = \frac{1}{15} - \frac{1}{6} = -\frac{3}{30}$$
$$\therefore \frac{v}{1} = -\frac{30}{3}, \text{ or } v = -10$$

Thus the image is 10 cm from the mirror, and, from the $-$ sign, the image is *virtual*.

  2. An object is placed in front of a convex mirror of focal length 10 cm, and the image is 6 cm from the mirror. Find the object distance.
  Here we should note that the image in a convex mirror is always *virtual* (p. 122). Thus
$$v = -6$$
$$f = -10 \text{ (convex mirror)}$$
Substituting in
$$\frac{1}{v} + \frac{1}{u} = \frac{1}{f}$$
$$\therefore \frac{1}{(-6)} + \frac{1}{u} = \frac{1}{(-10)}$$
$$\therefore \frac{1}{6} + \frac{1}{u} = -\frac{1}{10}$$
$$\therefore \frac{1}{u} = -\frac{1}{10} + \frac{1}{6} = \frac{2}{30}$$
$$\therefore \frac{u}{1} = \frac{30}{2}, \text{ or } u = 15$$

Thus the object is 15 cm from the mirror

Substituting in
$$\frac{1}{v} + \frac{1}{u} = \frac{1}{f}$$
$$\therefore \frac{1}{v} + \frac{1}{(-18)} = \frac{1}{(-15)}$$
$$\therefore \frac{1}{v} - \frac{1}{18} = -\frac{1}{15}$$
$$\therefore \frac{1}{v} = -\frac{1}{15} + \frac{1}{18} = -\frac{1}{90}$$
$$\therefore \frac{v}{1} = -\frac{90}{1} \text{ or } v = -90$$

Thus the image is 90 cm on the left of the mirror.
  (ii) In this case
$$u = -6 \text{ (object of left of mirror)}$$
$$f = -15$$
$$\therefore \frac{1}{v} + \frac{1}{(-6)} = \frac{1}{(-15)}$$
$$\therefore \frac{1}{v} - \frac{1}{6} = -\frac{1}{15}$$
$$\therefore \frac{1}{v} = -\frac{1}{15} + \frac{1}{6} = \frac{3}{30}$$
$$\therefore \frac{v}{1} = \frac{30}{3}, \text{ or } v = 10$$

Since v is positive, the image is 10 cm on the *right* of the mirror, i.e. a virtual image.

  2. An object is placed in front of a convex mirror of focal length 10 cm, and the image is 6 cm from the mirror. Find the object distance.
  The image in a convex mirror is always virtual (p. 122), and hence it is on the *right* of the mirror.
$$v = -6$$
$$f = -10 \text{ (convex mirror)}$$
Substituting in
$$\frac{1}{v} + \frac{1}{u} = \frac{1}{f}$$
$$\therefore \frac{1}{(-6)} + \frac{1}{u} = \frac{1}{(-10)}$$
$$\therefore -\frac{1}{6} + \frac{1}{u} = -\frac{1}{10}$$
$$\therefore \frac{1}{u} = -\frac{1}{10} + \frac{1}{6} = -\frac{2}{30}$$
$$\therefore \frac{u}{1} = \frac{30}{2}, \text{ or } u = -15$$

Thus the object is 15 cm. on the left of the mirror.

Magnification Formula

When a curved mirror is used, it usually makes the object look bigger or smaller. The *linear* or *transverse magnification, m,* is defined by

$$m = \frac{\text{length of image (I)}}{\text{length of object (O)}} \quad . \quad . \quad . \quad \text{(i)}$$

and it can be shown the linear magnification can always be calculated from the formula

$$m = \frac{v}{u} \text{ numerically} \quad . \quad . \quad . \quad \text{(ii)}$$

Thus if a concave mirror image is 45 cm from the mirror and the object is 9 cm away, then, numerically,

$$m = \frac{v}{u} = \frac{45}{9} = 5.$$

The image is thus 5 times the length of the object. If the image distance in a convex mirror is 6 cm and the object distance is 10 cm, then, numerically,

$$m = \frac{v}{u} = \frac{6}{10} = 0 \cdot 6.$$

Thus the image is 0·6 times the length of the object.

Summary

1. The *centre of curvature* and *radius of curvature* of a spherical mirror are respectively the centre and radius of the sphere of which the mirror forms a part.
2. The *pole* of a mirror is the centre of the reflecting surface.
3. The *principal axis* of a spherical mirror is the line joining the pole to the centre of curvature.
4. The *principal focus* of a spherical mirror is that point on the principal axis to which all rays parallel and close to the principal axis converge for a concave mirror, or from which they appear to diverge after reflection from the mirror for a convex mirror.
5. The *focal length* of a spherical mirror is the distance between the principal focus and the pole of the mirror, and is equal to half the radius of curvature.
6. For a *concave or converging* mirror:
    (*a*) the principal focus is real,
    (*b*) the image is real and inverted when the object is at a distance from the mirror greater than the focal length.
    (*c*) the image is erect, virtual and magnified when the object is at a distance from the mirror less than the focal length.

7. For a *convex or diverging* mirror, the image is always erect, virtual and diminished for all positions of the object.

8. The *formula* is $\frac{1}{v} + \frac{1}{u} = \frac{1}{f}$. A plus or minus sign must be attached to the figures when substituting for the letters, according to a sign convention.

Magnification, m, $= \frac{v}{u}$ (numerically).

EXERCISES

1. What do you understand by the terms, (*a*) centre of curvature, (*b*) pole, (*c*) principal axis of a spherical mirror? Draw a labelled diagram in illustration.

2. Define (*a*) principal focus, (*b*) focal length of a spherical mirror. How does the focal length of a spherical mirror compare with its radius of curvature? Give diagrams to illustrate your answer.

3. Using the laws of reflection, show by geometry that the focal length of a convex mirror is equal to half its radius of curvature.

4. Name the three most important incident rays, together with their corresponding reflected rays, which are used in constructing ray diagrams for spherical mirrors.

5. Give diagrams to show how (*a*) a magnified inverted image, (*b*) a magnified erect image is formed by a concave mirror.

6. Explain, with the aid of a diagram, why a convex mirror is to be preferred to a plane mirror for use in car driving.

7. Find by a graphical method the nature, position and size of the image of an object 1 cm tall placed 25 cm from a concave mirror of focal length 20 cm.

8. By means of a ray diagram, find out all you can about the image formed when an object 0·5 cm tall is placed 7 cm from a convex mirror of focal length 4 cm.

9. A candle flame 7·5 mm high is situated 26 mm from a concave mirror of radius of curvature 80 mm. Obtain all the information you can about the image formed.

10. Write a short essay on the reflecting telescope.

11. Describe an experiment to measure the focal length of a concave mirror.

12. An object is placed (i) 10 cm and then (ii) 4 cm in front of a concave mirror of 6 cm focal length. Find the image distance from the mirror in each case, and the magnification in each case.

13. The image in a convex mirror of radius of curvature 20 cm is 4 cm from the mirror. Find the object distance from the mirror, and the magnification. (*Hint.—* The image in a convex mirror is virtual.)

14. The image in a concave mirror is erect and magnified, and 16 cm from the mirror. If the focal length is 4 cm, find the object distance and the magnification.

15. The image in a concave mirror is real and three times the size of the object. If the image distance from the mirror is 24 cm, find the focal length of the mirror.

16. By means of a diagram, show how a motor-car headlamp can produce a fairly parallel beam of light.

A concave mirror has a focal length of 12 cm, and an object 4 cm high is placed 18 cm from the mirror. Draw a diagram showing how the image is formed, and find its distance from the mirror and its magnification.

17. What is meant by (i) a real, (ii) a virtual image? By means of ray diagrams, show how each type may be formed by a concave mirror.

An object is 60 cm from a concave mirror, and an image is formed 30 cm in front of the mirror. By means of a scale drawing, find the focal length of the mirror and the magnification. Check your result by calculation.

18. State as many facts as you can about the appearance of the image of an object in a convex mirror. Draw a ray diagram to show how the image is formed.

An object is placed 45·0 cm in front of a convex mirror, and the image is formed 15·0 cm from the mirror. Calculate the new distance of the image from the mirror if the object is moved 20·0 cm towards the mirror.

CHAPTER THIRTEEN

Refraction of Light

A swimming-bath looks much shallower than it actually is; a straight stick appears bent when placed half in and half out of water; and the landscape "shimmers" on a hot summer's day. These, and many other equally curious effects, are due to a phenomenon known as the refraction of light.

When light from a ray box is incident on a rectangular slab of glass, experiment shows that the ray is "bent" or *refracted* on passing from the air to the glass (Fig. 122). At the same time, a little of the light is reflected from the surface of the glass.

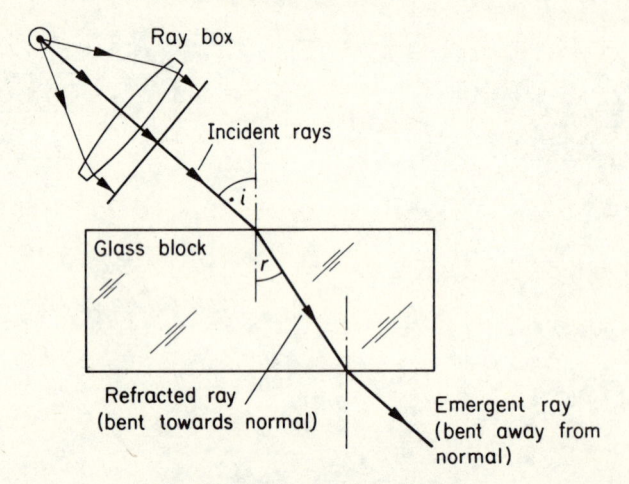

Fig. 122. Refraction through glass

The technical terms used in connection with refraction are illustrated in Fig. 123, which represents the passage of a ray of light from air to glass. The *angle of incidence, i,* is the angle between the incident ray and the normal at the point of incidence. The *angle of refraction, r,* is the angle between the refracted ray and the normal.

It is important to remember that, when a ray passes from one medium to a more optically dense medium, the ray bends towards the

REFRACTION OF LIGHT · 131

normal. Conversely, a ray passing from glass or water into air is bent away from the normal, as shown in Fig. 122.

```
AO   = Incident ray
OB   = Refracted ray
NON' = Normal
∠AON = Angle of incidence
∠BON' = Angle of refraction
```

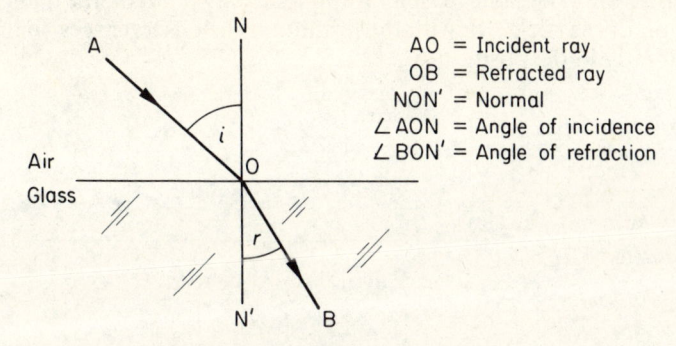

Fig. 123. Incidence and refraction

Wave Tank Observations

It can be shown in the wave tank that refraction is the result of a change in speed of waves when they enter a less transparent material. If a thick piece of glass is placed in the tank, so that the water only just covers it, then it will be seen that the waves travel more slowly when they pass from the normal depth of water to the shallow depth over the glass. If the glass is now placed so that its edge is not parallel to the parallel waves being generated, the refraction of these waves can be investigated.

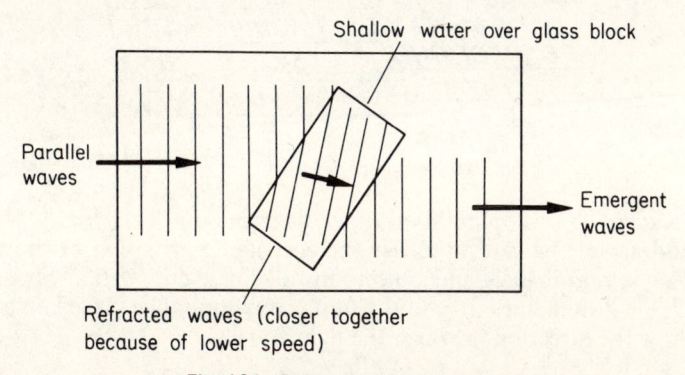

Fig. 124. Refraction in a wave tank

Some Effects of Refraction. Apparent Depth

The apparent upward bending of a stick when placed in water is shown in Fig. 125. Rays of light from the end B of the stick pass from water to air, and are bent away from the normal since they are passing to a less optically dense medium. Entering the eye, the rays appear to be coming from a point C above B. C is thus the image of B as a result of refraction. The same reasoning applies to any point on the immersed portion of the stick AB, with the result that the observer sees an image apparently in the position AC.

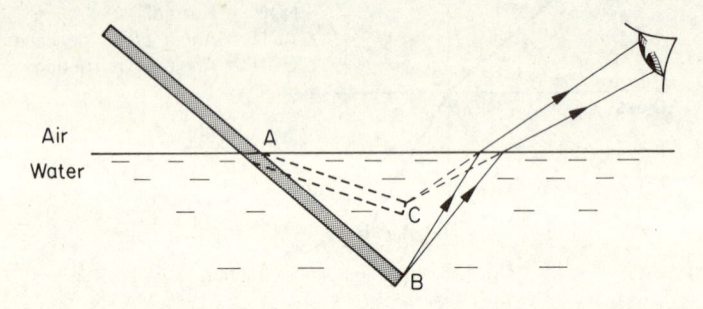

Fig. 125. Apparent bending of an object in water

Fig. 126 illustrates the appearance of print viewed through the top of a piece of thick glass placed over it. Since rays are refracted away from the normal when they pass from glass to air, the print and the bottom of the glass appear raised. The apparent raising of the print thus occurs for the same reason that a stick appears to be bent upwards when placed in water, as explained in the previous paragraph.

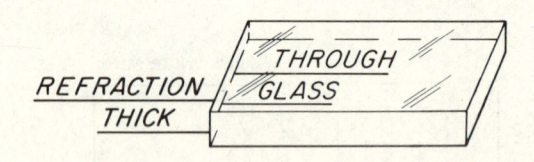

Fig. 126. Apparent depth in thick glass

To avoid confusion in this and ray diagrams similar to Fig. 125, one should always be careful to use the accepted convention of drawing real rays, real images and objects in full lines, and virtual rays and images in dotted lines. In addition, an arrow should be placed on a ray to show the direction in which the light travels.

Experiments on Refraction

A straight line SS′, to represent the surface of separation between air and glass, is drawn on a sheet of drawing paper on a drawing board, together with a normal ON and several lines at various angles to ON to represent incident rays (Fig. 127).

REFRACTION OF LIGHT · 133

A ruler is placed along SS' and a rectangular glass block carefully placed in contact with it in the position shown in Fig. 127. The ruler is now transferred to the lower edge of the block and the block is then removed.

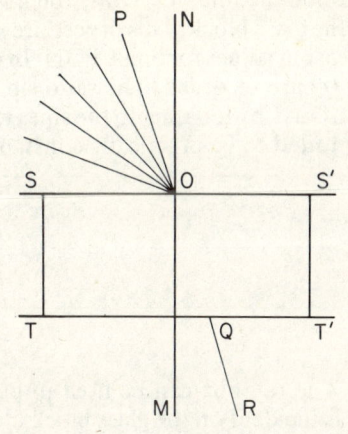

Fig. 127. Experiment to establish the laws of refraction

A line TT', to represent the lower edge of the block, is now drawn. Without moving the ruler, the block is now placed carefully in contact with the ruler. The two lines SS' and TT' should now coincide exactly with the upper and lower vertical faces of the block.

This is a better method than simply drawing round the block with a pencil. The block is thick and its edges are usually bevelled, which

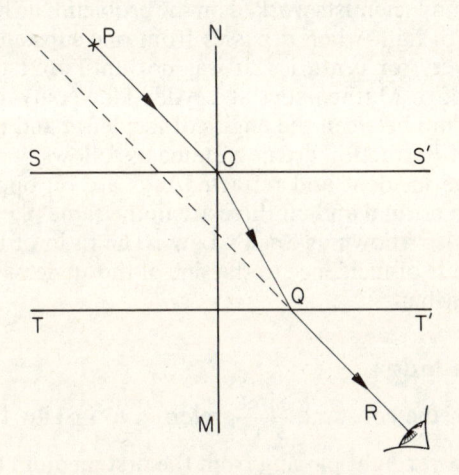

Fig. 128. A refracted ray

renders it difficult to draw lines to coincide exactly with the block faces.

A line OP is drawn on the paper, the angle PÔN being about 20°. On looking into the face TT′ of the block, line OP will be seen through the glass. A ruler is now placed on the paper in position QR such that QR appears to continue the line PO. Draw the line QR and join OQ, after first removing the glass block. This procedure is followed for other lines OP, using increasing values for angle PÔN. In each case the angles PÔN (i) and MÔQ (r) are recorded. The ratio $\sin i / \sin r$ may now be found for each pair of rays by looking up the sines in tables (see p. 000). The ratio should be found to be practically constant.

i	r	$\sin i$	$\sin r$	$\dfrac{\sin i}{\sin r}$

Ray box method. The ray box can be used in place of a ruler. It is turned to that a ray is incident on the glass block along one of the lines drawn (Fig. 127). The points or crosses are marked on the emerging ray. The block is then removed and the two points are joined to intersect the lower edge of the glass. The refracted ray is the line joining the point of intersection to the point of incidence on the other edge, and i and r can now be measured. This is repeated for other rays, $\sin i / \sin r$ is calculated for each, and the result should be fairly constant.

The Laws of Refraction

Although many scientists worked on the problem, the laws governing the refraction of light when it passes from one substance to another resisted discovery for centuries. It was not until 1621 that Willibrod Snell, Professor of Mathematics at Leyden University, discovered the exact relationship between the angles of incidence and refraction.

The Laws of Refraction are now stated as follows:

Law I. The incident and refracted rays are on opposite sides of the normal and all three are in the same plane.

Law II. (Also known as Snell's Law.) The ratio of the sine of the angle of incidence to the sine of the angle of refraction is a constant.

Refractive Index

The value of the constant, $\dfrac{\sin i}{\sin r}$, referred to in Law II is called the *refractive index* for light passing from the first medium to the second, and we shall denote it by the letter n.

If the medium is air (or more strictly a vacuum), then n is called the refractive index of the second medium. For example, if a ray passes from air to water, then,

$$\text{Refractive index of water } n = \frac{\sin i}{\sin r}$$

The refractive index of the glass used for making the lenses is required in the manufacture of high-grade telescopes and microscopes. For crown glass, n is about 1·52; for flint glass it is about 1·65. The refractive index of water is 1·33.

The Principle of Reversibility of Light

The principle of the reversibility of light, which states that the paths of light rays are reversible, has already been mentioned in connection with reflection in Chapter 12. The same holds true for the case of refraction and, indeed, for rays passing through any optical system.

The refractive indices for a ray passing from air to glass and from glass to air may be distinguished by using the symbols $_an_g$ and $_gn_a$ respectively.

Thus, using Fig. 123,

$$_an_g = \frac{\sin i}{\sin r}$$

and by the principle of reversibility of light,

$$_gn_a = \frac{\sin r}{\sin i}$$

Hence,

$$_gn_a = \frac{1}{_an_g}$$

This equation will be used later on in the chapter in connection with critical internal reflection. If $_an_g = 1·5$, it follows that $_gn_a = 1/1·5 = 0·67$.

Total Internal Reflection.   Critical Angle

When we first considered the refraction of light through a glass block earlier in this chapter, we mentioned the reflection which occurs at the surface of the glass at the same time. In Fig. 129 the reflected rays have been drawn in to make the story complete. It will be noticed that there is an external reflected ray BE, and an internal reflected ray CF inside the glass. All of these rays may be produced and examined by using a ray box and a glass slab.

Now there is a very important difference between (1) reflection at the surface of an optical medium denser than that in which the light is travelling, and (2) reflection at the surface of a less optically dense medium.

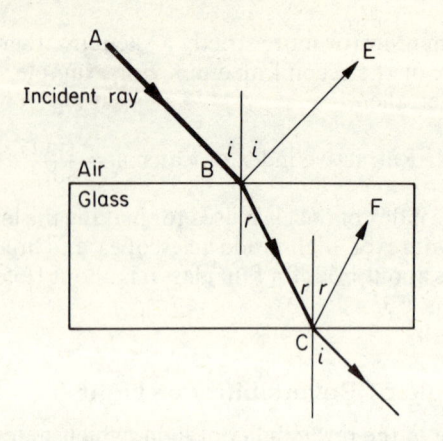

Fig. 129. Refraction and reflection in a glass block

Let us suppose that the angle of incidence for a ray passing from glass to air, an optically less dense medium, is small as in Fig. 130 (i). Here we get both a refracted and a reflected ray, the latter, however, being relatively weak.

Suppose now the angle of incidence is gradually increased. The angle of refraction also increases until, for a certain critical angle of incidence, c, the angle of refraction is just $90°$. This special case is shown in Fig. 130 (ii). Up to now, a comparatively weak reflected ray is

(i) Refraction and internal reflection
$i < c$

(ii) Critical internal reflection
$i = c$

(iii) Total internal reflection
$i > c$

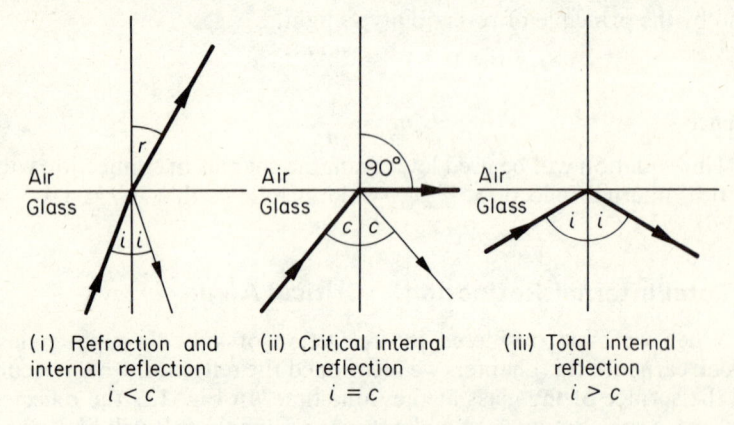

Fig. 130. A boundary of optical media

obtained internally in the glass, and a strong refracted ray passes out into the air. Now it is clearly impossible to have an angle of refraction greater than $90°$. Thus for angles of incidence greater than the critical angle *all* the light is totally internally reflected. There is now no refracted ray at all and we have only a *strong* internally reflected ray (see Fig. 130 (iii)).

Relation Between Critical Angle and Refractive Index

We have already seen that $_g n_a = 1/_a n_g$, and hence, from Fig. 130 (ii).

But
$$\frac{\sin c}{\sin 90°} = \frac{1}{_a n_g}$$
$$\sin 90° = 1$$

Therefore
$$\sin c = \frac{1}{_a n_g}$$

or
$$_a n_g = \frac{1}{\sin c}$$

For crown glass of refractive index $_a n_g = 1.5$, the critical angle c is about 42°. This is obtained from the above equation, using a table of sines.

Two Methods of Measuring Critical Angle and Refractive Index of Glass

(1) *Using a ray box*. A semicircular glass block and a ray box are placed on a sheet of paper on a drawing board so that the ray from the box enteres the block radially. For small angles of incidence both a refracted ray and an internally reflected ray are obtained. For larger angles of incidence there is total internal reflection.

The ray box is carefully adjusted, still keeping the ray passing through the block along a radius, until a direction for the incident ray is found for which the angle of refraction just reaches 90 and suddenly disappears

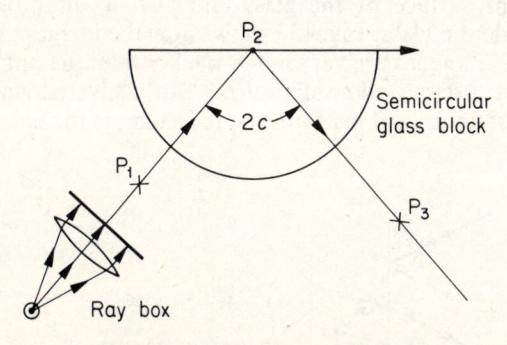

Fig. 131. Measuring critical angle

(Fig. 131). The positions of the incident and critical reflected rays are then marked by pencil crosses at P_1, P_2 and P_3. The block and ray box are removed, and P_1P_2 and P_2P_3 are joined. Then angle $P_1P_2P_3$ is twice the critical angle, which can thus be found.

(2) *By drawing*. A pin O is fastened with adhesive tape to the centre of the plane face AB of a semicircular glass block (Fig. 132).

The pin is viewed through the block by moving the eye to-and-fro along the path indicated. A position for the eye is found for which the image of O is just on the point of disappearing. This position is marked by placing a ruler on the paper in line with O and the eye. Line QP is drawn along the ruler, then AB is drawn in in pencil and the block removed. The normal ON is drawn and OP joined. Then PON is the critical angle.

In each of these experiments a value for the critical angle should be found and the refractive index of glass calculated from $n = 1/\sin c$.

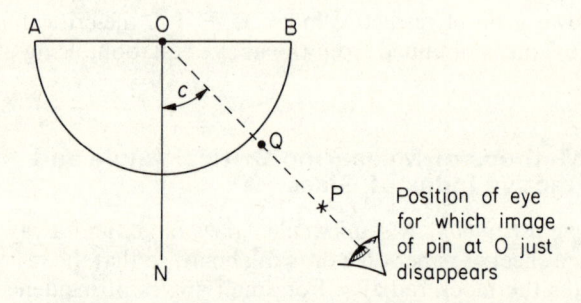

Fig. 132. Graphical measurement of critical angle

Multiple Images Formed by a Silvered Glass Mirror

Ordinary mirrors, made by silvering the back face of a sheet of glass, suffer from the disadvantage that extra images are formed by reflection from the front surface of the glass and also by multiple internal reflection inside the glass. Fig. 133 shows how the images are formed. Ordinarily these images are very much weaker than the image formed by the silvered surface and go unnoticed. But if silvered glass mirrors are used in certain optical instruments, for example the episcope, they

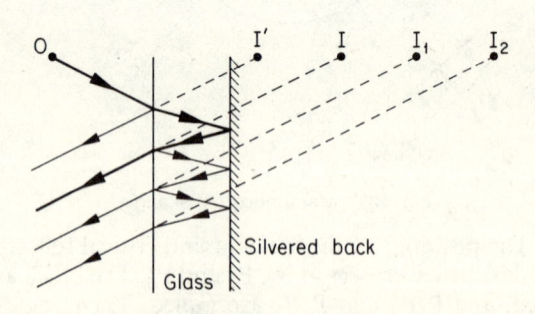

Fig. 133. Multiple reflections in a mirror

are a nuisance. For this reason episcope mirrors are silvered on the front surface. Care is needed in handling such mirrors as the silver is easily damaged. Tarnishing is prevented by a very thin coating of lacquer. In Fig. 133, I is the brightest image.

Total Internal Reflection in Prisms

The problem of providing an untarnishable mirror which gives one image only has been solved in the submarine periscope by using 45° right-angled glass prisms, as shown in Fig. 134 (*a*). Actually a submarine periscope is a combined periscope and telescope, but for simplicity in the diagram the lenses have been omitted. Light enters the faces of the prisms normally and falls on the hypotenuse face internally at an angle of incidence of 45°. Total reflection occurs here, since the critical angle for ordinary glass is about 42° (p. 137).

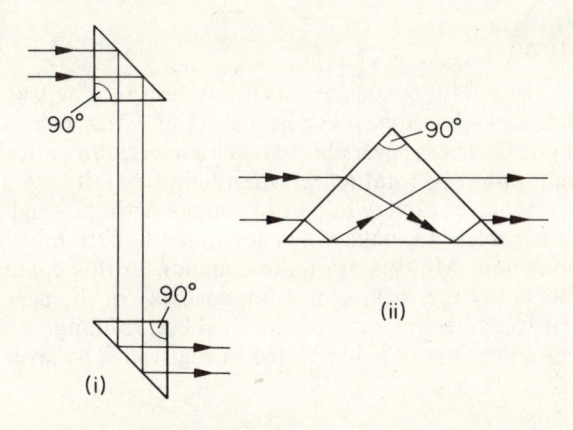

Fig. 134. Total internal reflection in right-angle prisms

For reasons explained in Chapter 14, it is necessary to place slides or films upside down in a projector in order to obtain a picture the right way up on the screen. It is not always possible to do this, since it is occasionally necessary to project an image of a thin glass cell containing a liquid. For example, polarisation on the copper plate of a simple cell (see p. 49) may be demonstrated to a class by this method. In such cases the image may still be obtained on the screen the correct way up by placing an *erecting prism* in front of the projection lens. Fig. 134 (ii) shows how a right-angled prism is used for this purpose. Light enters the face of the prism approximately parallel to the base or hypotenuse face. Total reflection occurs at the base, with the result that the rays passing through are inverted.

140 · ELEMENTARY PHYSICS

A third method of employing total internal reflection in right-angled prisms is used in prism binoculars. A prism binocular is simply a pair of telescopes conveniently shortened in length by causing the light to traverse the tube three times instead of once. If light is incident perpendicular to the hypotenuse face of the prism it will undergo two internal reflections, finally emerging parallel to its original path but travelling in opposite direction. Fig. 135 indicates how two prisms are used in this manner in the binocular.

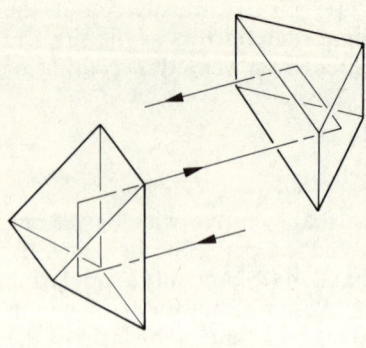

Fig. 135. Optical arrangement of prism binoculars

The Mirage

Mirages are usually associated with hot deserts. The traveller in a desert often sees what appears to be a sheet of water a short distance ahead of him. This he is never able to reach since it is an optical illusion. It is brought about by total reflection of light from the sky at the less optically dense layer of very hot air in contact with the sand.

It is not necessary to make a journey to the Sahara in order to see this phenomenon. Mirages are quite common in this country. On a hot summer's day the surface of a hot roadway in the near distance may appear wet and shiny as though it had been raining.

How this comes about is illustrated in Fig. 136. The layer of air in

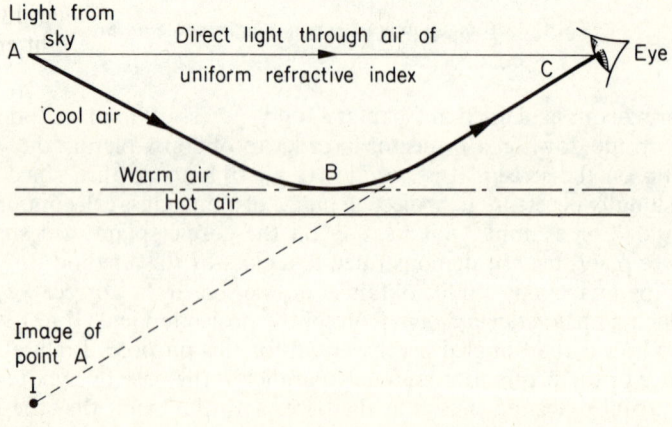

Fig. 136. A mirage

contact with the hot road surface becomes very hot and expands, thus becoming optically less dense than the cooler layers above. A ray of light AB coming from the sky through the cool air layers bends upwards slightly as it enters the layers of warm air of decreasing refractive index nearer the ground. The light thus bends upwards progressively as it traverses the lower layers, until it meets a hot surface layer near the ground at an angle of incidence greater than the critical angle. Total reflection then occurs, and light enters the eye along the direction BC. A virtual image of the point A in the sky is therefore seen at I. The hot surface layer of air thus acts as a mirror in which an image of the sky is seen. Since we are accustomed to seeing the sky mirrored in the surface of still water, the natural assumption made when viewing the mirage is that the ground surface is wet.

Deviation of Light by a Triangular Prism

Triangular glass prisms are of considerable importance in the study of light, as we shall see later in Chapter 15.

Unlike a rectangular block which simply displaces the emergent light parallel to its incident direction (Fig. 137), a triangular prism causes the light to be *deviated*.

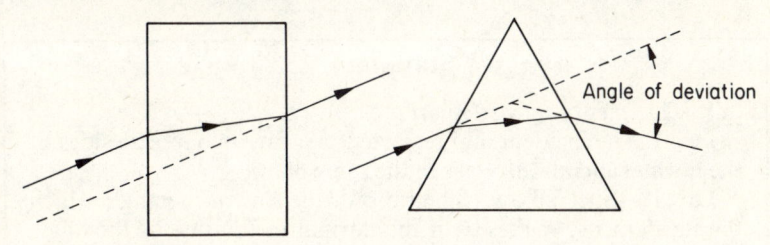

Fig. 137. *Displacement* of a ray by a rectangular prism; *deviation* of a ray by a triangular prism

The *angle of deviation* is the angle between the incident and emergent rays. The deviation is least when the light passes symmetrically through the prism, that is to say, when the angle of incidence is equal to the angle of emergence. This may be shown to be true by a simple experiment.

A 60° prism is placed with one face in contact with a pin P_1 stuck vertically in a sheet of paper on a drawing board (Fig. 138). This pin and a second pin P_2 are then viewed by refraction of light through the prism, so that they appear to have images at I_1 and I_2. The prism is then rotated to and fro about the pin P_1, and a position found for which the angle between P_1P_2 and I_1I_2 is a minimum. Two more pins E_1 and E_2 are then stuck in the paper in line with I_1 and I_2. The position of the prism is drawn on the paper with pencil, after which the prism is

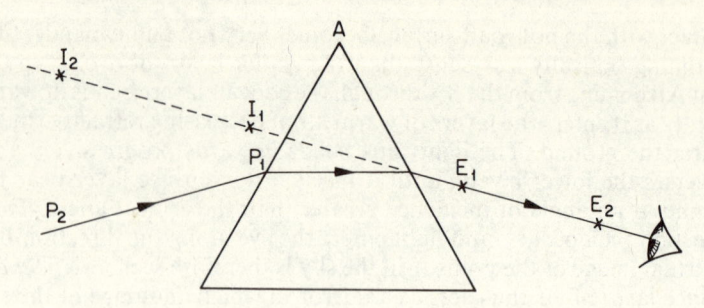

Fig. 138. Minimum deviation occurs with symmetrical rays

removed. On joining P_1P_2 and E_1E_2 it will be found that these lines, which represent the incident and emergent rays respectively, cut the prism at points equidistant from the refracting edge A. It follows that, in the minimum deviation position, the light passes symmetrically through the prism. Thus if normals are constructed and the angles of incidence and emergence measured they will be found to be equal.

Summary

1. The *laws of refraction* are:

Law I. The incident and refracted rays are on opposite sides of the normal and all three are in the same plane.

Law II. (Snell's Law.) The ratio of the sine of the angle which the incident ray makes with the normal to the sine of the angle which the refracted ray makes with the normal is a constant.

2. $n_m = \dfrac{\sin i}{\sin r}$ for a ray passing from air (or more strictly a vaccum) to the medium.

3. The *critical angle* for a ray passing from one medium to a less optically dense medium is that angle of incidence for which the angle of refraction in the less dense medium is 90°.

4. For a ray passing from a medium of refractive index $_an_m$ to air (or more strictly a vacuum) the critical angle is given by

$$\sin c = \frac{1}{_an_m}$$

5. In the case of light travelling from one medium to a less optically dense medium, *total internal reflection* occurs for all angles of incidence greater than the critical angle.

REFRACTION OF LIGHT · 143

EXERCISES

1. What do you understand by the refraction of light? Explain why a pool of water appears shallower than is actually the case.

2. Explain, with the aid of a ray diagram, why a straight ruler appears to be bent when placed in water at an angle of 45°, with half its length immersed.

3. State the laws of refraction and describe an experiment to verify them, using a glass block and pins, or a ray box.

4. What is meant by *refractive index?* By means of a graphical construction, find the angle of refraction for a ray entering the surface of water from air at an angle of incidence of (i) 30°, (ii) 50°. Check your answers by calculation ($_an_w = 1\cdot33$).

5. Calculate the angle of refraction when light is incident at 30° from (i) air to glass, (ii) glass to air ($_an_g = 1\cdot5$).

6. What is meant by (*a*) critical angle, (*b*) total internal reflection? Draw diagrams to explain your answer.

7. The refractive index of water is $1\cdot33$. Calculate the critical angle for a ray travelling from water to air.

8. An empty test-tube is held at an angle of about 45° to the horizontal and lowered into a beaker full of water. When viewed from above it has the appearance of being filled with mercury. Explain this phenomenon.

9. Describe an experiment to measure the critical angle for glass using a semicircular glass block and a ray box. What information about the glass can you obtain from a knowledge of its critical angle?

10. Show by means of ray diagrams how you would use a glass prism to turn a ray of light through an angle of (*a*) 90°, (*b*) 180°. Give examples of practical use made of prisms in these two ways.

11. What kind of prism would you use as an erecting prism? Give a diagram to show a practical use of an erecting prism.

12. Explain why the dry surface of a road on a hot day sometimes has the appearance of being wet.

13. Describe and explain the multiple images obtained with a thick mirror.

CHAPTER FOURTEEN

Lenses

Magnifying glasses or lenses have been in use for centuries; spectacles were in use in Europe in the 13th century. Lenses of many different types play an important part in our own everyday life. Apart from the benefit of spectacles which enable millions of people to read in comfort, our lives would be vastly changed if we had no cameras, projectors, microscopes or telescopes, all of which function by means of lenses.

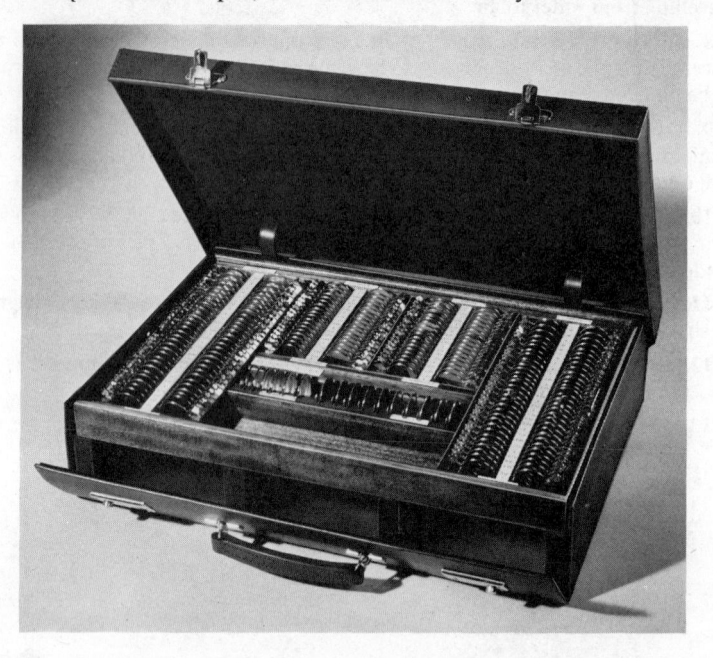

Plate 25. An optician's box of lenses: converging and diverging lenses of many different focal lengths are used to test for defects of vision

Not all lenses can be used as magnifying glasses. There are some, used in opera glasses and in spectacles for short-sighted persons, which always give a diminished, erect virtual image. These are referred to an concave or diverging lenses, while magnifying glasses are called convex

LENSES · 145

or converging lenses. The two types can be readily distinguished from one another; converging lenses are thickest in the middle while diverging lenses are thinnest in the middle. Fig. 139 illustrates some of the more common types of lenses.

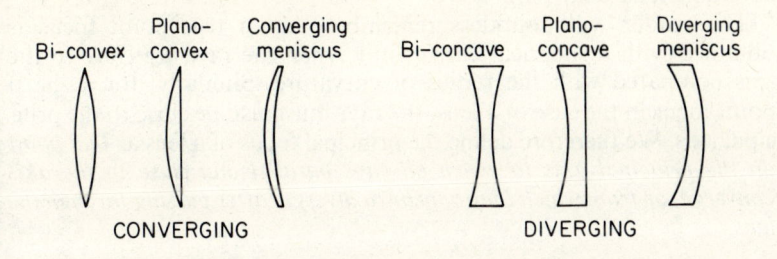

Fig. 139. Converging and diverging lenses

Principal Focus of a lens

A simple lens is usually a piece of glass bounded by spherical surfaces.

The *principal axis* of a lens is the line joining the centres of curvature of its surfaces.

If a parallel beam of light, parallel to the principal axis, is incident on a converging lens, the rays, after passing through the lens, all

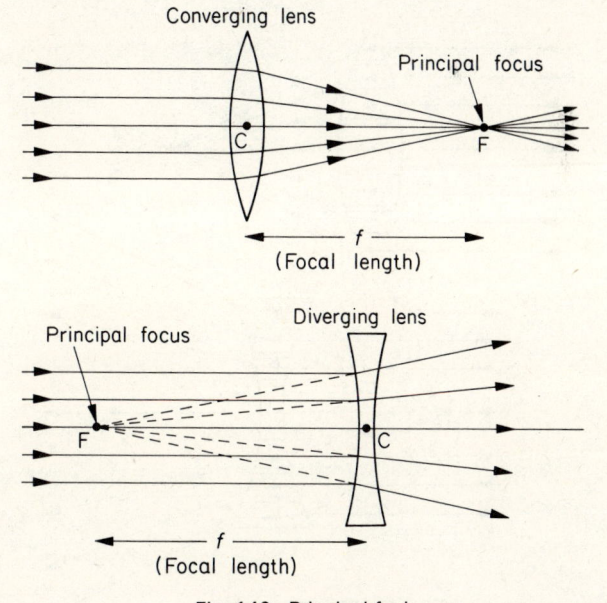

Fig. 140. Principal foci

converge to a point on the axis which is called the *principal focus*. In the case of a diverging lens, the rays will spread out after passing through the lens, as if diverging from a focus behind the lens. The principal focus is thus real for a converging lens and virtual for a diverging lens (Fig. 140).

The reader will doubtless remember that a true point focus is obtained with a spherical *mirror* only when the rays are *close* to the axis compared with the radius of curvature. Similarly, for a sharp point focus in the case of a lens, the rays must also be close to the principal axis. We therefore define the principal focus of a lens as *that point on the principal axis to which all rays parallel and close to the axis converge, or from which they appear to diverge, after passing through the lens.*

Lenses compared with Prisms

In Chapter 14 we saw how a triangular glass prism causes light to be deviated on passing through it. Now a lens may be regarded as being made up of a very large number of portions of triangular prisms, the angles of which decrease from the edges of the lens to its centre. As a result, light is deviated more at the edges of a lens than at the centre. This will explain how a beam of light parallel to the principal axis of a lens is either brought to a real focus in the case of a converging lens, or diverges from a virtual focus in the case of a diverging lens (see Fig. 141).

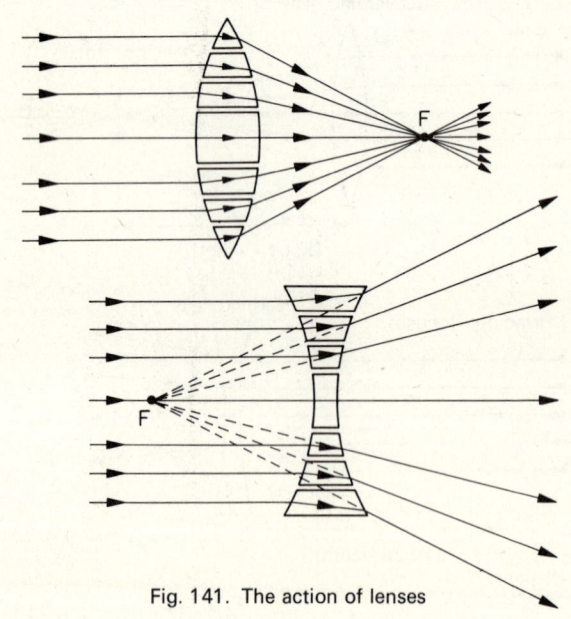

Fig. 141. The action of lenses

Optical Centre of a Lens. Focal Length

The central portion of a lens may be regarded as a small part of a parallel-sided slab, so that rays passing through it are not deviated but only slightly displaced parallel to their original direction. When the lens is thin, this displacement is sufficiently small to be ignored, so that in all our diagrams rays going through the centre of the lens are drawn straight. The centre of a thin lens may then be called the *optical centre*.

The *focal length* of a lens is the distance between the optical centre C and the principal focus (see Fig. 140).

A Lens has Two Principal Foci

Since light may pass through a lens in either direction, there will be two principal foci, one on either side of the lens. These are denoted by the symbols F and F'.

Apart from their use in locating the principal axis of a lens, the centres of curvature of the faces of a lens are not of particular importance in elementary work. We shall see later that two points on the axis which are important are situated respectively at a distance of twice the focal length from the optical centre on either side of the lens.

Special Rays for Locating Images

Three particular classes of rays are used in geometrical constructions to locate the image formed by a converging lens:
1. Rays parallel to the principal axis will pass through the principal focus after refraction through the lens.
2. Rays through the principal focus will emerge parallel to the principal axis after refraction through the lens.
3. Rays through the optical centre are undeviated.

Two of these rays only are sufficient to locate an image, and which particular pair are chosen is merely a matter of convenience.

Figs 142 to 147 are a series of diagrams to show the type of image formed as the object is moved progressively along the principal axis, starting at a point between the lens and the principal focus. As is usual in optical diagrams the object is represented by a vertical arrow OA standing on the principal axis. IB represents the image formed.

The Magnifying Glass.
Images Formed by Converging Lens

Fig. 142 illustrates the use of a lens as a magnifying glass. Used in this way it is sometimes called a *simple microscope* to distinguish it from the compound microscope, which is a more powerful instrument consisting of two or more lenses mounted in brass tubes (p. 154). It will be noticed that the image in this case is erect, virtual and magnified, and on the same side of the lens as the object.

Fig. 144 is of particular interest, since a lens is used in this way to throw magnified real image of a slide or film on a large screen. The image is inverted and hence a slide must be put upside down in the projector.

Fig. 146 illustrates the manner in which the lens of a camera produces a small, real, inverted image on a sensitive plate or film.

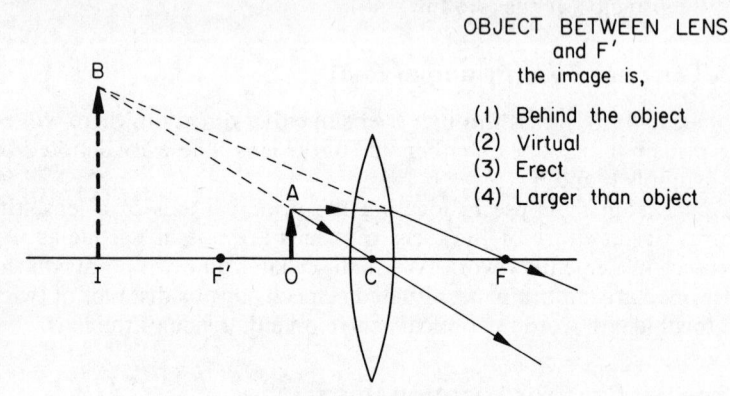

OBJECT BETWEEN LENS and F'
the image is,
(1) Behind the object
(2) Virtual
(3) Erect
(4) Larger than object

Fig. 142. A magnifying glass

OBJECT AT F'
the image is at infinity

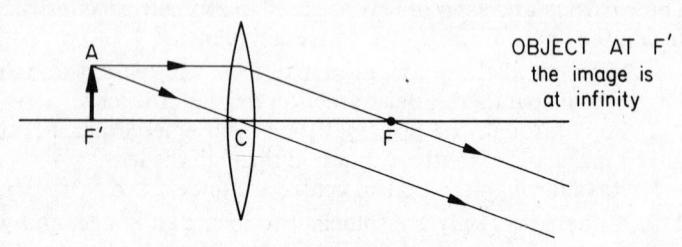

Fig. 143. Object at the focus

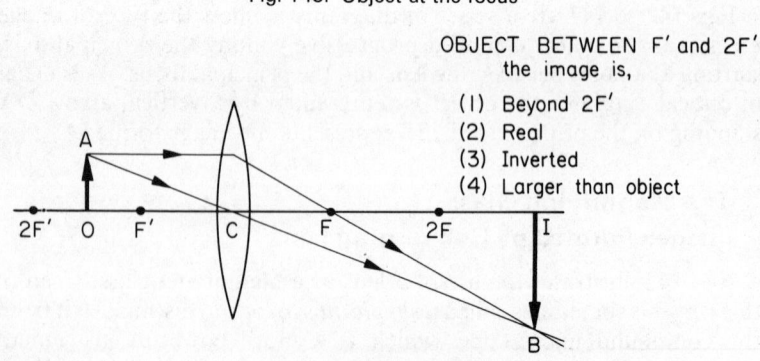

OBJECT BETWEEN F' and 2F'
the image is,
(1) Beyond 2F'
(2) Real
(3) Inverted
(4) Larger than object

Fig. 144. Real image

Image Formed by a Diverging Lens

Fig. 148 illustrates the formation of an image by a diverging lens. For all positions of the object, the image is virtual, erect and smaller than the object, and is situated between the object and the lens.

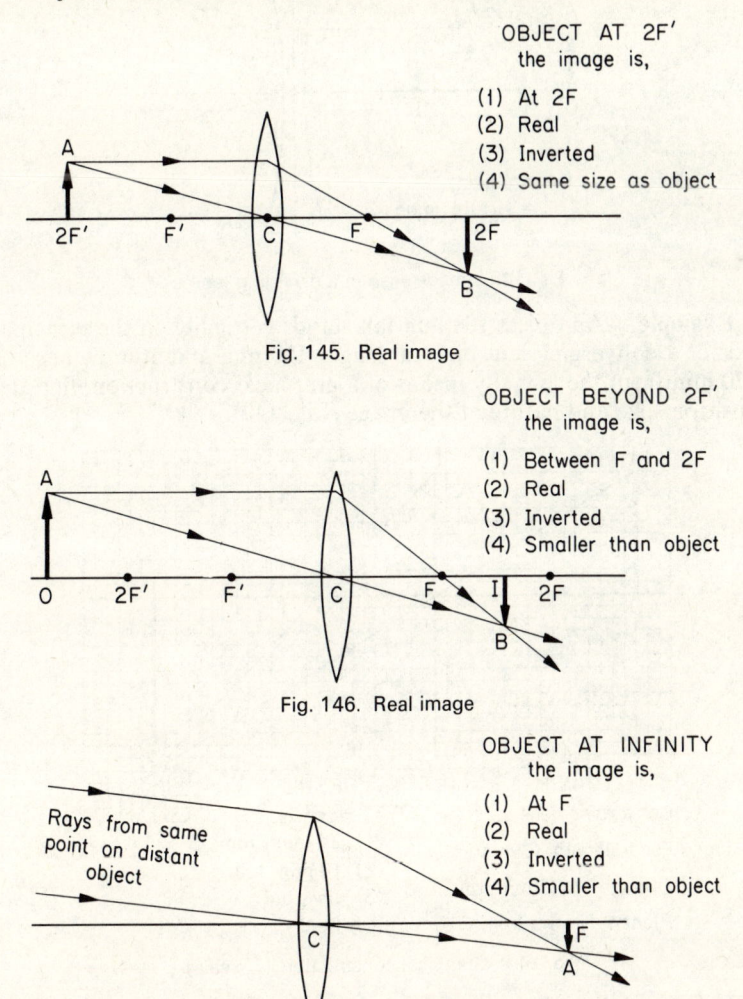

OBJECT AT 2F′
the image is,
(1) At 2F
(2) Real
(3) Inverted
(4) Same size as object

Fig. 145. Real image

OBJECT BEYOND 2F′
the image is,
(1) Between F and 2F
(2) Real
(3) Inverted
(4) Smaller than object

Fig. 146. Real image

OBJECT AT INFINITY
the image is,
(1) At F
(2) Real
(3) Inverted
(4) Smaller than object

Fig. 147. Real image

Accurate Construction of Ray Diagrams

In ray diagrams for finding the position of an image formed by a thin lens, the lens is represented by a straight line, the actual path of the rays through the lens itself being ignored. We are justified in doing this since the lenses used are thin.

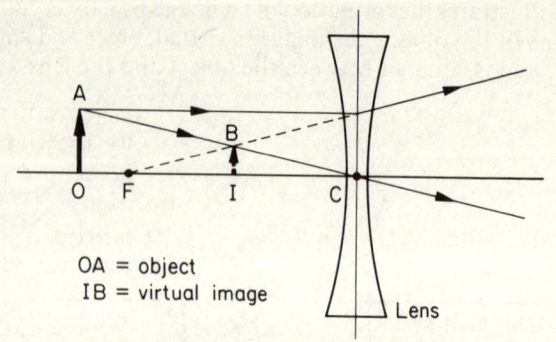

Fig. 148. Image seen in a diverging lens

OA = object
IB = virtual image

Example.—An object 100 mm tall stands vertically on the principal axis of a converging lens of focal length 100 mm and at a distance of 170 mm from the lens. By means of a graphical construction, find the position, size and nature of the image (Fig. 149).

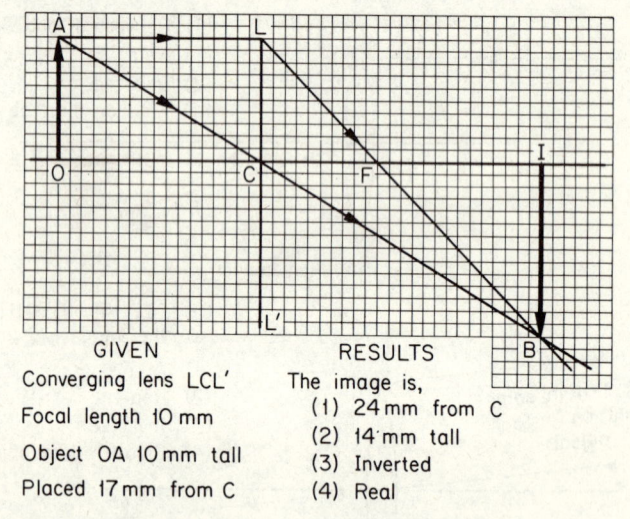

GIVEN
Converging lens LCL'
Focal length 10 mm
Object OA 10 mm tall
Placed 17 mm from C

RESULTS
The image is,
(1) 24 mm from C
(2) 14 mm tall
(3) Inverted
(4) Real

Fig. 149. Graphical construction ($\frac{1}{10}$ scale)

Using graph paper with 1 mm squares, a horizontal straight line OCI represents the principal axis with LCL' at right angles to it to represent the lens. The principal focus F is marked 10 mm from C. A perpendicular OA, 10 mm long, is drawn to OC at a distance of 17 mm from C. The two rays used to locate the image are:

(1) ACB through the optical centre (undeviated), and
(2) AL parallel to the principal axis, which emerges along LFB.

LENSES · 151

The intersection B of the two emergent rays is the image of A.

IB, perpendicular to the axis, will therefore represent the image of OA.

The data given, and the measurements made on the diagram, should be recorded on the graph paper as shown in the figure.

Magnification

As we have seen, the size of the image produced by a lens varies according to the position of the object. The *linear magnification* is the ratio of the height of the image to the height of the object, and is usually denoted by the letter m. Thus

$$m = \frac{\text{Height of image}}{\text{Height of object}}$$

It is useful to know how m depends on the distances of the image and object from the lens. Referring to Figs 144 and 148, it will be found easy to prove that the angles of triangle CIB are respectively equal to the angles of triangle COA.

Hence the triangles CIB and COA are similar, and it follows that,

$$\frac{\text{IB}}{\text{OA}} = \frac{\text{IC}}{\text{OC}}$$

or

$$m = \frac{\text{Distance of image from lens}}{\text{Distance of object from lens}}$$

It is customary to denote the image and object distances from the lens by the letters v and u respectively, so that,

$$m = \frac{v}{u} \text{ numerically (see also p. 127)}.$$

Determination of Focal Length of Convex Lens, using Plane Mirror

A plane mirror is set up behind a lens held in a suitable stand so that light passing through the lens is reflected back again (Fig. 150). The

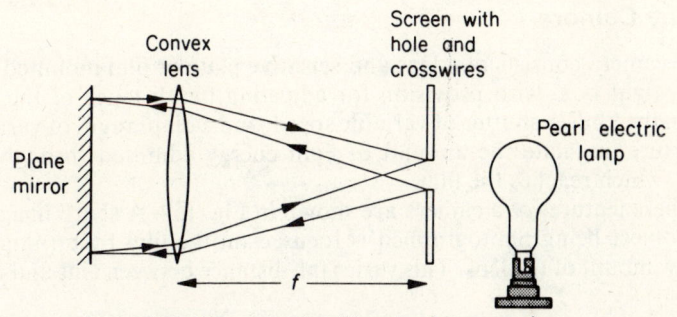

Fig. 150. Measuring focal length of a convex lens

object used in this experiment is a hole and cross-wire in a white screen, illuminated by a pearl electric lamp.

The lens holder is moved backwards and forwards along the bench until a sharp image of the object is formed on the screen alongside the object itself. This can only take place when the object is situated in the focal plane* of the lens. Under these conditions, rays from any point on the object will emerge from the lens as a parallel beam. They will therefore be reflected back through the lens as a parallel beam and be brought to a focus in the same plane as the object.

The distance between the lens and screen now gives the focal length of the lens.

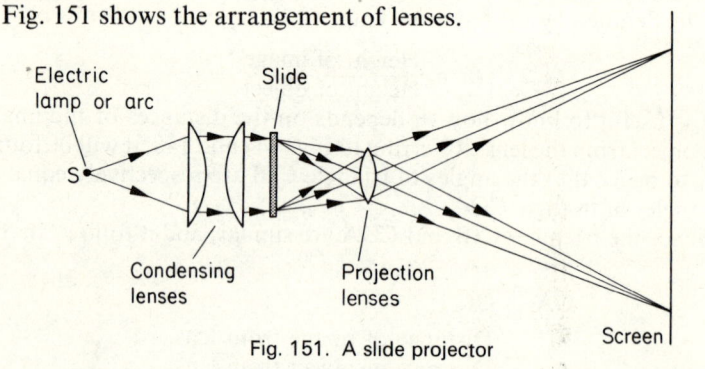

Fig. 151 shows the arrangement of lenses.

Fig. 151. A slide projector

The illuminant is a special lamp having two or three short stout filaments arranged close together to give a small but very concentrated source of light. In order to obtain a brilliant picture on the screen, two plano-convex lenses collect light which would otherwise spread out and be wasted, and cause it to converge on to the slide. The projection lens then forms an image of the slide on the screen.

The projection lens is mounted in a sliding tube, so that it may be moved axially to focus a sharp image on the screen.

The Camera

A camera consists of a lens and sensitive plate or film mounted in a light-tight box, with provision for adjusting the distance of the lens from the film. A shutter of variable speed, and a diaphragm of variable aperture, regulate the amount of light energy admitted through the lens, which reaches the film.

These features of a camera are shown in Fig. 152. A sharp image of the object being photographed is focused on the film by turning the screw mount of the lens. This varies the distance between lens and film.

---

* The focal plane of a lens is a plane through the principal focus at right angles to the principal axis.

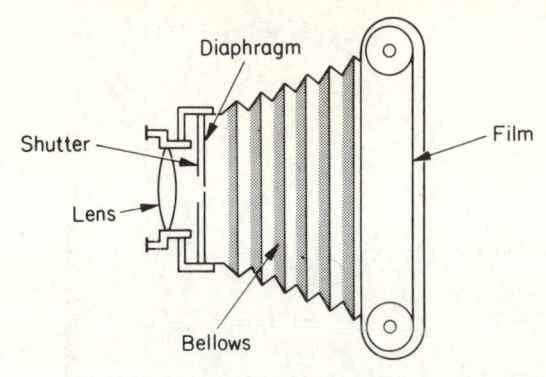

Fig. 152. A simple camera

The correct setting of the lens for an object at a given distance from the camera is obtained on a scale engraved on the lens mount.

The Eye

Fig. 153 is a simplified diagram of the human eye. In many respects it is similar to the camera. An image is formed by the eye lens on the sensitive retina at the back of the eye, whence a message is transmitted to the brain by way of the optic nerve.

Plate 26. The lens arrangement in a reflex camera

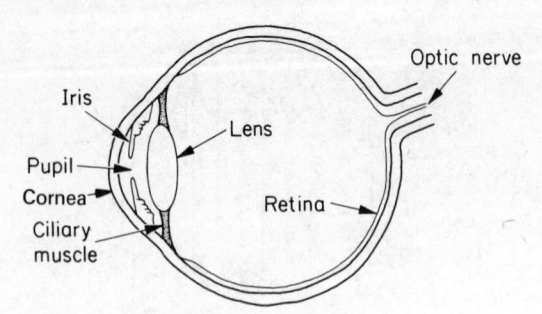

Fig. 153. Human eye

According to the intensity of the light falling on it, the iris or coloured portion of the eye automatically adjusts the size of the pupil or circular opening in its centre. This protects the retina from being harmed by too bright a light. Focussing of the image on the retina is effected by an alteration in the focal length of the eye lens. This is done by the ciliary muscles, which vary the thickness and consequently the focal length of the eye lens. In this respect the eye differs from the camera, since, as we have already seen, focusing in the camera is brought about by varying the distance of the fixed focus lens from the film.

The Compound Microscope

This instrument employs two lenses of short focal length arranged as shown in Fig. 154. The first of these, called the objective, produces an enlarged, real, inverted image I_1 of a small object O.

The image I_1 then acts as an object for the eyepiece, which gives a virtual, erect image I_2 which is still further enlarged. This is the image which is seen by the eye.

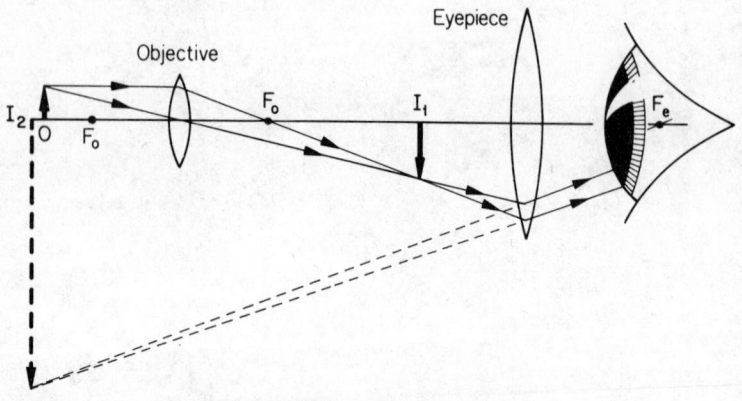

Fig. 154. Compound microscope

Telescopes

A telescope is an instrument for viewing distant objects. In its basic form it has two lenses. The front lens pointing at the object is called the *objective;* its purpose is to collect the light from the distant object, and it forms an image in front of the second lens, which is called the *eyepiece*. The eye is placed behind the eyepiece, and this lens acts like a magnifying glass through which the final image is seen.

In all telescopes, the objective O has a long focal length, and the eyepiece E has a short focal length; this arrangement produces high magnifying power. The *astronomical telescope* has a convex lens objective and eyepiece, and the final image is upside down (Fig. 155(i)). The *Galilean telescope,* used in opera glasses, has a convex lens objective but a concave lens eyepiece (Fig. 155(ii)). This gives a final image the right way up. In *prism binoculars*, which are short telescopes, the objective and eyepiece are convex lenses as in the astronomical telescope, but the two total reflecting prisms make the final image the right way up and the right way round Fig. 155(iii)). Since a point on

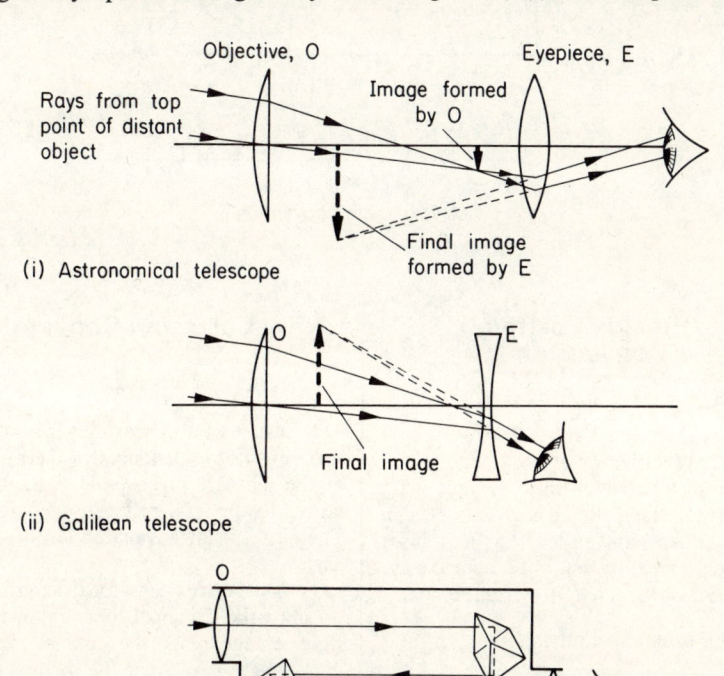

Fig. 155. Forms of refracting telescope

a distant object sends rays parallel on arrival at the telescope, the drawings in Fig. 155 (i), (ii) begin with parallel rays from the top point of the object.

The largest telescope in the world is the Hale telescope at Mount Palomar, which utilises a 5 m diameter parabolic mirror.

Lens Formula and Calculations

In Chapter 12 we mentioned formulae used in calculations with curved spherical mirrors. If u is the object distance, v is the image distance, and f is the focal length, the formulae used with *lenses* on the respective sign conventions are:

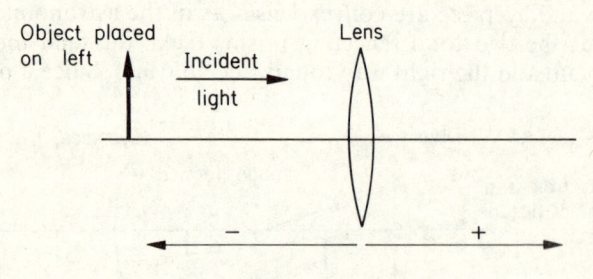

Fig. 156. Sign convention

"Real is Positive" Convention

1. $$\frac{1}{v} + \frac{1}{u} = \frac{1}{f}$$

2. When an object or image is real, the distance is given a + sign; when virtual, the distance is given a − sign.

Thus a convex lens has a + focal length (real focus), but a concave lens has a − focal length (virtual focus).

3. Magnification, $m = \dfrac{v}{u}$ numerically.

Examples 1. An object is placed (i) 14 cm, (ii) 8 cm in front of a convex lens of focal length 10 cm. Find the image distance and magnification in each case.

New Cartesian Convention

1. $$\frac{1}{v} - \frac{1}{u} = \frac{1}{f}$$

2. Distances are measured from the lens (Fig. 156). Distances to the right of the lens are given a + sign; distances to the left are given a − sign. The object is always placed left of the lens.

Thus a convex lens focal length is + since the principal focus is on the right of the lens; the concave lens focal length is − since the focus is on the left of the lens.

3. Magnification, $m = \dfrac{v}{u}$ numerically.

Examples 1. An object is placed (i) 14 cm, (ii) 8 cm in front of a convex lens of focal length 10 cm. Find the image distance and magnification in each case.

(i) We have
$u = +14$ (real object)
$f = +10$ (convex lens)
Substituting in
$$\frac{1}{v} + \frac{1}{u} = \frac{1}{f}$$
$$\therefore \frac{1}{v} + \frac{1}{(+14)} = \frac{1}{(+10)}$$
$$\therefore \frac{1}{v} + \frac{1}{14} = \frac{1}{10}$$
$$\therefore \frac{1}{v} = \frac{1}{10} - \frac{1}{14} = \frac{2}{70}$$
$$\therefore \frac{v}{1} = \frac{70}{2}, \text{ or } v = 35 \text{ cm.}$$

Also, $m = \frac{v}{u} = \frac{35}{14} = 2\cdot 5$

(ii) Here
$u = +8$ (real object)
$f = +10$
$$\therefore \frac{1}{v} + \frac{1}{(+8)} = \frac{1}{(+10)}$$
$$\therefore \frac{1}{v} + \frac{1}{8} = \frac{1}{10}$$
$$\therefore \frac{1}{v} = \frac{1}{10} - \frac{1}{8} = -\frac{1}{40}$$
$$\therefore \frac{v}{1} = -\frac{40}{1}, \text{ or } v = -40 \text{ cm}$$

The minus means the image is *virtual* (p. 21).
Also $m = \frac{v}{u} = \frac{-40}{8} = 5$ (numerically)

2. A convex lens used as a magnifying glass gives an image 24 cm from the lens. If the focal length is 6 cm, find the object distance and magnification.

We have
$v = -24$ (*virtual* image, p. 230)
$f = +6$ (convex lens)
Substituting in
$$\frac{1}{v} + \frac{1}{u} = \frac{1}{f}$$
$$\therefore \frac{1}{(-24)} + \frac{1}{u} = \frac{1}{(+6)}$$
$$\therefore -\frac{1}{24} + \frac{1}{u} = \frac{1}{6}$$

Examples 1. An object is placed (i) 14 cm, (ii) 8 cm in front of a convex lens of focal length 10 cm. Find the image distance and magnification in each case.

(i) We have
$u = -14$ (object left of lens)
$f = +10$ (convex lens)
Substituting in
$$\frac{1}{v} - \frac{1}{u} = \frac{1}{f}$$
$$\therefore \frac{1}{v} - \frac{1}{(-14)} = \frac{1}{(+10)}$$
$$\therefore \frac{1}{v} + \frac{1}{14} = \frac{1}{10}$$
$$\therefore \frac{1}{v} = \frac{1}{10} - \frac{1}{14} = \frac{2}{70}$$
$$\therefore \frac{v}{1} = \frac{70}{2}, \text{ or } v = 35 \text{ cm.}$$

Also, $m = \frac{v}{u} = \frac{35}{-14} = 2\cdot 5$ (num.)

(ii) Here
$u = -8$ (object left of lens)
$f = +10$
$$\therefore \frac{1}{v} - \frac{1}{(-8)} = \frac{1}{(+10)}$$
$$\therefore \frac{1}{v} + \frac{1}{8} = \frac{1}{10}$$
$$\therefore \frac{1}{v} = \frac{1}{10} - \frac{1}{8} = -\frac{1}{40}$$
$$\therefore \frac{v}{1} = -\frac{40}{1}, \text{ or } v = -40 \text{ cm}$$

The minus means that the image is 40 cm. on the *left* of the lens, i.e. the image is virtual (p. 148).

Also $m = \frac{v}{u} = \frac{-40}{8} = 5$ (numerically)

2. A convex lens used as a magnifying glass gives an image 24 cm from the lens. If the focal length is 6 cm, find the object distance and magnification.

We have
$v = -24$ (image *left* of lens)
$f = +6$ (convex lens)

$$\therefore \frac{1}{u} = \frac{1}{6} + \frac{1}{24} = \frac{5}{24}$$

$$\therefore \frac{u}{1} = \frac{24}{5}, \text{ or } u = 4.8 \text{ cm}$$

$$\therefore m = \frac{v}{u} = \frac{-24}{4.8} = 5 \text{ (numerically)}$$

Substituting in
$$\frac{1}{v} - \frac{1}{u} = \frac{1}{f}$$

$$\therefore \frac{1}{(-24)} - \frac{1}{u} = \frac{1}{(+6)}$$

$$\therefore -\frac{1}{24} - \frac{1}{u} = \frac{1}{6}$$

$$\therefore \frac{1}{u} = \frac{1}{6} + \frac{1}{24} = \frac{5}{24}$$

$$\therefore -\frac{u}{1} = \frac{24}{5}, \text{ or } u = -4.8 \text{ cm.}$$

$$\therefore m = \frac{v}{u} = \frac{-24}{-4.8} = 5$$

Summary

1. Thin spherical lenses are divided into two classes:
   (a) Converging or convex (thickest in the middle).
   (b) Diverging or concave (thinnest in the middle).

2. The *principal axis* of a lens is the line joining the centres of curvature of its faces.

3. The *principal focus* of a lens is that point on the principal axis to which all rays parallel and close to the principal axis converge, or from which they appear to diverge, after passing through the lens.

4. The *focal length* of a lens is the distance between the optical centre and the principal focus.

5. A converging (convex) lens produces either a real inverted image or a virtual erect image according as the object is at a distance from the lens greater or less than the focal length.

6. A diverging (concave) lens always produces a virtual erect image of a real object.

7. The linear magnification of a lens, m,

$$= \frac{\text{Height of image}}{\text{Height of object}}$$
$$= \frac{\text{Distance of image from lens}}{\text{Distance of object from lens}} = \frac{v}{u} \text{ (num.)}$$

8. The lens formula is $\frac{1}{v} + \frac{1}{u} = \frac{1}{f}$ (R.P. convention),

or
$$\frac{1}{v} - \frac{1}{u} = \frac{1}{f} \text{ (N.C. convention).}$$

EXERCISES

1. What is a lens? Draw sketches of a diverging (concave) and a converging (convex) lens, and state briefly why the names "diverging" and "converging" are used.

2. Define (*a*) principal axis, (*b*) optical centre of a lens. Draw diagrams showing what happens when two rays, one parallel to the principal axis and the other through the optical centre, are incident on (i) a convex and (ii) a concave lens.

3. Define the principal focus and the focal length of (*a*) a converging (convex) les, (*b*) a diverging (concave) lens, illustrating your definitions with a diagram in each case.

4. Describe an experiment to measure the focal length of a convex lens.

5. What is meant by the magnification of a lens? Explain, with the aid of a diagram, how the magnification is related to the distances of object and image from the lens in the case of (*a*) real and (*b*) virtual images.

6. Show by means of ray diagrams how a converging lens may produce a magnified virtual image.

7. Find by means of an accurate ray diagram the nature, position and size of the image of an object 20 mm high, placed 60 mm from a converging lens of focal length 35 mm.

8. A real image, half the height of the object, is formed by a converging lens. If the distance between the object and image is 140 mm, find the focal length of the lens and its distance from the object.

9. An object 15 mm tall is placed 34 mm from a convex lens of focal length 60 mm. Find by drawing a ray diagram the nature, position and size of the image formed.

10. An object 30 mm tall is placed 115 mm from a lens of focal length 75 mm. What type of lens is being used if the image formed is between the object and the lens? Draw an accurate ray diagram to locate the image and state its nature, position and size.

11. What is the difference between a simple microscope and a compound microscope? Give ray diagrams to show the way in which each gives a magnified image.

12. Give simple diagrams of (*a*) the human eye and (*b*) the camera, showing how an image is formed in each case. Give an account of any points of similarity or dissimilarity between them.

13. By means of a diagram show how an enlarged image of a picture in a book may be projected on to a screen by the aid of a powerful light source, a plane mirror and a lens.

14. An object is placed (i) 120 mm and then (ii) 60 mm in front of a converging (convex) lens of focal length 100 mm. Calculate the image distance in each case and the magnification.

15. An enlarged erect image is produced 200 mm from a convex lens of focal length 50 mm. Calculate the object distance and the magnification.
(*Hint.*—Is the image real or virtual?)

16. An object is placed (i) 160 mm, (ii) 40 mm in front of a diverging lens of focal length 120 mm. Find the image distance in each case and the magnification.

17. Draw ray diagrams showing how (i) an astronomical telescope (ii) a Galilean telescope work. What are the differences between the two telescopes, and how also do they differ in their action on the rays of light which pass through the instruments?

CHAPTER FIFTEEN

Dispersion and Colour

It had been known for centuries that small fragments of colourless glass and precious stones glittered in bright colours when white light passed through them, but it was not until after the middle of the seventeenth century that Sir Isaac Newton investigated the problem experimentally.

Newton's work in this direction was prompted by the need to find a way of removing coloration from the images seen through a telescope. This instrument had been invented around 1600 by a Dutch spectacle maker called Lippershey.

Newton's Experiment with a Prism

Newton began his experiments by making a small circular hole in one of the window shutters of his room at Cambridge. Light from the sun streamed through this hole and made a circular white patch on the opposite wall. On placing a triangular glass prism before the hole, an elongated coloured patch of light was formed on the wall. Newton called this a *spectrum*, and noted that the colours formed were in the order Red, Orange, Yellow, Green, Blue, Indigo and Violet (Fig. 157).

The theory which he put forward to explain the spectrum was that white light consists of a mixture of seven different colours. The refractive index of glass is different for each colour, so that when white light falls on the prism, each colour in it is refracted at a different angle,

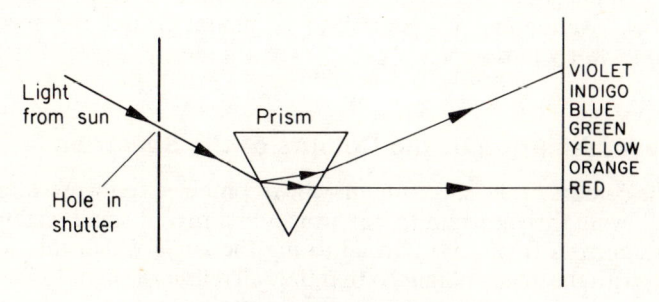

Fig. 157. Newton's experiment

with the result that the colours are spread out to form a spectrum. It should be noted that when the light is incident towards the apex of a prism, it is refracted towards the base of the prism, the violet being refracted most and the red least. The "splitting up" of white light by the prism is called *dispersion*. Strictly speaking, there are many shades of each colour in the spectrum, each shade merging almost imperceptibly into the next.

Production of a Pure Spectrum

The spectrum formed in Newton's first experiment is impure. This was recognised as being due to the fact that it consisted of a series of circular coloured images all overlapping.

Later Newton devised the arrangement shown in Fig. 158 for producing a fairly pure spectrum. A converging lens L is placed so as to

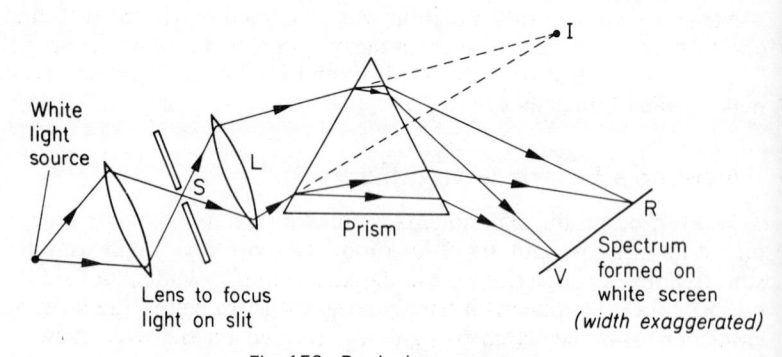

Fig. 158. Producing a spectrum

form an image I of a narrow slit S brightly illuminated with white light. A prism is then placed in the path of the light from the lens. As a result, the light is deviated and dispersed through the prism so as to form a spectrum VR on a white screen. This spectrum consists of a series of coloured images of the slit all touching one another. If the slit is made narrow, overlapping is reduced to a minimum and the spectrum becomes fairly pure.

Recombination of the Colours of the Spectrum

The colours of the spectrum may be recombined to form white light by allowing the spectrum to be formed on a row of small rectangular plane mirrors (Fig. 159). On adjusting the angle which the mirrors make with the incident light so that they all reflect the light to the same place on a screen, a white patch of light results.

DISPERSION AND COLOUR · 163

Newton showed the recombination of the colours to form white light in another way. He painted the colours of the spectrum in sectors on a disc. When rotated at high speed the disc appears white. It is only fair to say that the whiteness thus obtained is not too good, but generally is of a greyish tint. This is due to the fact that it is difficult to obtain coloured pigments which are strictly pure colours. The experiment works on account of what is called the "persistence of vision". The impression of an image on the retina of the eye is retained by the brain for a small fraction of a second after the image has disappeared. Consequently the brain sums up and blends together the rapidly changing coloured images of the disc and thus produces the sensation of a stationary white image.

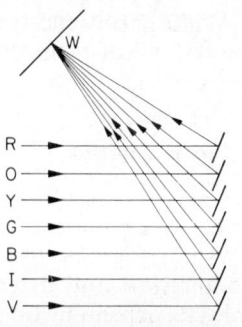

Fig. 159. Recombination of colours

It should also be mentioned that persistence of vision is responsible for the picture seen on the television screen. Here a constant succession of images is thrown on the screen at the rate of 50 per second. The eye retains the sensation of each image until it receives the next, so producing an impression of continuity.

Colour of Objects in White Light

When white light falls on any particular body, then either all the colours in the white light may be reflected from the body, when it appears white, or only some of them may be reflected while the others are absorbed. In the latter case the body appears coloured. The energy of the light absorbed is generally converted into heat so that the body becomes slightly warmer. The colour which the body presents to the eye is the colour of the light which it reflects. Thus the green leaves of plants have this appearance since they reflect green light and absorb the other colours.

Plate 27. A spectrometer. A triangular prism is placed on the circular table and the tube on the left (the collimator) is used to produce a beam of parallel rays from a light source; the resulting spectrum is examined through the telescope on the right

White paper reflects all the colours of the spectrum while black paper absorbs all of them. Blackness is thus due to the absence of light of any colour.

Light Filters

Interesting results are obtained when light filters consisting of sheets of gelatine coloured with various dyes are placed, in turn, in front of the slit in Fig. 158. By this means, the light transmitted by the filter can be analysed into its component colours. It is observed that certain colours, depending on the colour of the filter, are now absent from the spectrum. The missing colours are those of light which has been absorbed by the filter while the remaining colours have been transmitted.

Now one would expect red gelatine to transmit only red light, green gelatine only green light, and so on. Indeed, this generally proves to be so when tested by experiment. But an unusual result is obtained with yellow gelatine. The spectrum of the light passing through most types of yellow gelatine is found to consist of red and green as well as yellow. What is even more striking is that this particular yellow light looks just the same to the eye as that which comes from a filter passing only pure yellow. To distinguish between the two, the former kind of yellow is called "compound" yellow light.

Experiment shows that the yellow petals of flowers and most yellow paints are examples of compound yellow.

Appearance of Coloured Objects in Coloured Light

A convenient source of light of various colours may be obtained by placing an ordinary lamp in a box with an opening which may be covered with gelatine sheets of different colours. By means of such a lamp the appearance of different coloured objects in different colours of light may be examined in a dark room.

Then it is found that red bodies look red in red light while green and blue ones look black since they have absorbed the red light. In like manner a red poppy appears black in green light. On the other hand, the compound yellow petals of a daffodil appear black only in blue or violet light. The daffodil appears yellow only in yellow or white light. In red light it looks red and in green light, green.

Primary and Secondary Colours

Although yellow may be produced by mixing red and green lights, it is not found possible to produce either red, green or blue by mixing two other colours. For this reason, red, green and blue are called *primary* colours.

Yellow is called a *secondary* colour. The other two secondary colours are cyan, made by mixing green light and blue light, and magenta, by mixing red light and blue light.

Mixture of Coloured Lights

Before proceeding further it must be pointed out that mixing coloured paints is an entirely different thing from mixing coloured lights. Paints will be dealt with later.

The effect of mixing coloured lights may be investigated by using three projectors fitted with slides of various coloured gelatine sheets, and arranged so as to produce overlapping images on a white screen.

In this way it may be shown that a mixture of the three primary colours, red, green and blue, gives a white patch on the screen. However, a successful result is obtained only by using the right kind of red, green and blue gelatine for producing the colour and by having each light in the correct intensity. This can only be done by experimenting with different types of gelatine and by having lamps of the appropriate brightness.

By using two projectors the following facts may also be verified:

$$Red + Green = Yellow$$
$$Red + Blue = Magenta$$
$$Blue + Green = Cyan$$

A consideration of these results, together with the result that a mixture of the three primaries, red, green and blue, gives white, leads us to expect that:

$$Red + Cyan = White$$
$$Green + Magenta = White$$
$$Blue + Yellow = White$$

A further experiment with two projectors using appropriate gelatines shows that these results are correct.

Two colours such as those described above which give white light when added together are called *complementary* colours.

Mixing Coloured Pigments

One of the first things that the young student of painting learns is that green paint can be made by mixing yellow and blue paint.

This would not be possible if the paints available were pure yellow and pure blue. The success of this method of making green paint depends on the fact that the pigments in common use are impure colours. As we have already seen, yellow paint does, in fact, send a mixture of red, yellow and green light to the eye. Similarly, blue paint sends a mixture of blue and green light to the eye.

When the two paints are mixed, the yellow paint absorbs blue light out of the white light falling on it and the blue paint absorbs red and yellow light. The only remaining colour which both paints reflect is green. Consequently the mixture appears green.

Summary

1. Ordinary white light is composed of 7 different colours, namely, red, orange, yellow, green, blue, indigo and violet. These may be remembered by the letters VIBGYOR.

2. The refractive index of glass depends on the colour of the light used, being greatest for violet and least for red light.

3. When white light passes through a triangular prism the light is spread out into a patch of seven colours, called a spectrum. The violet light is deviated most and the red least.

4. A *fairly pure* spectrum of white light may be obtained by the use of a source of white light, a slit, a lens, a prism and a white screen.

5. The colour of a body is the colour of the light it reflects.

6. The primary colours are: red, green and blue. The secondary colours are: yellow, cyan and magenta.

7. Red + Green + Blue = White
Red + Green = Yellow
Green + Blue = Cyan
Red + Blue = Magenta

8. Complementary colours are two colours which added together give white. Thus the complementary colours are:
Red and Cyan
Green and Magenta
Blue and Yellow

EXERCISES

1. Describe Newton's experiment with a triangular glass prism. What conclusions may be drawn from it?

2. Explain why the spectrum obtained in Newton's first experiment with a prism is impure. Show by means of a labelled diagram how you would produce a pure spectrum of white light on a screen.

3. Describe two methods of recombining the colours of the spectrum to form white light.

4. A spectrum of white light is formed on a white screen. Describe its appearance. The white screen is then replaced in succession by (*a*) a red, (*b*) a yellow, (*c*) a black screen. State and explain what you would expect to observe.

DISPERSION AND COLOUR · 167

5. What are (*a*) primary colours and (*b*) secondary colours? Describe experiments to support your answer.

6. What are complementary colours? Describe an experiment to illustrate your answer.

7. Explain why a white screen illuminated by blue light and yellow light appears white, while a mixture of blue paint and yellow paint appears green.

8. A red poppy and a yellow daffodil are successively moved through the spectrum of white light which has been formed on a screen. Describe and explain the appearance of each flower in the various parts of the spectrum.

Plate 28. Part of the Curved (Parabolic) Mirror used at the world's largest solar furnace at Mont Louis in the French Pyrenees. It has about 3500 small mirrors, which concentrate the sun's rays.

(Courtesy of B.I.P.S. Ltd.)

Part Two

CHAPTER SIXTEEN

Radiation

The last chapter was concerned with visible light, or luminous energy. This is energy which is radiated from luminous objects. Because of the structure of our eyes, we can *see* only a very small fraction of all the energy which is carried by radiation. We can *feel* radiation from a hot object, but the majority of energy transmitted in this way can only be detected by instruments such as photocells and thermocouples. This whole range of energy radiation is called an energy spectrum.

Radiation does not require a material medium to carry it, and it is the means by which energy travels from the sun across the empty space beyond the earth's atmosphere. Radiation consists of waves which are able to pass through a vacuum. These waves are partly reflected and partly absorbed by objects on which they fall. The part which is absorbed becomes converted into heat. Radiant heat which has passed through a vacuum can be easily felt by holding the hand near to a vacuum-filled electric lamp when the current is switched on.

Detecting Thermal Radiation: Thermocouples

Radiant energy may be detected by converting it into electrical energy. A simple experiment serves to show how this is done. A copper and an iron wire are twisted together to form a junction, while the free ends of the wires are connected to the terminals of a sensitive galvanometer. On warming the junction an electric current is produced in the circuit and the galvanometer gives a deflection. This is called the thermoelectric effect (Fig. 160).

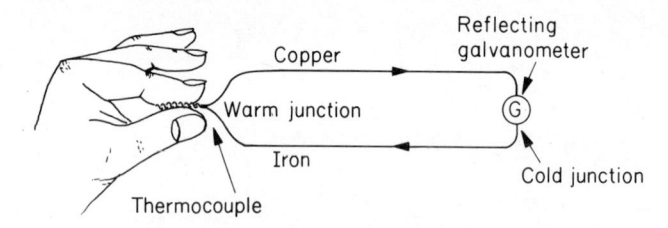

Fig. 160. A thermocouple, with electron current

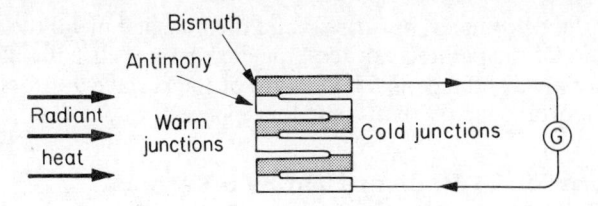

Fig. 161. A thermopile, with electron current

Bismuth and antimony are two metals which show the thermoelectric effect in a marked degree, and they are used for the detection of radiant heat in an instrument called a *thermopile*. In order to magnify the effect as many as 64 pairs of antimony and bismuth bars are joined in series, to give 64 junctions on which the radiant heat is allowed to fall. The bars are placed side by side, insulated from one another by paper, and their ends are soldered together. The whole is mounted in electrical insulating material, and provided with two terminals connected to the free ends of the two end bars (Fig. 161).

Comparing the Radiation from Different Surfaces

The rate at which a body radiates energy depends on its temperature and the nature and area of its surface. It is found that, for a given temperature, a body radiates most energy when its surface is dull black and least when its surface is highly polished.

A comparison of the radiating powers of different surfaces was first made by John Leslie of Edinburgh towards the end of the eighteenth century. Leslie used a hollow copper cube, each side of which had a different surface. One may be highly polished metal, another coated with carbon by holding it in the flame of a candle, while the remaining two surfaces may be painted in a light and dark colour respectively (Fig. 162).

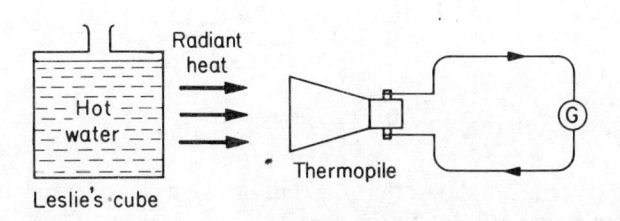

Fig. 162. Comparing radiating surfaces

The cube is filled with hot water and a thermopile placed at the same distance from each face in turn. In each case the steady deflection obtained on the galvanometer is recorded. The results show that the dull black surface produces the largest, and the polished metal the smallest deflection. Of the painted surfaces, the darker one is usually better but this is not always the case. The texture of the surface appears to be a more important factor than its colour.

Absorption of Radiant Heat by a Surface

As we have stated earlier in this chapter, radiant heat falling on a surface is partly absorbed and partly reflected. The absorbing powers of a dull black and a polished surface may be compared by using two sheets of tinplate, one polished and the other painted dull black. On the reverse side of each plate, a cork is fixed by means of a little melted paraffin wax. The plates are then set up vertically, a short distance apart, with a bunsen burner midway between (Fig. 163). When the burner is lit, both surfaces receives equal quantities of radiant heat. In a very short time the wax on the dull black plate melts and the cork slides off. The polished plate however remains cool and the wax unmelted.

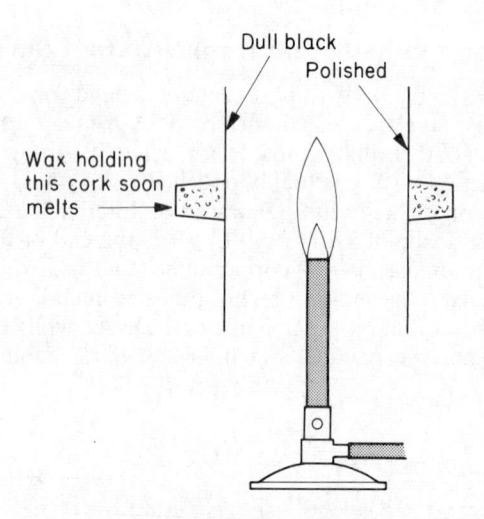

Fig. 163. Radiation absorption

This experiment shows that the dull black surface is a much better absorber of radiation than the polished surface. The polished surface is therefore a good reflector of heat, since little energy is taken in.

The experiment should be repeated with other types of surface whose radiating powers have been previously compared by the Leslie cube experiment. In every case it is found that the better radiator is also the better absorber of heat.

RADIATION · 171

Practical Uses of Thermal Radiation

The investigations on radiation and absorption described above have a number of useful applications. Buildings which are whitewashed or painted in light colours keep cooler in summer, since the light surfaces reflect radiant heat from the sun. Many factory roofs are aluminium-painted. The bright surface reduces the heat lost in winter, and keeps the interior cool in summer. We ourselves choose light-coloured clothing in summer for the same reason, and in hot countries such as India white clothing is generally the rule.

Brightly polished objects retain their heat for a long period. For this reason a silver teapot is to be preferred to others.

The so-called "radiators" of a hot water system do, in fact, emit most of their heat by convection (see chapter 19). Nevertheless, in order to increase the proportion of heat radiated they should be painted in a dark colour.

The Vacuum Flask

The vacuum flask is known to most of us as the Thermos flask, which is the trade name used by a large manufacturing firm. Originally, it was devised by Sir James Dewar for the purpose of storing liquefied gases. Liquid oxygen, for example, boils at the very low temperature of $-183°$ C., so that if it is placed in an ordinary flask it rapidly boils away. It is necessary therefore to keep it in a vessel through which heat cannot pass.

The vacuum flask consists of a double-walled glass vessel having a vacuum between the walls. Both walls are silvered (Fig. 164). No heat

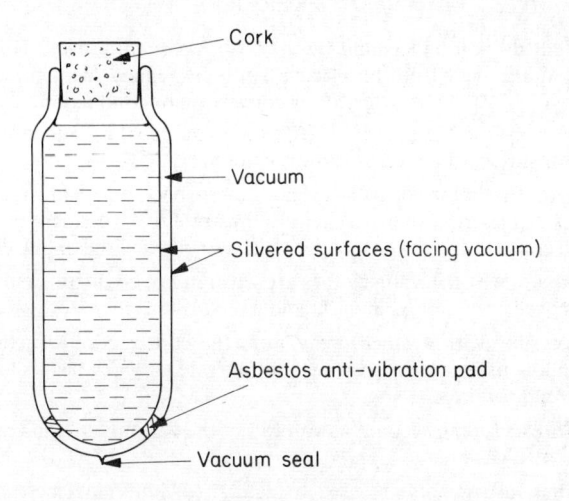

Fig. 164. A vacuum flask

can enter or leave the inner flask by conduction or convection across the vacuum. A certain amount of heat can be gained by the flask through radiation, but this is reduced to a minimum on account of the silvering. In addition there will be a little heat transmitted by conduction through the thin glass walls at the neck, and through the poorly conducting cork. The sum total of this heat transfer is very small so that a cold liquid inside remains cold for a very long period.

The vacuum flask is equally suitable for keeping liquids hot. There must be few people indeed who have not enjoyed the advantage of having a vacuum flask filled with hot tea or coffee when out on a picnic.

Summary

1. Radiation is the transmission of energy from one place to another by invisible waves which do not require a material medium for their conveyance.

Radiated energy includes radio, thermal, luminous, X-rays and gamma radiation.

2. Matt dark-coloured surfaces are better radiators of heat than highly polished light-coloured surfaces.

3. Surfaces which are good radiators also make good absorbers of radiant energy. Poor radiating surfaces absorb little energy and reflect most of the radiant energy falling on them.

4. The vacuum flask is designed to minimise heat transfer to or from its contents by radiation, convection and conduction.

EXERCISES

1. What do you understand by the term *radiation of heat*? How would you show that the heat from an electric lamp suspended from the ceiling passes downwards by radiation, and not by convection or conduction?

2. Describe the thermopile. How would you use it to compare the radiating powers of surfaces painted in various colours?

3. "Good radiators of heat are good absorbers, and bad radiators are bad absorbers." Describe an experiment to illustrate this statement in the cases of a polished copper surface and a copper surface coated with lampblack.

4. Explain why (*a*) white clothes are worn in hot countries, and (*b*) hot water radiators are best painted in dark colours.

5. Describe, with a labelled diagram, the construction of a vacuum flask. Explain how its construction minimises the rate at which heat is lost from a hot liquid contained in it.

6. Write as full an account as you can of the various ways in which a room is warmed by a gas fire.

7. What instruments are used to detect: (*a*) luminous energy, (*b*) radiated thermal energy, (*c*) radio transmissions.

CHAPTER SEVENTEEN

Measurement of Temperature

When an object absorbs thermal energy, its *temperature* usually rises; temperature can be regarded as the level of energy in the object. We know instinctively that the temperature of a bar of chocolate is greater than that of ice-cream, but we cannot say by how much until their temperatures are measured by a thermometer. Temperature measurement is needed on many occasions; for example, the doctor takes the temperature of a patient as a preliminary check on his health, and the temperature of a refrigerator must reach a certain value to become effective. The main purpose of this chapter is to discuss the common way of measuring temperature.

Measurement of Temperature

Most people are familiar with the mercury- or alcohol-in-glass thermometers for domestic use. These usually have spherical bulbs and are mounted on boxwood or metal scales. In contrast, laboratory thermometers have cylindrical bulbs for easy insertion through holes in corks, and have their scales engraved directly on the stem. When the bulb is heated the liquid expands and rises up the fine bore of the stem, and the temperature is read on the scale from the level of the mercury thread.

The mercury-in-glass thermometer is not accurate enough for research work. In this case the change in pressure of a gas with temperature, or of the change in the electrical resistance of a platinum wire with temperature, are used. These methods are dealt with in more advanced books.

Making a Mercury Thermometer

One end of a length of clean capillary tubing is heated in a bunsen flame until the glass softens and seals the end of the tube. The tube is then withdrawn from the flame and immediately blown to form a small bulb at the end. By repeating this process the size of the bulb may be increased as desired.

The correct size of bulb will, of course, depend on the bore of the tube and the temperature range for which the thermometer is required.

Although this method is that used in elementary laboratories, it should be noted that, in commercial practice, bulbs of the correct size are often made separately and afterwards fused on to the stem.

The next stage is the filling of the thermometer. A small glass funnel is connected to the stem by a short rubber tube, or better still, a short length of wide quill tubing is fused on to act as a funnel. A small quantity of pure mercury is poured into the funnel and the bulb gently heated. Air inside the bulb expands and bubbles through the mercury, and on allowing the bulb to cool, some mercury runs down into the bulb. By repeating this process of alternate heating and cooling, the bulb and stem may be completely filled with mercury.

The bulb is now heated to a temperature somewhat higher than the maximum which the thermometer is to record and the funnel removed. Still maintaining this temperature, the end of the stem is rotated in a small blowpipe flame, drawn out and sealed off.

The thermometer is now ready for graduation. It is advisable, however, to keep the thermometer for several months before this is finally carried out, since, as a result of the violent heat treatment it has received, the glass goes on slowly contracting for a considerable time.

The Fixed Temperature Points

The principle underlying the graduation of all types of thermometer is first to choose two fixed and easily obtained temperatures called the *upper* and *lower fixed points*, and then to divide the interval between them into a number of equal parts or degrees.

The upper fixed point is the temperature of steam from water boiling under standard atmospheric pressure equal to 760 mm of mercury in the barometer. The temperature of the boiling water itself is not used as a fixed point for two reasons. Firstly, local overheating may occur accompanied by "bumping" as the water boils; and secondly, any impurities which may be present will raise the boiling-point. The temperature of the steam just above the water will always be constant and will depend only on the barometric pressure at the time.

The lower fixed point is the temperature of pure melting ice. Here again, the ice must be pure since any impurities will lower the melting-point.

The Celsius Scale

The difference in temperature between the two fixed points is called the Fundamental Interval. For scientific purposes this interval is divided into 100 equal degrees, the lower point being called 0° and the upper 100°. This method of dividing the interval was suggested by a Swedish astronomer named Celsius and is called the Celsius (or, formerly, centigrade) scale. Temperatures on it are called "degrees Celsius" (° C).

MEASUREMENT OF TEMPERATURE · 175

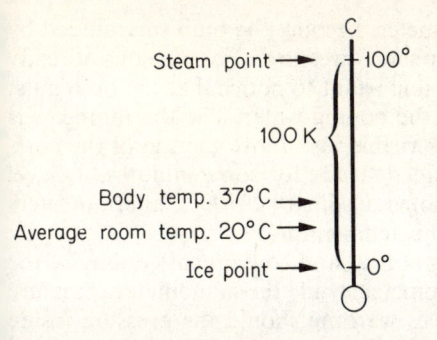

Fig. 165. The Celsius scale

- Steam point → 100° C
- 100 K
- Body temp. 37° C
- Average room temp. 20° C
- Ice point → 0°

While actual temperatures are measured in "degrees Celsius" the difference between two temperatures is measured in kelvin (K). Thus between the ice point (0° C) and the steam point (100° C) there is a temperature difference (or interval) of 100 K. Note that the symbol is written without the degree sign.

In more advanced scientific work another scale, called the absolute scale, is used. Temperatures on this scale are called "degrees kelvin" (K).

Another method of dividing the interval was devised by Fahrenheit of Danzig. On the Fahrenheit scale the ice point was called 32° and the steam point 212°, so that there were 180 degrees in the fundamental interval. The Fahrenheit scale is hardly ever used now, and never for accurate measurement in scientific work.

Testing the Upper Fixed Point

Laboratory thermometers should be tested for accuracy from time to time. The upper fixed point may be checked by pushing the thermometer through a hole in a cork and placing it inside a double-walled copper vessel called a *hypsometer* (Fig. 166). Water is steadily boiled

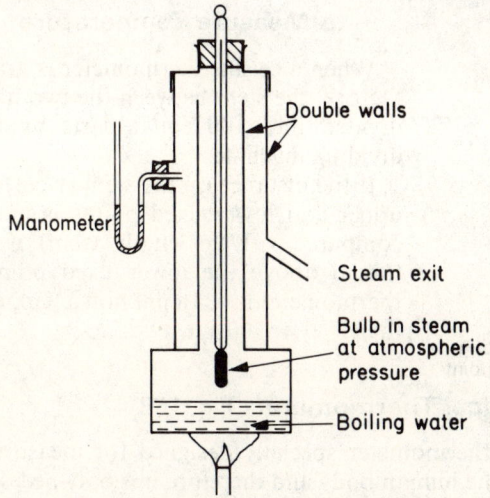

Fig. 166. Testing the upper fixed point

in the lower part of the hypsometer, keeping the bulb surrounded by pure water vapour at atmospheric pressure. For reasons already mentioned in this chapter, it is important to notice that the bulb must not be allowed to project into the boiling water. The thermometer is adjusted until the 100° mark is visible just above the top of the cork, and when the thread has remained steady for some minutes, its level relative to the 100° C mark is noted. Ordinary 0–100° C thermometers may show up to 1 K error at this temperature.

The double wall reduces loss of heat and consequent cooling of the vapour surrounding the thermometer, while the manometer (pressure gauge) seen in the diagram gives warning should the pressure inside the hypsometer differ from atmospheric pressure. If the barometric pressure at the time of the experiment is not equal to 760 mm height of mercury, then the true boiling-point for the prevailing pressure must be ascertained from a table showing the variation of boiling-point with pressure, and allowance made when marking the stem.

Lower Fixed Point

The thermometer is next placed in a glass funnel kept full of pure ice shavings, a beaker being placed underneath to catch the water. The thermometer is allowed to remain with the mercury thread just showing above the level of the ice. When the level of the thread has remained steady for some time its position is noted as before (see Fig. 167).

Pure melting ice

Using a Thermometer to Measure Temperature

When a celsius thermometer is graduated in a factory, the stem between the two fixed points is divided into 100 equal parts by means of a dividing machine.

If the distance on the stem (y cm) between the upper and lower fixed points is measured, and compared with the length (x cm) of the mercury thread above the lower fixed point when the thermometer is at an unknown temperature $\theta°$ C, then $\theta = 100\,x/y$

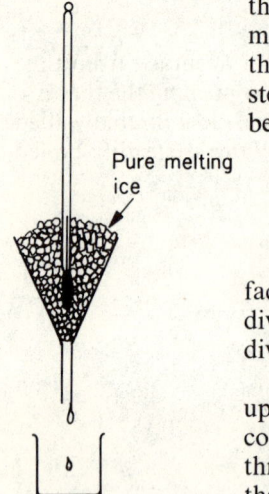

Fig. 167. Testing the lower fixed point

The Clinical Thermometer (Fig. 168)

This is a thermometer specially designed for measuring the temperature of the human body and therefore it is only necessary for it to have a range of a few degrees on either side of this temperature. It is

MEASUREMENT OF TEMPERATURE · 177

customary to place the thermometer beneath the patient's tongue and to leave it there for about 2 minutes to ensure that it fully acquires the body temperature.

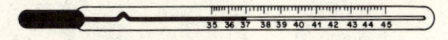

Fig. 168. A clinical thermometer

On removing the thermometer from the mouth, the mercury thread does not contract back into the bulb, but remains standing in the stem, thus enabling the recorded temperature to be read at leisure. This occurs since the stem has a narrow constriction in the bore just above the bulb. When the thermometer is taken out of the warm mouth, the sudden cooling and contraction of the mercury in the bulb causes the thread to break at the constriction and so leaves the thread in the stem at its original reading. Before the thermometer is used a second time, the mercury in the stem must be returned to the bulb by shaking.

Normal body temperature is 37° C.

Six's Maximum and Minimum Thermometer (Fig. 169)

This thermometer is used at meteorological stations but is also very popular amongst gardeners for use in greenhouses. Its purpose is to enable the user to ascertain the maximum and minimum temperatures

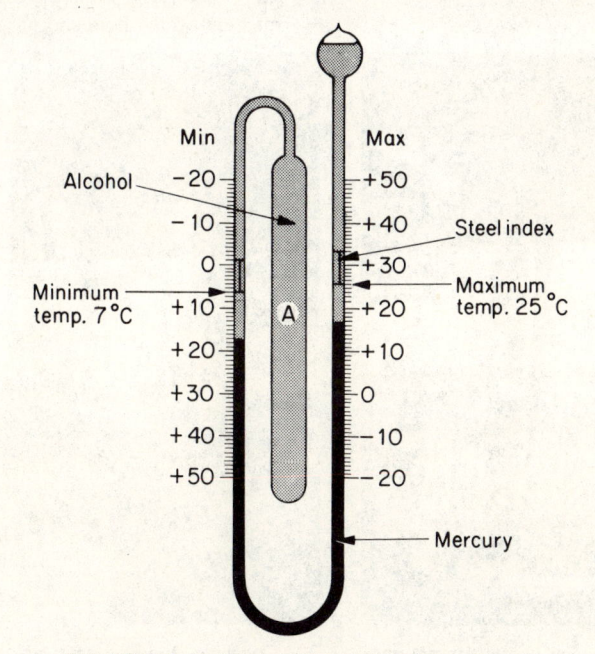

Fig. 169. A maximum and minimum thermometer

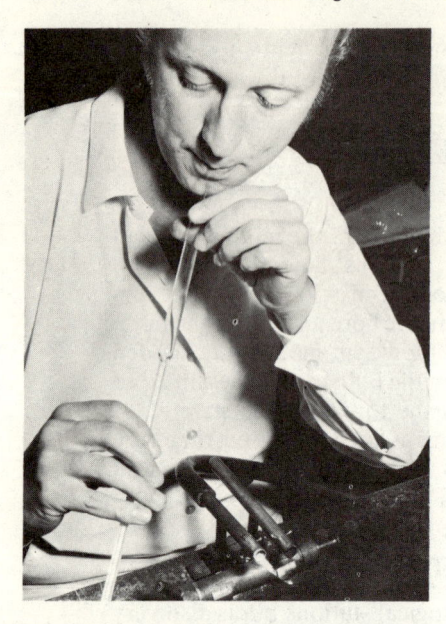

Plate 29. Stages in the manufacture of Thermometers

A.—Blowing the bulb on a thermometer; the bulb is fused on to the end of the capillary tube with another piece of glass

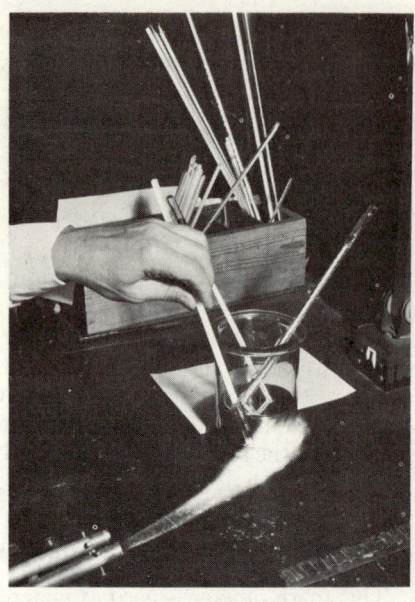

B.—Filling the thermometer with mercury; as shown, the bulb is heated to boil the mercury and thus expel the air. The open end is then quickly inverted in mercury, which rises and fills the tube.

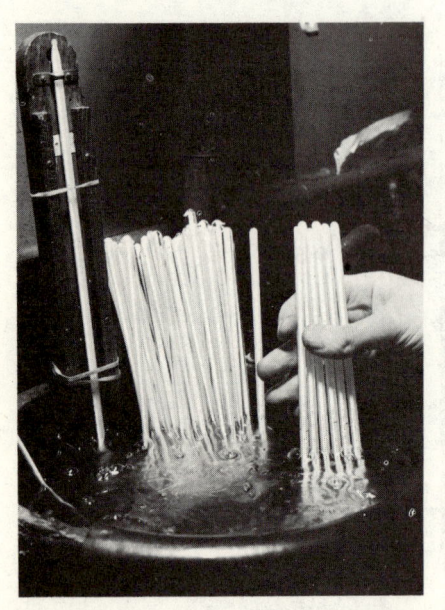

C.—Checking the ice-points of thermometers by immersion in melting ice.

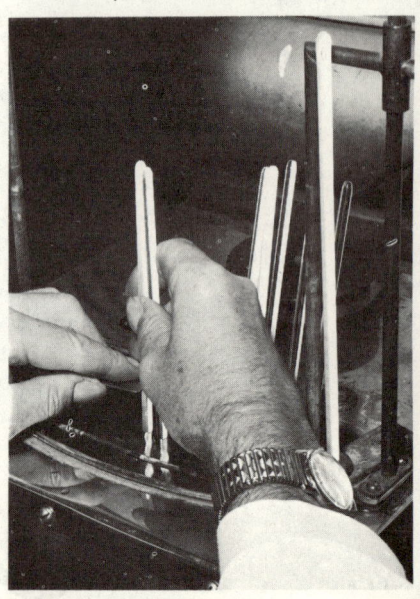

D.—Checking the intermediate points of thermometers against a standard (National Physical Laboratory) thermometer.

(*Courtesy of H. G. Zeal Ltd.*)

reached since the thermometer was last read. Generally speaking, a minimum temperature occurs during the night and a maximum during the day.

Invented by James Six towards the end of the eighteenth century, the thermometer consists of a fairly large cylindrical bulb A full of alcohol, connected by a U-shaped stem to a second bulb also full of alcohol except for a small air bubble. The bend of the U contains a thread of mercury. Two scales are provided, one against each limb of the tube, so that the temperature may be read against either of the mercury surfaces.

Resting on each of the mercury surfaces are small steel indexes provided with light springs to hold them in position against the glass. Expansion or contraction of the alcohol in A causes a movement of the mercury thread in one direction or the other. As a result, the appropriate index is pushed forward by the mercury and left in the extreme position reached. Thus the lower end of the index on the left indicates the minimum and that on the right the maximum temperature attained.

After a reading has been taken, the indexes are re-set in contact with the mercury by the aid of a small magnet.

It is important to notice that this is an alcohol thermometer, the mercury is used purely as a visible indicator.

The Choice between Mercury and Alcohol

The decision to use mercury or alcohol in a thermometer rests on the range of temperature required to be measured. Mercury freezes at $-39°$ C and boils at $359°$ C while alcohol freezes at $-115°$ C and boils at $78°$ C. It is essential therefore to use alcohol thermometers in places like Northern Canada and Russia where winter temperatures of $-40°$ C are not uncommon. Alcohol also possesses the advantage of having a coefficient of expansion about six times that of mercury.

Apart from these advantages, however, mercury is to be preferred to alcohol as a thermometric liquid for the following reasons:

(1) It does not wet glass. Alcohol tends to cling to the wall of the tube, particularly when the thread is falling.

(2) It does not, like alcohol, vaporise and distil on to the upper parts of the bore.

(3) It is opaque and therefore easily seen, whereas alcohol has to be coloured.

(4) It is better conductor of heat than alcohol and therefore responds more rapidly to changes in temperature.

Summary

1. *Temperature* is the level of internal energy in an object.
2. *A scale of temperature* is the interval between two fixed temperature points, divided into a chosen number of equal degrees.
3. The *lower fixed point* is the temperature of pure melting ice.

The *upper fixed point* is the temperature of steam from water boiling under standard atmospheric pressure of 760 mm height of mercury.

4. In the *Celsius scale* the interval between the two fixed points is divided into 100 equal parts, the lower fixed point being called 0° C and the upper, 100° C.
5. The *clinical thermometer* has a fine constriction and a short temperature scale. The *maximum and minimum thermometer* has alcohol and a mercury thread, with steel indexes to mark the maximum and minimum temperatures.
6. Normal body temperature is 37° C and average room temperature about 20° C.

EXERCISES

1. Describe how you would construct a mercury thermometer for measurement of temperatures between 0° and 100°C.

2. Define the two fixed points (ice point and steam point) of a temperature scale. Given a mercury thermometer, describe how you would test the accuracy of the fixed points, and then use it to measure temperatures in degrees C.

3. When placed in steam from boiling water, the mercury in an ungraduated thermometer reaches to a point 3 cm from the top of the stem. When placed in pure melting ice, the mercury reaches to a point 25 cm from the top of the stem. When allowed to acquire the temperature of the room, the mercury level in the stem is 21·7 cm from the top of the stem. Find the room temperature.

4. Give two reasons why water is not suitable for use as the liquid in a thermometer.

5. Describe some form of thermometer for indicating the maximum and minimum temperatures which have been reached since readings were last taken.

6. What is a clinical thermometer? Describe how a reading is taken with it. With the aid of a diagram, explain any noteworthy feature.

7. What are the advantages and disadvantages of mercury and alcohol for use in thermometers?

CHAPTER EIGHTEEN

Thermal Expansion

With a few exceptions, materials expand when heated. The action of a mercury or alchohol thermometer depends on the expansion of the thermometric liquid when it is heated; a flask fitted with a rubber bung and a length of glass tubing may be used to show the expansion of a liquid (Fig. 170). The flask is filled with water or other liquid, and the bung pushed into the neck of the flask until the level of the liquid comes a short distance up the tube. On plunging the flask into a can of hot water it is noticed that the level of the liquid at first falls slightly and then starts to rise steadily. The initial fall in level is due to the expansion of the glass, which becomes heated and expands before the heat has had time to be conducted through the glass into the liquid.

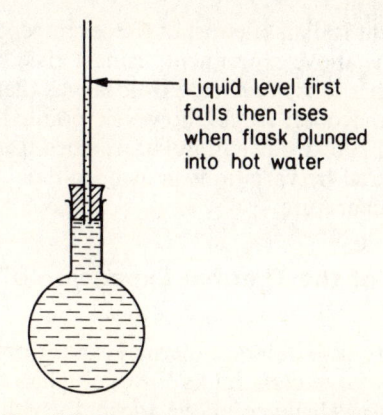

Fig. 170. Thermal expansion of a liquid

Gas Expansion

A simple experiment illustrates how gases expand compared with liquids. A flask fitted with a rubber bung and a length of glass tubing is inverted with the end of the tube dipping beneath the surface of some water in a beaker. If a warm hand is now placed over the flask, the air inside becomes heated and expands so that bubbles of air are seen emerging from the end of the tube. When the warm hand is removed,

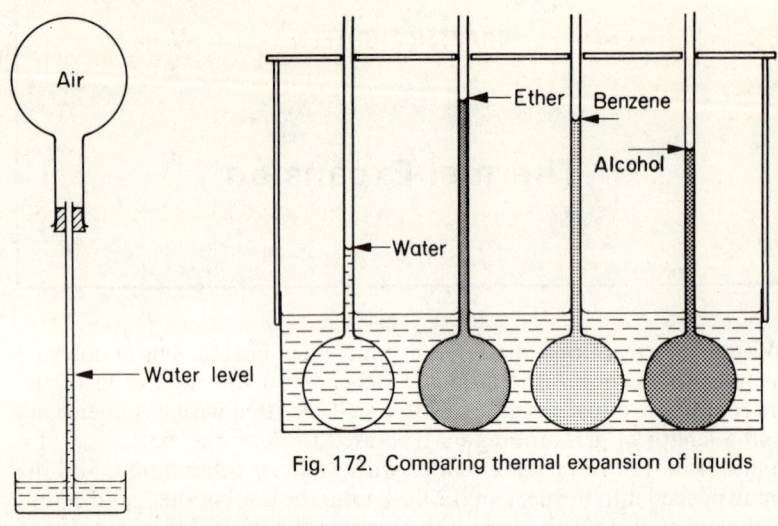

Fig. 171. Thermal expansion of a gas

Fig. 172. Comparing thermal expansion of liquids

the air in the flask contracts and water rises in the tube (Fig. 171). This shows that gases expand much more than liquids when their temperature changes.

Galileo, the great Italian scientist of the seventeenth century, was the first to perform the above experiment, using a glass bulb about the size of a hen's egg with a tube attached. His idea was that it should be used as a thermometer. Robert Boyle, however, pointed out that such an instrument would be extremely unreliable, since the level of the liquid in the tube is altered by variations in atmospheric pressure as well as by changes in temperature.

Comparison of the Thermal Expansion of Different Liquids

Different liquids have different thermal expansions. To demonstrate this, several fairly large glass bulbs to which glass tubes are attached are filled to a short distance above the bulb with different liquids. Fig. 172 shows the apparatus used, in which the bulbs contain water, alcohol, ether and benzene respectively. It is important to have the bulbs all of the same volume and with stems of the same internal diameter. The bulbs are immersed in a metal trough containing cold water and left until all the liquids have acquired the temperature of the bath. A little extra liquid should now be added, where necessary, to make all the levels the same. The bath is now heated and well stirred to ensure a uniform temperature. When the bulbs and their contents have acquired the new temperature of the bath, it will be seen that the liquid levels have risen by different amounts; of the four liquids used in this experiment, ether has the greatest expansion and water the least, while benzene expands more than alcohol. Thus, for a given rise in temperature, equal volumes of different liquids show different expansions in volume.

The Cubic Expansivity of a Liquid or Gas

At a given temperature a liquid or gas has a fixed volume and takes up the shape of the vessel which contains it. In the case of all fluids therefore, we can measure volume changes when they are heated. The coefficient of volume expansion or *cubic expansivity* of a fluid is defined as the increase in volume of unit volume per degree rise in temperature. "Unit volume" may be 1 cm^3 or 1 litre or 1 m^3, as convenient.

Any attempt to measure the expansion of a liquid directly is complicated by the fact that the containing vessel itself expands. However, since liquids must always be kept in some kind of vessel, it is generally convenient to know the *apparent expansion of a liquid,* which is the difference between its own expansion and that of the vessel. We therefore find it useful to measure the apparent cubic expansivity, which is the apparent increase in volume of unit volume per degree rise in temperature, when heated in an expansible vessel. To distinguish between the two values, the former is called the real or absolute cubic expansivity.

Measuring the Apparent Expansivity

Method. A direct though not accurate, method of measuring the apparent expansivity is to place an inverted 2 cm^3 pipette in a rubber cork at the top of a flask of known volume, filled with the liquid (Fig. 173). A thermometer is placed in another hole in the cork to measure the liquid temperature. The pipette is pushed down until the liquid level reaches M, the 2 cm^3 mark. The thermometer is now read, the liquid is gently warmed, and when the liquid rises to the top of the pipette the temperature is again observed.

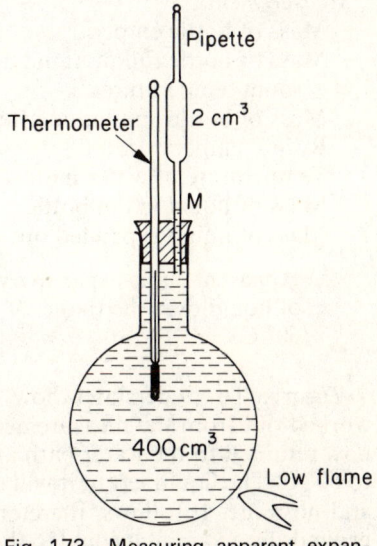

Fig. 173. Measuring apparent expansivity

Measurements.
$$\text{Volume of pipette} = 2 \text{ cm}^3$$
$$\text{Volume of liquid filling flask} = 400 \text{ cm}^3$$
$$\text{Initial liquid temperature} = 19°\text{ C}$$
$$\text{Final liquid temperature} = 36°\text{ C}$$

Calculation. Temperature rise $= 36 - 19 = 17$ K

400 cm³ for a 17 K rise expands by 2 cm³

$\therefore$ 1 cm³ for a 1 K rise expands by $\dfrac{2}{400 \times 17} \dfrac{\text{cm}^3}{\text{cm}^3 \text{ K}}$

$$= 0 \cdot 0003$$

Result Apparent cubic expansivity $= 0\cdot0003$ per K

Alternative method. The mass of a dry relative density bottle is first found when empty, and then, when full of liquid, at room temperature. This temperature is recorded and the bottle, together with a thermometer, is then placed in a beaker of water. Using a tripod, gauze and bunsen burner the water is then heated slowly to about 60° C stirring all the time to keep the temperature uniform. By having a very small flame, removed from time to time as necessary, the temperature of the water bath is kept constant at about 60° C for some minutes, to ensure that the liquid has fully acquired the temperature of the bath. The bottle is then removed from the bath, dried on the outside, allowed to cool and its mass found. The readings should be entered in the notebook as shown below.

Measurements.

Mass of bottle empty	$= 20$ g
Mass of bottle full of liquid at room temperature	$= 30$ g
Mass of bottle and liquid after heating	$= 28$ g
Room temperature	$= 20°$ C
Temperature of water bath	$= 60°$ C
Mass of liquid left in bottle	$= 8$ g
Mass of liquid expanded out	$= 2$ g

Apparent cubic expansivity of of liquid over the range 20° to 60° C. $= \dfrac{2}{(8 \times 40)} = \dfrac{1}{160}$ per K

Theory. To understand how the apparent cubic expansivity is worked out from the measurements, let us suppose that the bottle is now returned to the water bath and its temperature once more raised to 60° C. The liquid left in it will expand so as to fill the bottle exactly and no more. It follows, therefore, that the *volume left in* the bottle expands by an amount equal to the volume of that which expanded out during the experiment.

Thus if V = volume of liquid left in the bottle,
v = volume expanded out,
θ = *rise* in temperature,

Apparent cubic expansivity of methylated spirit $= \dfrac{v}{V \times \theta}$ per K

But since in this case the volumes are proportional to their masses (the liquid density being unchanged) we may write instead,

Apparent cubic expansivity of liquid $= \dfrac{\text{mass lost}}{\text{mass left} \times \text{temp. rise}}$

Expansion of Solids

With a few exceptions, substances expand when heated. In most cases the expansion is small and not easily seen unless steps are taken to magnify it. The expansion in length of a metal rod may be demonstrated by the simple apparatus of Fig. 174. A rod of brass or other metal about 0·5 m long is clamped at one end while the other rests on

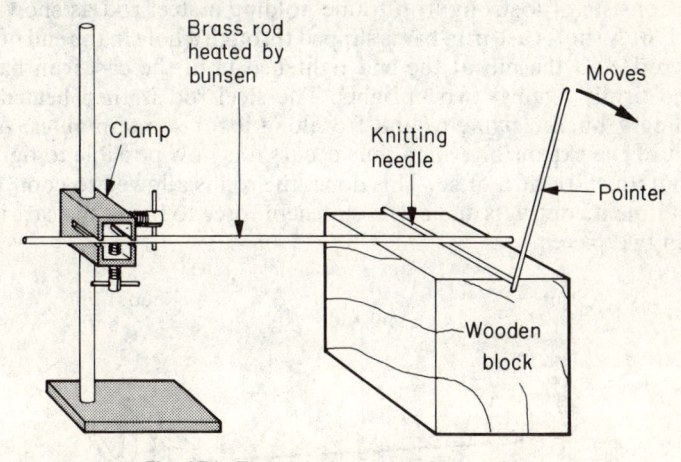

Fig. 174. Thermal expansion of a metal bar

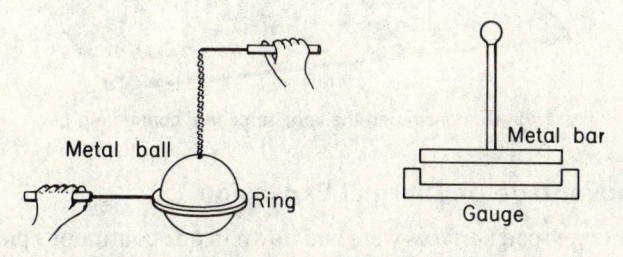

Fig. 175. Demonstrating the thermal expansion of metals

a knitting needle placed on a block of wood. A piece of wire or a drinking straw is fixed at right angles to the knitting needle to act as a pointer. When the rod is heated, it expands and causes the knitting needle to roll slightly. This results in quite a large movement of the pointer.

A *ball and ring,* or a *bar and gauge,* can also be used to show the expansion of metals (Fig. 175). The metal ball just passes through the ring, but on heating it is found to be too large to pass through. Similarly, the metal bar just fits into the gauge, but on heating it is found to be too long to fit.

Large Forces in Expansion

Large forces may be set up when a body expands or contracts. Sometimes these forces prove very inconvenient, but often they can be turned to practical advantage as will be decribed later.

The force of contraction when a hot steel rod contracts on cooling may be shown in the laboratory by a device known as a "bar breaker". This consists of a strong iron frame holding a steel rod as shown in Fig. 176. A short cast-iron bar is slipped through a hole in the end of the steel rod, and the nut at the end tightened until the cast-iron bar is pulled firmly against two uprights. The steel rod is then heated by running a bunsen flame to and fro along it for some minutes. As a result of the expansion which thus occurs it is now possible to tighten the nut an extra turn or so. This done, the rod is allowed to cool. In a short time it contracts and exerts sufficient force to break the cast-iron bar in two pieces.

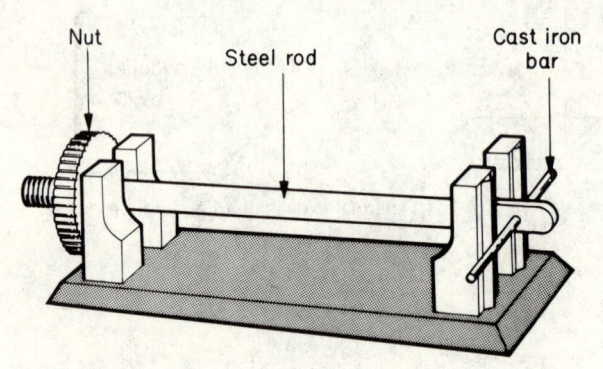

Fig. 176. Demonstrating the large force in a contracting bar

Disadvantage of Thermal Expansion

If concrete road surfaces were laid down in one continuous piece the concrete would crack due to expansion and contraction between the

THERMAL EXPANSION · 187

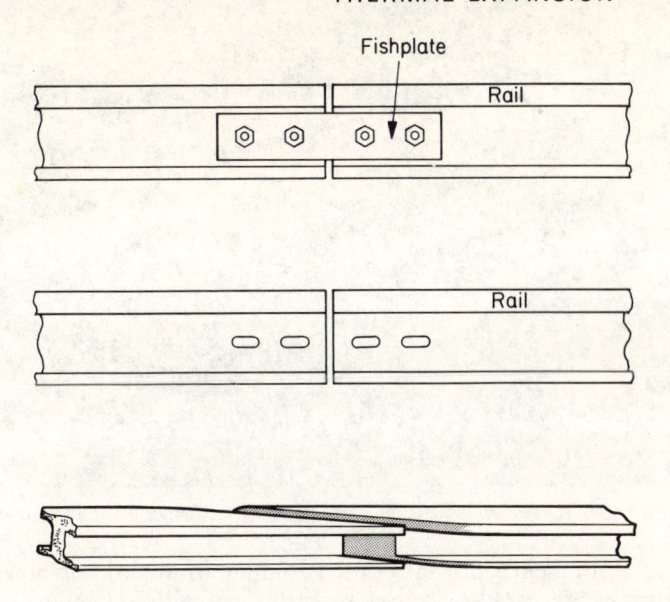

Fig. 177. Allowing for thermal expansion in railway lines

summer and winter temperatures. To avoid this, the surface is laid in small sections, each one being separated from the next by a small gap filled in with a compound of pitch. On a hot day this material will often be seen to have squeezed out of the joints as a result of the expansion.

Allowance has also to be made for the expansion of successive lengths of railway line. If this is not done, expansion will cause the rails to

Plate 30. Railway lines buckled by eccessive temperature

Plate *31*. A railway expansion joint designed for smooth running over long lengths of welded rail

buckle. With the recently introduced continuous welded rail, however, buckling is prevented by a very powerful method of clamping which allows virtually no movement. The clamping is done at a mean atmospheric temperature so that over the year the rail tends to contract as often as it tends to expand. To allow for free movement at the rail joints the bolt holes in the rails are slotted as shown in Fig. 177.

Allowance must be made also for the expansion of bridges and of the roofs of buildings made of steel girders. Various methods are used to overcome the difficulty, a common one being to have one end only of the structure fixed while the other rests on rollers, thus permitting free movement in either direction (Fig. 178).

Plate *32*. "Creeping" lead on the roof of Westminster Abbey: alternate thermal expansion and contraction has caused the metal sheets to stretch and buckle

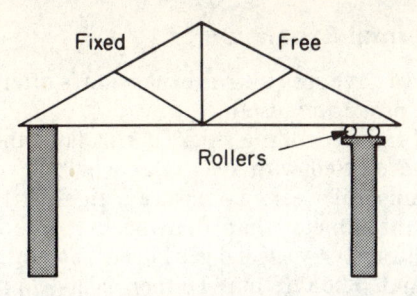

THERMAL EXPANSION · 189

Fig. 178. Allowing for expansion in a steel structure

Over a very long period of years, expansion and contraction results in the "creeping" of lead on sloping roofs. The illustration shows a portion of the roof of Westminster Abbey before it was repaired. Heated by the sun, the lead expands and tends to move down the roof under its own weight. On cooling and contracting, strain is caused in the lead, since the force of contraction is opposed by the weight of the lead and friction between it and the roof planking. As a result the lead undergoes a very slight permanent stretch. After many years of continual expansion and contraction, the lead stretches more and more, forms into folds and may even break. When this has occurred, the only remedy is to remove the lead and recast it into new sheets.

Plate *33*. Heating the steel tyre of a railway wheel with gas burners before fitting it to the wheel centre

Uses of Thermal Expansion

Although, as we have seen above, expansion is often troublesome, it can nevertheless prove very useful.

The wheels of railway rolling stock, particularly the driving wheels of locomotives, are fitted with steel tyres which have to be renewed periodically because of wear. To ensure a tight fit the tyre is made slightly smaller in diameter than the wheel. Before being fitted, the tyre is heated uniformly by special gas burners arranged in a ring. This causes it to expand. The tyre may be then easily slipped over the rim of the wheel, and on cooling it contracts and makes a tight fit.

The force of contraction when hot metal cools is also utilised in riveting together the steel plates and girders used in ship-building and other constructional work. The rivets are first made red-hot. This renders them soft and therefore easily burred into a head by pneumatic hammers, and their contraction on cooling serves to pull the plates tightly together.

Bimetal Strips

When rods of the same length but of different substances are heated through the same range of temperature, experiment shows that their expansions are not equal. Thus brass expands about one and a half times as much as iron or steel; aluminium expands about twice as much as steel. A metal alloy called *invar*, invented about 1904, has an exceptionally small expansion when its temperature rises, and it is therefore used in watches and thermostats. Glass has a smaller expansion than iron, and silica glass and Pyrex have a very low expansion. See also pp. 193, 195.

The difference in the expansions of brass and iron may be shown by riveting together a strip of brass and an equal strip of iron (Fig. 179).

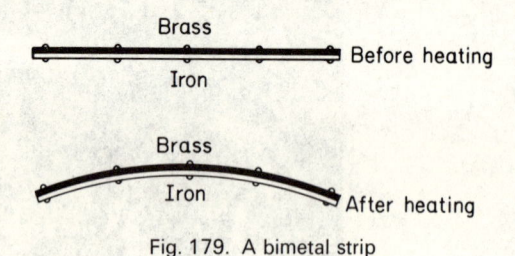

Fig. 179. A bimetal strip

When this bimetal strip is heated the strip bends, with the brass on the outside of the curve. The brass has thus become longer than the iron, showing that brass expands more than iron under equal temperature change.

THERMAL EXPANSION · 191

The bimetal strip has many useful applications, one of the most important being the electric thermostat, which is a device for maintaining a steady temperature. Fig. 180 shows the type of thermostat used in electric blankets. An electric blanket consists of a long resistance

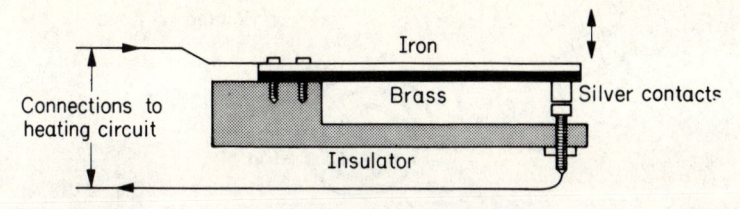

Fig. 180. A bimetal thermostat

wire, insulated by asbestos sleeving, and sewn in the form of a grid between two layers of blanket material. When the current is switched on, the wire becomes warm and heats the blanket. The circuit through the wire is completed through two silver contacts on the thermostat, one of which is fixed while the other is attached to the end of a bimetal strip. The whole device is enclosed in a small insulating box, and is sewn up inside the blanket so that it acquires the surrounding temperature. Should the blanket become too warm, the strip bends, separates the contacts and cuts off the current. On cooling, contact is re-made and the current again passes. This cycle of operations is repeated, with the result that the temperature of the blanket varies by only a few degrees.

Thermostats working on the same principle are used for maintaining a pre-determined temperature in hot water tanks, aquaria for tropical fish and electric irons.

Figs. 181, 182 illustrate two other uses of the bimetal strip. Fig. 181 shows the principle of an electric flashing unit. The current in the lamp circuit flows through a heating coil wound round a bimetal strip. As the strip becomes heated it bends and opens the contacts, thus cutting off both current and heat. On cooling, contact is re-established

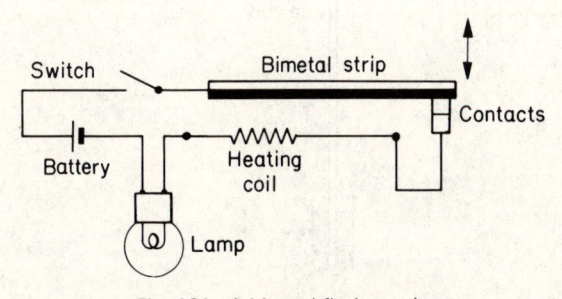

Fig. 181. A bimetal flasher unit

and the process repeats itself, with the result that the lamp flashes on and off.

Fig. 182 shows the principle of the bimetal thermometer. One end of a spiral of thin bimetal is fixed, the other end being attached to the

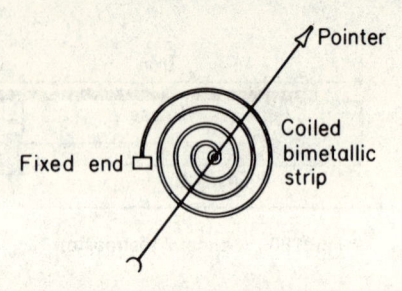

Fig. 182. A bimetal thermometer

spindle of a pointer moving over a scale of degrees. The metals used are brass and invar, and the spiral tends to curl in a clockwise direction as the temperature increases. For simplicity, the coil in the diagram is shown as a flat spiral, but in practice it is much longer than is shown and is wound in a cylindrical form.

Compensation for Expansion in Clocks and Watches

During the seventeenth century Galileo showed that the time of swing of a pendulum depends on its length and, furthermore, that the time of swing for a given length is always the same provided the swings are not too large. This discovery led to the development of clocks controlled by pendulums.

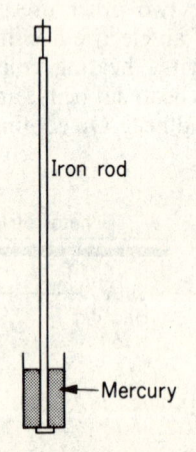

Fig. 183. Compensating pendulum

As would be expected, it is found that clocks tend to go slower during warm weather due to expansion in length of the pendulum. Several different methods have been devised to compensate for this, one of the most successful being the mercurial pendulum invented by George Graham in the eighteenth century. Graham's pendulum (Fig. 183) consists of a cylindrical glass vessel of mercury supported by an iron rod. The depth of mercury is adjusted so that the downward expansion of the rod is exactly compensated by the upward expansion of the mercury.

The timekeeping of watches is controlled by a balance. This is a small wheel with a heavy rim which oscillates to and fro under the action of a hairspring. An increase in temperature causes the watch to lose time for two reasons. Firstly the diameter of the wheel increases and secondly the elasticity of the hairspring decreases. Compensation is effected by making the rim of the wheel of bimetal strip and having it divided into two portions, as shown in Fig. 184. A rise in temperature

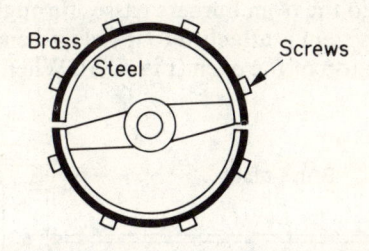

Fig. 184. Compensating balance-wheel

results in the strip bending inwards by an amount which compensates not only for the outward expansion of the spokes but also for the weakening of the hairspring.

Thermal Expansion in the Kitchen

Most people know that hot water should never be poured into thick glass tumblers or dishes since they are liable to crack. Glass is a poor conductor of heat so that when hot liquid is poured into the glass, the inside becomes hot while the outside remains cold. As a result, expansion of the inside sets up a strain which cracks the glass.

Very often cold jam-jars will crack when hot jam is poured into them. Fortunately, however, this may be prevented if the jars are first heated slowly in a warm oven before filling them.

It is worth noting that glassware for use in kitchen and laboratory can be obtained which is made of a special glass of low expansivity value. Pyrex is an example. Even when very hot, dishes and beakers made of this glass may be plunged into cold water without cracking.

Glass stoppers in bottles frequently become tightly fixed and attempts to remove them by force generally result in breakage. The following treatment invariably enables a stopper to be removed easily.

Two pairs of hands are needed, one to hold the bottle firmly on the table, while with the other pair, a strip of cloth wrapped once round the neck of the bottle is rapidly pulled to and fro. Energy expended against friction between cloth and glass becomes converted into heat. This causes the neck to expand sufficiently for the stopper to be withdrawn easily.

The Gas Thermostat

Oven temperature control in the modern gas cooker is effected by utilising the exceedingly low thermal expansion of an alloy of steel with 36 per cent of nickel. As will be seen from the table on page 195, this alloy, which is invar, expands by only one millionth of its length per kelvin rise in temperature.

The flow of gas to the oven burners passes through a valve A having an invar stem. This stem is attached to the closed end of a brass tube B projecting into the top of the oven (Fig. 185). When the burners are lit

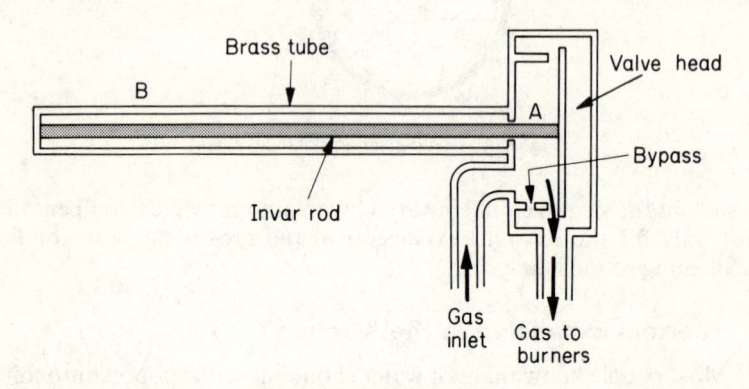

Fig. 185. A gas thermostat

the oven begins to warm up and the brass tube expands. The expansion of the invar is negligible and so it moves to the left, partially closing the valve opening and reducing the gas supply. Should the temperature of the oven fall, the brass tube contracts and the invar rod moves to the right, thus increasing the gas supply. The thermostat is provided with a rotating knob, not shown in the diagram, with which to adjust the minimum opening of the valve and hence arrange for any particular steady temperature to be maintained.

Measuring Expansion in Solids

As with liquids and gases, the volume of a solid increases with temperature. With solids, however, length is easier to measure than volume, and so we define *linear expansivity* as the increase in length of unit length by which a rod of any material expands when heated through 1 kelvin. Values of linear expansivity for a number of different substances are shown below.

Iron	0·000 012 per K
Brass	0·000 019
Aluminium	0·000 026
Invar	0·000 001
Glass	0·000 008 5
Silica	0·000 000 42
Concrete	0·000 011

Method. One method for measuring the linear expansivity of a metal in the form of a rod is shown in Fig. 186. A brass rod about 0·5 m long is carefully measured with a metre rule and is then enclosed in a steam jacket, between a fixed stop S and a micrometer M.

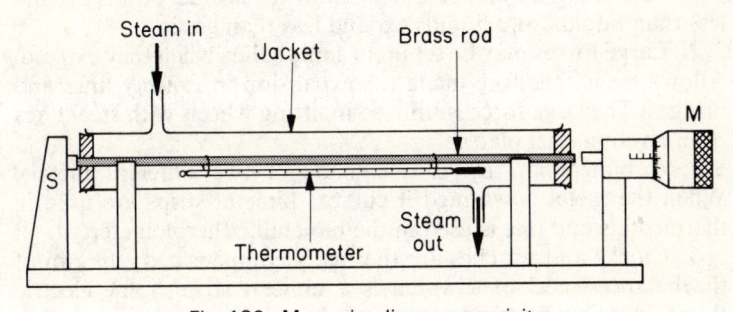

Fig. 186. Measuring linear expansivity

The rod is pushed against the stop S and the micrometer screw advanced until it just touches the end of the rod. The micrometer reading is recorded and at the same time the temperature of the rod is noted from a thermometer enclosed within the jacket.

The micrometer is then unscrewed for several turns and a current of steam from a boiler passed through the jacket for some minutes. The micrometer is once more adjusted until it again touches the end of the rod and its new reading taken. As a precaution, the micrometer should be unscrewed again and the steam flow continued for a further few minutes. A final reading of the micrometer will make certain whether or not the rod had fully acquired the steam temperature in the first instance. Lastly, the temperature of the steam in the jacket is recorded.

Measurements. A typical set of readings for this experiment is given below.

Original length of brass rod	= 502 mm
Initial temperature of rod	= 16·6° C
Final temperature of rod	= 99·5° C
1st micrometer reading	= 4.27 mm
2nd micrometer reading	= 3·48 mm

Calculation.

Rise in temperature of rod	= 99·5 − 16·6 = 82·9 K
Expansion of rod	= 4·27 − 3·48 = 0·79 mm

$$\text{Linear expansivity} = \frac{\text{length increase}}{\text{original length} \times \text{temp. rise}}$$

$$\therefore \text{Linear expansivity of brass} = \frac{0 \cdot 79}{502 \times 82 \cdot 9} \frac{\text{mm}}{\text{mm} \times \text{K}}$$

$$= 0 \cdot 000\,019 \text{ per K}$$

Summary

1. Solids, liquids and gases expand when heated. Solids expand less than liquids, and liquids expand less than gases.

2. Large forces may be set up in some solids when they expand. Allowance is therefore made for expansion in railway lines and bridges. The large force is utilised in fitting wheels with steel tyres or in riveting steel plates.

3. A bimetallic strip is one made of two different metals. When the metal is warmed it curves; bimetal strips are used in thermostats and one is used in the bimetallic thermometer.

4. Clocks and watches are thermally compensated; the rim of the balance-wheel of a watch is a bimetal strip. Some electric thermostats have a bimetal strip made of brass and invar.

5. The linear expansivity of a solid is the increase in length of unit length for 1 kelvin temperature rise; it can be measured with the aid of a micrometer screw gauge.

6. The volume expansivity of a gas, liquid, or solid is the increase in volume of unit volume for 1 kelvin temperature rise; the apparent expansivity can be measured by a volume (pipette) or relative density bottle method.

EXERCISES

Expansion of solids

1. Describe an experiment to show that a metal rod expands when heated.

2. What is a bimetallic strip? Describe one practical application of such a strip.

3. Describe two cases in which thermal expansion is troublesome, and explain the steps which may be taken to overcome it.

4. What is the effect of a change in temperature on the time-keeping of (a) a pendulum clock and (b) a pocket watch? What alterations in design may be made to compensate for the effects you describe?

5. Describe an experiment to show that considerable force may be exerted when a hot metal cools. Brifly describe two useful applications of this force.

6. Describe, with the aid of a simple diagram, the construction and action of a gas thermostat.

7. Define linear expansivity. Describe how you would measure it for a metal in the form of a rod or tube.

8. What gap should be left between 30 m lengths of steel railway line, laid down at a temperature of 10° C, if the maximum summer temperature expected is 40° C? (Linear expansivity of steel = 0·000 012 per K.)

9. Using the table of linear expansivities on page 195 find, in millimetre, the change of length of 3 metre of:
  (a) brass for a temperature rise of 100 K
  (b) iron for a temperature rise of 50 K
  (c) glass for a temperature rise of 45 K

10. An iron plate has a circular hole which is 50·0 mm in diameter when the temperature is 15° C. To what temperature must the plate be raised so that a cylindrical plug of diameter 50·3 mm will just fit into the hole? (Linear expansivity of iron = 0·000 012 per K.)

11. Two rods of brass and iron respectively are fixed to a short cross-bar as shown in Fig. 187. If the iron rod is 1 metre long, what must be the length of the brass rod so that the distance AB between the free ends of the rods remain constant at all temperatures? (Linear expansivity of iron 0·000 012, of brass 0·000 019 per K.)

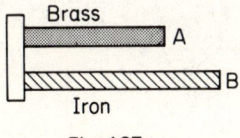

Fig. 187

Expansion of liquids and gases

12. Describe and explain what you would expect to observe when a flask, filled with water and fitted with a rubber bung and a length of glass tubing, is suddenly plunged into a can of hot water.

13. Explain the difference between the real and the apparent expansion of a liquid. Describe a method of measuring the apparent cubic expansivity of water, and explain how the result is calculated by using imaginary measurements.

14. Describe an experiment to show the relatively large expansion of a gas when warmed. Describe Galileo's air thermometer. Why did it prove unsatisfactory for measuring temperature?

15. A liquid X of volume 400 cm^3 expands by 3 cm^3 when warmed from 10° C to 70° C, and another liquid Y of volume 1000 cm^3 expands by 5 cm^3 when warmed from 20° C to 70° C. Calculate the cubic expansivity of X and Y.

16. A relative-density bottle was found to have mass 23·64 g empty, and 65·35 g when full of alcohol at 9·9° C. After having been kept in a water bath at a steady temperature of 60·0° C for some time, the bottle and its contents are found to weigh 63·19 g. Find the apparent cubic expansivity of alcohol.

17. The volume of the mercury in a thermometer is 0·60 cm^3 when the temperature is 0° C. If the mean area of cross-section of the bore of the stem is 0·000 40 cm^2, find the distance between the 0° and 100° C graduations on the thermometer. (Apparent cubic expansivity of mercury = 0·000 156 per K.)

CHAPTER NINETEEN

Convection

The heating of large rooms depends principally on one of the effects of thermal expansion of the air in the room. The effect can be made visible if a liquid is heated instead of air.

Convection in Liquids

When a vessel containing a liquid is heated at the bottom, a current of hot liquid moves upwards and its place is taken by a cold current moving downwards. Unlike conduction, where heat is passed on from one section of the substance to another by vibration of the particles (p. 206), the energy is here actually carried from one place to another in the liquid by the movement of the liquid itself. This phenomenon is called *convection*. The same process occurs when a gas such as air is heated.

Convection currents in water may be shown by filling a large spherical flask with water and dropping a single large crystal of potassium permanganate to the bottom of it through a length of glass tubing. A finger is placed over the end of the tube, which is then removed, together with the coloured water it contains. This method of introducing the crystal ensures getting it in the centre and also prevents it from colouring the water before it is required. On heating the bottom of the flask with a very small gas flame, as shown in Fig. 188, an upward current of coloured water will be noticed rising from the place where the heat is applied. This coloured stream reaches the top and spreads out. After a short time it descends down the sides of the flask, showing that a circulation has been set up.

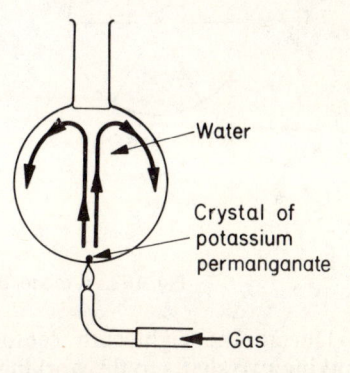

Fig. 188. Convection in a liquid

Explanation of Convection Currents

When a portion of liquid near the bottom of a vessel is heated, it expands; that is, its volume increases. A unit of volume of the liquid (say, 1 mm^3) therefore contains less mass than 1 mm^3 of unexpanded liquid. Hence the cold liquid is heavier per unit volume and the warm liquid rises. Thus a warm convection current moves upwards; for the same reason a cork rises in water or a hydrogen-filled balloon rises in air. See also Chapter 30.

If, on the other hand, some liquid in a vessel is heated at the top, the liquid there expands and remains floating on the denser liquid beneath. No convection current is set up, and the only way in which heat can travel downwards under these conditions is by conduction (see p. 206).

Convection in Air

The air convection current rising from an electric lamp may be shown by the aid of a small windmill. A suitable windmill may be cut with scissors from thin card or aluminium foil to the pattern of Fig. 189. The vanes are slightly bent and the mill, pivoted on a piece of bent wire, is held over the top of an electric lamp. When the lamp is switched on the windmill rotates in the hot upward air current. A device similar to this is often used to produce a flickering effect in domestic electric heaters of a type which are intended to resemble glowing coal fires.

Pattern of windmill

Hot upward air current from lamp

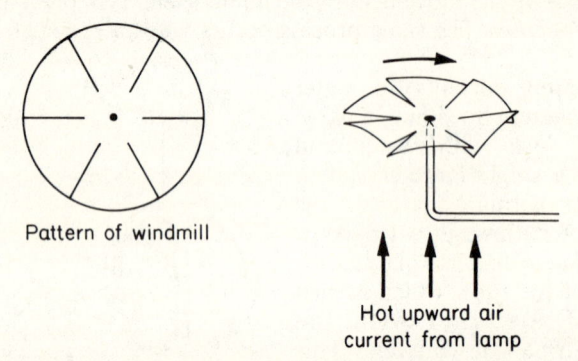

Fig. 189. A model depending on air convection

During the eighteenth century, coal mines were ventilated by sinking two shafts to the workings, known as the upcast and downcast shafts respectively. A fire was lit at the bottom of the upcast shaft which caused the air in it to become heated and rise. Fresh air entered the downcast shaft and passed through the passages of the mine workings before it, in turn, became heated and passed out through the upcast shaft. In this way a constant flow of fresh air was maintained through the mine. Fig. 190 shows a laboratory model to illustrate this

CONVECTION · 201

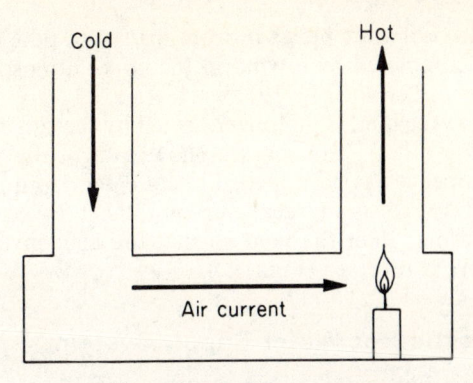

Fig. 190. Ventilation by air convection

method of ventilation. It consists of two wide glass tubes projecting from the top of a rectangular wooden box with a removable glass front. A short piece of candle is lit at the base of one of the tubes. When a piece of smouldering brown paper is held over the top of the other tube, the direction of the convection currents will be rendered visible by the passage of smoke through the box.

Land and Sea Breezes

At places on the coast in summer time it is noticeable that a breeze generally blows in from the sea during the daytime, while at night the direction of the wind is reversed. These breezes are local convection currents.

During the day the land is heated by the sun to a higher temperature than the sea. The reason for this is twofold. Water has a higher specific heat capacity than earth. This means that the sea maintains a fairly constant temperature, whilst the land temperature fluctuates between hot in daytime and cold at night. In addition, the surface of the sea is in constant motion, leading to mixing of the warm surface water with the cooler layers below. Air over the land is therefore heated, expands

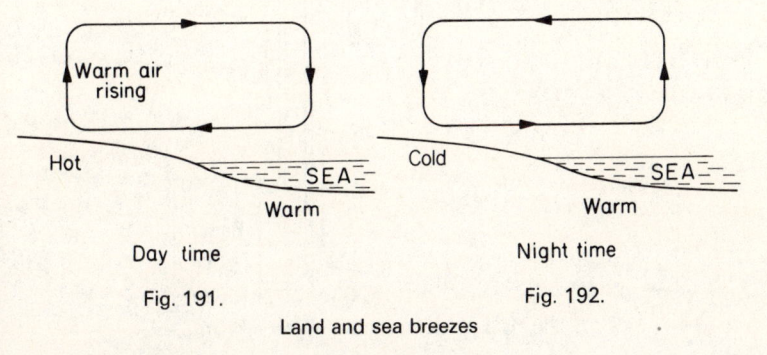

Day time

Fig. 191.

Night time

Fig. 192.

Land and sea breezes

and rises while cooler air blows in from the sea to take its place. The circulation is completed by a wind in the upper atmosphere blowing in the opposite direction (Fig. 191).

At night-time the land is no longer heated by the sun and cools very rapidly. On the other hand the sea shows practically no change in temperature, since it has been heated to a greater depth than the land, and consequently acts as a larger reservoir of heat. By comparison, the sea is now warmer than the land so that the air convection current described above is reversed (Fig. 192).

The Domestic Hot Water Supply System

The domestic hot water supply system consists of a *boiler*, a *hot water storage tank* and a *cold supply tank* interconnected by pipes arranged as shown in Fig. 193. When the boiler fire is alight a convection

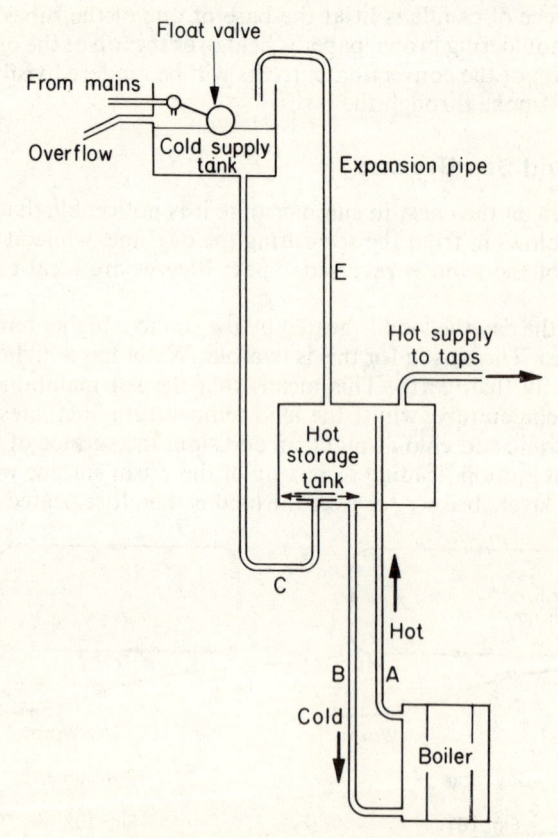

Fig. 193. A domestic hot water system

current of hot water rises up the flow pipe A while cold water descends to the boiler through the return pipe B, where it becomes heated in turn. In this way a circulation is set up, with the result that the hot water storage tank gradually becomes filled with hot water from the top downwards. It is important to notice that the flow pipe A leaves the boiler at the top and projects up into the hot tank, while the return pipe B connects the bottom of the hot tank to the bottom of the boiler.

Hot water for use in kitchen and bathroom is taken from a pipe leading from the top of the hot tank. When hot water is run off, an equal volume of water from the cold supply tank enters the hot storage tank at the bottom through the pipe C. The whole system is thus kept constantly full of water and no air can enter. The water level in the cold tank is maintained by a supply from the mains which enters through a float valve.

An expansion pipe E rises from the top of the hot tank and is bent twice at right angles so that its end is over the cold tank. this is a safety precaution; if the fire is allowed to burn so fiercely that the water boils, steam and hot water are discharged harmlessly into the cold tank and no damage results. The expansion pipe also permits the escape of dissolved air which comes out of the water when it is heated, as otherwise this might cause troublesome air locks in the pipes.

Fig. 194 shows a glass model which demonstrates the convection currents described above. To begin with, the water in the lower flask is coloured with blue ink while the tubes and upper vessel are full of colourless water. When the flask is steadily heated with a bunsen burner a hot convection current of coloured water rises up one tube. After a short time a distinctly visible layer of hot coloured water collects at the top of the upper vessel. Eventually this layer increases in depth until the upper vessel is entirely filled with hot coloured water. Finally, warm coloured water will be seen descending the straight tube.

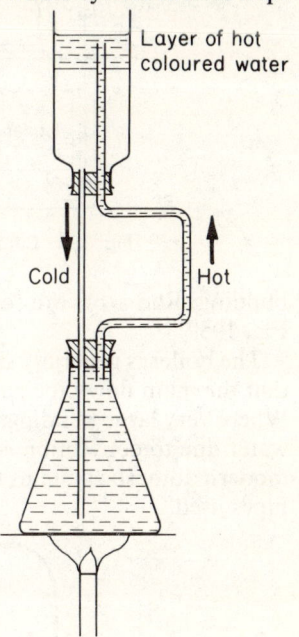

Fig. 194. Demonstration of convection in water

The Hot Water Central Heating System

In many respects a central heating system is similar to a domestic hot water system, except that there is no hot tank, and hot water circulates through a pipe passing through the various rooms of the

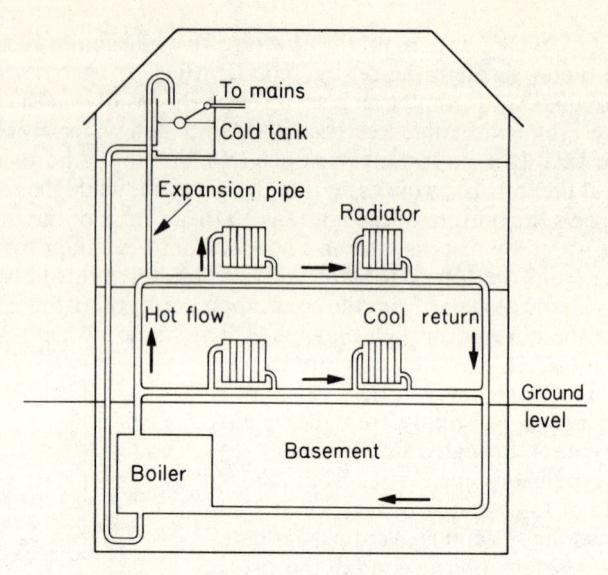

Fig. 195. Central heating by convection of water

building. Radiators are connected to this pipe at intervals as shown in Fig. 195.

The boiler is generally situated in the basement and it will be noticed that the main flow pipe passes directly to the top floor of the building. Where very large buildings are concerned the natural circulation of the water due to convection is assisted by pumps. A pump is also used in modern domestic systems to overcome the liquid friction in the narrow pipes used.

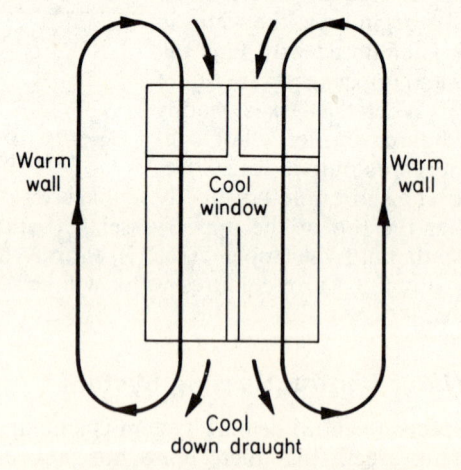

Fig. 196. Air convection near a window

One very important aspect of the layout of a heating system is the position chosen for the radiators. These are normally placed directly beneath the windows. By reason of the thinness of glass, heat from a room is conducted more rapidly through glass than through the much thicker walls. Consequently the air in contact with windows is much cooler than that adjoining the walls. The tendency therefore in winter is for a convection current to be set up in the air of a room in the neighbourhood of windows as shown in Fig. 196. This creates an unpleasantly cold draught on the heads of persons sitting beneath windows. and is particularly noticeable in large public halls and churches. The trouble may be prevented by placing radiators beneath the windows to counteract the down-draught by an upward current of warm air.

Summary

1. Convection is the name given to the transfer of heat through a liquid or gas by the movement of the particles themselves, which carry the heat with them.

2. A hot water circulation system transfers heat by convection currents in water. Hot water radiators warm a room largely by convection currents in the air.

3. Convection currents are the result of hot fluid being displaced by heavier cold fluid.

EXERCISES

1. Describe experiments to show how thermal energy is transmitted through (*a*) a liquid, (*b*) air.

2. Draw a labelled diagram of a domestic hot water supply system using wide. pipes, and explain the circulation of the water.

3. Explain why the hot water pipes of a central heating system are usually placed near the floor, while the cold pipes in a refrigerating chamber are placed near the ceiling.

4. Explain how sea and land breezes are formed. Draw diagrams in illustration.

5. Explain how coal mines were formerly ventilated by a convection method. Draw a diagram illustrating the method.

6. A kettle of water is warmed by a burner. Explain the processes by which all the water becomes hot.

7. The tube C in Fig. 193 enters the bottom of the tank and not the side, and ends in a T-piece. Suggest reasons for this procedure.

CHAPTER TWENTY

Thermal Conduction

If a steel poker is pushed into a fire and left there for a time, the handle becomes warm. The heat has travelled through the metal. The process by which energy is transmitted through the metal is called *conduction*.

If heat is given to a substance it makes the molecules move faster than before. Generally, the molecules in solids move to-and-fro, or vibrate, and the vibration becomes more vigorous as the temperature rises. In the case of the poker referred to above, its molecules are set into vigorous vibration owing to contact with the very strongly vibrating molecules of the glowing fuel. The hot molecules at the end of the poker will cause their immediate neighbours to vibrate more vigorously and so appear hotter also. In this manner an increased vibration is transmitted from molecule to molecule along the poker, until finally the handle becomes warm.

Copper conducts about eight times better than steel. If the poker had been made of copper, we should probably have found the handle too hot to touch.

Good and Bad Conductors of Heat

Most metals are good conductors of heat, silver and copper being outstandingly good. At the other end of the scale, substances like cork, wood, cotton and wool are very bad conductors, or insulators.

In general, thermal conductors are also electric conductors and insulating materials are equally effective thermally and electrically. Both good and bad conductors have their uses. Kettles for use on an open fire were made of copper since heat is conducted most rapidly through this metal. The "bit" of a soldering iron is also made of copper, so that when its tip is cooled through contact with the work, heat is rapidly conducted from the body of the bit to restore the temperature of the tip and maintain it above the melting-point of solder.

Bad conductors have a very wide application. Beginning with our own personal comfort, we prevent loss of heat from ourselves by a covering of poorly conducting material. Textiles are bad conductors of heat since they are full of tiny pockets of air enclosed by the fibres of the material. Air, in common with all gases, is a very bad conductor of heat. We say in ordinary conversation that wool is warmer than cotton. Technically, of course, we imply that it has a lower thermal conductivity than cotton.

Lagging

Loss of heat by conduction through the walls of an oven is reduced by constructing the oven with inner and outer walls and packing the space between with glass wool. Glass wool is not only a very poor conductor but has the merit of being non-inflammable. Material of low thermal conductivity used in this way for the purpose of preventing the escape of heat is called *lagging*. Another example is the covering of hot water storage tanks and pipes with a layer of plaster mixed with asbestos. Cold water pipes which are likely to be exposed to low winter temperatures where they run through roofs or along outside walls are generally wrapped in strips of felt or sacking. This prevents loss of heat, and consequent freezing, during winter.

Handling Good and Bad Conductors

If one stands in bare feet on linoleum, the latter feels cold, but a carpet on the same floor feels comfortably warm. The difference is due to the fact that linoleum is a better conductor of heat than carpet.

To begin with, both linoleum and carpet are at the same temperature. This may be verified by placing a thermometer in contact with each in turn and noting that the same reading is obtained. The feet are, however, warmer than either linoleum or carpet, and consequently heat tends to flow from the feet. Linoleum, being the better conductor, conveys heat more rapidly from the feet than carpet. As a result, the feet feel cold on the linoleum, but warm on the carpet.

Precisely the same effect is experienced when handling a garden fork in winter. The iron part of the fork feels cold but the wooden handle warm.

Ignition Point of a Gas

An inflammable gas will burn if its temperature reaches a value known as the "ignition point". The effect of a metal on the burning of a gas can be shown by placing a wire gauze about 50 mm above a bunsen burner. If the gas is turned on and lighted underneath the gauze it is noticed that the flame does not pass through the gauze. The wires of the gauze conduct the heat of the flame away so rapidly that the hot gases passing through the gauze are cooled below the ignition temperature (Fig. 197).

The gas is now turned out and the gauze allowed to cool. Afterwards the gas is again turned on and lit above the gauze. This time the flame

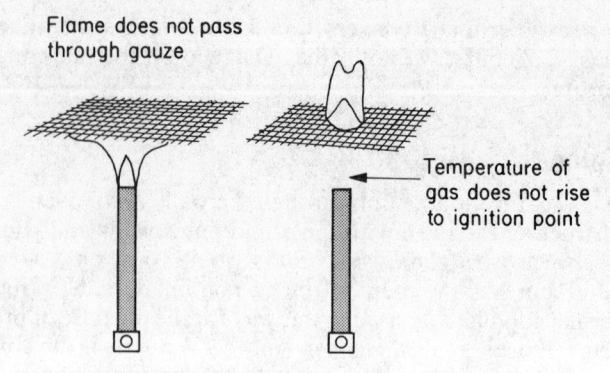

Fig. 197. Thermal conduction by a metal gauze

continues to burn above the gauze. As in the previous case, the wires conduct heat rapidly away, with the result that the temperature of the gas in contact with the underneath surface of the gauze is not raised to its ignition point. The flame will only pass through the gauze if it should become red-hot. As we shall now show, this experiment illustrates the principle of the Davy safety lamp.

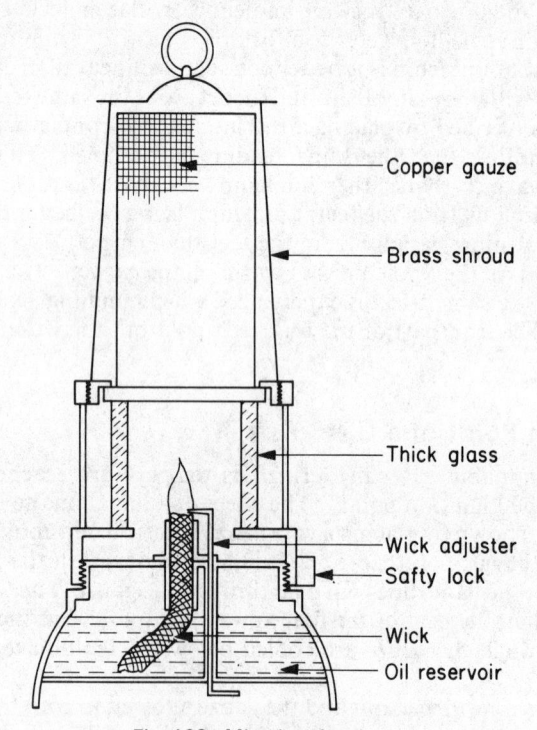

Fig. 198. Miner's safety lamp

The Miner's Safety Lamp

The enormously increased output of coal for industrial purposes towards the end of the eighteenth century brought with it a corresponding increase in the number of fatal mine accidents. An inflammable gas called methane or fire-damp is often found in coal mines. This, when mixed with the air of the mine, often exploded when it came into contact with the naked flames of the candles which, at that time, were used for illumination.

In 1813 a society was formed to study methods for preventing these explosions, and Sir Humphry Davy was approached for advice. Davy investigated the problem and eventually found a remedy in the safety lamp. In its original form this consisted of a simple oil burner completely surrounded by a cylinder of wire gauze. The gauze, however, threw undesirable shadows, and later a thick cylindrical glass window was added, still keeping the gauze above, but encased in a brass shroud to protect it from damage (Fig. 198).

Should the atmosphere surrounding the lamp contain methane, its presence will be indicated by the flame becoming surrounded by a bluish haze. This is due to the methane burning when it comes into contact with the flame. The flame cannot extend beyond the gauze and cause an explosion since the wires of the gauze, being good conductors of heat, conduct the heat away extremely rapidly. Thus the temperature of the gauze never rises to the ignition temperature of the gas-air mixture in the mine.

Variation in Conductivity

The difference in conductivity of various materials can be shown by the apparatus of Fig. 199. Rods of the same diameter and length of

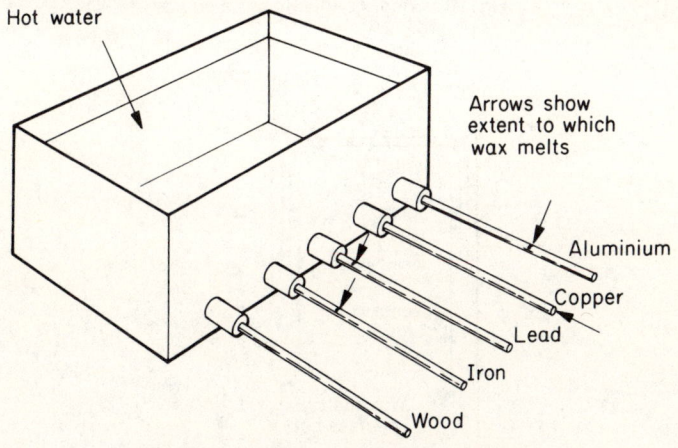

Fig. 199. Comparing thermal conductivities

aluminium, copper, lead, iron and wood are made to project from corks inserted in holes in the side of a metal trough. The rods are first dipped into molten paraffin wax and withdrawn to allow a coating of wax to solidify on them. Boiling water is then poured into the trough so that the ends of the rods are all heated to the same temperature. After some minutes have elapsed it is noticed that the wax has melted to different distances along the rods, indicating differences in their thermal conductivities.

Conduction of Heat through Liquid

All ordinary liquids, with the exception of mercury, which is a metal, are poor conductors. Nevertheless, heat can be transmitted very quickly through liquids by convection.

To prevent convection, and to confine the process of heat transmission to conduction only, it is necessary to heat a liquid at the top.

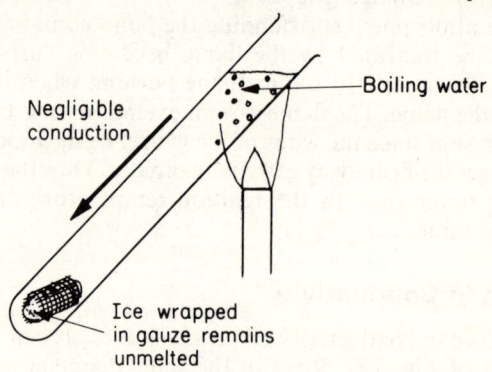

Fig. 200. Poor conduction in a liquid

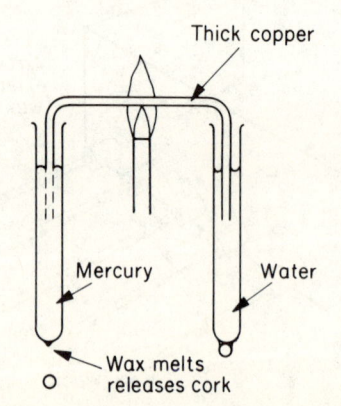

Fig. 201. Comparing conductivities of liquids

Thus we may show water to be an extremely bad conductor of heat by wrapping a piece of ice in gauze to make it sink and placing it at the bottom of a test-tube nearly full of water. By holding the top of the tube in a bunsen flame, the water at the top may be caused to boil vigorously while the ice at the bottom remains unmelted (Fig. 200).

Mercury may be shown to be a better conductor than water by taking two test-tubes containing mercury and water respectively and attaching a cork to the bottom of each with melted wax (Fig. 201). A piece of thick copper wire bent twice at right angles is then placed with one leg in each of the two liquids. On heating the centre of the wire with a bunsen flame, heat is conducted through the metal equally into the water and mercury. In a very short time the wax on the mercury-filled tube melts and the cork falls off. Very prolonged heating is necessary before the same occurs with the water-filled tube.

It may be noted that *gases* are far worse conductors of heat than liquids.

Summary

1. Conduction is the name given to the process by which heat energy is transmitted through a substance, by the handing on of kinetic energy of vibration from one molecule to another, without the molecules moving from their mean positions.

2. Generally speaking, metals are good conductors of heat while non-metals are poor conductors.

3. Liquids, with the exception of mercury, are poor conductors.

4. The miner's safety lamp is based on the principle that metal gauze is a good conductor of heat, thus preventing the gas outside reaching its ignition point.

EXERCISES

1. A metal bar is heated at one end by means of a bunsen burner. Explain the process by which heat travels through the bar to the far end.

2. Explain why, (*a*) the bit of a soldering iron is made of copper, (*b*) cold water pipes are sometimes wrapped in sacking.

Mention two examples of practical uses of good and bad conductors of heat.

3. A workman picks up a shovel on a winter day and notices that the metal part of the handle feels much colder than the wooden part. Give reasons for this.

4. A piece of wire gauze is placed over a bunsen burner and the gas ignited underneath. Some minutes elapse before the flame passes through the gauze. Explain the delay.

5. Describe, with the aid of a labelled diagram, the construction and action of a miner's safety lamp.

6. Describe experiments to compare the heat conducting properties of (*a*) copper and wood, (*b*) water and mercury.

7. Describe an experiment to show that water is a bad conductor of heat.

8. Explain why (*a*) a carpet feels warmer to the bare feet than linoleum, (*b*) wool is warmer than cotton.

9. Name three good conductors of heat and three poor conductors. Explain (*a*) why birds "fluff" their feathers more in winter than in summer, (*b*) why, in polar climates, wooden huts must not be built with steel bolts passing right through them.

10. Explain why the presence of double walls and attics help to keep a house cool in summer and warmer in winter.

CHAPTER TWENTY-ONE

Measurement of Length, Volume and Mass

Measurements in Physics

Physics is a subject which deals with energy and the properties of materials. In all branches of Physics very little real progress was made until *measurements* were attempted, and today a physicist must be able to measure accurately distances, volumes, masses, times and temperatures as well as numerous other quantities such as electric current and voltage. It may therefore be said that Physics is concerned with the measurement of energy. The National Physical Laboratory at Teddington, Middlesex, and the Department of Industrial and Scientific Research are two government organisations in which trained physicists are engaged on measurements.

Scientists and Technologists in countries all over the world have agreed to use the international system (SI) of measurement of length

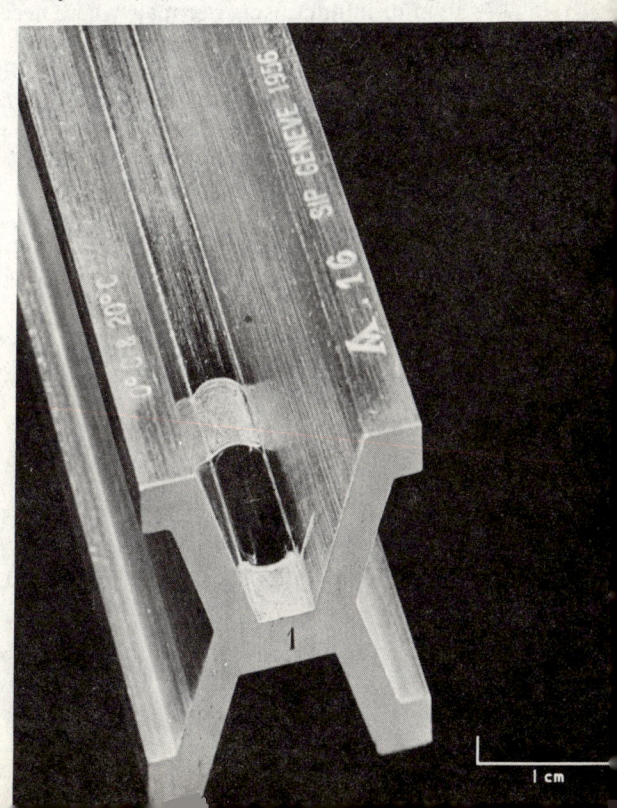

Plate *34*. The international metre: one end of copy no. 16, kept in London. The shape was designed to give maximum rigidity to the bar for minimum use of metal

and mass. This is why inches and pounds are not now used in science, although they formerly played a large part in everyday life.

This chapter introduces some of the instruments used for measuring length, volume and mass. We have already studied other instruments, for example thermometers for taking temperatures, and the different meters used in electrical experiments. Measuring instruments are the scientist's tools and are used by all technologists, and everyone should know how to use and read them as accurately as possible.

Measuring the Larger Distances

In laboratories, the longer lengths are usually measured by means of metre or $\frac{1}{2}$ metre boxwood scales. Originally the metre was defined as the distance between two lines ruled near the ends of a bar of platinum kept at Paris. This standard metre was made in the year 1799, and since then metre scales used all over the world have had to agree with it. Copies of the standard metre are kept at the National Physical Laboratory.

The relation of the metre to the other units of length is shown in the following table:

$$1 \text{ kilometre (km)} = 1000 \text{ metre.}$$
$$1 \text{ metre (m)} = 1000 \text{ millimetre.}$$

The centimetre (cm), equal to 10 mm, is also used sometimes.

A length is never expressed in centimetres and millimetres, but either in m or in mm, using decimals where necessary.

Great care should always be taken in handling metre sticks, as they do not have the short ungraduated portion usually left at the end of an ordinary ruler to take the wear. In any case, wherever possible it is best to start from, say, the 10 mm graduation and subtract 10 mm from the reading at the other end. On account of the thickness of the wood, an error will result if the eye is not placed vertically above the mark being read on the scale. This is called an error due to parallax. Standing the scale on its edge avoids errors due to parallax. Fig. 202 shows a millimetre scale giving a reading of 283·7 mm. Since tenths of a millimetre

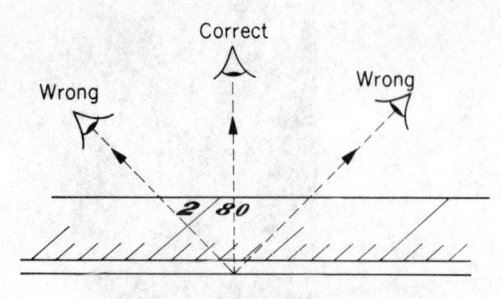

Fig. 202. Parallax error in measurement

MEASUREMENT OF LENGTH, VOLUME AND MASS · 215

are not marked on the scale the last figure has to be estimated by eye.

Dimensions of a Solid Body

Distances on a solid object, for example the diameter of a ball, cannot be measured directly with an ordinary scale. For such measurements as this, calipers are employed. These consist of a pair of hinged, curved steel jaws as shown in Fig. 203. The jaws are closed until they both touch the object in the position for which a measurement is required, and the distance between them is afterwards measured on a suitable scale.

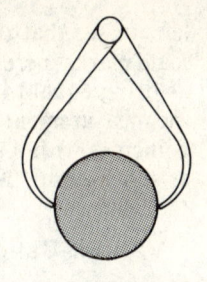

Fig. 203. Calipers

The Vernier

About 350 years ago Pierre Vernier invented a simple method for obtaining the second decimal place in millimetre measurements such as we have described, without having to estimate fractions of a division by eye.

For use with a scale of millimetres, the vernier is a short scale 9 mm long divided into 10 equal parts, so that the difference in length between a vernier division and a scale division is 0·1 mm. The vernier slides along the scale until its zero mark just touches the end of the object being measured (Fig. 204).

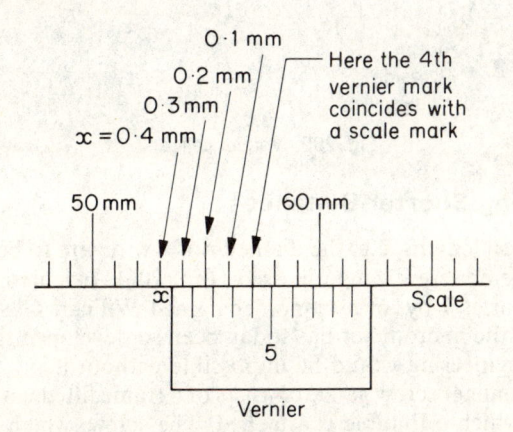

Fig. 204. A vernier scale

Our diagram shows a scale and vernier giving a reading of 53·4 mm. The fraction of a scale division shown as x gives the second decimal place. Looking along the vernier, we notice that the *fourth* vernier mark coincides with a scale mark. Counting back from this mark towards the left we see that the differences between successive vernier marks and scale marks increase by 0·1 mm each time, finally giving the distance x as being equal to 0·4 mm. It follows that the second decimal place in the measurement made is given by the number of a vernier mark which coincides with a scale mark. Verniers are used on Fortin barometers, as shown on p. 298, and in vernier calipers.

Vernier Calipers

Fig. 205 illustrates a pair of vernier or slide calipers. These consist of a steel scale with a fixed jaw at one end. Objects to be measured are placed between this and a sliding jaw carrying a vernier. It will be noted that, in addition, inside jaws are provided for such measurements as the inside diameter of tubes

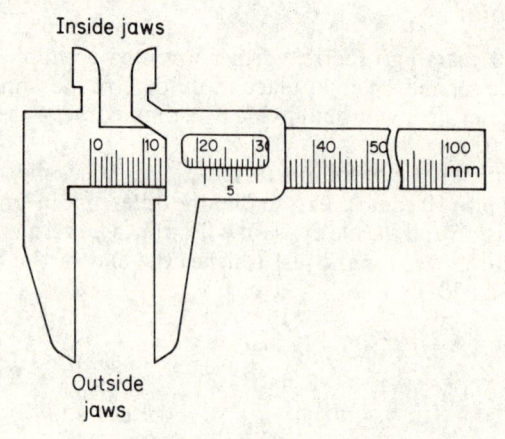

Fig. 205. Vernier calipers

Measuring Shorter Distances

When small lengths, e.g. the diameter of a wire, are to be measured, the micrometer screw gauge is used (Fig. 206). Invented during the reign of Charles I by an astronomer named William Gascoigne, the principle of the micrometer has today been so developed that modern precision engineering would be impossible without it.

The micrometer screw gauge consists of a frame fitted with a screwed spindle to which a thimble is attached. The screw, which is the most important part, is totally enclosed to protect it from damage. It has a pitch of 0·5 mm, so that for each complete turn the spindle moves through 0·5 mm. Fractions of a turn are indicated on the thimble, which has a scale of 50 equal division. Each division on the thimble therefore represents a screw travel of one-fiftieth of half a millimetre or 0·01 mm.

MEASUREMENT OF LENGTH, VOLUME AND MASS · 217

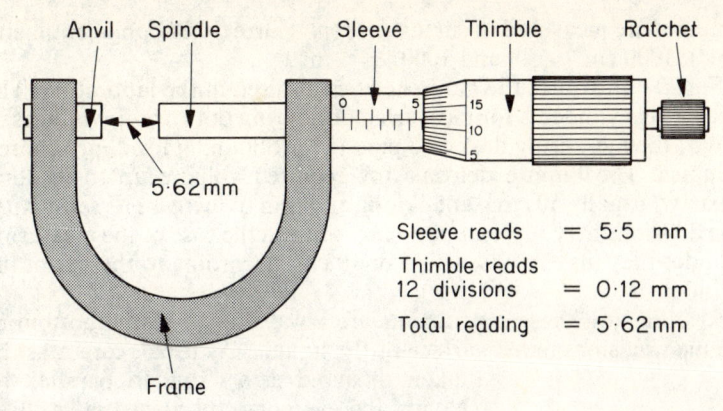

Fig. 206. Micrometer gauge

Sleeve reads = 5·5 mm
Thimble reads 12 divisions = 0·12 mm
Total reading = 5·62 mm

To take a reading, the object being measured is gripped very gently between the anvil and spindle. Some gauges have a ratchet which slips when turned and prevents undue pressure which would strain the gauge. Expert users however prefer to work by their sense of touch. The sleeve has a scale in $\frac{1}{2}$ millimetres which are gradually uncovered by the thimble, one for each complete turn of the screw. The sleeve and thimble readings are noted. Expressing the result in mm it follows that the sleeve reading gives the units and the first decimal place while the thimble reading gives the second decimal place.

Volume of Liquids

For measuring the volume of a liquid, different graduated glass vessels are available, the choice of which depends on the circumstances.

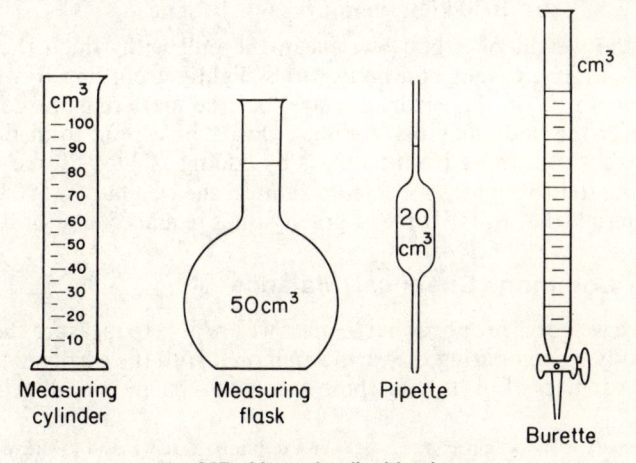

Fig. 207. Measuring liquid volume

Volumes are measured in cubic metre (m^3), litre (l), or cubic centimetre (cm^3). 1000 cm^3 = 1 l and 1000 l = 1 m^3.

Fig 207 illustrates the graduated vessels used in the laboratory. The measuring cylinder is for measuring or pouring out various volumes of liquid; the measuring flask and pipette for obtaining fixed, pre-chosen volumes. The burette delivers any required volume up to its total capacity, usually 50 cm^3, and is long and thin to increase its sensitivity. The divisions may represent 0·1 cm^3, while in the case of the measuring cylinder they may represent 1, 5 or 10 cm^3 according to the size of the cylinder.

Readings on these instruments are always taken to the bottom of the meniscus or curved surface of the liquid.* As usual, care must be taken to avoid errors due to parallax by having the eye correctly placed (Fig. 208). The pipette and burette are held upright, but the cylinder and flask should always be stood on a horizontal bench when being read, or errors are almost certain to result from tilting.

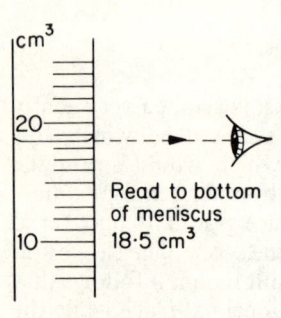

Fig. 208. Reading the meniscus level

Read to bottom of meniscus 18·5 cm^3

Mass and Weight

By the mass of a body we mean the quantity of matter it contains; the unit of mass is a lump of platinum kept at Paris together with the standard metre already mentioned. It is called the standard kilogramme.

1000 milligramme (mg) = 1 gramme
1000 gramme (g) = 1 kilogramme
1000 kilogramme (kg) = 1 tonne

By the weight of a body we mean the pull with which the earth attracts it. The weight of a body varies slightly according to where it happens to be on the earth's surface, but the mass remains constant wherever the body may be. We must always be careful to distinguish the weight of a thing from its mass by adding "f" for "force" when referring to its weight, so that, for example, the weight of a 500 g mass of material (that is, the force of gravity on it) equals 500 gf or 0·5 kgf.

The Common (Chemical) Balance

Since weight is proportional to mass we are able to measure the mass of a body by comparing the earth's pull on it with the earth's pull on a standard mass. For this purpose we use a balance and a box of

---

* Mercury with its convex meniscus is an exception. Here we read to the top of the meniscus.

MEASUREMENT OF LENGTH, VOLUME AND MASS

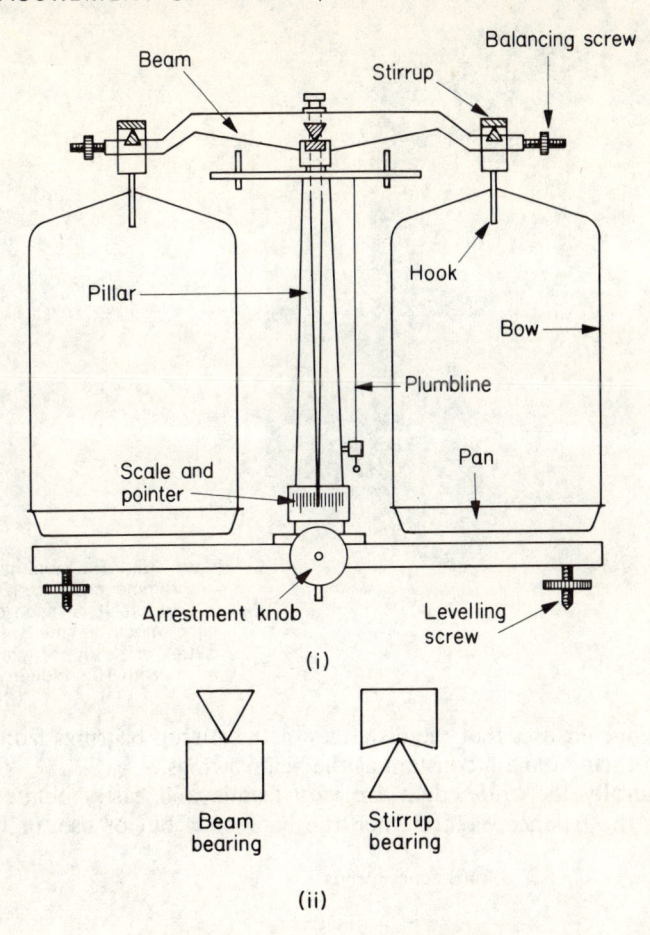

Fig. 209 (i & ii). A chemical balance

"weights". To be strictly scientific it would be better to call the latter a box of "masses".

Balances used in laboratories differ from those used in shops in that they are more sensitive. This means that they respond to much smaller changes of weight in the pans. The most important and delicate parts of a balance are the bearings of the beam and scale-pan stirrups. These are made of agate, a very hard semi-precious stone. Fig. 209 (ii) shows the arrangement of the agates. The beam is supported on an agate knife-edge resting on agate planes, while the stirrups have V-shaped agates resting on knife-edges at the ends of the beam. Such bearings possess very little friction, so that the beam swings freely and no sticking occurs. In addition the accuracy of the balance is increased, since the

Plate *35*. The international kilogramme: copy no. 18, kept in London. It is made of the same metal as the standard metre, an alloy of platinum with 10% iridium

knife-edge ensures that the distances of the stirrup bearings from the beam bearing remain constant as the beam swings.

Naturally the knife-edges are very fragile and easily blunted by jolting the balance. Hence when the balance is out of use, or when

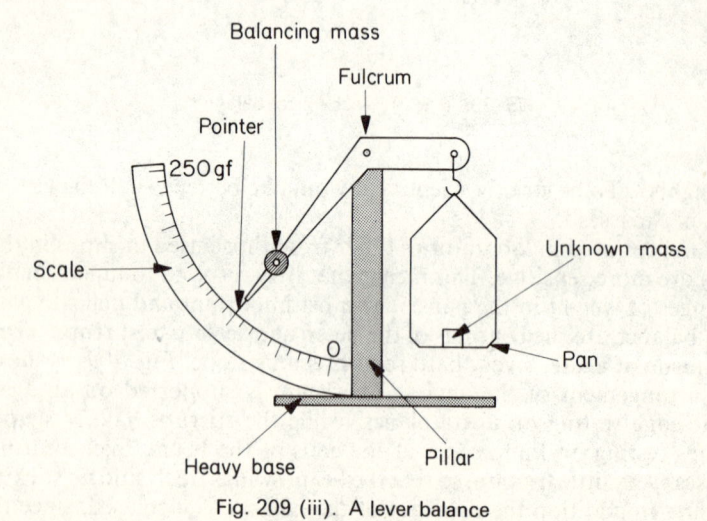

Fig. 209 (iii). A lever balance

MEASUREMENT OF LENGTH, VOLUME AND MASS · 221

weights are being transferred to or from the pans, the beam is brought to rest by a special handle or knob which lowers it on to supports and brings the knife-dges out of contact with their planes.

Fig. 209(i) shows the main parts common to most balances. Those in your own laboratory may differ from this by having either a rider or chain attachment for getting fractions of a gramme. The balancing screws shown in the diagram at the ends of the beam should not be adjusted without consulting your teacher. You will be shown how to use a balance and the precautions to observe before making measurements.

In brief, the object to be weighed is placed in the left-hand pan, and standard masses in the other. The beam is raised and, if necessary, one pan may be gently fanned with the hand to set it swinging. The standard masses are adjusted until the pointer swings equal numbers of divisions on either side of the zero. The masses in the two pans will then be equal.

Let us conclude by reminding you of some important rules.
1. Always adjust the plumbline by turning the levelling screws at the base of the balance before you start to measure.
2. Never touch the masses with your fingers. Use the tweezers.
3. Never touch the balance when the beam is swinging.
4. Never weigh anything wet or hot on the balance. Always dry the outside of the containing vessel thoroughly when liquids are weighed.

For many measurements in Physics a lever-arm balance is sufficiently accurate, and very much easier and quicker to use. Many chemistry laboratories now use an electric balance which adjusts the standard masses automatically and gives a reading of high accuracy.

The Spring Balance

Experiment shows that the extension of a spiral spring is proportional to the force applied to it, provided the force is not too large to strain the spring.

Now the weight of an object is the force on it due to gravity, or, in other words, the force with which the earth pulls it. The extension of a spring is therefore proportional to the weight of the body attached to it.

Calibration of a spring balance to measure weight. Fig. 210 illustrates a convenient form of the apparatus used for this experiment. A spiral spring is attached to a screw at the top of a piece of wood on which is stuck a strip of millimetre squared paper. The lower end of the spring carries a light scale-pan to which weights may be added. The extension of the spring for a given load is found by taking the difference between two readings of the bottom coil of the spring against the millimetre scale.

The apparatus is held vertically in a clamp and stand, and the reading of the bottom coil of the spring noted on the millimetre scale.

222 · ELEMENTARY PHYSICS

This will be the zero load reading. Weights are then added to the pan, increasing the load by, say 10 gf each time, and the corresponding scale readings recorded. A second set of readings should be taken as the pan is unloaded. The results are tabulated as shown below and the mean extensions calculated for the various loads.

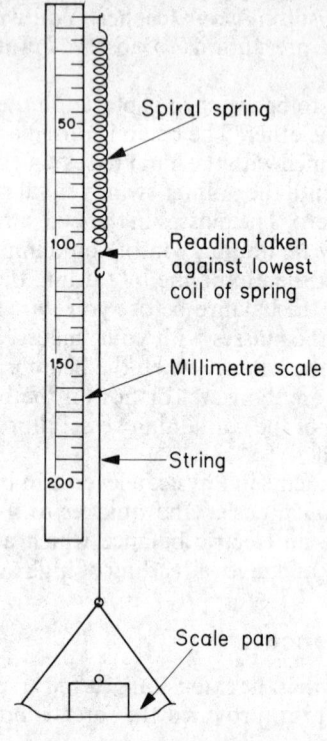

Fig. 210. Measuring the extension of a spring

A graph of extension against load is found to be a straight line passing through the origin showing that, for a spiral spring,

Extension is proportional to Load

or $$\frac{\text{Extension}}{\text{Load}} = \text{constant}.$$

Use of the spring and graph to find the weight of an object. Fig. 211 shows a typical graph obtained in the above experiment. Its practical use to measure weight may best be illustrated by the following example to find the weight of a piece of metal.

MEASUREMENT OF LENGTH, VOLUME AND MASS · 223

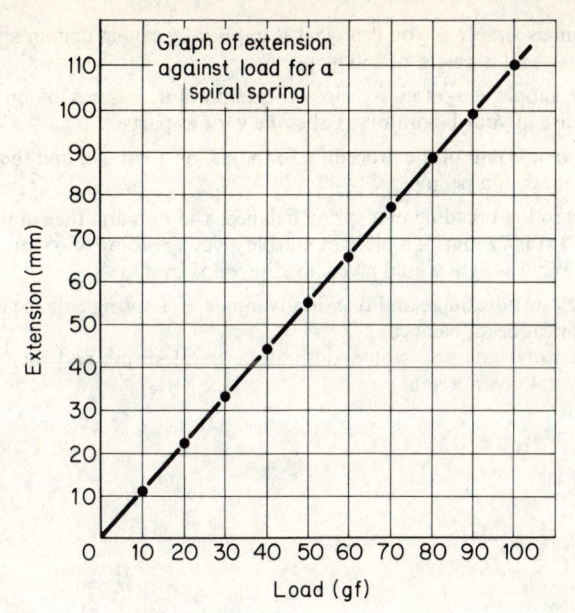

Fig. 211. Graph of extension and load

$$\text{Zero load reading of balance} = 72 \text{ mm}$$
$$\text{Reading with metal in pan} = 134 \text{ mm}$$

Therefore,
$$\text{Extension} = 62 \text{ mm}$$

From the graph, an extension of 62 mm corresponds to a load of 56·5 gf.

Hence,
$$\text{Weight of metal} = 56 \cdot 5 \text{ gf}.$$

EXERCISES

1. Explain why a wooden rule should usually be placed on its edge and not flat when measuring a distance on an object.

2. Draw a diagram of a scale and vernier which are giving a reading of (i) 134 mm (ii) 687 mm.

3. Name and describe the instrument you would choose to measure the diameter of a steel ball (about 50 mm) to a tenth part of a millimetre. Explain how you read the instrument.

4. How would you measure the diameter of a knitting needle or a piece of wire as accurately as possible? Explain the principle of the instrument used.

5. How would you measure out the following volumes of water into a beaker, (a) 25 cm^3, (b) 72 cm^3, (c) 13·4 cm^3, (d) 500 cm^3?
Give a simple sketch together with the name of the vessel used in each case.

6. Explain as simply as you can what is implied by saying that an apple has a mass of 250 g and a weight of 250 gf.

7. Draw simple diagrams to show the important features of one type of balance in use in your laboratory. Label the various parts.

8. Give an account of the procedure for adjusting a balance and then using it to find the mass of a penny.

9. The zero load reading of a spring balance is 45 mm and the reading with a load of 50·0 gf is 72 mm. If a piece of marble gives a reading of 65 mm calculate its weight. What weight would give a reading of 51 mm?

10. Give one advantage and one disadvantage of a spring balance compared with a chemical beam balance.

Describe fully how you would calibrate a spiral spring and then use it to measure an unknown weight.

CHAPTER TWENTY-TWO

Stationary Forces

Forces

When you hit a ball with a bat, a force is exerted which you hope will send the ball flying. On the other hand, a string supporting a picture exerts a force which should keep the picture quite still. These are two of the numerous examples of forces. A very common force is the force due to *gravity*; this is the force which pulls us to the ground if we are tackled in a rugger match and knocked off-balance. The force of gravity on an object is called the *weight* of the object, and forces,

Plate *36*. The Forth railway bridge: hundreds of triangular frames give the structure its strength

Types of Forces

In structural engineering and building, forces are encountered in girders or ropes such as those in cranes and suspension bridges. A simple force is that in a rope or string OB, when every force has a direction, as well as magnitude (size), and the direction of the force is always shown by an arrow in diagrams. Thus the weight W is shown acting vertically downwards in Fig. 212(i); the tension T prevents the weight from falling down and acts vertically upwards, as shown. In Fig. 212(ii), an object C is held still on a smooth inclined plane by a rope CD acting up the plane. The weight W is again shown acting vertically downward, and the tension P in the rope acts up the plane. In this case there is a force R on C due to the plane, and this is called the **reaction** of the plane. In Fig. 212(iii) part of a girder system rests on a support at A. The forces at A are the reaction R of the support, the tension Q in AC, and the thrust P in AB.

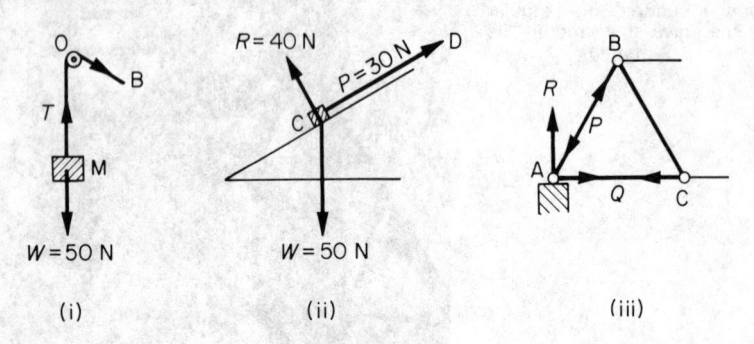

Fig. 212. Static forces

How Forces are Represented

The Forth bridge, the Tay road-bridge, the Severn bridge and others like them were constructed with the aid of many diagrams showing the size of the forces and the direction in which they acted. If a load has a weight Q of 50 N, it can be represented by a line 50 mm long on a scale of 1 N to 1 mm. As the weight always acts vertically downwards, a vertical line ab is drawn, and an arrow placed on it to show the force

---

* Actually it is 9·8 N, but 10 N is near enough for the present purpose.

STATIONARY FORCES · 227

direction (Fig. 213(i)). In Fig. 213(ii) the three forces Q, P and R are 50, 30 and 40 N respectively, and are represented by ab, bc and ca respectively. These are the forces W, P, R also shown in Fig. 212(ii).

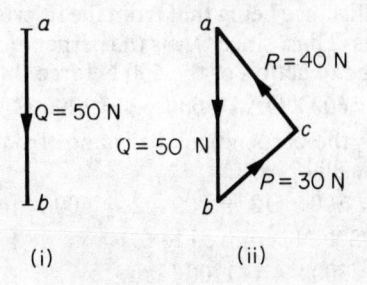

Fig. 213. Force diagrams

Turning Moments, or Torque

In this chapter we shall study particularly the *turning-effect* of forces. When you open a door, you are exerting a force which has a turning-effect. There are numerous examples of forces which have turning-effects because wheels of all descriptions, whether in lathes, cars or roller-skates, are turned by forces. Wheels usually rotate about their centre, and the turning-effect of the force about the centre is called the *torque* or *moment* of the force about that axis or point. The axis or point is also called the *fulcrum*. When a door is opened it turns about the hinges; the fulcrum is thus the line passing through the hinges.

How Moments are Calculated

If a person weighing 600 N sits at a point A 2 m from the rocking-point or fulcrum O, he can not balance a lighter person of 300 N at B, the same distance from O on the other side (Fig. 214). The torque

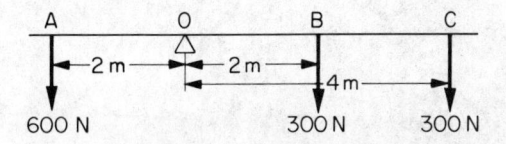

Fig. 214. Turning forces (torque, or moments)

of 600 N about O is thus greater than the torque of 300 N about O. If the lighter person moves further along the see-saw from B, however, he can counter-balance the heavier person at A. This occurs when he reaches C, where OC is 4 m. The moment or torque of a force about a point such as O thus depends on two factors: (1) the magnitude (size) of the force, (2) the distance of the force from the turning-point. The rule for calculating the moment or torque is as follows:

Torque = Force × Perpendicular distance

the perpendicular distance being that from the fulcrum to the line along which the force acts. Thus, since OA is the perpendicular distance from O to the vertical line of action of the 600 N force,

Torque about O = $600 \times OA = 600 \times 2 = 1200$ N m . . (1)

Again, since OB is the perpendicular distance from O to the vertical line of action of the 300 N at O,

Torque about O = $300 \times OB = 300 \times 2 = 600$ N m . . (2)

When the force of 300 N is moved to C,

Torque about O = $300 \times 4 = 1200$ N m. . . . (3)

Clockwise and Anticlockwise Moments

The 600 N force at A tends to turn the beam about O in an anticlockwise direction. The 300 N force at B tends to turn the beam about O in a clockwise direction. From (1) and (2), it follows that the anticlockwise moment is greater than the clockwise moment, and thus the beam will tilt about O in an anticlockwise direction. When the 300 N force is moved to C, it follows from (3) that the clockwise moment is now exactly equal to the anticlockwise moment, and thus the beam will now balance and remain horizontal.

Plate 37. Level-crossing barrier: the torque of the lifting arm is balanced by that of a heavy weight inside the wire cage

Experiment to Demonstrate Definition of Torque

An experiment to illustrate the importance of the perpendicular in the definition of "torque" is shown in Fig. 215. AC is a light ruler pivoted at its mid-point O. A string AB is attached at A to one end, and has a scale-pan with a weight Q in it at the other end passing over a pulley B. A weight P is placed on the other side of the pivot O, and is

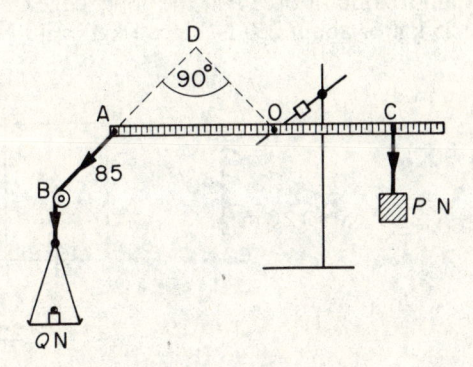

Fig. 215. Balancing torques

moved until the ruler is balanced horizontally. The distance OC is then measured. The force in the string AB is Q, and the *perpendicular distance* OD from the pivot O to the direction of the force is measured with the aid of two rulers, one of which is placed along AB and the other along OD.

In one experiment, the following measurements were taken:
Q (and scale-pan weight), 85 N; P, 100 N; OD, 385 mm; OC, 326 mm.

$$\therefore Q \times OD = 85 \times 385 = 32700 \text{ N mm (approx.)} = 32 \cdot 7 \text{ N m}$$
$$\text{and} \quad P \times OC = 100 \times 326 = 32600 \text{ N mm} \quad\quad = 32 \cdot 6 \text{ N m}$$

Thus, to a good approximation, the moment of Q about O = the moment of P about O when the ruler is balanced.

Other Examples of Torque

If a bicycle is ridden properly, the foot on the pedal P will always exert a force perpendicular to the crank-shaft OP (Fig. 216(i)). Suppose the force is 60 N and the distance from P to the axle O is 0·25 m. Then, since OP is perpendicular to the direction of the force,

$$\text{Torque about O} = 60 \times 0 \cdot 25 = 15 \text{ N m}$$

If the pedal is turned so that the force is applied vertically downwards, the perpendicular distance from O to the direction of the force is now

shorter than OP, as shown in Fig. 216 (ii). Suppose it is 0·20 m. Then
$$\text{Torque about O} = 60 \times 0{\cdot}20 = 12 \text{ N m}$$
The moment about O is thus less than before, and it can easily be seen that the greatest moment about O is obtained when the force is exerted perpendicularly to the crank, as in Fig. 216 (i).

In Fig. 216 (iii) a heavy case ABCD 2·5 m tall and of 25 kg mass is being tilted by a horizontal Force P at the upper edge C. The weight at M is therefore 25 kgf or about 250 N, since 1 kgf $\simeq$ 10 N. The force at

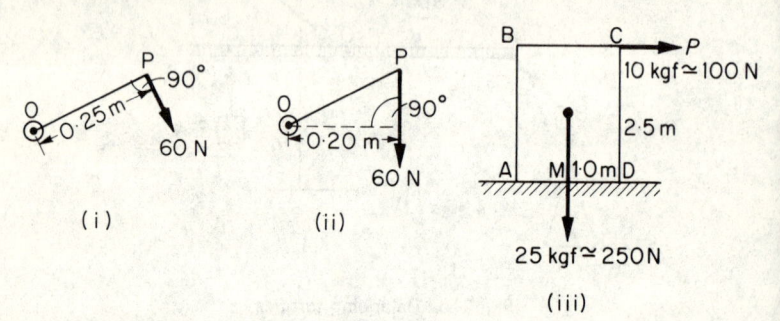

Fig. 216. Examples of torque

P will be 10 kgf or about 100 N. If DM = 1·0 m, then the torque of 250 N about the lower edge D
$$= 250 \times \text{MD} = 250 \times 1 = 250 \text{ N m}$$
The moment of the force P about D
$$= 100 \times 2{\cdot}5 = 250 \text{ N m}$$

One torque therefore balances the other and the case will turn freely about D.

Principles of Levers

A "lever" is a machine in which a rigid rod or body moves about a pivot or fulcrum. It is generally used to overcome a large weight or resistance by applying only a small effort. Examples of levers include crowbar, scissors, wheelbarrow, and bottle-openers as we shall see.

To cut string directly requires a considerable force. When scissors are used to cut string, however, a force P is applied at B, and the string is cut at A as the arms of the scissors rock about the hinge O (Fig. 217 (i)). Suppose OA = 25 mm, OB is 75 mm and the force to be overcome at A is 30 N. The moment of P about O = $P \times \text{OB} = P \times 75$; the moment of the 30 N force about O = $30 \times 25 = 750$. Thus when the scissors are used,
$$P \times 75 = 750 \text{ or } P = 10 \text{ N}$$

Plate *38*. The force applied by the signalman to these levers produces a torque which can apply a larger force to operate distant points and signals

A 30 N resistance is thus overcome by using a 10 N force. We say that the *mechanical advantage* of the scissors in this case is 30 N/10 N or 3. The mechanical addvantage can be increased by placing the string nearer the hinge O.

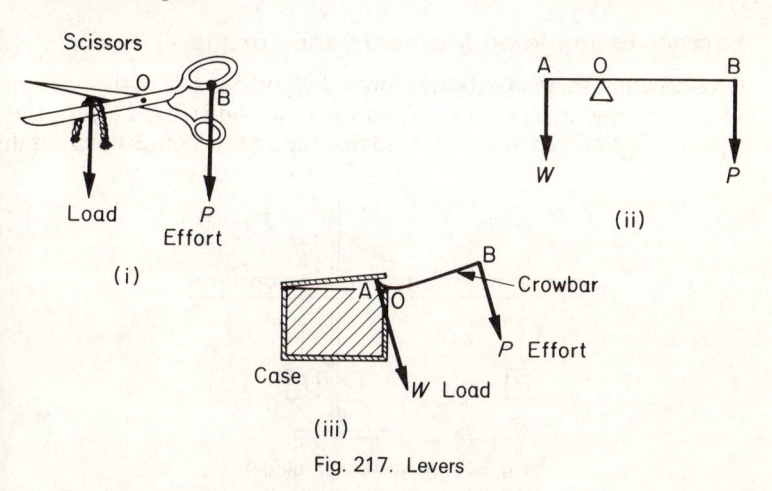

Fig. 217. Levers

232 · ELEMENTARY PHYSICS

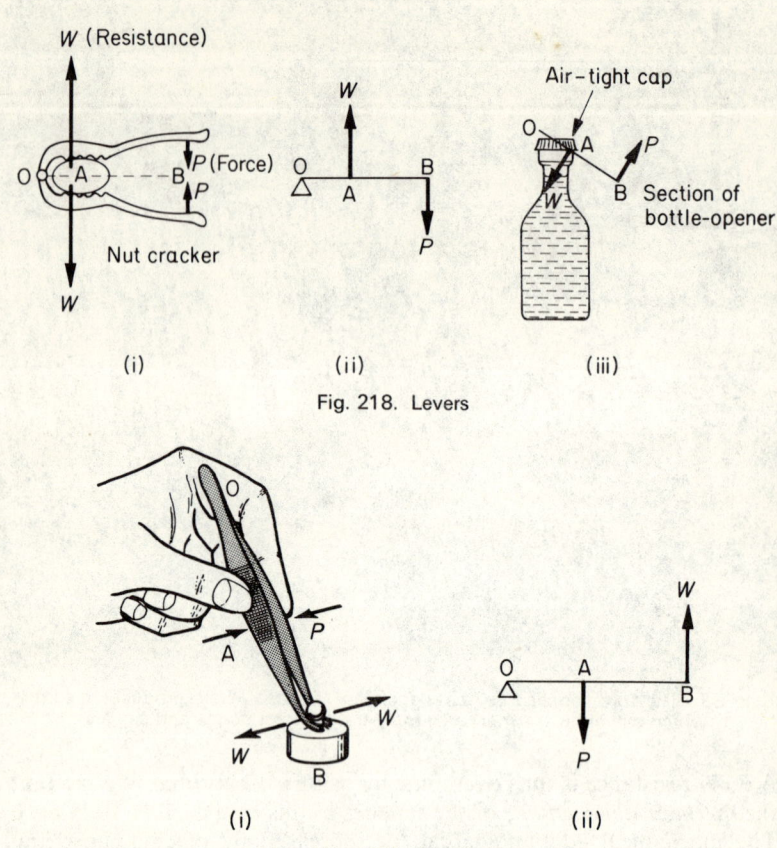

Fig. 218. Levers

Fig. 219. Levers

Further Example on Moments and Torque

On occasions, there may be two forces P, Q on one side of the fulcrum O of a lever, and a single force R on the other side (Fig. 220). In this case, when R is moved to a point C so that the lever becomes horizontal,

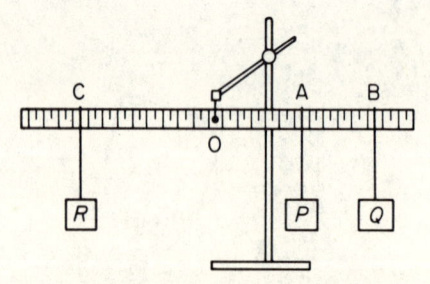

Fig. 220. Moments (or torque)

the turning moment of R about O is equal to the sum of the clockwise turning moments of P and Q about O. Thus

$$R \times OC = P \times OA + Q \times OB.$$

As an illustration, suppose $P = 50$ N, $Q = 100$ N, $R = 120$ N, $OC = 400$ mm, $OB = 350$ mm. Then the length OA is given by

$$120 \times 400 = 50 \times OA + 100 \times 350$$
$$\therefore 48\,000 = 50 \times OA + 35\,000$$
$$\therefore 13\,000 = 50 \times OA, \text{ or } OA = 260 \text{ mm}$$

Equilibrium of Parallel Forces

When traffic passes over a bridge, the weights of the various vehicles act vertically downwards. The forces R, S at the supports M, N of the bridge act vertically upwards, therefore, to counter-balance the effect of the weights of the vehicles on the bridge (Fig. 221). Suppose three

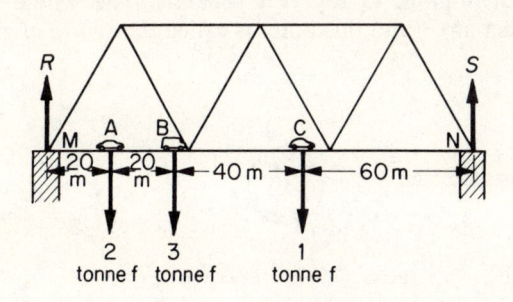

Fig. 221. Parallel forces

vehicles, of masses 2, 3 and 1 tonne respectively, are situated at an instant at A, B, C, where MA is 20 m, AB is 20 m, BC is 40 m and CN is 60 m. The weights and the forces R, S are parallel forces, and as the total upward force must balance the total downward force, then

$R + S = 2 + 3 + 1 = 6$ tonne f, or about 60 kN   (1 tonne = 1000 kg)

We cannot yet work out R or S. However, another relation between the forces can be found by considering moments. Since the bridge is in equilibrium, *the total clockwise moments of the forces about any point must balance the total anticlockwise moments.* We can take moments about any point we choose. If we take moments about N, the force S will have zero moment since N is a point on S, and we are then left with an equation in which only the force R appears. Thus

Total clockwise moment
about N $= R \times MN = R \times 140$

Total anticlockwise moment
about N
$$= 2 \times AN + 3 \times BN + 1 \times CN$$
$$= 2 \times 120 + 3 \times 100 + 1 \times 60 = 600$$

$$\therefore R \times 140 = 600, \text{ or } R = \frac{600}{140} = 4\tfrac{2}{7} \text{ tonne f}$$

But $R + S = 6$
$$\therefore S = 6 - R = 6 - 4\tfrac{2}{7} = 1\tfrac{5}{7} \text{ tonne f}$$

Thus the forces at the supports, called the *reactions,* are $4\tfrac{2}{7}$ and $1\tfrac{5}{7}$ tonne f respectively; the total reaction being 6 tonne f, which is equal to the total downward force.

Position of Centre of Gravity

If we try and balance a ruler on the edge of a knife, we usually find it balances at the middle. With trial and error, the ruler can be balanced on a compass-point, and in this case the whole weight of the ruler is supported at a point G say (Fig. 222(i)). The whole weight thus appears to act at G, and this point is called the *centre of gravity* of the ruler.

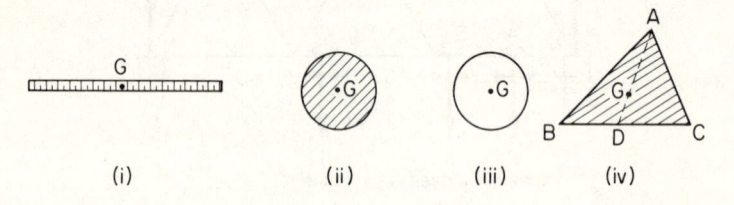

Fig. 222. Centres of gravity

The centre of gravity of a circular *disc* is at its centre Fig. 222(ii)). The centre of gravity of a *ring* is at its centre (Fig. 222(iii)). The centre of gravity of a triangular sheet (known as a triangular "lamina") is the intersection of the medians, and this is two-thirds of the distance along any median measured from the corresponding point of the triangle. The median is the line joining one point of a triangle to the mid-point of the opposite side; thus if D is the mid-point of BC, then $AG = \tfrac{2}{3} AD$ (Fig. 222(iv)).

Locating Centre of Gravity

The centre of gravity of an irregular sheet of cardboard ABCD or other material can be located by making a hole H in it, and suspending it at H by a pin P (Fig. 223). The hole is made a little wider than the pin so that the sheet can swing freely. A *plumb-line,* a length of thread or string with a weight W at one end, is now attached to P, and the line of the thread, which is vertical, is marked on ABCD.

Since the centre of gravity G is somewhere on the vertical line below H, the experiment is repeated by suspending ABCD from a hole K at another place, and the new vertical line KL is drawn. G is then the point of intersection of the two lines drawn, as shown.

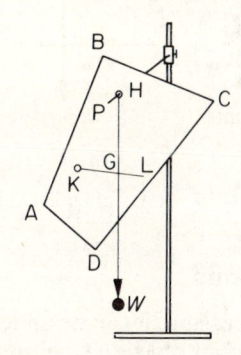

Fig. 223. Locating the centre of gravity

Stable, Unstable, Neutral Equilibrium

If we are not careful when walking on slippery ground, the vertical line through our centre of gravity may fall outside the feet. Our weight can then suddenly pull us over, owing to the moment exerted about the feet, which is anticlockwise in Fig. 224. In this case we are said to be "unstable".

An object which moves further away from its position when displaced is said to be in *unstable equilibrium*. Conversely, an object which returns to its original position when displaced, such as a punch-ball on a stand, is said to be in *stable equilibrium*. An object which remains in its displaced position, such as a ball rolled to another position on a horizontal plane, is said to be in *neutral equilibrium*.

A bunsen burner B can be used to illustrate the three types of equilibrium mentioned. If it is placed with its base on the table in the usual way, and the base then tilted about one side O, the burner will return to its original position when released (Fig. 225(i)). This is stable equilibrium. The weight, acting through the centre of gravity G, has an anticlockwise (restoring) moment about O. On the other hand, suppose the burner is turned upside down, as shown in Fig. 225(ii). If the burner is now tilted slightly and released, it topples over. The weight through G now has a clockwise moment about X, which causes the burner to move further away from its original position. This is unstable equilibrium. If the

Fig. 224. Unstable equilibrium

burner is turned on one side, so that the base is Y (Fig. 225(iii)), it remains in its new position when pushed. The burner is now in neutral equilibrium.

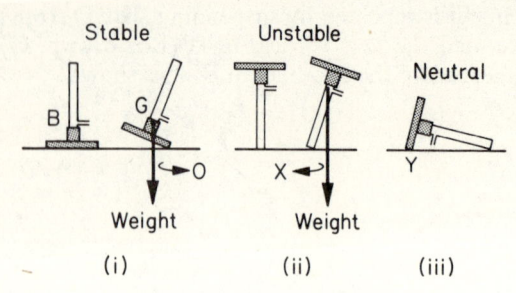

Fig. 225. States of equilibrium

Practical Applications

From our previous discussion, it can be understood that the position of the centre of gravity of an object has an important influence on its stability. *The lower the centre of gravity, the more likely is stable equilibrium.* On this account racing-cars are built low, and lamp-stands have heavy bases to bring down their centres of gravity. Tests have

Plate *39*. Tilt test on a double-deck bus: with the upper seats filled with sandbags to represent passengers, the centre of gravity of the vehicle must be low enough for it to tilt through 30° angle before falling over

Plate *40*. The Triumph TR6 is designed to have a low centre of gravity to give stability when cornering at high speed

shown that the centre of gravity of a bus with standing passengers on it is liable to be dangerously high, and with such a load the vehicle may overturn on rounding corners. By regulation, therefore, standing passengers are not allowed on the tops of buses.

Summary

1. *Forces* are measured in newton (N) or sometimes in kgf. 1 kgf is the force of gravity on 1 kg mass, and is equal to about 10 N.

2. A *force is represented* in drawings by a straight line with an arrow on it; this is drawn in the direction along which the force acts, and the length of the line must represent to scale the magnitude of the force.

3. The *torque* or *moment* of a force is the turning-effect of the force, and is measured by

Force × *Perpendicular distance* from fulcrum to the force

4. When a lever is in equilibrium, the total clockwise moment about the fulcrum is equal to the total anticlockwise moment.

5. The *centre of gravity* of an object is the point through which the whole weight appears to act.

6. An object is in *stable* equilibrium if it returns to its original position when slightly displaced; it is in *unstable* equilibrium if it moves further away, and in *neutral* equilibrium if it remains in its displaced position. Generally, an object will tend to be in stable equilibrium if its centre of gravity is low, and in unstable equilibrium if its centre of gravity is high.

EXERCISES

1. The handle of a door is pulled with a force of 4 N acting perpendicularly to the door. If the handle is 1·0 m from the line joining the hinges, calculate the moment exerted. When is a smaller moment exerted, although the force may again be 4 N?

2. A light ruler AB (negligible mass) is suspended at its mid-point O. A mass of 40 g is tied to a point 35 cm to the left of O, and a mass of 65 g is tied to a point 18 cm to the right of O. The ruler is held horizontally. Calculate the moment of each force about O and state if it is clockwise or anticlockwise.

3. A uniform light rod AB, 1·0 m long, is suspended at its centre O. A mass of 120 g is placed at A.
   (i) At what distance from O must a mass of 200 g be placed for perfect balance?
   (ii) What mass will balance the rod if it is placed 20 cm from O?

4. The claws of a hammer of length 240 mm are used as a lever to pull up a nail whose perpendicular distance from the fulcrum is 20 mm. If the resistance of the nail is 50 N, what force must be applied to the end of the hammer, and perpendicular to it, just to raise the nail?

5. In Fig. 226 (i) ABC is a light rod pivoted at O, and P, Q, R are weights at A, B, C which keep it balanced.
   (i) If OA = 1·8 m, OB = 0·6 m, OC = 2·0 m, find R when P = 50 N, Q = 20 N.
   (ii) If OA = 30 mm, OC = 24 mm, calculate OB when P = 30 N, Q = 30 N, R = 60 N.
   (iii) If AB = 6 cm, BO = 4 cm, BC = 12 cm, find P when Q = 80 N, R = 100 N.

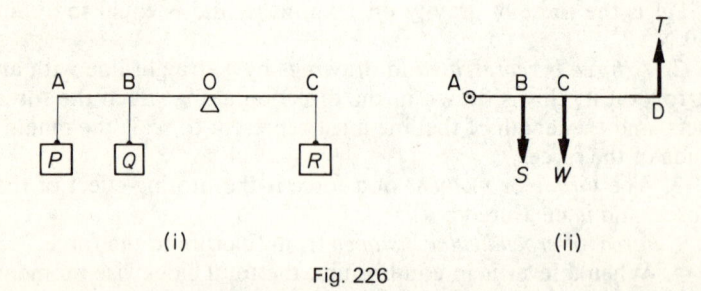

Fig. 226

6. In Fig. 226 (ii) ABCD is a heavy rod whose weight W acts at C. T is the force required just to tilt the beam about A when a load S is placed at B.
   (i) If AB = 3 m, BC = 4 m, CD = 5 m, find T when S = 30 N, W = 20 N.
   (ii) If AB = 80 cm, BC = 60 cm, CD = 100 cm, find S when T = 500 N, W = 400 N.
   (iii) If AB = 5 m, BC = 6 m, find CD when T = 6 N, S = 16 N, W = 8 N.

7. Describe and explain how (i) a pair of scissors, (ii) a wheelbarrow act on the lever principle. Draw diagrams, and show, by giving estimated numbers to the distances and forces concerned, how the effort is calculated.

9. What is the *centre of gravity* of an object? Draw sketches showing the positions of the centre of gravity of (i) a circular disc, (ii) a rectangular sheet of metal, (iii) a rod of wood of the same width and thickness throughout, (iv) a ring of metal.

Describe fully an experiment to find the centre of gravity of a sheet of metal of an irregular shape.

10. Draw a diagram of a cone or funnel in *stable, unstable,* and *neutral* equilibrium. What do you understand by these three types of equilibrium?

11. A bunsen burner is placed (*a*) inverted, (*b*) the right way up, *jc*) on its side, with the curved end of the base resting on the table. In each case the burner is tilted slightly. Describe and explain what happens, and state which type of equilibrium each case represents.

12. Draw labelled diagrams to illustrate three classes of levers. Give one example of each, and work out the *mechanical advantage* in each case by taking estimated numerical values for distances and forces.

Assume that the force of gravity on 1 kg mass is 10 N.

CHAPTER TWENTY-THREE

Moving Forces: Work, Energy, Power

Work and Energy

In everyday conversation the word "work" is used to refer to almost any kind of physical and mental activity, but in the sciences it has one meaning only. An engine pulling a train is said to do work; the engine exerts a force on the train, and the force moves through a distance. For work to be done, therefore, two things are necessary. We must have a force and it must produce motion. Atlas, the Greek god who spent his time supporting the world on his shoulders, doubtless grew very tired on account of his labours, but technically speaking he did no work at all since he merely exerted an upward force on the world and did not move it.

Work is thus said to be done when the point of application of a force moves, and is measured by the product of the force and the distance moved in the direction of the force. We may therefore write

Plate *41*. British Rail class 86 electric locomotive. One hundred of these locomotives were built for the lines from Liverpool and Manchester to London. Electric energy is taken from the overhead cable at 25 kV a.c. and a transformer and rectifier converts this to a lower voltage for driving the d.c. traction motors, of which there are four—one to each pair of wheels. The power available is 2600 kW ($\frac{3}{4}$ kW = 1 hp); the locomotive can pull with a force of 260 kN, its mass is 81 000 kg (81 tonne), and it is designed to work at up to 160 km/h (100 mph).

MOVING FORCES: WORK, ENERGY, POWER · 241

Energy expended = Work = Force × Distance moved
= Force × Displacement

Thus an engine exerting a pull of 4000 N and moving through a distance of 20 m does work equal to 4000 × 20 or 80 000 N m.

Energy and its Sources

Anything which is able to do work, as we have defined it above, is said to possess *energy*, so we define energy as the capacity to perform work.

The world we live in abounds in energy in a variety of different forms. Perhaps the most important of these is chemical energy. It is generally admitted that man's utilisation of the latent chemical energy in coal or oil, released in the form of heat to drive steam turbines or internal combustion engines, has had more influence on the development of modern civilisation than any other factor.

Another important form of energy is electrical energy. Of recent years, large hydro-electric power installations have been built not only in this country, but all over the world. "Hydro-electric" means the production of electricity by dynamos driven by water turbines. The rapid flow of water required for this purpose comes from the vast reservoirs formed by building dams across valleys.

Windmills which convert the energy of wind into mechnical energy have long been in use for working water pumps as well as for milling grain or sawing timber. In some parts of the world where the sun shines uninterruptedly for long periods, large concave mirrors have been set up to collect energy directly from the sun by focusing its rays on to special steam boilers which provide power for running small dynamos.

At present we are in an age in which *nuclear energy*, resulting from the splitting or *fission* of the nuclei of certain atoms, as well as from the *fusion* of nuclei, is bringing about a further revolution in our material way of living.

Mechanical Energy

In mechanics, energy is measured in two ways; as kinetic energy or energy of motion, and potential energy or energy of position.

An example of the former is the energy of a moving projectile such as a bullet or of a moving hammer head. These are able to do work by overcoming forces when they strike an object. A heavy flywheel stores energy in the form of motion and so keeps an engine running smoothly in between the working strokes of its pistons. Heat also is a form of kinetic energy since the heat of a body consists solely of the vibration of the molecules of which it is composed. In this sense the difference between a cold soldering iron and a hot one is that the molecules of the latter are in a state of more violent agitation.

In general, potential energy is the name given to the energy stored in bodies when they are raised above the earth's surface. But in addition, we find it convenient also to describe as potential the energy of such things as a wound clock-spring or a cylinder of compressed air. A practical example which comes readily to mind is the energy stored in the weights of a grandfather clock. When the weights are raised, work is done as energy is expended against the gravitational force of attraction of the earth on them. This energy becomes stored in the weights in the form of potential energy, and is subsequently converted into kinetic energy in the moving parts of the clock as the weights descend.

At this stage we may well ask what has become of the original potential energy of the weights when the clock has completely run down. The answer is that it has all become converted into heat energy, largely as the result of work done against friction between the wheel spindles and their bearings. The clock therefore becomes slightly warmer, and ultimately gives up any excess heat to the atmosphere.

The Conservation of Energy and Mass

Einstein's work on the theory of relativity which he put forward early in the present century has altered our ideas regarding mass and energy as being separate and distinct from one another. In this book we cannot even begin to explain the meaning of relativity. Suffice it to say that Einstein has simplified our picture of the universe by showing that mass and energy can be converted from one to the other. This view has been supported by a number of experiments. It has been demonstrated, for example, that atoms radiating energy are losing mass. It has been calculated that the complete conversion of 1 gramme of matter into energy would provide as much energy as that obtained by burning about 3000 tonne of coal!

Until this theory was put forward, two fundamental laws were accepted by physicists. Firstly the Law of Conservation of Matter, which states that the total quantity of matter in the universe is fixed and cannot be increased or decreased by human agency. Secondly the Law of Conservation of Energy, which affirms that the total quantity of energy in the universe is likewise constant and can be neither created nor destroyed. Nowadays, in the light of relativity theory, these two laws have become fused into one, and we accept the principle that the sum total of mass plus energy in the universe is fixed and unalterable.

Transformation of Energy from One Kind to Another

It is interesting to study in reverse the series of energy transformations which lead to the release of luminous energy by pressing an electric switch.

MOVING FORCES: WORK, ENERGY, POWER

The light is given out from a thin incandescent tungsten filament inside a glass bulb. The thermal energy required to raise the temperature of the tungsten wire is derived from the energy expended when the electric current moves against the resistance offered to its passage through the wire.

The electric current itself is generated by a dynamo run by a steam turbine. The turbine in turn is driven by expanding high-pressure steam from a coal-fired boiler.

Now coal consists mainly of carbon and is formed from the remains of giant fern forests which flourished millions of years ago. Changes in the earth's crust led to these forests becoming submerged beneath layers of sediment and subjected to pressure. The plants from which the coal is formed derived their growth from the action of the sunlight in which they were bathed.

The reader may for himself trace the energy changes back to the sun in the case where dynamos are run by water power.

It is thus striking to reflect that the light and power from electricity and gas, which are daily used in home and industry, come from energy poured out by the sun millions of years ago and, so to speak, bottled up in coal and oil.

In the examples of energy transformation we have considered above, the last link in the energy chain is the production of heat. This is found to be true in all cases. Even the light from the lamp finally turns back into heat when it is absorbed by bodies on which it falls. This fact is referred to as the "degradation" of energy into heat and has led physicists to suppose that the end of life, as we know it, will come when all the energy in the universe is uniformly distributed as heat at the same temperature.

Measurement of Work and Energy

Earlier in this chapter it was pointed out that the potential energy of a body raised above the earth's surface is equal to the work done against its weight in lifting it. It is convenient to use as a unit the energy expended in moving a force of 1 newton through a distance of 1 metre. This unit of energy is called the joule (J). Since the gravitational force on 1 kg mass is approximately 10 N (actually 9·8 N), the energy expended in lifting a 1 kg mass vertically through 1 m is about 10 joule (actually 9·8 J).

Power

Machines may be classified by the speed with which they do work; thus there are motor-car engines of small "power", as they are rated, or large power. Power is defined as *the rate of doing work*, which is the same as *energy transferred per second*. Thus a pump moving 50 kg

Plate *42*. Stephenson's "Rocket" locomotive, built for the Liverpool and Manchester Railway in 1829. Its mass was 4500 kg and it could pull a train on level track at 24 km/h (15 mph). As a result of the Rocket's success in trials at Liverpool in October 1829, locomotive designs were based on Stephenson's system for the following hundred years and more

mass of water through a vertical height of 8 m in 5 seconds transfers 500 N (approx.) through 8 m = 4000 J in 5 s. That is 800 J in 1 s, or a power of 800 joule per second. A power of 1 joule per second is called 1 watt. Hence the power calculated above is 800 J/s or 800 W.

The horsepower was first measured by James Watt, who, during the eighteenth century, made numerous improvements to steam pumping machinery. Before the introduction of steam, pumps for removing water from mines were worked by horses. James Watt wished to measure the power of the new engines in terms of the power of a horse. He accordingly harnessed a horse to a rope passing over a pulley at the top of a deep mineshaft, and found the time taken to raise a known load through the vertical height of the shaft. From this he defined 1 horsepower, which is equal to about 750 watt or 0·75 kilowatt.

Summary

1. *Work* is said to be done when a force moves, and is measured by the product of the force and the distance moved in the direction of the force.

2. Work is the energy transferred in any process.

MOVING FORCES: WORK, ENERGY, POWER · 245

3. *Mechanical energy* is measured as:
   (a) *kinetic energy* or energy of motion, or
   (b) *potential energy* or energy of position.
4. The *Law of Conservation of Energy* states that the sum total of energy of all forms in the universe is fixed and cannot be increased or decreased.
5. The unit of energy is the joule. It is the energy transferred when a force of 1 newton moves through a distance of 1 metre in any direction.
6. *Power* is the rate of energy transfer.
7. The unit of power is the watt. 1000 W = 1 kW. 1 horsepower is approximately equal to 750 watt.

EXERCISES

1. What is meant by *work*? How is it measured? Define the joule.
2. Define (a) *power*, (b) *watt*.
3. State the Law of Conservation of Energy. Give an example of the application of the law.
4. Find the work done in moving (a) 12 N through 15 m, (b) 2 N through 20 m, (c) 2 tonne f through 5 m.
5. A grandfather clock has two weights each 10 kg mass, which are raised once a week through a height of 1·5 m. Neglecting work done against friction, find approximately the total work done annually in winding the clock.
6. A crane lifts a load of 2 tonne f through 20 m in 40 seconds. Find (a) the total work done, (b) the work done per second, (c) the power output of the crane.
7. A boy whose mass is 40 kg runs up a flight of 30 steps each 150 mm high in 6 seconds. Find approximately (a) the total work done in raising his own weight, (b) the useful average power he develops.
8. Explain the meaning of (a) kinetic and (b) potential energy. Give two examples of each.
9. A stone of 15 kg mass is raised to a height of 20 m above the ground. What is its potential energy?
The stone is afterwards allowed to fall freely. Find its potential and kinetic energies (a) when halfway to the ground, (b) at the instant of striking the ground.
10. An electric pump having a useful power output of $\frac{2}{3}$ h.p. is used to pump water from a well into a raised tank of capacity 2·5 m^3*. If the discharge outlet from the pump is 20 m above the surface of the water in the well, find the time taken to fill the tank.
(1 m^3 of water has mass 1 tonne = 1000 kg)

*about 550 gallons, since 1 gallon = 4·5 litre, and 1 m^3 = 1000 l.

CHAPTER TWENTY-FOUR

Thermal Energy Measurement

The previous chapter showed how energy, measured in joule, is expended when a force (measured in newton) moves some object through some distance (measured in metre) from its former position. This may be summarized as:

energy transferred (J) = force (N) × displacement (m).

It was also shown that power (measured in watt) is equal to the energy transferred per second, or:

power (W) = energy transferred (J)/time taken (s).

The power of an electric heater is usually marked on the name-plate; it might be, for example, 1 kilowatt or 2 kilowatt—that is, 1000 watt or 2000 watt. Suppose it is 1000 watt (1 kW), then we can say that it

Plate *43*. Joule calorimeter showing the outer jacket, heater, and stirrer

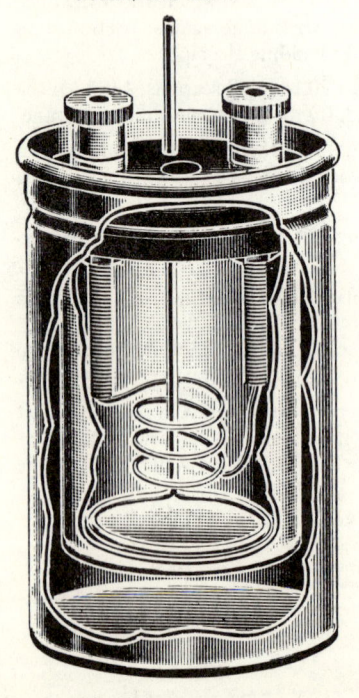

Plate *44*. A joule meter, for use on 12 volt A.C., records energy directly

will transfer energy at the rate of 1000 joule every second from electrical energy in the wire to thermal energy in the room. What matters now is, what effect on temperature does all this thermal energy have?

This chapter is concerned with the way in which the temperature of a material depends on the energy it receives.

Calorimeters; Prevention of Thermal Losses

In simple thermal experiments, it is usual to transfer the energy to some water contained in a small highly polished copper can, called a *calorimeter,* and to measure the rise in temperature of the water with a thermometer. There is always the difficulty in experiments of this kind that, if we are not careful, some energy will escape before we have had time to measure it.

In earlier chapters we discussed the various processes by which a body can lose thermal energy. Radiation losses from the calorimeter are reduced to a minimum by having it highly polished. Secondly, it is always suspended inside a larger can or jacket to protect it from draughts and to prevent the setting up of cold air convection currents along its sides. The method of suspending the calorimeter varies. It may be supported by hooks or else stood on a poor conductor such as a flat cork. In either case the heat lost by conduction will be very small (see Fig. 227). Finally, it is desirable to have a cover over the calorimeter to prevent losses both of heat and liquid by evaporation.

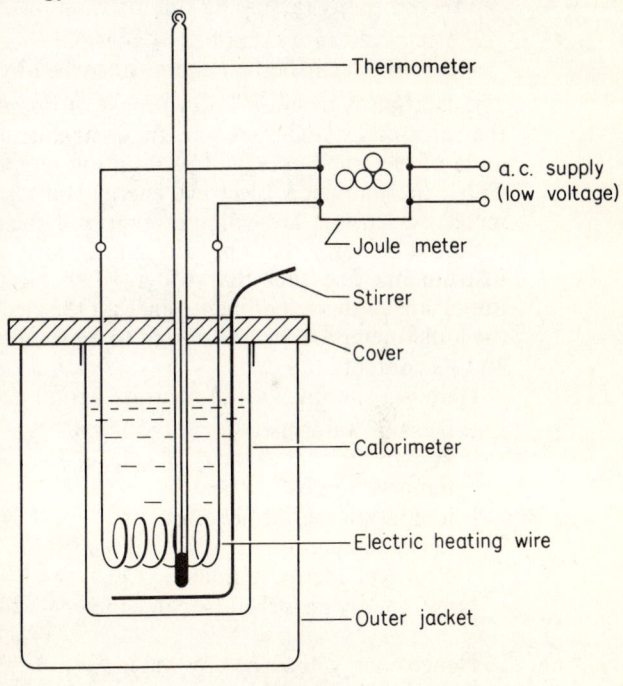

Fig. 227. A joule calorimeter as set up for measurements

The calorimeter itself is made of copper, which is a very good conductor. This ensures that the calorimeter and its contents will attain a uniform steady temperature with the least possible delay after a hot body has been placed in it.

Thermal Capacity

When we speak of the capacity of a bottle we mean the volume of liquid which it can hold when full. In like manner we refer to the *thermal capacity* of a particular body. This, of course, does not mean the total quantity of heat energy it can hold since we cannot fill a body with heat in the same sense that we can fill a bottle with water. We define the thermal capacity of a body as *the quantity of thermal energy required to raise its temperature by* 1 *kelvin* (K).

In thermal experiments the calorimeter itself takes up heat energy, so it is important to be able to find its thermal capacity, if this is not already known.

The joule-calorimeter illustrated in Fig. 227 can be used to find how the temperature of a liquid depends on the energy supplied to it. In such an instrument the energy absorbed by the metal calorimeter vessel can be allowed for because its thermal capacity is already known. We can therefore say (assuming that thermal losses are negligible) that:

electrical energy supplied = thermal energy absorbed by the calorimeter + thermal energy absorbed by the liquid.

The method is to put a known mass of liquid, water for example, in the calorimeter and pass into the instrument a measured number of joule of electrical energy. The resulting temperature rise is measured with a thermometer. Electrical energy is measured directly on a joule-meter, which is a low-voltage version of the domestic energy meter; it should be noted that only alternating current must be used with this instrument. The fact that water is an electrical conductor is not important in this experiment, since all the electric energy measured by the joule-meter will be transferred to thermal energy in the calorimeter and its contents.

Here is a specimen set of measurements:

mass of water used = 180 g
known thermal capacity of calorimeter = 240 J per K
temperature before heating = 15° C
temperature after heating = 20° C
hence temperature rise = 5° C
electrical energy supplied = 5000 J

Now, energy absorbed by calorimeter = 240 joule for 1 K rise,
= 1200 joule for 5 K rise.
Hence energy absorbed by water = 5000 − 1200 J
= 3800 joule for 5 K rise.
Therefore thermal capacity of 180 g of water = 3800/5
= 760 J per K.

Specific Heat Capacity

If we take *equal masses* of water and oil and warm them in separate beakers by the same burner it is found that the oil temperature may rise by 10 kelvin in 3 minutes but the water may only rise by 5 kelvin. Since the rate of supply of heat is the same in the two cases, it is clear that oil has a smaller thermal capacity than an equal mass of water. Similarly, experiment shows that about 0·4 joule raises the temperature of 1 gramme of copper by 1 kelvin, that about 1 joule raises the temperature of 1 gramme of aluminium by 1 kelvin, and that about 2 joule raises the temperature of 1 gramme of aniline by 1 kelvin. We say that different substances have different *specific heat capacities*, and we define the specific heat capacity of a substance as *the quantity of heat energy required to raise the temperature of* 1 *gramme of it by* 1 *kelvin*.

From the figures given above, it follows that the specific heat capacities of copper, aluminium and aniline are respectively 0·4, 1, and 2 joule per gramme kelvin. The specific heat capacity of water is easily found from the above measurements as follows.

Thermal capacity of 180 g of water = 760 joule per kelvin, hence energy to raise the temperature of 1 g of water by 1 K is 760/180 J = 4·2 J approximately.

That is, the specific heat capacity of water is approximately 4·2 joule per gramme kelvin. This is usually stated in the form: 4·2 J/g K or as 4200 J/kg K (approximately).

We now have two important relations for thermal energy:
1. **Thermal capacity = mass × specific heat capacity.**
2. **Thermal energy transfer = mass × specific heat capacity × temperature difference.**

An Experiment to Find the Thermal Capacity of a Calorimeter

A copper calorimeter together with a stirrer made of copper wire is first weighed empty and then when about half-full of cold water. Meanwhile, some water in a beaker is heated to about 40° C. A thermometer is placed in the calorimeter and allowed to remain until it gives a steady reading for the temperature of the cold water. The calorimeter should be placed where it will not receive heat by radiation from the bunsen burner. The thermometer is then transferred to the warm water in the beaker and the temperature carefully read to a tenth of a degree. Warm water at this known temperature is then immediately poured into the calorimeter until it is nearly full. The mixture is stirred to ensure thorough mixing and the final steady temperature is recorded. Lastly the calorimeter and its contents are weighed.

The following is a typical set of results from this experiment.

Weighings.
Calorimeter and stirrer = 55 g
Calorimeter, stirrer and cold water = 121 g
Calorimeter, stirrer and mixture = 189 g

Temperatures.
  Cold water   = 13·7° C
  Warm water   = 40·7° C
  Mixture   = 26·9° C

Calculations.
  Mass of cold water = 66 g
  Mass of warm water = 68 g
  Fall in temperature of warm water = 40·7 − 26·9 = 13·8 K
  Rise in temperature of cold water,
    calorimeter and stirrer = 26·9 − 13·7 = 13·2 K
  Energy transfer =
    mass × specific heat capacity × temperature difference
Hence, energy given up by warm water = 68 × 4·2 × 13·8 = 3948 J
   energy received by cold water = 66 × 4·2 × 13·2 = 3654 J

Plate *45*. Gas burners in use to heat a steel tyre before fitting to a wheel centre. The tyre is then held in place by the force of its thermal contraction

The calorimeter and stirrer receive the difference between the heat energy given up by the warm water and the heat energy received by the cold water, i.e. $3948 - 3654 = 294$ J, so that 294 J raise the temperature of the calorimeter and stirrer by 13·2 kelvin. Hence

$$\text{thermal capacity of calorimeter and stirrer} = \frac{294}{13\cdot2}$$
$$= 22\cdot26 \text{ joule per kelvin.}$$

Measuring the Power of a Gas Burner

The heat energy supplied per second by a bunsen burner can be found approximately by pouring 250 g of water into an aluminium mug or a beaker, using a measuring cylinder for the purpose (1 cm^3 of water has mass 1 g). The mug is placed on a gauze and tripod over a bunsen burner, and the rise in temperature measured in, say, 4 minutes.

Suppose the temperature of the cold water was 15° C and that after 4 minutes it had risen to 85° C. The *rise* in temperature is $(85-15) = 70$ kelvin. The number of joule transferred is $250 \times 4\cdot2 \times 70 = 73\,500$ J. and therefore the rate of supply of heat energy from the burner to the water

$$\frac{73500 \text{ J}}{4 \times 60 \text{ s}} = 306 \text{ joule per second} = 306 \text{ watt.}$$

The rate of supply of energy depends on the size of the flame and the pressure of the gas. The result we obtain will not, of course, represent the total power of the burner, since we have ignored the heat which has escaped round the sides of the vessel and also that used in heating the tripod, gauze and the vessel itself.

Calculation of Heat Energy Lost or Gained

As an example of how thermal loss is calculated, let us find how many joule are given out when a piece of iron of mass 50 g and specific heat capacity 0·5 joule per gramme degree C cools from 80° C to 20° C.

To say that the specific heat capacity of iron is 0·5 J/g K means that 1 g of iron gives out or takes in, as the case may be, 0·5 J when its temperature *changes* by 1 kelvin.

It follows that 50 g of iron in cooling through 1 kelvin will give out
$$50 \times 0\cdot5 \text{ joule}$$
Hence 50 g of iron in cooling from 80° to 20° C will give out
$$50 \times 0\cdot5 \times (80-20) \text{ joule} = 1500 \text{ joule}$$
If we write our last expression in words we get the useful formula:
Heat energy lost or gained
$$= \text{Mass} \times \text{Specific Heat capacity} \times \text{Change in temperature}$$

Thus if 120 g of copper of specific heat capacity 0·4 J/g K is warmed from 14° C to 100° C, the heat energy gained
= 120 × 0·4 × (100 − 14)
= 4128 joule

Experiment to Find the Specific Heat Capacity of Copper

The specific heat capacity of a solid can usually be found in the laboratory by warming it to a high temperature, and then quickly transferring it to a calorimeter containing cold water. The water then becomes warmer and the solid cooler; both finally reaching the same temperature. The solid has lost some heat to the water and the calorimeter. We shall see shortly that the *method of mixtures,* as it is called, enables the specific heat capacity of the solid to be calculated.

Suppose the specific heat capacity of copper is required. Since this is the same material as that of the calorimeter, the experiment can be performed without first finding the thermal capacity of the calorimeter.

A fairly large piece of copper with a thread attached is put into a beaker or mug of water, which is kept boiling gently with a bunsen burner.

While the temperature of the copper is thus being raised to 100° C a copper calorimeter is first weighed empty and then when about two-thirds full of cold water. The calorimeter is then placed inside its jacket and a thermometer placed in it.

When the copper has been in the boiling water long enough to reach a temperature of 100° C, the temperature of the cold water is noted, and the hot copper is then lifted by the thread and transferred to the calorimeter.

To enable this to be done with as little loss of heat as possible the calorimeter is held fairly close to the hot bath and the copper transferred quickly, but without splashing; just before it is placed in the calorimeter, the copper is given a slight shake to remove adhering hot water.

The mixture is then stirred by slowly lifting the copper up and down by the thread, always keeping it immersed in the water, and the final steady maximum temperature noted. The piece of copper used may be weighed either before or after the experiment.

The following set of results is given to show how the readings may be recorded and the specific heat of copper calculated.

Weighings.
Copper = 150 g
Calorimeter = 50 g
Calorimeter and water = 140 g

Temperatures.
Hot copper = 100° C
Cold water = 13·5° C
Mixture = 24·4° C

THERMAL ENERGY MEASUREMENT · 253

Calculations. As we have already seen, the heat energy given out or taken in by a substance is given by mass × specific heat capacity × change in temperature.

If the specific heat capacity of copper = c J/g K
and specific heat capacity of water = 4·2 J/g K

In calculating the result, it is useful to note that, with masses in g: we have:

$$\begin{aligned}
\text{Heat energy given out by hot copper} &= 150 \times c \times (100-24\cdot 4) \\
&= 11\,340 \times c \text{ joule} \\
\text{Heat energy received by water} &= 90 \times 4\cdot 2 \times (24\cdot 4 - 13\cdot 5) \\
&= 4120 \text{ joule} \\
\text{Heat energy received by calorimeter} &= 50 \times c \times (24\cdot 4 - 13\cdot 5) \\
&= 545 \times c \text{ joule}
\end{aligned}$$

Now
  Heat energy given out by hot copper
        = heat energy received by water and calorimeter

Therefore, $11\,340c = 4120 + 545c$
∴ $10\,795c = 4120$
∴ $c = 0\cdot 38$ J/g K

This result is affected, of course, by errors inherent in the experiment, such as the inevitable small loss of heat in transferring the hot copper to the calorimeter.

Calculation of Thermal Capacity of Calorimeter

Since the specific heat capacity of a substance is the thermal capacity of 1 gramme of it, it follows that the thermal capacity of any other mass of the substance is given by multiplying the mass m by the specific heat capacity c, or in symbols,

Thermal capacity = mc joule per kelvin. If SI is strictly observed, then m will be in kg and c in J/kg K. In any event, the same mass unit must be used through the calculation.

To Find Specific Heat Capacity of a Metal other than Copper

This experiment is carried out by the method of mixtures in exactly the same manner as that for copper, except that the copper is replaced by a sample of some other metal, for example iron.

The results are recorded in the usual way, c denoting the specific heat capacity of iron.

In calculating the result, it is useful to note that, with masses in g:
Heat energy given out by hot iron
        = Mass of iron × c × Fall in temperature
Heat energy received by water
        = Mass of water × 4·2 × Rise in temperature

Heat energy received by calorimeter
= Mass of calorimeter × 0·4 × Rise in temperature.

An equation is made from these results, similar to that for copper, from which c is calaculated.

To find the Specific Heat Capacity of a Liquid

The most convenient way of doing this is to transfer a piece of copper which has been heated to 100° C to a calorimeter about two-thirds full of the chosen liquid. The results are recorded as in the previous

Remembering that, in the present case, the heat energy given out by the hot copper is equal to the heat energy received by the liquid plus the heat energy received by the calorimeter, an equation is made out between the following heat quantities. The equation is then solved for c, the specific heat capacity of the liquid. With masses in g:

Heat energy given out by the hot copper
= Mass of copper × 0·4 × Fall in temperature
Heat energy received by liquid
= Mass of liquid × c × Rise in temperature
Heat energy received by calorimeter
= Mass of calorimeter × 0·4 × Rise in temperature

Plate 46. The six-cylinder engine of a Triumph TR6. Energy to drive the car is obtained from burning petrol; the chemical energy in the fuel is released as thermal energy which forces the pistons down as the gas in the cylinder expands. Piston movement transmits mechanical energy through the crankshaft and gearbox to the driving wheels

THERMAL ENERGY MEASUREMENT

Table of Specific Heat Capacities in joule per kg kelvin

Aluminium	925	Mercury	140
Brass	390	Methylated spirit	2440
Copper	390	Tin	237
Ice	2100	Turpentine	1770
Iron	460	Water	4200
Lead	130	Zinc	390

In the above table it will be seen that water has the unusually high specific heat capacity of 4200 J/kg K. Very few substances have a higher specific heat than this, the most notable being liquid hydrogen which has a specific heat capacity of 25 000 J/kg K, and mixtures of certain alcohols with water.

Summary

1. The joule is the unit for all forms of energy.
2. 4200 joule will raise the temperature of 1 kg of water through 1 K.
3. The power of a heater (in watt) is the number of joule transferred per second.
4. The *thermal capacity* of a body is the quantity of heat energy required to raise the temperature of the body through 1 degree.
5. The *specific heat capacity* of a substance is the number of joule required to raise the temperature of unit mass of it through 1 kelvin.
6. The number of joule lost or gained by m kg of a substance of specific heat capacity c J/kg K undergoing a temperature *change* of t kelvin is given by energy transfer = mass × specific heat capacity × temperature difference.

EXERCISES

Specific heat capacities, when required, should be obtained from the table on page 255.

1. Find the number of joule required to raise the temperature of
    (a) 23·5 g of water from 10° to 13·6° C,
    (b) 62 g of brass from 15° to 35° C,
    (c) 45 g of aluminium from 2° to 27° C,
    (d) 50 g of lead from 15° to 100° C.

2. Describe an experiment to find the useful heat energy obtained per minute from a bunsen burner when heating water in a metal can. State the various ways in which heat is wasted in this experiment.

3. What is the thermal capacity of (a) a copper calorimeter of mass 90 g, (b) an aluminium calorimeter of mass 30 g?

4. Place the following in order of decreasing thermal capacity:
   (a) 150 g of lead,
   (b) 50 g of iron,
   (c) 30 g of mercury,
   (d) 20 g of water.

5. Calculate the final steady temperature of the following mixtures, neglecting heat losses and heat received by the containing vessel:
   (a) 40 g of water at 80° C and 60 g of water at 11° C,
   (b) 100 g of copper at 100° C and 40 g of water at 10° C,
   (c) 50 g of zinc at 100° C and 20 g of turpentine at 10° C,
   (d) 80 g of iron at 50° C and 40 g of methylated spirit at 10° C.

6. Which has given out more heat energy when both have cooled to room temperature of 15° C, 20 g of iron at 300° C or 20 g of water at 50° C?

7. Define specific heat capacity.

8. Describe fully an experiment to measure the specific heat capacity of aluminium. In particular explain the precautions taken to get an accurate result and show how the result is calculated.

9. Explain the following:
   (a) the jam in a tart taken freshly from the oven is liable to burn the tongue, while the pastry does not do so.
   (b) the incandescent sparks from a grindstone do not cause a burn when they fall on the hand.

10. A piece of iron of mass 50 g is held in a bunsen flame until it has acquired the temperature of the flame. It is then quickly transferred to a copper calorimeter of mass 40 g containing 120 g of water at 14° C. If the final steady temperature of the calorimeter and its contents is 33° C, calculate the temperature of the bunsen flame. (Take sp. ht. capacity of copper as 0·4 J/g K.)

11. An electric heating coil of power 10 watt is immersed in a thin copper calorimeter containing 90 g of oil. The temperature rises from 10° C to 25·4° C in 6 minutes. Neglecting any heat lost to the atmosphere and the heat taken up by the calorimeter, calculate the specific heat capacity of the oil.

12. Describe fully an experiment to measure the temperature of a bunsen burner. Write out the thermal equation in words, *or* give imaginary measurements and calculate the result.

13. A piece of aluminium is heated to 100° C and then transferred to a copper calorimeter of mass 50 g containing 65 g of water at 20° C. The final steady temperature of the water is 28° C. Find the mass of the aluminium used. (Sp. ht. cap. of copper = 0·4 J/g K.)

14. A piece of metal weighing 150 g is heated in boiling water to a temperature of 100° C and then quickly transferred to a copper calorimeter of mass 40 g containing 50 g of water at 15° C. After stirring, the final steady temperature is found to be 21·6° C. Calculate the specific heat capacity of the metal used. What metal do you suppose was used? (Sp. ht. cap. of copper = 0·4 J/g K.)

CHAPTER TWENTY-FIVE

Latent Heat

Latent Heat of Vaporisation

When a kettle is put on a gas ring to boil, the temperature of the water rises until it reaches 100° C. At this temperature it starts to boil, that is to say bubbles of vapour form at the bottom of the kettle and rise to the surface, where they burst and escape as steam.

Once the water has begun to boil, the temperature remains constant and ceases to rise above 100° C. All the same, heat energy is being steadily absorbed from the gas flame by the water as it boils. This heat, which is going into the water but not increasing its temperature, is the energy needed to turn the water from the liquid state to the vapour state.

Experiment shows that 2257 joule are required to convert 1 gramme of water at its boiling-point to steam at the same temperature. This is known as the *specific latent heat of steam*. "Latent" means hidden or concealed, and this name was given to the heat years ago since it did not indicate its presence by producing a rise in temperature when water is converted to vapour.

When the steam condenses to form water, the latent heat is given out. For this reason a scald from steam is more painful than from boiling water. Other liquids besides water have latent heats. For example, 860 joule are needed to convert 1 gramme of alcohol at its boiling-point to vapour at the same temperature, while 358 joule are required in the case of ether. These quantities of heat energy are called the specific latent heats of vaporisation.

The *specific latent heat of vaporisation* of a substance is *defined* as *the energy required to convert unit mass of the substance from the liquid to the vapour state without change of temperature.*

Latent Heat of Fusion

Just as latent heat is taken in when water changes to vapour at the same temperature, so the same thing occurs when ice melts to form water. Here the latent heat is not so great. It requires only 334 joule to convert 1 gramme of ice at 0° C to water at the same temperature. Likewise, when water at 0° C. freezes into ice, 334 joule are given up for

Plate 47. Calder Hall nuclear power station. In a power station, the boilers supply latent heat to change water into steam. Part of this energy is released in the steam turbines, which drive the generators, and the remainder is lost to the atmosphere when the used steam is condensed back to water in these cooling towers. The mist rising from the towers consists of droplets of cooled water, which are absorbed by the air

every gramme of ice formed. This is called the *specific latent heat of ice*.

As mentioned on p. 257, the phenomenon of latent heat is not confined to water alone. Other substances also absorb latent heat when they melt or evaporate. Conversely, they give out latent heat on solidifying or condensing.

In general, the heat energy needed to convert a substance from the solid to the liquid state is called latent heat of fusion.

The *specific latent heat of fusion* of a substance is *defined* as *the energy required to convert unit mass of the substance from the solid to the liquid state without change of temperature.*

Cooling Curve and Melting-point of Naphthalene

The latent heat given out when a molten substance freezes to the solid state may be shown by the following experiment with naphthalene. Naphthalene is a white crystalline solid obtained from coal tar. It has a characteristic smell and is familiar in the form of moth balls.

A test-tube containing naphthalene is held vertically by a clamp and stand (Fig. 228). The naphthalene is then heated gently with a very small bunsen flame until it just melts. A thermometer is inserted in the

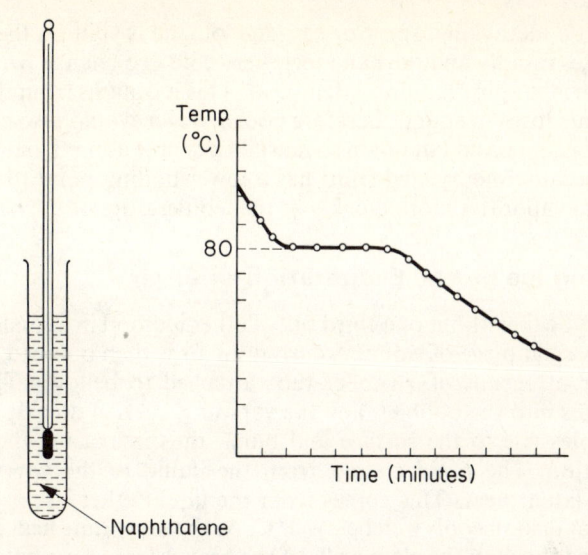

Fig. 228. Testing the melting-point of naphthalene by its cooling curve

naphthalene and the heating continued until the temperature of the melted naphthalene is about 100° C. The bunsen flame is then removed, and readings of the thermometer are taken at minute intervals as the tube and its contents are cooling. It is noticed that when the freezing-point, or what is the same thing, the melting-point, of the naphthalene is reached the temperature remains constant at 80° C until all the naphthalene has solidified. After this the temperature again falls. The temperature changes are illustrated most strikingly by plotting a graph of temperature against time (Fig. 228). The flat portion of the graph represents the time during which the naphthalene is solidifying. Here its temperature remains constant at 80° C although heat energy is steadily being lost by convection and radiation all the time. The heat energy lost is exactly compensated by the latent heat of fusion of the naphthalene, which is being given out during the change from the liquid to the solid state.

This experiment also shows how the *melting-point* of a pure solid can be found. As in the naphthalene experiment, the solid is heated until it all melts, and a cooling curve is obtained. The melting-point corresponds to the temperature of the flat portion of the curve, as in Fig. 228.

Cooling Produced by Evaporation

Some liquids have a low boiling-point, and thus change from liquid to vapour quite easily at ordinary temperatures. These are called *volatile liquids*. Methylated spirit and ether are examples.

If a little methylated spirit or eau-de-Cologne is spilt on the hand it evaporates rapidly and the hand feels very cold. To change from liquid to vapour, the spirit requires latent heat. This it obtains from the hand, which thus loses heat and therefore cools. Water would also cause the hand to become cold but not in so marked a degree as methylated spirit. This is because methylated spirit has a lower boiling-point than water and so it evaporates more quickly at the temperature of the hand.

Making Ice by the Evaporation of Ether

A glass beaker about one-third full of ether is stood in a small pool of water on a flat piece of wood. A current of air is then bubbled through the ether by means of a rubber tube attached to bellows. The ether evaporates into the bubbles, and the vapour is carried quickly away as the bubbles rise to the surface and burst, thus increasing the rate of evaporation. The rapid change from the liquid to the vapour state requires latent heat. This comes from the liquid ether itself, with the result that it soon cools well below $0°$ C. At the same time heat becomes conducted through the glass walls of the beaker from the pool of water below it, and eventually the water cools to $0°$ C. After this it begins to lose latent heat, and freezes.

The Refrigerator

The cooling inside the cabinet of a domestic refrigerator is brought about by the forced evaporation of a volatile liquid inside a copper coil E. This requires latent heat which is taken from the air surrounding the coil (Fig. 229). As the liquid evaporates, the vapour is removed by an electric pump, and under the reduced pressure, the liquid evaporates very rapidly.

The vapour is not wasted but passes into a second coil C outside the cabinet, where it is compressed by the pump and condenses back to liquid. Here, of course, latent heat is given out. To enable this heat to be dissipated quickly, the coil is fitted with copper fins. Heat is conducted into the fins and thence into convection currents in the surrounding air.

From the condensing coil C, the liquid passes back into the evaporator coil inside the cabinet. In this manner a continuous circulation of liquid and vapour is set up. The rate of evaporation and consequently the degree of cooling produced is controlled by a thermostat switch (not shown in the diagram), which switches the pump motor on and off at intervals. The switch is adjustable, and is provided with a dial which may be set to give any desired low temperature inside the cabinet.

A different type of refrigerator is also in common use which, instead of a pump, employs a gas flame or electric heater to provide the energy necessary to maintain the circulation of liquid and vapour. The method of producing the circulation is somewhat more complex than that described above. Nevertheless the basic principle, namely cooling by absorption of latent heat, remains the same.

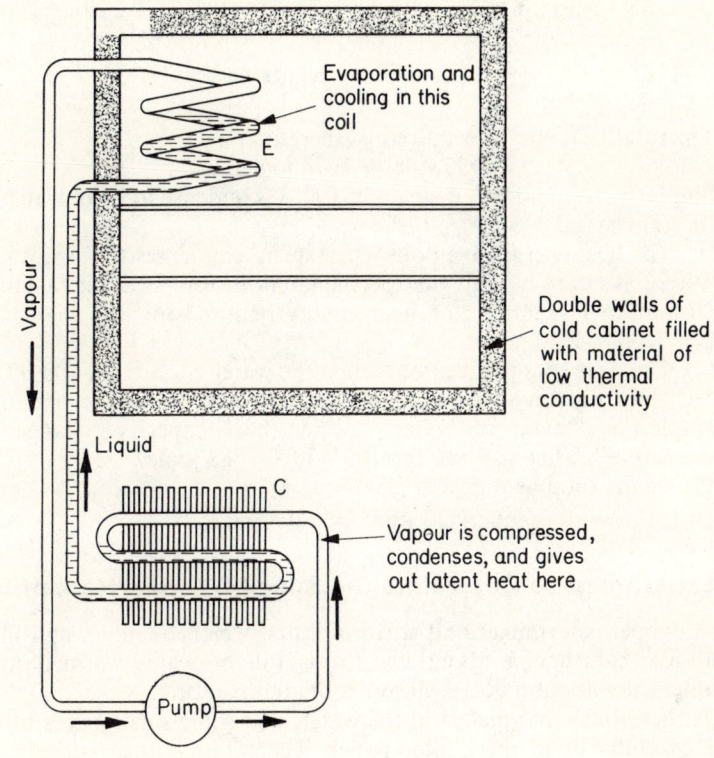

Fig. 229. A refrigerator

Latent Heat Calculations

Suppose 3 g of ice at $0°$ C is melted and finally becomes water at $7°$ C. The quantity of heat energy required is calculated in two separate stages:

(1) The heat energy required to change the ice to water at $0°$ C is latent heat (Fig. 230). If the specific latent heat of ice is taken as 330 joule per gramme, the heat energy required for this change $= 3 \times 330 = 990$ J.

(2) The heat energy to change the water at $0°$ C to water at $7°$ C does *not* involve latent heat, but is given simply by "mass of water $\times$ specific heat capacity $\times$ change of temperature". This quantity of energy $= 3 \times 4 \cdot 2 \times (7-0) = 88 \cdot 2$ joule.

```
    3g
   Ice            Water              Water
  ┌─────┐  Add  ┌─────┐   Add     ┌─────┐
  │ 0°C │ ───▶ │ 0°C │  ────▶   │ 7°C │
  │     │ 990J │     │   88 J    │     │
  └─────┘      └─────┘           └─────┘
```

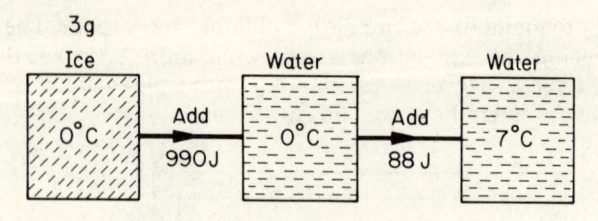

Fig. 230. Latent heat and heat capacity

The total heat energy required is, therefore,
$$990 + 88 = 1078 \text{ joule}.$$

Similarly, suppose 2 g of steam at 100° C condense to form water at 30° C. Then,

(1) The heat energy given out when steam condenses to form water at 100° C is latent heat. If the specific latent heat of steam is taken as 2260 joule per gramme, the heat energy required for this change is $= 2 \times 2260 = 4520$ joule.

(2) The heat energy given out when the water cools from 100° C to 30° C does not involve latent heat but is given, as in the previous example, by "mass of water × specific heat capacity × change in temperature". That is, $2 \times 4 \cdot 2 \times (100 - 30) = 588$ joule.

Hence the total heat energy given out
$$= 4520 + 588 = 5108 \text{ joule}$$

Experiment to Determine the Specific Latent Heat of Ice

A copper calorimeter and stirrer are first weighed empty, and then with the calorimeter about two-thirds full of water warmed to a temperature about 6 degree above room temperature.

A thermometer is placed in the water, and some small pieces of ice are carefully dried on a filter paper. The water is then stirred, the temperature noted, and immediately the dry ice is added. Stirring continuously, sufficient ice is added to bring the final steady temperature down to about 6 degrees below room temperature. This final steady temperature is noted and the calorimeter and its contents weighed.

The following is a typical set of results obtained for the experiment.

Weighings.
    Calorimeter and stirrer   = 55·0 g
    Calorimeter, stirrer and water   = 148·0 g
    Calorimeter, stirrer, water and ice   = 161·4 g

Temperatures.
    Warm water   = 22·2° C
    Final steady temperature of mixture = 10·0° C

Calculations.

Mass of warm water	= 93·0 g
Mass of ice	= 13·4 g
Let the specific latent heat of ice	= l joule per gramme, and

assume the specific heat capacity of copper = 0·42 J/g K

In this experiment, the heat energy given out by the calorimeter, stirrer and water in cooling from the initial to the final temperature is equal to the heat energy received by the ice. Now the ice may be regarded as receiving two lots of heat energy. Firstly, the latent heat necessary to melt it to form water at 0° C; and secondly, the heat energy to raise the temperature of the now melted ice from 0° C to the final temperature 10·0° C. Thus

Heat energy given out by calorimeter
 and stirrer = 55 × 0·42 × 12·2 joule
and Heat energy given out by warm water = 93 × 4·20 × 12·2 joule
Also,
Heat energy received by ice to melt it
 to water at 0° C = 13·4 × l joule
and Heat energy received by melted ice to
 raise it from 0° to 10·0° C = 13·4 × 4·2 × 10·0 joule

Equating the heat energy received to the heat energy given out,
(13·4 × l) + (13·4 × 4·2 × 10·0)
 = (55 × 0·42 × 12·2) + (93 × 4·2 × 12·2)
Whence l = 334 joule per gramme

The difficulties encountered in preventing loss of heat in a calorimeter experiment have already been pointed out. In this experiment it is purposely arranged that the calorimeter is for approximately half the time above room temperature and for the remainder of the time the same number of degrees below room temperature. As a result the heat gains and losses of the calorimeter from and to the surroundings cancel each other out.

An Experiment to Determine the Specific Latent Heat of Steam

In this experiment steam is passed into cold water in a calorimeter, where it condenses and gives out latent heat.

The supply of steam may be obtained from water kept boiling in a flask fitted with a rubber bung and delivery tube, but a copper boiler is better if one is available. To ensure that only dry steam enters the calorimeter a *water trap* is used. The arrangement of the apparatus is shown in Fig. 231. Any water droplets which come over due to condensation of the steam in the rubber tube from the boiler are caught in the trap, and are unable to enter the calorimeter. To reduce the cooling of the steam as far as possible the apparatus is well lagged. Strips of felt or other suitable material of low thermal conductivity are wrapped round the water trap and delivery tubes.

The boiler is started in good time so that the apparatus has time to warm up and produce a steady flow of dry steam. A calorimeter and stirrer are weighed empty and then when the calorimeter is about three-quarters full of cold water. The calorimeter is placed inside a jacket,

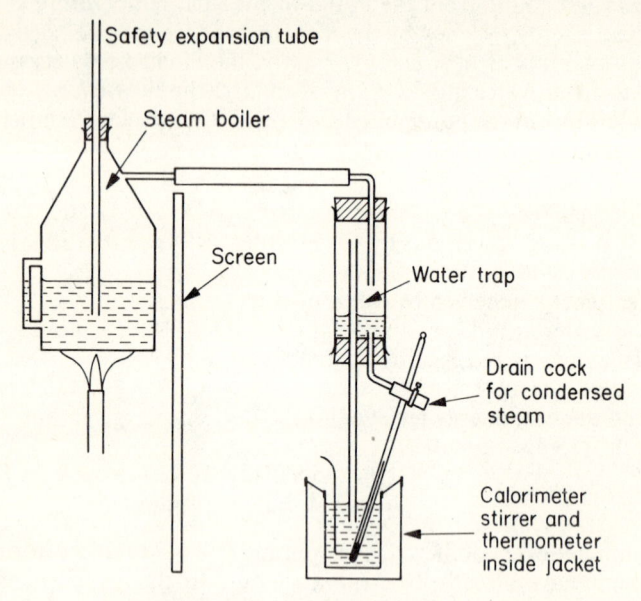

Fig. 231. Measuring specific latent heat of steam

and in addition, a screen is placed so as to shield it from direct radiation from the hot boiler. The calorimeter is brought up to the steam supply, and its temperature noted immediately before inserting the steam nozzle just below the surface of the water. This is most conveniently done by holding the calorimeter in the hand and lifting the calorimeter, rather than by placing the calorimeter down on the bench and adjusting the nozzle so as to project into it. During the passage of steam the water is constantly stirred to ensure thorough mixing. When the temperature has risen by about 30° C, the calorimeter is removed from the steam and the final maximum steady temperature of the water is noted.

The following set of restuls for this experiment is given in order to show the method of calculating the specific latent heat of steam.

Weighings.

    Calorimeter and stirrer   = 55·0 g
    Calorimeter, stirrer and water   = 149·3 g
    Calorimeter, sitrrer, water and condensed steam = 154·4 g

Temperatures.
Before passing steam = 16·2° C
After passing steam = 46·4° C

Calculations. It will be remembered that, in the last experiment, we regarded the ice as receiving two lots of heat during the experiment. In the present experiment it is helpful to treat the condensation of the steam as occurring in two distinct stages. Firstly, each gramme of steam gives out l joule in condensing to form water at 100° C; and afterwards this water cools from 100° C to the final steady temperature, giving out 4·2 joule per gramme kelvin fall in temperature as it does so.

Taking the specific latent heat of steam as l joule per gramme, and the specific heat capacity of copper as 0·42 joule per gramme kelvin we have:

Mass of water in calorimeter = 149·3 − 55·0 = 94·3 g
Mass of steam passed in = 154·4 − 149·3 = 5·1 g

Heat energy given out by steam in condensing to water at 100°C = $5·1 \times l$ joule

Heat energy given out by condensed steam in cooling from 100° C to 46·4° C = $5·1 \times 4·2 \times (100 - 46·4)$ joule

Heat energy received by water in calorimeter = $94·3 \times 4·2 \times (46·4 - 16·2)$ joule

Heat energy received by calorimeter and stirrer = $55·0 \times 0·42 \times (46·4 - 16·2)$ joule

Equating the energy given out to the energy received, we obtain
$(5·1 \times l) + (5·1 \times 4·2 \times 53·6) = (94·3 \times 4·2 \times 30·2) + (55 \times 0·42 \times 30·2)$
whence $l = 2260$ joule per gramme

Summary

1. The *specific latent heat of vaporisation* of a substance is the energy required to convert unit mass of the substance from the liquid to the vapour state without change of temperature.

2. The *specific latent heat of fusion* of a substance is the energy required to convert unit mass of the substance from the solid to the liquid state without change of temperature.

In the case of water, these two latent heats are generally called the "specific latent heat of steam" and the "specific latent heat of ice" respectively.

3. The *melting-point* of a pure solid can be found from a cooling curve.

4. Volatile liquids are used in *refrigerators*. These have low boiling-points, and absorb latent heat on evaporation.

EXERCISES

Note. When required in the following examples, the specific latent heat of ice should be taken as 330 joules per gramme, and the specific latent heat of steam as 2260 joules per gramme.

1. Define (*a*) the specific latent heat of steam, (*b*) the specific latent heat of ice.

2. Find the number of joules required to convert:
    (*a*) 5 g of ice at 0° C to water at 0° C.
    (*b*) 14 g of ice at 0° C to water at 56° C.
    (*c*) 6 g of water at 100° C to steam at the same temperature.
    (*d*) 15 g of water at 12° C to steam at 100° C.

3. Calculate the heat energy given out when
    (*a*) 7 g of water at 0° C turns to ice at 0° C.
    (*b*) 6 g of water at 21° C turns to ice at 0° C.
    (*c*) 8 g of steam at 100° C condenses to water at 100° C.
    (*d*) 9 g of steam at 100° C condenses to water at 23° C.

4. A few drops of ether spilt on the hand gives rise to a very cold sensation. This does not occur if olive oil is used instead of ether. Give an explanation.

5. Give reasons for the following:
    (*a*) underclothing should be well aired before it is put on,
    (*b*) an athlete puts on a sweater when resting after violent exercise which has caused him to perspire, even though he does not feel cold.

6. How many joules are required to convert 15 g of ice at 0° C to steam at 100° C?

7. A piece of iron of mass 250 g and specific heat capacity 0·46 J/g K is heated to 100° C and then placed on the surface of a block of ice at 0° C. Ignoring all heat changes except those between the iron and ice, calculate the mass of ice melted.

8. What mass of steam at 100° C must be passed into 150 g of turpentine (sp. ht. cap. 1·77 J/g K) to raise its temperature from 5° C to 89° C?

9. An electric kettle contains 1 litre of water together with a lump of ice of mass 200 g, all at 0° C. The electric heater is rated at 1 kW. Neglecting heat losses to the surroundings and the heat absorbed by the kettle itself, find the time taken after switching on
    (*a*) until the ice has just melted,
    (*b*) until the kettle boils dry.

10. Give a simple diagram to show the essential features of a refrigerating unit and explain its action.

11. 50 g of melted wax at its melting-point (62° C) were poured into a copper calorimeter of mass 40 g with 80 g of water at 15° C. The mixture was well stirred and the final temperature found to be 44·0° C. If the sp. ht. cap. of wax and copper are 1·6 and 1·4 J/g K respectively, calculate the specific latent heat of fusion of wax.

12. A few gramme of beeswax were placed in a test-tube together with a thermometer and gently heated until the wax had all melted. The following temperature readings were then taken as the wax was allowed to cool.

Time in minutes	Temperature in °C	Time in minutes	Temperature in °C
0	81·0	7	62·0
1	73·0	8	62·0
2	68·5	9	61·7
3	65·2	10	60·8
4	63·2	11	59·5
5	62·3	12	58·5
6	62·0		

Plot a cooling curve for beeswax. From it, find the melting-point of beeswax and explain the shape of the graph.

13. Describe an experiment to find the specific latent heat of ice. Explain the precautions taken to ensure a good result, and show how the result is calculated.

14. Give a diagram to show the apparatus used to determine the specific latent heat of steam. Describe how you use it and state the readings taken. Write out, in words, the heat equation used for calculation of the final result.

15. 6·2 g of steam at 100° C was passed into a copper calorimeter of mass 90 g containing some water at 10·2° C. The final steady temperature was 42·0° C. Find the original mass of water in the calorimeter. (Take sp. ht. cap. of copper as 0·4 J/g K.)

16. 25 g of dried ice at 0° C was added to a copper calorimeter of mass 80 g containing 70 g of water at 60° C. The mixture was stirred until the ice had just melted. What was the final steady temperature? (Take sp. ht. cap of copper as 0·4 J/g K.)

CHAPTER TWENTY-SIX

Machines

To many people the word "machine" conjures up visions of a more or less complicated piece of mechanism composed of gear wheels, levers, screws and the like. But however complex a machine may appear at first sight, its various parts can be shown to be applications of a few simple mechnical principles. This will be discussed shortly.

Machines are not confined to factories and workshops. Even within the home we use a large range of machines; they vary in complexity from screwdrivers and tin-openers to sewing machines and refrigerators. All these devices have one property in common. By their aid we are enabled to perform work more easily or more quickly than could be done directly by hand, if indeed it could be done by hand at all.

The Lever

In Chapter 22 we considered one of the oldest and most widely used mechanical principles, that of the lever. The use of levers was known to the ancient Greeks, and it is reported that Archimedes once remarked. "Give me a lever long enough and I will move the world!"

A lever is a rigid rod pivoted about a point called the fulcrum. A force called the effort is applied at one point on the lever and this overcomes a force called the load at some other point. It may here be noted that the terms effort and load are used in connection with all machines and are not confined specially to levers.

Levers are divided for convenience into three classes or orders depending on the position of the fulcrum with respect to the effort and load. Fig. 232 illustrates some simple machines based on the lever principle.

Mechanical Advantage

When an effort of 50 N is applied to a lever and a load of 300 N is overcome, the mechnical advantage of the lever is 300/50 or 6. In any machine the mechanical advantage (M.A.) is defined as the ratio of the load to the effort. Thus

$$\text{M.A.} = \frac{\text{Load force}}{\text{Effort force}}$$

MACHINES · 269

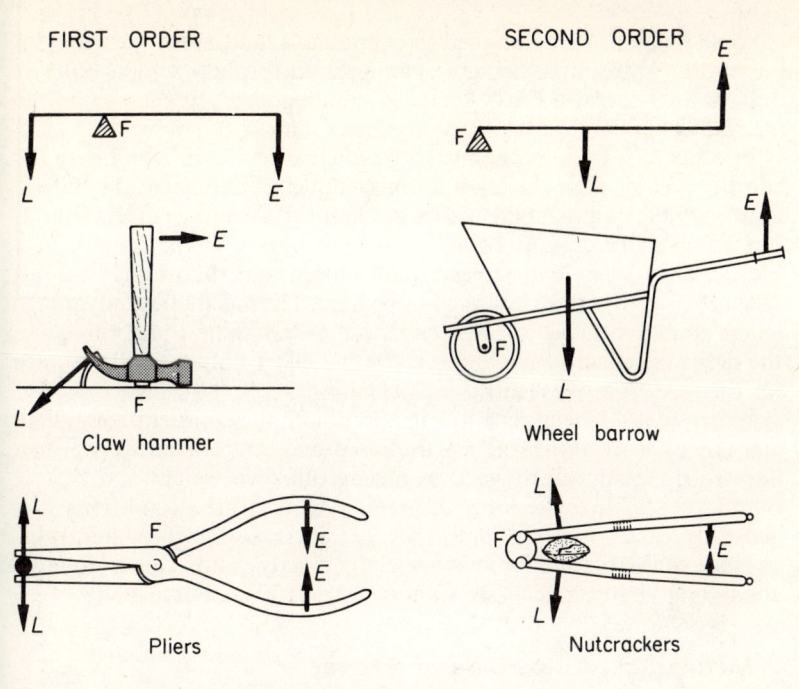

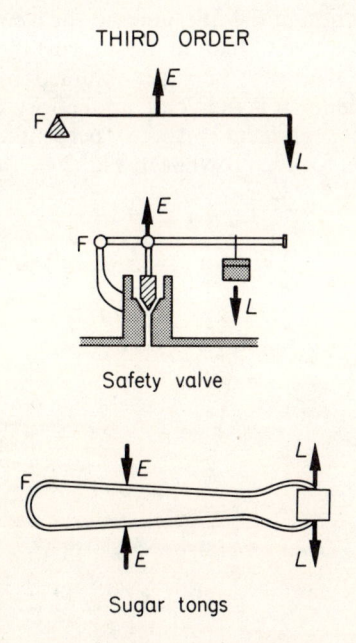

FIRST ORDER

Claw hammer

Pliers

SECOND ORDER

Wheel barrow

Nutcrackers

THIRD ORDER

Safety valve

Sugar tongs

Fig. 232. Levers classified by positions of the forces

Some machines are designed to overcome a load much greater than the effort, an example being a spanner used to undo a tight bolt, or pulleys used to raise heavy loads at building sites. In such cases the mechanical advantage has a value greater than 1.

In other cases the mechanical advantage is less than 1 and here the effort is greater than the load. Strange though it may seem the bicycle is an example of a machine with a mechanical advantage of less than 1. Under ordinary conditions the resistance opposing the motion of a bicycle on a level road is very small indeed and the mechanical advantage therefore does not need to be high. The mechanical advantage is less than 1 because the velocity ratio is less than 1 and this gives the desirable effect of having to move the effort only a small distance for the load to move a much greater one.

When we are ascending a hill, in addition to the comparatively small amount of work done against frictional and air resistances, we now have to do vastly more work in raising our own weight and that of the bicycle against the force of gravity. Under these conditions it is generally easier to walk, unless we can increase the mechanical advantage of the bicycle by increasing its velocity ratio. This is done by changing to a lower gear (see train of gears in Fig. 244).

Mechanical Advantage of a Lever

If we neglect friction at the fulcrum and the weight of the lever itself (both being comparatively small in most cases) the mechanical advantage in any particular case may be obtained by writing down the equation of moments for the load and effort about the fulcrum. Remembering that "moment = force × perpendicular distance from fulcrum", we have, for the crowbar in Fig. 233,

$$L \times 0 \cdot 2 = E \times 1 \cdot 4$$

whence
$$\text{M.A.} = \frac{L}{E} = \frac{1 \cdot 4}{0 \cdot 2} = 7$$

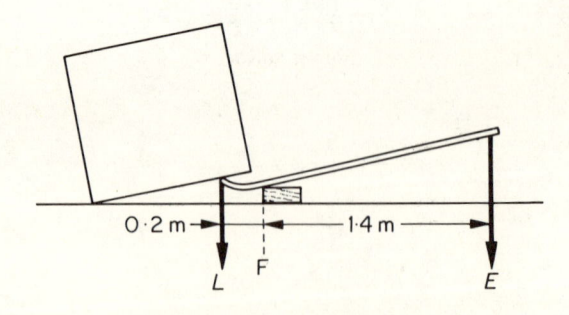

Fig. 233. Mechanical advantage

Pulleys

A pulley is a wheel with a grooved rim. For practical purposes one or more pulleys may be mounted in a framework called a block. The effort and load are applied to ropes passing over the pulleys, one or more strings being used according to the system in operation.

The Single Fixed Pulley (Fig. 234)

This is often seen in use for the purpose of raising small loads contained in a bucket or basket to the top of a building during constructional or repair work. The tension is the same throughout the rope, so that, neglecting the weight of the rope itself and any friction in the bearings of the pulley,

$$\text{Load} = \text{Effort}$$

and

$$\text{Mechanical advantage} = \frac{\text{Load}}{\text{Effort}} = 1.$$

Fig. 234. Single fixed pulley

In this case, although the effort applied is equal to the load raised, we obtain the greater convenience and ease of being able to stand on the ground and pull downwards, instead of having to haul the load upwards from the top of the building.

The Single Moving Pulley

This is illustrated in Fig. 235. Here the tension throughout the string or rope is equal to the effort applied, so that the total upward pull on the pulley is twice the effort E.

Suppose a load of 4 kgf is supported by the pulley and that the weight of the pulley block and string is negligible. Then since the load is supported by the tension in two sections of string, the tension in the string, or the effort applied, need only be 2 kgf. Thus

$$\text{Mechanical advantage} = \frac{\text{Load}}{\text{Effort}} = \frac{4\,\text{kgf}}{2\,\text{kgf}} = 2$$

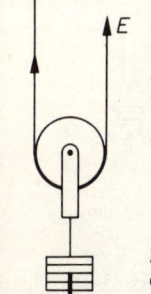

Fig. 235. Single moving pulley

Direction of a Tension in a String

In all our pulley diagrams some thought has to be given to the direction in which the force arrows are drawn on the strings.

Suppose we consider the simple case of 2 kgf supported by a string held in the hand (Fig. 236). The tension in the string is 2 kgf and acts equally both upwards and downwards. The arrow pointing upwards represents the force

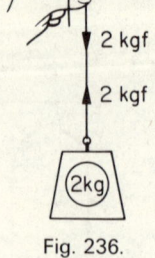

Fig. 236. Direction of forces in a string

which the string exerts on the load while the arrow pointing downwards shows the force exerted by the string on the hand. This is a straightforward example of Newton's law that "Action and Reaction are equal and opposite".

In general, we do not put in both arrows but only the one giving the direction of the force in which we are interested. Thus in Fig. 235 both arrows are drawn upwards as we wish to indicate the force exerted by the string on the load. We are not here concerned with the downward pull of the string on the support.

The First System of Pulleys

This is an arrangement of single moving pulleys. Fig. 237 shows two such pulleys in use. Theoretically we can go on increasing the mechanical advantage of this system by increasing the number of pulleys, but in practice, difficulties then arise through the strings becoming entangled. Moreover, the system becomes unwieldy on account of the great length of string required to obtain a reasonable movement of the load and for this reason the system is never used in practice.

The fixed pulley A is put in for the convenience of obtaining a downward pull for the effort. It does not alter the mechanical advantage of the system.

If an effort of 10 N (about 1 kgf) is applied to the string passing over pulley A, there will be an upward force of 20 N on pulley B since it is supported by *two* sections of string in which there is a tension of 10 N. Likewise, the total upward pull on pulley C is 40 N. Hence pulley C can support a load of 40 N (or about 4 kgf).

It can now be seen that if an effort of E newton is applied to the string passing over pulley A, there will be an upward force on B of $2E$ newton, and the the total upward force on pulley C is $4E$ newton which is the load it can support. Thus

$$\text{Mechanical advantage} = \frac{4E}{E} = 4$$

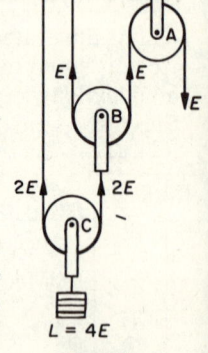

Fig. 237. System of pulleys

In a practical case, however, the mechanical advantage is always less than 4, as we have not allowed for friction in the string and pulleys and the weight of the strings and pulleys. An experiment for measuring the *practical* mechanical advantage of a pulley system will be described later.

MACHINES · 273

The Second System of Pulleys

This arrangement is by far the most important of all, being commonly used on lifts and cranes.

Two blocks are employed containing, in practice, up to eight pulleys in each, but for simplicity, Fig. 238 illustrates the system with only two pulleys in each block. In order to simplify the diagram, the pulleys are shown mounted on separate axles and placed one above the other. In practice, however, the pulleys in each block are side by side and run independently on a common axle (see also Fig. 239). A single string is used which passes round each pulley in turn.

Examination of Fig. 238 shows that the lower block is supported by four sections of string. Incidentally, the number of sections of string supporting the block is always equal to the total number of pulleys in the two blocks together. It follows that, if an effort E is applied to the free end of the string, then the total upward force on the load will be $4E$.

As in the previous cases considered we will neglect friction and the weight of the moving parts of the system, and therefore

$$\text{Mechanical advantage} = \frac{4E}{E} = 4$$

Fig. 238. System of pulleys

Velocity Ratio (or Speed Ratio)

In the pulley systems we have already considered where the mechanical advantage is greater than 1, it might appear at first sight that we are getting more out of the machine than we are putting into it. While in such cases the load overcome is greater than the effort applied, nevertheless the effort has to be applied through a greater distance than that through which the load moves. The energy or work obtained is then equal to the energy or work expended, less any work wasted against friction in the machine. This is discussed below.

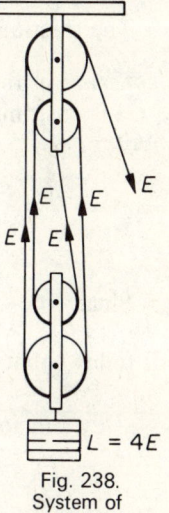

In the second system shown in Fig. 238 it will be clear that, in order to raise the load by 1 m, each string supporting the load must be shortened by 1 m. The effort must therefore be applied through a total distance of 4 m.

The ratio of the distance moved by the effort to the distance moved by the load in the same time is called the *velocity ratio* of the machine, i.e.

$$\text{Velocity (or speed) ratio} = \frac{\text{Distance moved by effort}}{\text{Distance moved by load in same time}}$$

Work Done by a Machine. Efficiency

In the case we have just considered, if the system were a "perfect" machine, i.e. composed of weightless and frictionless strings and pulleys, then a load of 4 N would be raised a distance of 1 m by an effort of 1 N exerted over a distance of 4 m.

The work done (or energy expended) by the machine on the load is then $4 \text{ N} \times 1 \text{ m}$, which is equal to 4 N m (= 4 joule), while the work done by the effort is $1 \text{ N} \times 4 \text{ m}$, which equals 4 joule. These are equal, as we should expect for a perfect machine. In practice, machines are not perfect and some work is always wasted in overcoming friction and in raising moving parts. The useful work done by a machine is always less than the work done by the effort.

The fraction, $\dfrac{\text{Useful energy obtained from the machine}}{\text{Total energy put into the machine}}$, is called the *efficiency* of the machine.

It is customary to express this fraction as a percentage, so we may write

$$\text{Efficiency} \left(\frac{\text{energy output}}{\text{energy input}}\right) \times 100 \text{ per cent.}$$

Since
$$\text{Work} = \text{Force} \times \text{Distance moved,}$$
it follows that

$$\text{Efficiency} = \frac{\text{Load} \times \text{distance load moves}}{\text{Effort} \times \text{distance effort moves}} \times 100\%$$

$$= \text{M.A.} \times \frac{1}{\text{Velocity ratio}} \times 100\%$$

or
$$E = \frac{M.A.}{V.R.} \times 100 \text{ per cent}$$

This equation will be found very useful for working out problems, but it should be remembered that it is not a definition of efficiency and should not be used as such.

Experiment to show how the Practical Mechanical Advantage and Efficiency of a Pulley System vary with the Load

Any system of pulleys may be used for this experiment but we will assume that a system having two pulleys in each block is being employed.

The pulleys are set up as in Fig. 239, scale-pans being provided for the addition of weights to represent load and effort. Since the scale-pans are more or less an essential convenience, they are best treated as part of the whole machine itself. Some people, however, prefer to weigh the pans and add their weights to the load and effort respectively. Whichever course is adopted should be mentioned in the account of the experiment.

An initial load of say 50 gf is added to the load pan, and weights are then added to the effort pan until the load just rises slowly with a steady velocity. The load and effort are recorded in a table, and the experiment repeated for a series of increasing loads.

The velocity ratio of this machine may be found by measuring a pair of corresponding distances moved by effort and load. For each pair of

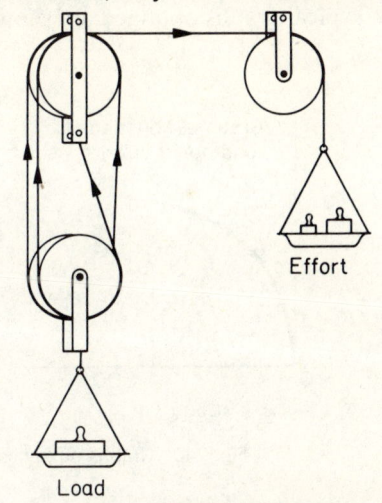

Fig. 239. Measuring mechanical advantage and efficiency

readings of effort and load obtained, the mechanical advantage and the efficiency should be calculated from the appropriate formulae and entered in the table.

Load in gf	Effort in gf			
		M.A. = $\dfrac{\text{Load}}{\text{Effort}}$	Efficiency = $\dfrac{\text{M.A.}}{\text{V.R.}} \times 100\%$	

In connection with this experiment, the following points should be noticed:

(1) The useless load consists of the weight of the moving pulley block, and friction has also to be overcome. The former is constant, while the latter, though it increases with load, is small. The total useless load may therefore be regarded as being practically constant. As, therefore, the useful load increases, it becomes a larger fraction of the total load lifted. Consequently the mechanical advantage increases with load.

(2) The efficiency also increases with load for the same reasons as above.

(3) On account of the work wasted in overcoming friction and in raising the moving pulley block, the efficiency cannot reach 100 per cent. Also since there are only 4 pulleys the mechanical advantage cannot exceed 4.

Graphs should be plotted of M.A. against load, and efficiency against load. The shape of the curves obtained will illustrate the above remarks. Typical graphs obtained are shown in Fig. 240.

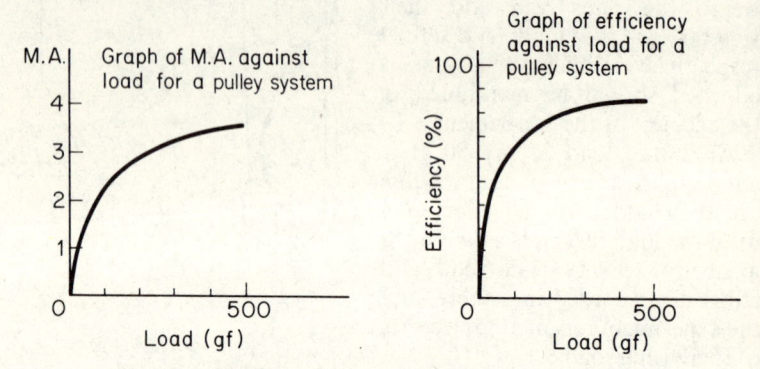

Fig. 240. Graphs of mechanical advantage and efficiency

The Inclined Plane

A heavy load may be raised more easily by pulling it up along a sloping surface than by lifting it vertically.

Heavy barrels are often loaded into vans by passing two ropes round them and hauling them up an incline formed by two stout planks held apart by iron stays. As will be seen from Fig. 241, the use of ropes in this manner also brings in the principle of the moving pulley, the barrel in this case acting as its own pulley.

It is believed that the enormous blocks of stone used in the construction of the Egyptian pyramids were raised into position by

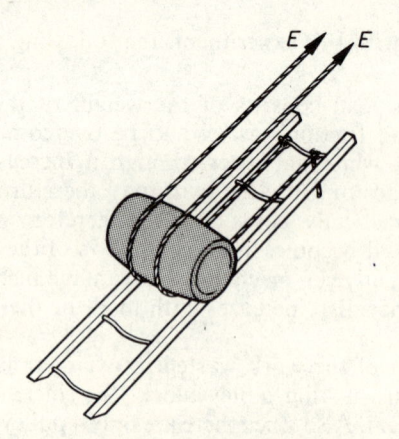

Fig. 241. Inclined plane

dragging them, on rollers, up a long ramp of earth built against the structure during course of erection. On completion of the building the earth was carried away.

Velocity Ratio and Mechanical Advantage of Inclined Plane

Fig. 242 shows a load being pulled up an inclined plane AB, friction being reduced by having the load on a trolley.

In order to raise the load through a vertical height h, the effort has to be exerted through a longer distance equal to the length of the plane l.

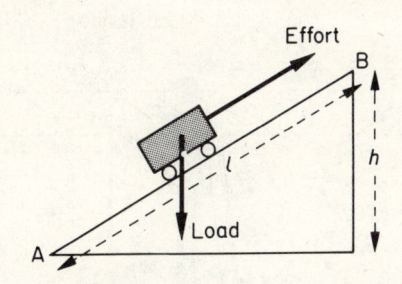

Fig. 242. Measurements on an inclined plane

It is important to realise that the distance through which the load is overcome is h and not l, because the weight of the load always acts vertically downwards.

It follows that the velocity ratio is given by

$$\text{V.R.} = \frac{\text{Distance moved by effort}}{\text{Distance moved by load}}$$
$$= \frac{\text{Length of plane}}{\text{Height of plane}}$$
$$= \frac{l}{h}$$

The mechanical advantage may be obtained by applying the Law of Conservation of Energy (or the Principle of Work). To do this in the simplest manner, we neglect the work done against friction and equate the work done on the load to the work done by the effort.

Thus, for a "perfect" inclined plane,

Load × Distance load moves = Effort × Distance effort moves

or $$\text{M.A.} = \frac{\text{Load}}{\text{Effort}} = \frac{\text{Distance effort moves}}{\text{Distance load moves}}$$

Thus $$\text{M.A.} = \frac{l}{h}$$

The Screw

Millions of screws and bolts are used daily for the purpose of holding together with considerable force the different parts of various structures. The principle of the screw is of the utmost practical importance. In addition to its use for micrometers it provides the essential feature of machines like vices and lifting jacks.

The distance between successive threads on a screw is called its pitch. For one complete turn, therefore, a screw moves through a distance equal to its pitch. As an example of the screw as a machine we will consider the working of a car jack. Fig. 243 shows a common type

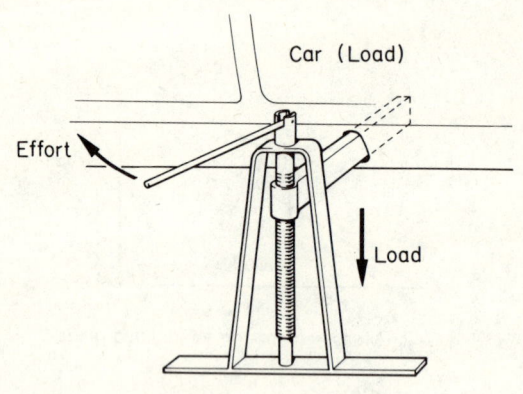

Fig. 243. A screw-jack

of jack, which consists of a long screw carrying a nut to which is hinged a short steel bar for fitting into a slot in the car chassis. To raise the car, the screw is turned by hand using a short steel bar known as a tommy bar.

Typical data for this type of jack are

Length of tommy bar: 200 mm
Pitch of screw: 2 mm
Load lifted: 500 kgf ≃ 5000 N

The effort required to lift the car may be obtained by ignoring friction and applying the Principle of Work. Thus

$$\text{Work done by effort} = \text{Work done on load}$$
$$\therefore \text{Effort} \times \text{Circumference of circle traced out by tommy bar} = \text{Load} \times \text{Screw pitch}$$
$$\therefore \text{Effort} \times 2 \times \tfrac{22}{7} \times 200 = 5000 \times 2$$

whence
$$\text{Effort} = 8 \text{ N (approx.)}$$

It must be pointed out that, in practice, the effort must be considerably greater than this in order to overcome friction. Even so, the total effort required will still be very small indeed compared with the load lifted.

The Wheel and Axle

The windlass used to raise buckets from wells, or the capstan used on board ship to raise the anchor, are examples of a machine called the *wheel and axle*. The wheel and axle is met with in a variety of forms, some of which are illustrated in Fig. 244.

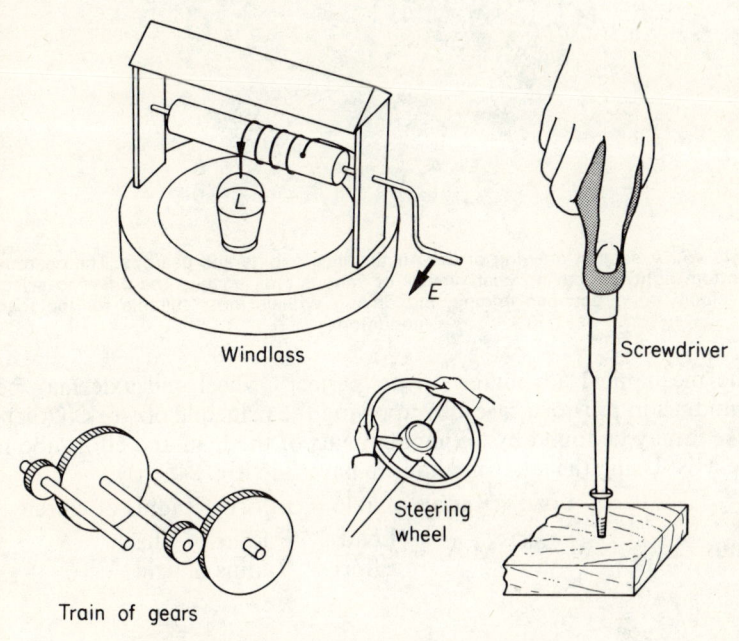

Fig. 244. Various wheel and axle arrangements

Essentially it consists of two wheels of different diameters rigidly fixed on the same axle. In Fig. 245(i), the effort is applied by a string attached to the rim of the larger wheel, while the load is raised by a string wound round the axle or smaller wheel. For one complete turn the effort and load move through distances equal to the circumferences of the wheel and axle respectively. The velocity ratio is therefore given by

$$\text{V.R.} = \frac{\text{Distance moved by effort}}{\text{Distance moved by load}}$$

$$= \frac{2\pi \times \text{Radius of wheel}}{2\pi \times \text{Radius of axle}}$$

$$= \frac{R}{r}$$

280 · ELEMENTARY PHYSICS

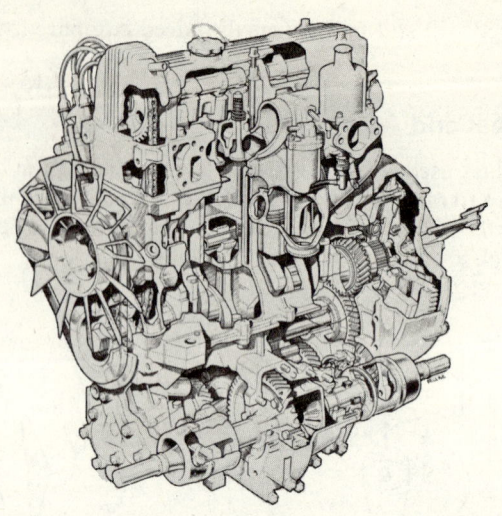

Plate 48. A section drawing of the Austin Maxi engine and gearbox. The gearbox (bottom right) by having gear-wheels of various radii enables the driver to select a velocity ratio between engine and driving wheels most suitable for the road conditions

The mechanical advantage for a "perfect" wheel and axle may be found, as in previous cases, by applying the principle of work. Otherwise it may be found by taking moments of the load and effort about the axis. Using the latter method we have (see Fig. 245 (ii)),

$$\text{Load} \times \text{Radius of axle} = \text{Effort} \times \text{Radius of wheel}$$

Thus
$$\text{M.A.} = \frac{\text{Load}}{\text{Effort}} = \frac{\text{Radius of wheel}}{\text{Radius of axle}} = \frac{R}{r}$$

Fig. 245. Measurements on a wheel and axle

MACHINES · 281

> **Summary**
>
> **1.** A *machine* is a device by means of which a force applied at one point may be used to overcome a force applied at some other point.
>
> **2.** The mechanical principles most commonly used in machines are those of the lever, the pulley, the inclined plane, the wheel and axle, and the screw.
>
> **3.** The Effort is the force applied to the machine. The Load is the force overcome by the machine.
>
> **4.** Mechanical advantage $= \dfrac{\text{Load}}{\text{Effort}}$
>
> Velocity ratio $= \dfrac{\text{Distance moved by effort}}{\text{Distance moved by load}}$
>
> Efficiency $= \dfrac{\text{Useful work done by machine}}{\text{Total work put into machine}} \times 100$ per cent.

EXERCISES

1. What is a machine? Define the terms *effort, load, velocity ratio* and *mechanical advantage*.

2. What is a lever? Explain with the aid of diagrams three machines based on the principle of the lever in which the effort, load and fulcrum are in different relative positions.

3. Define the *efficiency* of a machine. Show that the efficiency of a machine is also equal to the ratio of the mechanical advantage to the velocity ratio.

4. Give a diagram of a pulley system using (*a*) 4 pulleys and one string, (*b*) 4 pulleys and more than one string. In each case state the velocity ratio of the system.

5. Draw a diagram of a pulley system using 3 pulleys and one string. What is its velocity ratio?

6. A pulley system has an efficiency of 65 per cent and a velocity ratio of 6. Find its mechanical advantage. What effort would be required to raise a load of 100 kgf? Give a sketch of the system.

7. Find the efficiency of a system of pulleys having a velocity ratio of 4, if an effort of 40 kgf is required to raise a load of 120 kgf.

8. Give an example of the use of an inclined plane as a machine. A locomotive can exert a tractive effort (pull) of 2 tonne f. Assuming that no work is wasted, find the maximum weight of the train which it could haul up a slope which rises by 1 m for every 600 m travelled. (1 tonne = 1000 kg)

9. A packing case weighing 250 kgf is pulled by a rope up a wooden plank 3 m long, the upper end of which rests on the tailboard of a van 1 m from the ground. Neglecting friction, find the effort required.

Also find the effort required if the frictional force between packing case and plank is 30 N.

10. A force of 10 N is applied at right angles to the tommy bar of a vice at a distance of 80 mm from the axis of the screw. If the pitch of the screw is 1 mm. find the force of compression between the jaws of the vice (neglect friction).

11. The length of the crank of a windlass is 30 cm and the diameter of the axle is 10 cm. Find the effort required to raise a bucket of water weighing 20 kgf, if none of the work done is wasted.

12. In question 11, find the effort required if the efficiency of the windlass is 65 per cent.

Assume that the force of gravity on a mass of 1 kg is 10 N.

CHAPTER TWENTY-SEVEN

Density and Relative Density

Density

When handling balsa wood one is struck by its extreme lightness. On the other hand, the unusual heaviness of a bottle of mercury invariably surprises a person who lifts it for the first time. This unexpectedness is due to their relative masses; 10 cm^3 of mercury has mass 136 g but 10 cm^3 of balsa wood has only 2 g mass.

The *mass of unit volume* of a substance is called its *density*. From the figures above, the density of mercury is 13·6 g per cm^3, or 13 600 kg per m^3; for balsa wood it is 0·2 g per cm^3. The density of water is 1 g per cm^3, which is the same as 1000 kg per m^3.

The density of a sample of a given substance is therefore calculated by dividing the mass by the volume.

Thus $\quad$ Density = $\dfrac{\text{Mass}}{\text{Volume}}$, or $d = \dfrac{m}{V}$.

Also $\quad$ Mass = Volume × Density, or $m = V \times d$,

and $\quad$ Volume = $\dfrac{\text{Mass}}{\text{Density}}$, or $V = \dfrac{m}{d}$.

The densities of all common substances, solids, liquids and gases, and all chemical elements, have been carefully determined and are to be found recorded in books of physical and chemical constants. This information is of practical importance as the following examples will show.

Applications of Density

A knowledge of the densities of steel, concrete and other materials is necessary before an engineer can start to design a bridge or other building.

From the dimensions on his plans he can calculate the volume of any part of the structure, and this, multiplied by the density of the material, gives the mass and hence the weight. With this information he is now able to calculate the required strength of the foundations and supporting girders.

By the end of the last century it had been known for more than a hundred years that the density of nitrogen obtained from the air was slightly greater than that prepared in the laboratory from other substances. In all other respects the two kinds of nitrogen seemed to be identical. Lord Rayleigh and Sir William Ramsay suspected that the atmospheric nitrogen contained small quantities of a heavier gas. By experiments which cannot be described here, they succeeded in isolating a new gas which they called argon. This has since proved to be very useful, and nowadays it is used in gas-filled electric lamps. Its presence in the lamp at low pressure enables the filament to be run safely at a higher temperature than in a vacuum and so gives more light per unit of electricity used.

An Experiment to Determine the Density of Alcohol

A burette is filled with alcohol and its tap or clip opened and a little liquid allowed to run through in order to expel air from the pipe. The burette is then set up vertically in a stand and its reading noted.

A clean dry beaker is weighed and afterwards about 20 cm^3 of liquid is run into it from the burette. The second reading of the burette is noted and the beaker and liquid are weighed. By subtracting the mass of the empty beaker from the mass of the beaker plus liquid we obtain the mass of the liquid alone. We are now able to calculate the density of the liquid by dividing the mass by the volume.

The experiment should be repeated using different volumes of liquid each time, and a mean value for the density obtained. It will be found convenient to tabluate the results as below:

Mass of empty beaker =   g

Burette readings in cm^3		Volume of liquid in cm^3	Mass of beaker and liquid in g	Mass of liquid in g	Density of liquid in g per cm^3
(1)	(2)				

Mean value for density of alcohol =   g per cm^3 =   kg per m^3

To Find the Density of a Solid

The method described here is suitable for finding the density of any substance insoluble in water, and obtainable in pieces of irregular shape. Should the substance dissolve in water, then the same method may be used provided a non-solvent liquid such as white spirit (turpentine substitute) is used in the measuring cylinder.

DENSITY AND RELATIVE DENSITY · 285

A sample of the solid, e.g. a piece of coal, is weighed on a balance. A measuring cylinder is partly filled with water and the reading taken. The sample is gently lowered by a loop of cotton into the water so that it is completely immersed, and the new reading on the measuring cylinder is taken (Fig. 246). The difference between the two readings gives the volume of the coal. Should the sample be too large to go into a measuring cylinder, its volume may be found by the eureka can (Fig. 247). This is a cylindrical can with a short spout. Water is poured in

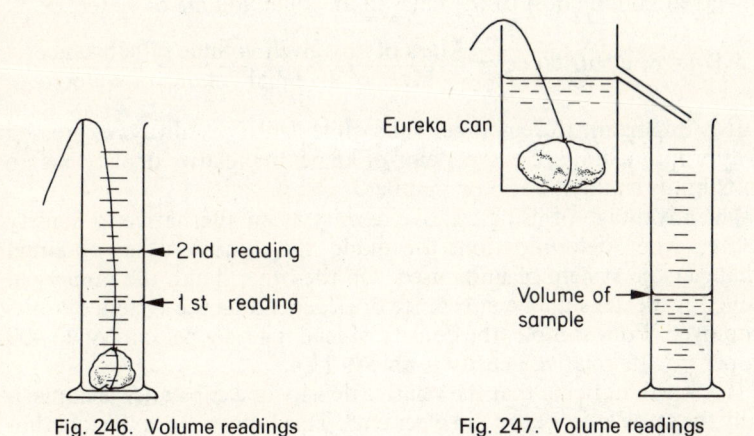

Fig. 246. Volume readings

Fig. 247. Volume readings

until it runs from the spout. When no more water drips from the spout, the sample is gently lowered into the can by a cotton loop. The water displaced is caught in a measuring cylinder and, when all dripping has ceased, the reading of the water level in the measuring cylinder will be the volume of the sample.

As in the previous experiment, the density is calculated from the equation,

$$\text{Density} = \frac{\text{Mass}}{\text{Volume}}$$

The density of several different substances should be found by this method and the results tabulated.

Substance	Mass in g	Measuring cylinder readings in cm^3		Volume in cm^3	Density in g per cm^3
		(1)	(2)		

Relative Density

Substances are frequently compared in mass to water, the most common liquid. To make the comparison a fair one, *equal* volumes of the substance and water are compared. Mercury is about 13·6 times the mass of an equal volume of water; cork is about 0·24 times the mass of an equal volume of water. Mercury is said to have a relative density of 13·6, and cork a relative density of 0·24.

The *relative density* of a substance is thus the ratio of the mass of any given volume of it to the mass of an equal volume of water, i.e.

$$\text{R.D. of a substance} = \frac{\text{Mass of any given volume of substance}}{\text{Mass of an equal volume of water}}$$

It is important to remember that while density is always expressed in appropriate units, e.g. g per cm^3 or kg per m^3 relative density has no units but is simply a ratio or number.

The advantage of using relative density as an alternative to density is that, when determinations are made, the same result is obtained whatever the system of units used. On the other hand, the numerical value for the density of a substance does depend on the system of units employed. For example, the density of lead is 11·4 g per cm^3 or 11 400 kg per m^3. Its relative density is always 11·4.

It is worth noticing that the relative density of a substance is numerically the same as its density in g per cm^3. This follows from the fact that the mass of 1 cm^3 of water is 1 g. Density in kg per m^3 is always relative density × 1000.

To Find the Relative Density of a Liquid

In accordance with the definition of relative density, we require to find the masses of equal volumes of the liquid and water. This is done by using a *relative density bottle* (Fig. 248), which is made of thin glass and fitted with a ground-glass stopper having a fine hole through its centre or a groove along its side. The special exact-fitting stopper enables the same volume of liquid to fill the bottle each time, as we shall shortly see.

Fig. 248.

The bottle is first weighed empty and then when full of the liquid and water respectively. Filling the bottle is carried out by pouring in the liquid carefully from a beaker, or better still by using a small funnel. When the stopper is inserted, excess liquid flows up through the hole and down the outside of the bottle. Before weighing, the bottle should be held by the neck only and wiped dry. One should avoid holding the bottle in the hand since the warmth of the hand will cause some of the liquid to expand out through the hole in the stopper and so lead to error.

DENSITY AND RELATIVE DENSITY · 287

The results should be recorded in the notebook, as below. As far as possible, equals signs, decimal points and so on should be arranged uniformly underneath each other. (See item 4 of *Hints to the Pupil* at the front of the book.)

Mass of empty R.D. bottle = g
Mass of bottle full of liquid = g
Mass of bottle full of water = g
Mass of liquid = g
Mass of water = g

$$\text{R.D. of liquid} = \frac{\text{Mass of liquid}}{\text{Mass of same vol. of water}}$$

$$= \frac{\text{g}}{\text{g}}$$

The Relative Density of a Solid

The relative density of a solid may be found by first weighing it, then weighing the water which it displaces from a Eureka can, and dividing the mass of the solid by the mass of the equal volume of water. A more accurate method, using Archimedes' Principle, is given in Chapter 30.

Summary

1. The density of a substance is the mass of unit volume of it. Density is usually expressed in gramme per cubic centimetre or kg per cubic metre.

2. The relation between the density, volume and mass of a piece of material is,

$$\text{Density} = \frac{\text{Mass}}{\text{Volume}}$$

3. The relative density of a substance is the ratio of the mass of any given volume of it to the mass of an equal volume of water. Thus,

R.D. of a substance =
$$\frac{\text{Mass of any given volume of the substance}}{\text{Mass of an equal volume of water}} = \frac{\text{density of substance}}{\text{density of water}}$$

4. Density in kg per m^3 = density in g per cm^3 × 1000.

EXERCISES

1. Define (*a*) density and (*b*) relative density of a substance.
2. Calculate the density of
   (*a*) glass if 120 cm^3 has a mass of 300 g.
   (*b*) gold if 10 cm^3 has a mass of 193 g.

(c) silver if 15 cm³ has a mass of 177·5 g.
(d) sea water if 1100 cm³ has a mass of 1155 g.

3. Find the volume of
   (a) 50 g of cork of density 0·25 g per cm³,
   (b) 270 g of paraffin wax of density 0·9 g per cm³,
   (c) 1 kilogramme of alcohol of density 0·79 g per cm³,
   (d) 1 tonne of oak of density 800 kg per m³.

4. What mass of petrol of relative density 0·72 is needed to fill a tank of capacity 50 litre?

5. A bar of chocolate is wrapped in a piece of aluminium which measures 150 mm × 100 mm and is 0·01 mm thick. Find the total mass of aluminium for 1000 bars. (Density of aluminium = 2·7 g per cm³.)

6. 153 cm³ of balsa wood of density 0·2 g per cm³ is used in the construction of a model aircraft. The total mass of the other materials, cement, paper, elastic, etc., used is 12 g. Find the mass of the complete model.

7. Draw a diagram of a relative density bottle and explain fully how it is used to find the relative density of seawater.

8. A relative density bottle has a mass of 14·62 g when empty, 57·43 g full of turpentine and 63·81 g when full of water. Find the relative density of turpentine.

9. A greenhouse roof contains 100 m² of glass of thickness 3 mm. If the density of glass is 2500 kg per m³, find the mass of glass supported in the roof.

10. A tangle of copper wire is found to have a mass of 64·5 g. By means of a screw gauge, the diameter of the wire is measured in several places and found to have a mean value of 1 mm. The density of copper is 8900 kg per m³. Find the length of wire in the tangle.

11. If provided with lead shot, describe how you would measure the density of lead. Give a list of imaginary measurements, and calculate the density from them.

CHAPTER TWENTY-EIGHT

Hydrostatics: Pressure

Atmospheric Pressure.   Crushing Can Experiment

Until the seventeenth century it was not realised that the atmosphere exerted a pressure and men explained its effects by saying that "nature abhorred a vacuum". Thus the common experience that, when air is sucked out of a bottle, it immediately tries to rush back in again, was explained by the theory that nature could not tolerate a vacuum. Nowadays, of course we say that the excess atmospheric pressure outside the bottle causes a flow of air into the bottle until the pressures inside and outside are equalised.

The large forces which can be produced by atmospheric pressure may be shown by means of a metal can fitted with an airtight stopper. The stopper having been removed, a small quantity of water is boiled in the can for a few minutes until the steam has driven out the air. The cork is then tightly replaced and simultaneously the flame beneath the can is turned out.

Cold water is then poured over the can. This causes the steam inside to condense, producing water and water vapour at very low pressure. As a result, the excess atmospheric pressure outside the can causes it to collapse inwards.

Meaning of Pressure

"Pressure" is a word we use from day to day without worrying too much as to its exact meaning. Thus we think of a steam engine as working by steam pressure. At home some of the cooking may be done in a pressure cooker. Before going out for a bicycle ride we make sure there is sufficient air pressure in the tyres.

In physics, however, we do not get very far until we are able to measure the things we talk about, so it becomes necessary to define or state the exact meaning of the words we use.

Pressure is defined as *the weight or force acting normally on unit area.* Thus if a brick of weight 2 kgf rests on an end of area 80 cm^2, the pressure exerted = $\frac{2}{80}$ = 0·025 kgf per cm^2. If the brick is turned so that it rests on another face of larger area, perhaps 250 cm², the new pressure = $\frac{\text{weight}}{\text{area}} = \frac{2}{250} = 0.008$ kgf per cm², which is less than before.

Pressure is usually expressed in newton per metre squared (N/m²). If 1 kgf is taken as about 10 N and 1 m² is 10 000 cm², then 4 kgf per cm² is equal to about 400 000 N/m².

Pressure of Air

We spend our time living at the bottom of a sea of air. Air has weight, and as a result it exerts a pressure of about 100 000 N/m², not only on the earth's surface but all over the surface of objects on the earth including ourselves. An average sized man having a surface area of 1·25 m² will thus have a total weight or thrust acting over his body of 1·25 × 100 000 = 125 000 N (or about 12·5 tonne f). He is not of course conscious of this enormous load since his blood exerts a pressure slightly greater than the atmospheric pressure and so a balance is more than effected. At high altitudes, where the pressure of the air is less, the

Plate *49*. The Magdeburg hemispheres experiment: a drawing of the scene, published in 1672

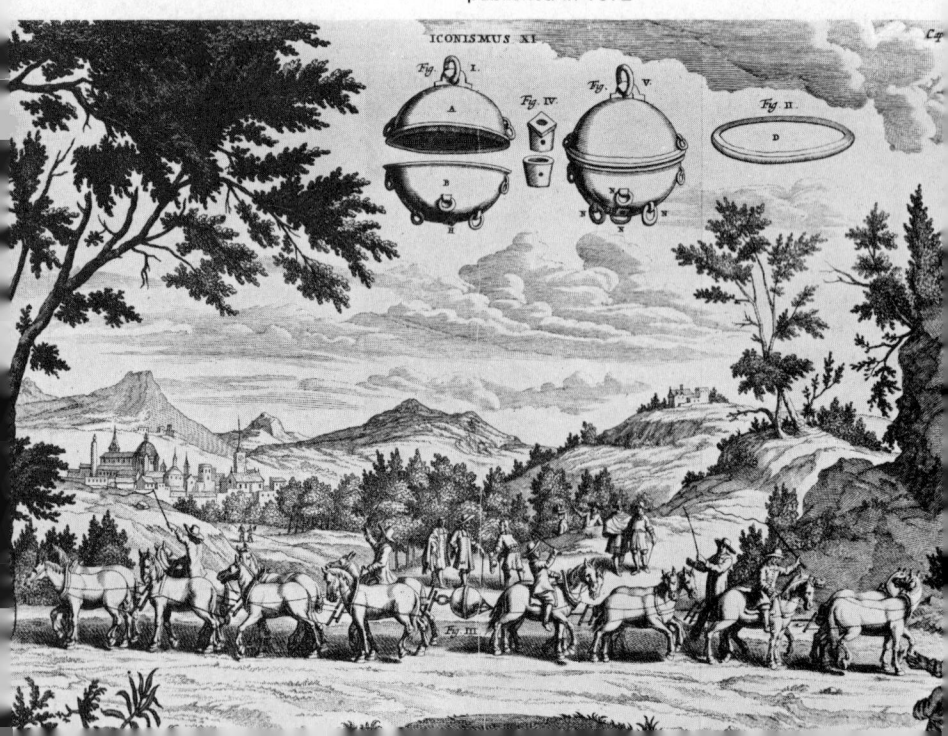

HYDROSTATICS: PRESSURE

pressure of the blood forces it through the membranes, and nosebleeding occurs if no precautions are taken.

The Magdeburg Hemispheres

In 1654, a German scientist named Otto von Guericke made two hollow bronze hemispheres one of which had a stopcock. After the rims of these had been placed together with a greased leather ring in between to form an airtight joint, the air was pumped out and the stopcock closed (Fig. 249).

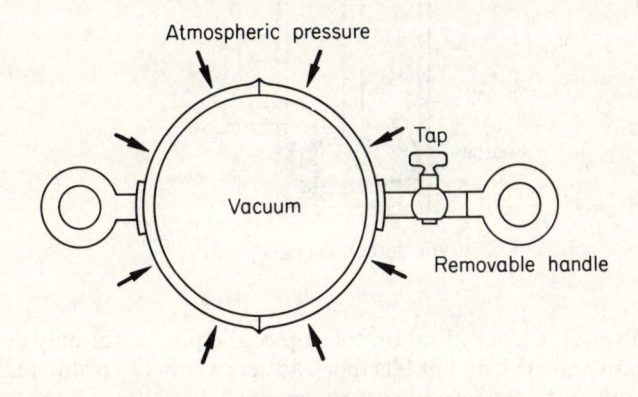

Fig. 249. The Magdeburg hemispheres

Before this was done the hemispheres could be pulled apart quite easily since the pressure outside was balanced by an equal pressure inside. On removal of the air from inside, the external atmospheric pressure alone acted, which caused the hemispheres to be pressed tightly together. This experiment was first performed before the Imperial court assembled at Ratisbon, on which occasion two teams of eight horses each were harnessed to the hemispheres and driven in opposite directions. They proved unable to separate the hemispheres until air had been re-admitted through the stopcock.

The Vacuum Pump

The big advances in the study of air pressure which were made during the seventeenth century followed the invention of the air pump by

Otto von Guericke. Fig. 250 shows the principle of a modern type of pump. Each time the piston is at the bottom of the cylinder some air from the vessel to be evacuated expands into the space above the piston. On each upstroke the air above the piston is carried out through

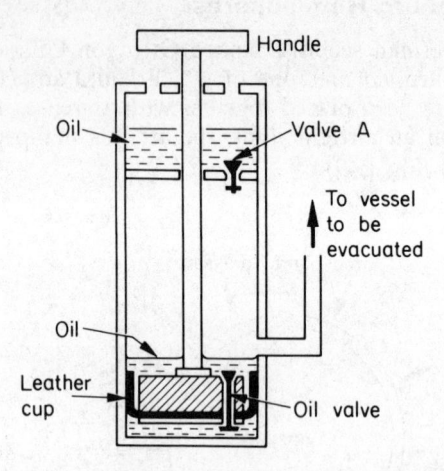

Fig. 250. A vacuum pump

the valve A. A layer of oil on the top of the piston not only acts as a lubricant and air seal, but fills the dead space between piston and valve at the top of the stroke and ensures removal of all the air trapped there.

Pressure in a Liquid

Liquids exert pressure as a result of their weight in the same way that air does. Later on in this chapter we shall have something to say about the pressure exerted by water on a diver.

The way in which pressure varies in a liquid may be shown by the apparatus of Fig. 251. Several thistle funnels bent at different angles have thin rubber tied securely over their mouths. One of these is connected by rubber tubing to a U-tube containing water. If the rubber is then pushed in with the finger the air inside is compressed and pushes up the water in the U-tube.

The funnel is now lowered into a tall jar full of water, when it will be noticed that, the deeper it goes, the greater is the difference in level, h mm, of the water in the two arms of the U-tube. It follows that the pressure in the water in the jar increases with depth.

Similar results are obtained if the thistle funnel is replaced by the others in turn, whose mouths are pointing in different directions. This

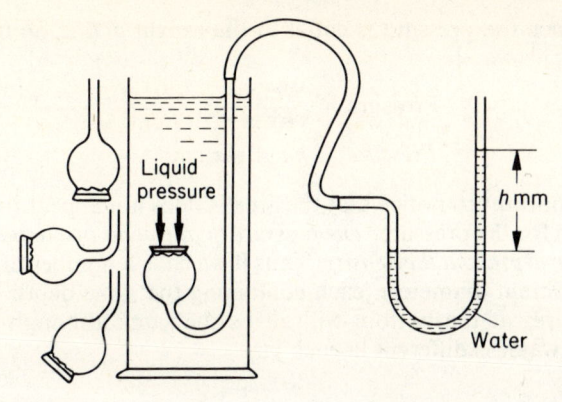

Fig. 251. Pressure in a liquid

shows that the pressure in water not only increases with depth but also acts in all directions. The same result is obtained with liquids other than water.

Finally, if a thistle funnel is lowered to the *same depth* in a number of different liquids in turn, it will be noticed that the greater the density of the liquid, the greater is the pressure.

Calculation of Pressure

Suppose we think of a horizontal area A cm^2 at a depth of h cm below the surface of a liquid (Fig. 252). Standing on this area and pressing down on it there is a volume of liquid hA cm^3. The mass of

Volume of liquid column = hA cm^3

Mass ,, ,, ,, = hAd g

Weight ,, ,, ,, = hAd gf

Pressure at depth h cm

$$= \frac{hAd}{A}$$

$$= hd \text{ gf per cm}^2$$

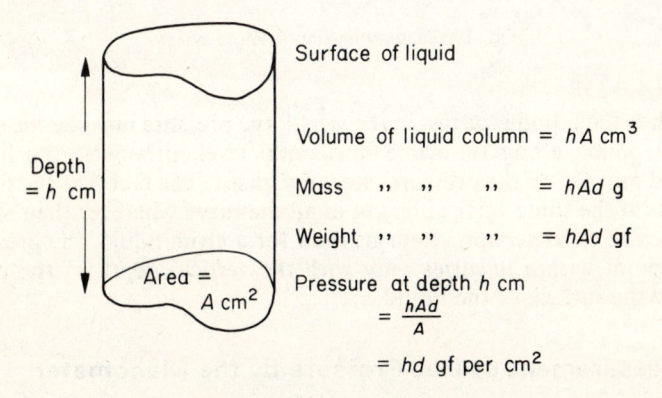

Fig. 252. Calculating pressure

this liquid, found by multiplying the volume by the density, d g per cm^3 of the liquid is equal to hAd g and hence its weight is hAd gf.

Now since the pressure is equal to the weight acting on unit area, we have,

$$\text{Pressure} = \frac{\text{Weight}}{\text{Area}} = \frac{hAd \text{ gf}}{A \text{ cm}^2}$$

or
$$\text{Pressure} = hd \text{ gf per cm}^2$$

It is important to notice that the area A does not appear in the final expression for the pressure. *The pressure at any point in a liquid depends only on the depth and the density*. Thus if we have a number of different jars of different diameters, each containing the same depth of water, the pressures at the bottom will all be the same although the total weight of water is different in each jar.

A Liquid Finds its Own Level

The result obtained in the last paragraph may be illustrated experimentally by means of the communicating tubes of a glass vessel (Fig. 253). Water or any other liquid poured into this vessel will be seen to stand at the same level in each tube, illustrating the popular saying that, "water finds its own level".

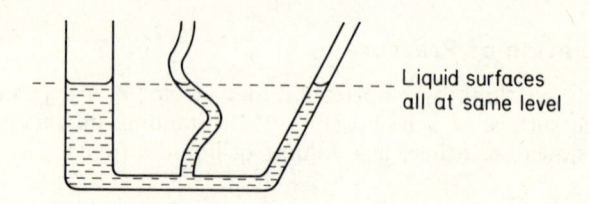

Fig. 253. Liquid level in a single system

When the liquid is at rest in the vessel, the pressure must be the same at all points along the same horizontal level, otherwise the liquid would move until the pressures were equalised. The fact that the liquid stands at the same vertical height in all the tubes whatever their shape or area of cross-section confirms that, for a given liquid, the pressure at a point within it varies only with the vertical depth of the point below the surface of the liquid.

Measurement of Gas Pressure by the Manometer

Earlier in this chapter it was stated that the pressure of the atmosphere was about 100 000 N per m². Before explaining how this is measured let us make a study of the *manometer*, an instrument for measuring the pressure of a gas.

HYDROSTATICS: PRESSURE

The manometer consists of a U-tube containing liquid, such as water. When both arms are open to the atmosphere, the same atmospheric pressure is exerted on the water surfaces A and B and these are at the same horizontal level (Fig. 254).

In order to measure the pressure of the gas supply in the laboratory, the side A is connected to a gas tap by a length of rubber tubing (Fig. 255). When the tap is turned on the gas pressure is exerted on the surface A, with the result that the level B rises until the pressure at C on the same horizontal level as A becomes equal to the gas pressure. Thus,

Pressure of gas = atmospheric pressure + pressure due to water column BC

It follows that the *excess* pressure of the gas above that of the atmosphere is given by the pressure of the water column BC, and is therefore equal to hd gf per cm^2 where h is the height of the column in centimetres and d is the density of water in g per cm^3.

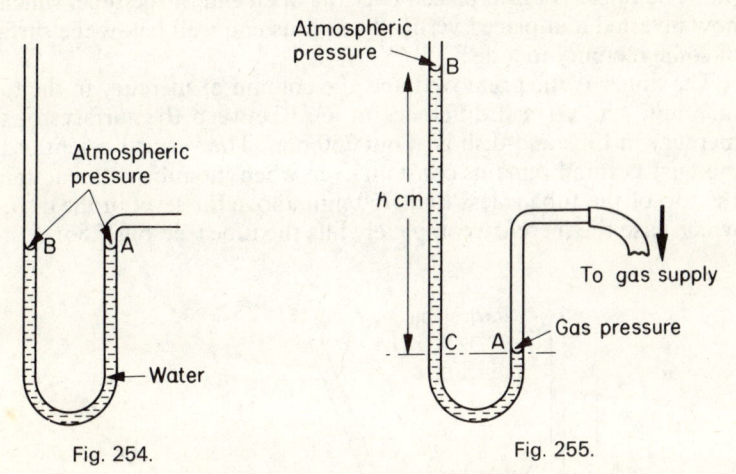

Fig. 254.

Fig. 255.

Measuring pressure with a manometer

The height h cm is called the *head of water* in the manometer and it is customary to use this height only as a measure of the excess pressure. We can therefore say,

Excess pressure of gas supply is equivalent to the pressure h cm of water.

For measuring higher pressures than in the example above, mercury (density 13·6 g per cm^3) is used in the manometer, while for lower pressures a liquid such as xylene (density 0·88 g per cm^3) is more suitable than water.

Torricelli's Experiment.   Simple Barometer

About the middle of the seventeenth century an Italian scientist named Torricelli, living at Pisa, suggested an experiment to discount the theory that nature abhorred a vacuum. Torricelli believed that nature's supposed horror of a vacuum was caused simply by atmospheric pressure. In a famous experiment, first performed in 1643, he set up the first *barometer,* an instrument for measuring the pressure of the air.

In the laboratory, a simple barometer can be made by taking a stout-walled glass tube about a metre long and closed at one end, and filling it almost to the top with clean mercury. This is done with the aid of a small glass funnel and short length of rubber tubing. Small air bubbles will generally be noticed clinging to the walls of the tube and these must be removed. With the finger placed securely over its open end, the tube is inverted several times so that the large air bubble left at the top of the tube travels up and down, collecting the small bubbles on its way. More mercury is then added so that the tube is completely full. The finger is again placed over the open end of the tube, which is now inverted and placed vertically with its end well below the surface of some mercury in a dish.

The finger is then removed and the column of mercury in the tube falls until the vertical difference in level between the surfaces of the mercury in tube and dish is about 750 mm. The vertical height of the mercury column remains constant even when the tube is tilted, unless the top of the tube is less than 750 mm above the level in the dish, in which case the mercury completely fills the tube (see Fig. 256).

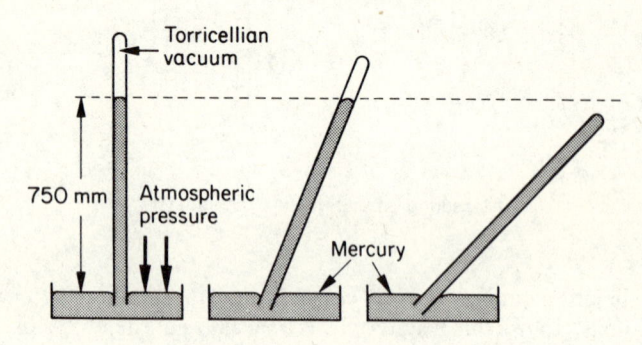

Fig. 256. A simple barometer

Torricelli explained that the column of mercury was supported in the tube by the atmospheric pressure acting on the surface of the mercury in the dish, and pointed out that small changes in the height of the column, which are noticed from day to day, are due to fluctuations in the atmospheric pressure. The space above the mercury in the tube is called a *torricellian vacuum;* it contains a little mercury vapour and in this respect differs from a true vacuum.

Calculation of Atmospheric Pressure from Barometric Height

Density of mercury = 13 600 kg per m^3

Pressure of the atmosphere = Pressure of a column of mercury 0·75 m high

$$= Hd \text{ kgf per m}^2$$
$$= 0.75 \times 13\,600 \text{ kgf per m}^2$$
$$= 10\,200 \text{ kgf per m}^2$$

But 1 kgf $\simeq$ 10 N, or, for accurate work, 1 kgf = 9·8 N.

Hence atmospheric pressure = 10 200 × 9·8
$$= 100\,000 \text{ N per m}^2$$

The above calculation shows how the pressure may be obtained from the height of the mercury column. For the most part however this is rarely done. It is customary to express the atmospheric pressure simply in terms of the height of the mercury column. The average value over a long period is 760 mm. We therefore say,

Normal or standard atmospheric pressure = 760 mm of mercury.
This pressure is also called *one atmosphere*.

Pascal's Experiments with Barometers

Torricelli died a few years after the barometer experiment had been performed and did not live to see his explanation of it, in terms of atmospheric pressure, generally accepted among scientists.

After Torricelli's death, Pascal repeated the experiment in France and set up two barometers. The first of these was placed at the foot of a mountain in Auvergne called the Puy du Dome, whilst the other was carried up the mountain side and the height of the column read at intervals on the way up. On account of the decreasing height of the atmosphere above this barometer, its mercury column showed a progressive fall on account of the reduced atmospheric pressure. The barometer at the foot of the mountain showed practically no change.

It was this final experiment which brought about the downfall of the theory that nature abhors a vacuum and established the principle that the atmosphere exerts a pressure.

The Fortin Barometer

The atmospheric pressure is often required accurately in laboratory experiments, and for a more accurate measurement of the barometric height than can be obtained with a simple barometer, the Fortin barometer is used (Fig. 257).

Here the tube containing the mercury is protected by enclosing it in a brass tube, the upper part of which is made of glass so that the mercury surface may be seen. Readings are taken by a vernier moving over a millimetre scale of sufficient length to cover the full range of variation in barometric height.

To overcome errors due to alteration in the lower mercury level when the mercury rises or falls in the tube, the dish of mercury used in the simple barometer is replaced in the Fortin by a leather bag which may be raised or lowered by a screw. Before taking a reading, this screw is adjusted until the lower mercury surface just touches an ivory pointer. This pointer has been fixed so that it coincides with the zero of the vertical millimetre scale, and the height of the mercury above the level in the bag is then read from the scale.

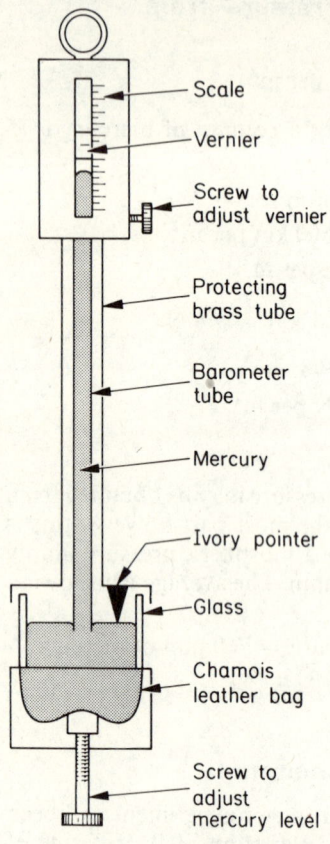

Fig. 257. A Fortin barometer

The Aneroid Barometer and Altimeter

Barometers of the aneroid (without liquid) type are commonly used as weather glasses. The essential part of an aneroid barometer is a flat cylindrical metal box or capsule, corrugated for strength, and hermetically sealed after having been partially exhausted of air (Fig. 258). Increase in atmospheric pressure causes the box to cave in slightly while a decrease allows it to expand. The movements of the box are magnified

HYDROSTATICS: PRESSURE · 299

by a system of levers and transmitted to a fine chain wrapped round the spindle of a pointer. The chain is kept taut by means of a hairspring attached to the spindle.

The dial of these instruments is usually calibrated as in Fig. 259. Low

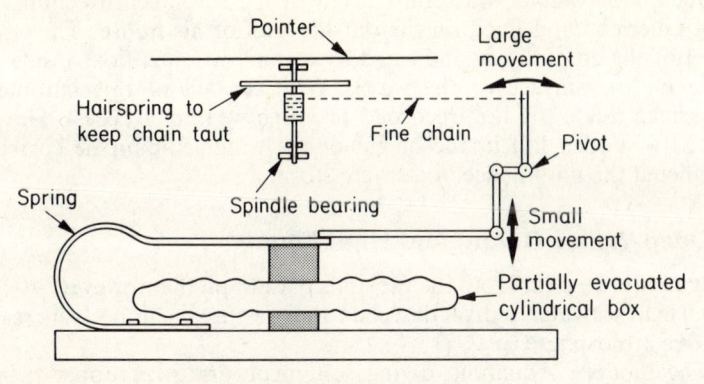

Fig. 258. Aneroid barometer

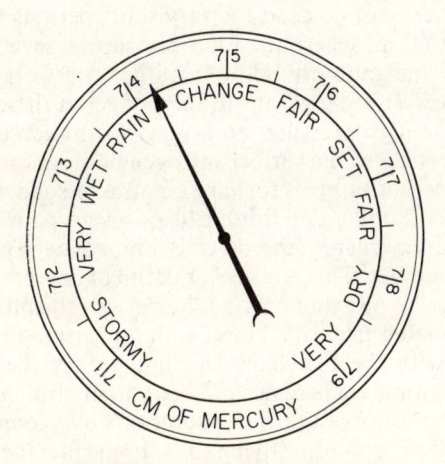

Fig. 259. Aneroid barometer scale

pressure, or a sudden fall in pressure, generally indicates unsettled weather whilst a rising barometer or high pressure is associated with a period of fine weather.

Aneroid barometer movements are used in the construction of altimeters for aircraft. In these the scale is calibrated in metre. Roughly speaking the atmospheric pressure falls by 25 mm for every 300 m of ascent.

The Water Barometer

Since the relative density of mercury is 13·6 it follows that if water were used as the liquid in a simple barometer, the water column would have to be (760 × 13·6) mm or 10·3 m long.

Such a barometer was constructed in the seventeenth century by von Guericke and fixed on the outside wall of his house. The upper level of the column was indicated by a small wooden float inside the tube on the surface of the water. With the aid of this barometer Guericke made the first recorded scientific weather forecast. Having noted a sudden fall in the height of the water column he correctly predicted the imminence of a severe storm.

Deep Water Diving and High Flying

It should be clear from the previous paragraph that for every 10·3 m (10·0 m in seawater) a diver descends, the pressure on his body increases by one atmosphere (p. 297).

The modern Aqualung diving suit incorporates a rubber helmet fitted with a circular window and supplied with air from compressed air cylinders carried on the wearer's back. Using this apparatus, experienced divers can descend for very short periods to a maximum depth of about 60 m, where the total pressure is seven atmospheres. At depths in the neighbourhood of 45 m they can work for periods of about 15 minutes. It is dangerous to stay longer at these depths, since, as a result of the high pressure, an excess of nitrogen dissolves in the blood, and on return to the surface nitrogen bubbles form in the blood in the same way that bubbles form in a bottle of soda water when the cork is removed. Such a condition causes severe pain or even death, and in cases of emergency the diver is immediately placed in a decompression chamber. This is a steel tank full of compressed air and by slowly reducing the pressure over a long period, the nitrogen becomes gradually eliminated from the blood without forming bubbles.

In contrast with the problems encountered by the diver, airmen flying at high altitudes experience difficulty in breathing on account of the low atmospheric pressure. The problem is overcome by the use of either "pressurised" cabins or flying suits. In the first method, all openings in the aircraft cabin are sealed and normal atmospheric pressure is maintained inside by air pumps. Where this method is not practicable the airman is enclosed in an airtight rubber suit fitted with a transparent helmet. Air is supplied to the suit from a cylinder of compressed air so that the occupant can breathe air at ordinary pressure.

Boyle's Law

As we have seen, the pressure of the atmosphere is regarded as being due to the weight of the air pressing downwards. The pressure of the air inside a closed vessel such as an inflated balloon or in a bicycle pump is looked at from another standpoint. Gases consist of billions of tiny molecules in a state of continual movement, colliding all the time with one another and bombarding the walls of their containing vessels. It is these billions of tiny blows on the walls of the vessel which cause the pressure. The greater the number of blows, the greater is the pressure. Thus, when the handle of a bicycle pump is pushed in, the volume of the air inside is decreased without altering the number of molecules present. There will now be more molecules per cm^3 and therefore more molecules bombarding each cm^2 of surface, with a consequent increase in pressure.

The law relating the pressure and volume of a fixed mass of gas was first studied experimentally by Robert Boyle who lived during the seventeenth century. Boyle made a glass tube in the form of a letter J having its shorter arm closed (Fig. 260(i)). Mercury was poured in so

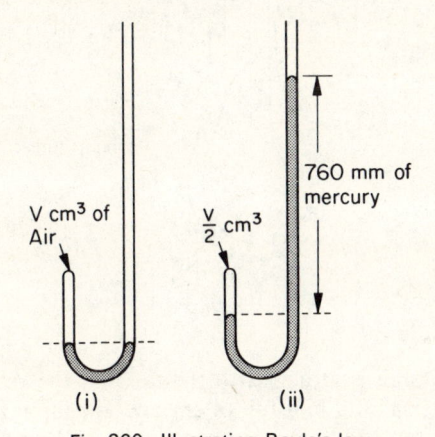

Fig. 260. Illustrating Boyle's law

as to trap air in the short arm and adjusted so that the levels were the same in both sides. This ensured that the pressure of the air was atmospheric. The volume of the trapped air was noted. More mercury was then added until the difference in mercury levels was equal to the barometric height (760 mm of mercury). The pressure of the air was thus *doubled* and it was now noticed that the volume of the air had been *halved* (Fig. 260(ii)). Other values of pressure were used and the corresponding volumes noted. Each time Boyle found that the product of pressure and volume was constant, from which he concluded that the volume and pressure were inversely proportional to each other.

Verification of Boyle's Law

Method. A modern form of apparatus for varying and measuring the pressure and volume of a fixed mass of dry air is shown in Fig. 261. It consists of a burette B connected by a length of rubber pressure tubing to a glass reservoir A containing mercury. With the tap T open, the reservoir is adjusted until the burette is full of mercury. A calcium

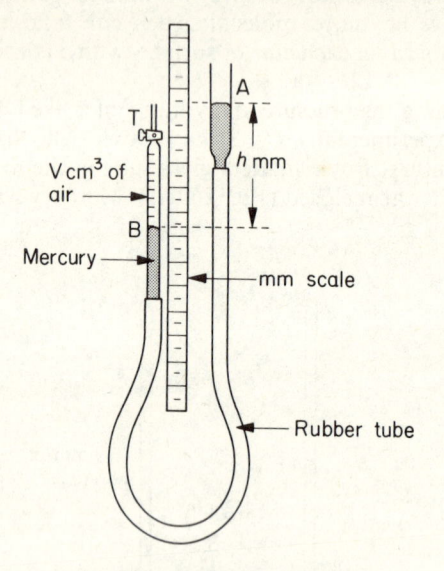

Fig. 261. Testing Boyle's law

chloride drying tube is attached to the tap and the reservoir lowered until the burette is about half full of dry air. The tap is then closed and the drying tube removed. The mercury levels in A and B are now the same, so that the air in B is at atmospheric pressure. The volume of the air in the burette (v cm³) is recorded, and at the same time the atmospheric pressure (H mm) of mercury is read from a Fortin barometer.

The reservoir A is now raised or lowered to a series of different positions, the volume, v cm³ and the mercury levels in A and B being recorded for each position.

The pressure of the gas is given by $p = H+h$ mm of mercury when A is above B and by $p = H-h$ mm of mercury when A is below B.

All the above readings should be tabulated as shown.

Measurements.
Atmospheric pressure = H =   mm of mercury.

Volume v cm³	Level A	Level B	mm	Pressure $p = H \pm h$ mm of mercury	$p \times v$	$\dfrac{1}{p}$

Result. If the experiment has been carefully carried out it will be found that the product of pressure and volume is, within the limits of experimental error, the same for each pair of values.

We therefore say

$$\text{Pressure} \times \text{Volume} = \text{Constant}.$$

This means that if the volume is halved the pressure is doubled, and so on. Such a relationship between p and v is called "inverse proportion", and it holds for all gases. *Boyle's Law* is often stated as follows: the pressure of a fixed mass of gas, at constant temperature, is inversely proportional to its volume.

Precaution. It is necessary to qualify the above statement by the words "at constant temperature". This is often overlooked. If the temperature alters during the experiment the gas will undergo thermal expansion (see p. 183) and Boyle's Law will not hold.

We generally assume that the temperature of the laboratory remains fairly constant during the experiment, but it would be better to take readings at intervals on a thermometer suspended near the gas burette as a check.

Verifying Boyle's Law by Plotting a Graph

We learn from mathematics, that if in the equation $y = mx$, where m is a fixed or constant number we give various values to x and calculate y, a straight line graph passing through the origin is obtained on plotting y against x.

Now if Boyle's Law is true

$$pv = c, \text{ a constant,}$$

or

$$v = c \times \frac{1}{p}$$

Comparing this equation with $y = mx$, and remembering that m and c are constants, we note that

$$\frac{1}{p} \text{ correponds to } x$$

and

$$v \text{ corresponds to } y.$$

Hence if Boyle's Law is true we should get a straight line passing through the origin by plotting v against $\frac{1}{p}$ (Fig. 262).

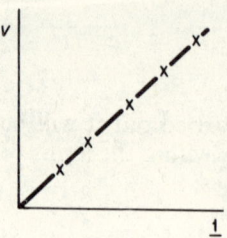

Fig. 262. Boyle's law graph

Values of $\frac{1}{p}$ should be found from a table of reciprocals and the graph plotted.

Worked example. Assuming that the temperature inside a motor tyre is the same as that of the air outside, find the volume of air at atmospheric pressure, 100 000 N/m² required to inflate the tyre to a pressure of 200 000 N/m² above atmospheric pressure. The volume of the inner tube is 0·01 m³

When the tyre is flat the pressure of the air inside it is equal to atmospheric pressure 100 kN/m² (1000 N = 1 kN). When it has been pumped up the pressure indicated on a gauge is 200 kN/m² and the absolute or total pressure inside the tyre is 300 kN/m².

Since the temperature is constant, Boyle's Law holds and the product pressure × volume, for the air entering the tyre, is also constant. Thus

$$p_1 v_1 = p_2 v_2,$$

where p_1 = atmospheric pressure
v_1 = volume of air at atmospheric pressure
p_2 = pressure inside tyre
v_2 = volume of tyre.

Hence $100 \times v_1 = 300 \times 0·01$

$$v_1 = \frac{300 \times 0·01}{100}$$
$$= 0·03 \text{ m}^3$$
$$= 30 \text{ litre}$$

Summary

1. *Pressure* = Force (or weight) acting normally per unit area.
2. The *pressure of a column of liquid* of density d g per cm³ and height h cm is given by

Pressure = hd gf per cm²

3. The *pressure of a gas* is measured with a water or mercury manometer.
4. The *pressure of the atmosphere* is measured by the height of a column of mercury in the simple barometer. The barometric height is normally 760 mm of mercury or 10·3 m of water, and is

equivalent to about 100 kN per m². The Fortin barometer is a simple barometer with the addition of an ivory pointer and vernier scale to enable the barometric height to be measured to a high degree of accuracy.

5. The *aneroid barometer* uses the movement of the lid of a metal box partially exhausted of air to measure the pressure of the atmosphere.

6. *Boyle's Law* states that the pressure of a fixed mass of gas, at constant temperature, is inversely proportional to its volume, or

$$\text{Pressure} \times \text{Volume} = \text{Constant}.$$

EXERCISES

1. Explain what is meant by pressure. Calculate the pressure exerted by the point of a drawing-pin, if it is pushed into a board with a force of 3 kgf the area of the point being 0·15 mm².

2. State three facts you know concerning pressure in a liquid and describe experiments to illustrate each of them.

3. A motor-car tyre is to be inflated to a pressure of 200 kN per m². The diameter of the pump barrel is 50 mm. Find the maximum force which will have to be exerted on the piston of the pump. ($\pi = \frac{22}{7}$.)

4. Describe a water manometer and explain how it may be used to measure the excess pressure of the laboratory gas supply above that of the atmosphere.

5. Give full details of the way in which you would set up a simple barometer and use it to measure the pressure of the atmosphere.
How would you test the barometer to make sure that there was no air in the space above the mercury?

6. On a certain day the barometric height was 762 mm of mercury. Express this pressure in N per m². (Density of mercury = 13 600 kg per m³.)

7. Give a labelled diagram of the Fortin barometer and describe how it is used to make an accurate determination of the barometric height.

8. If the air pressure is 100 kN per m², calculate the force due to this pressure on (i) a person's head of area 0·04 m², (ii) the faces of a cube whose sides are 0·5 m long.

9. Describe the construction and explain the action of an aneroid barometer.

10. State Boyle's Law and describe how you would verify it for pressures above and below atmospheric pressure.

11. A certain mass of gas occupies 1000 cm³ when the pressure is 800 mm of mercury. What would be the new volume if the pressure is changed to 300 mm of mercury, the final temperature being unchanged?

12. A steel cylinder of volume 0·1 m³ contains oxygen at 120 atmospheres pressure. What volume of gas is available for use at 5 atmospheres pressure at the same temperature?

13. A bubble of air of volume 0.5 cm^3 escapes from a diver's helmet at a depth of 20 m of water. Calculate the volume of the bubble immediately before it breaks at the surface, assuming no change in temperature. (Atmospheric pressure = 10 m of water.)

14. A simple barometer is set up in the usual way except that, instead of the customary stout-walled tube, a long burette with a well-fitting tap is used. The barometric height is found to be 750 mm of mercury.

The tap is then opened carefully and closed again when the height of the mercury has fallen to 660 mm. The volume occupied by the air now above the mercury is 15 cm^3. What volume of air, measured at atmospheric pressure and the same temperature, entered the burette when the tap was open?

Assume that the force of gravity on a mass of 1 kg is 10 N.

CHAPTER TWENTY-NINE

Applications of Atmospheric and Liquid Pressure

The Suction Pad

In this chapter we shall discuss some of the applications of atmospheric and liquid pressure. A very common application nowadays of atmospheric pressure is the circular shallow rubber cap or pad, about 25 mm in diameter, on which articles can be hung by a hook on the rubber. The suction pad is also used for attaching notices to shop windows and for similar purposes.

When the rubber is moistened to obtain a good air seal and pressed on a smooth flat surface, the cup is flattened and at the same time squeezes out the air from beneath it. Atmospheric pressure then holds the pad firmly to the surface.

The Common Pump

Pumps were used successfully to raise water from wells long before their action was properly understood. An alternative name for the

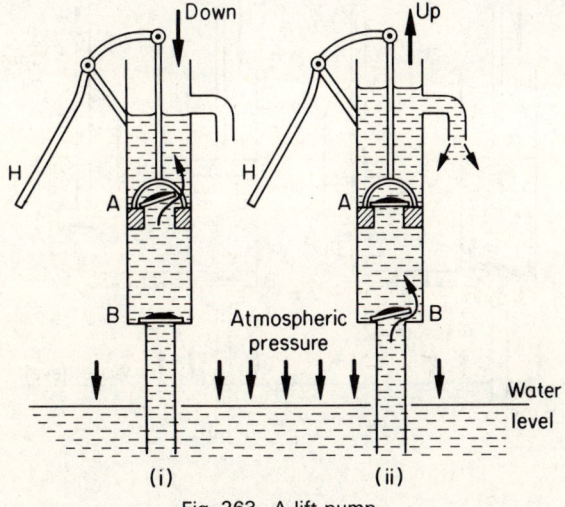

Fig. 263. A lift pump

common pump is the suction or lift pump (Fig. 263). It consists of a cylindrical metal barrel fitted near the top with a side tube to act as a spout. At the bottom of the barrel, where it joins a pipe leading down to the well, is a clack valve B. The latter is a hinged circular leather flap weighted by a brass disc so that it normally falls shut. A plunger carrying a leather cup and fitted with a second clack valve A is moved up and down inside the barrel by a handle H.

To start the pump working it is first primed by pouring some water on to the top of the plunger. This makes a good air seal and prevents leakage of air past the plunger during the first few strokes needed to fill the pump with water. Once the pump is filled the action is as follows.

The downstroke (Fig. 263(i)). When the plunger moves downwards the valve B closes under its own weight, while the water inside the pump passes upwards through the valve A into the space above the plunger.

The upstroke (Fig. 263(ii)). On the upstroke the valve A closes by its own weight and as the plunger rises, water is pushed up the pipe and through the valve B by atmospheric pressure on the surface of the water in the well. Simultaneously, the water above the plunger is raised and flows out of the spout.

Limitations of the common pump. Since the normal height of a water barometer is, as we have seen, about 10 m it means that this is the maximum height to which water can be raised by a common pump. An imperfect vacuum, however, is usually obtained on account of bubbles from dissolved air forming near the top of the water column. For this reason, the practical working height of a pump is rather less than 9 m.

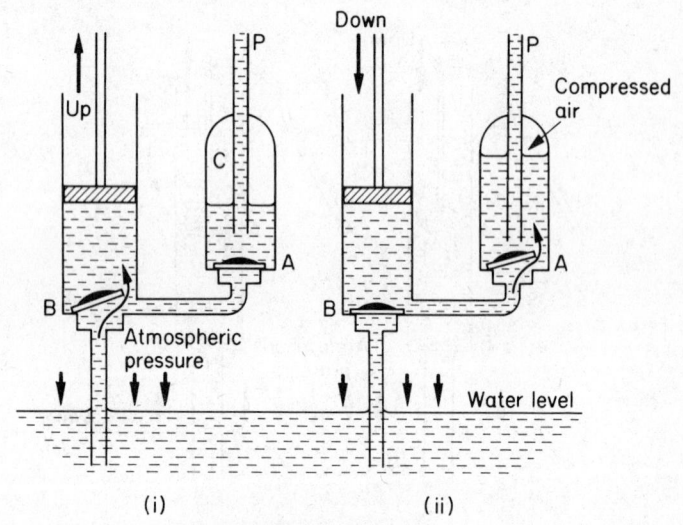

Fig. 264. A force pump

The Force Pump

For raising water to a height of more than 10 m, the force pump is used (Fig. 264). It consists of a pump with a solid plunger and foot valve B, connected by a pipe to a chamber C through a valve A.

The upstroke (Fig. 264(i)). On the upstroke, valve A closes and water is pushed up into the pump through valve B by atmospheric pressure.

The downstroke (Fig. 264(ii)). On the downstroke, valve B closes and water is forced into the chamber C through valve A by the pressure due to the mechanical force exerted on the plunger.

The exit pipe P projects into the chamber C so that some air becomes trapped at the top of the chamber. This is compressed and acts as a cushion, thus preventing a sudden jolt to the pump when the water column in P falls slightly and sharply closes valve A at the beginning of the upstroke. C also helps to expel water on the upstroke.

The maximum height to which water may be raised by this means depends on

    (*a*) The force which is exerted on the plunger during the downstroke.
    (*b*) The ability of the pump and its working parts to withstand the pressure of the long column of water in the exit pipe P.

The pump itself must be under 10 m above the water surface.

Early Fire Pumps

During the early nineteenth century, manual fire pumps were used which consisted of a pair of force pumps connected to a long handle and worked by a team of four men. Both pumps fed alternately into a

Plate 50. A modern diesel-driven fire pump

chamber with a compressed air-space similar to that described above. At the moment of change-over of feed from one pump to the other the compressed air expanded and so maintained a steady flow of water to the hoses.

The Preserving Jar

Atmospheric pressure can be put to use in the kitchen in connection with the preservation of fruit.

The preserving jar is a glass jar covered with a glass cap seated on a flat rubber ring. Clean fruit and water are placed in the jar, leaving a small air space at the top. Several of these jars are placed in a large vessel of cold water which is then slowly brought to the boil. During this process the glass caps with their rubber rings are loosely held in position by a metal screw cap. About 10 minutes' boiling is generally sufficient to sterilise the fruit and to cause air to be driven from the jars by steam from the water inside. The screw caps are then tightened and the jars removed from the water.

After cooling, the space at the top of the jar contains only water vapour at low pressure. As a result, the glass cap is then firmly pressed down by atmospheric pressure. No bacteria-laden air can afterwards enter and so the contents remain in good condition for a long period. It is important to notice that, when the jars have cooled, the presence of the metal screw cap is not strictly necessary as the seal is now maintained by atmospheric pressure (Fig. 265).

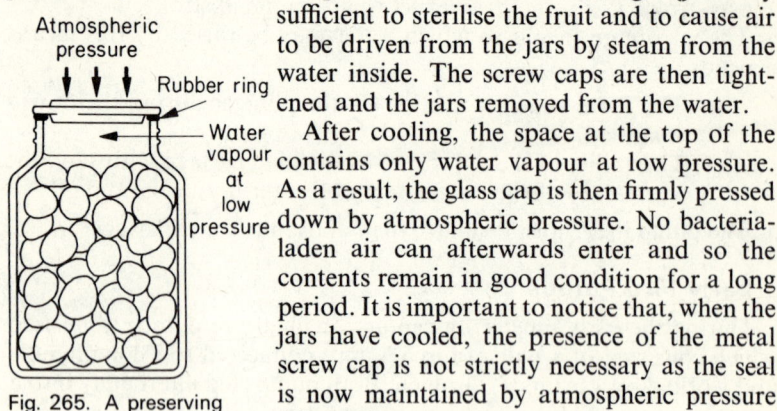

Fig. 265. A preserving jar

The Transmission of Pressure in Fluids.

When a fluid completely fills a vessel, and a pressure is applied to it at any part of its surface, for example by means of a cylinder and piston connected to the vessel, that pressure is transmitted equally throughout

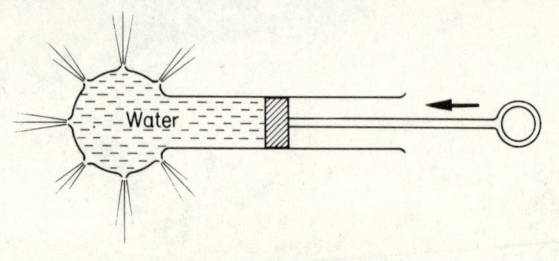

Fig. 266. Pressure in a fluid

the whole of the enclosed fluid. This fact, first recognised by the French scientist and philosopher, Pascal, in 1650, is called the Principle of Transmission of Pressure in fluids.

Fig. 266 shows a piece of apparatus to demonstrate this principle. It consists of a glass barrel fitted with a plunger and ending in a bulb pierced with holes of uniform size. It is filled with water by dipping the bulb in water and slowly raising the plunger. When the plunger is then pushed in, the water squirts equally out of all the holes. This shows that the pressure applied to the plunger has been transmitted uniformly throughout the water.

Nowadays the principle of transmission of pressure has many practical applications. Indeed, our lives may often be said to depend on it whenever we ride in a bus or motor-car, since the brakes of the majority of road vehicles are worked by hydraulic pressure.

This system of braking is shown diagrammatically in Fig. 267. The brake-shoes are expanded by a cylinder having two opposed pistons.

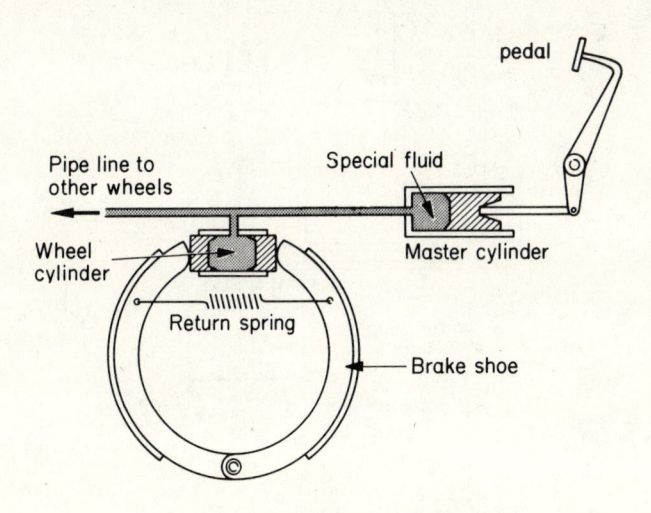

Fig. 267. Hydraulic brake system

These are forced outwards by liquid under pressure conveyed by a pipe from the master cylinder. The piston of the master cylinder is worked by the brake pedal. When pressure on the pedal is released, the brake-shoe pull-off springs force the wheel pistons back into the cylinders, and the liquid is returned to the master cylinder.

A very important advantage of this system is that the pressure set up in the master cylinder is transmitted equally to all four wheel cylinders so that the braking effort is equal on all wheels.

Hydraulic Pressure

Hydraulic presses have numerous uses, from the compression of soft materials like waste paper and cotton into compact bales, to the shaping of motor-car bodies and the forging of steel armour plate.

In its simplest form, the hydraulic press consists of a cylinder and piston of large diameter connected by a pipe to a force pump of much smaller diameter. Water from a supply tank is pumped into the cylinder and the piston moves out, exerting considerable force (Fig. 268). A release valve T is provided to run off water from the cylinder after the piston has done its work.

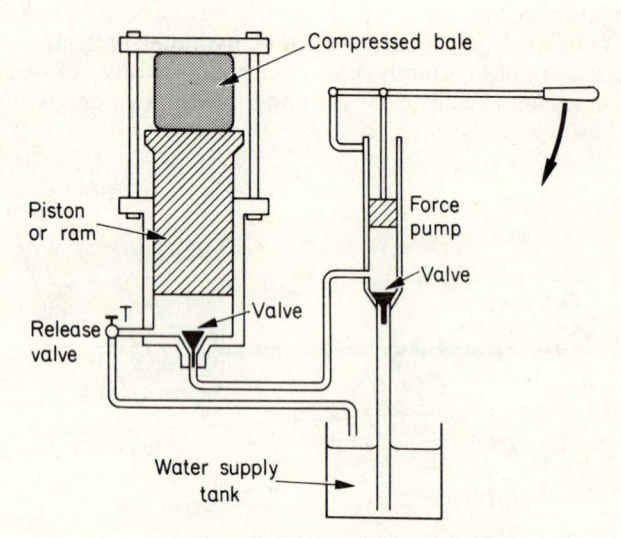

Fig. 268. A hydraulic press

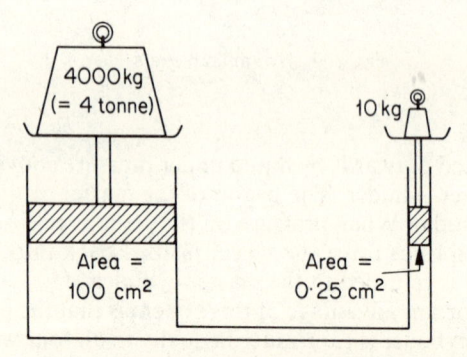

Fig. 269. The principle of a hydraulic press

Plate 51. A large hydraulic press in a steel works

In order to understand how enormous forces may be produced with ease by this press, look at Fig. 269, which is a simplification of Fig. 268, for the purpose of explaining the principle.

Suppose the pump barrel has an area of 0.25 cm^2 and that a force of 10 kgf is applied to its plunger. The applied pressure is equal to

$$\frac{\text{Force}}{\text{Area}} = \frac{10}{0.25} = 40 \text{ kgf per cm}^2$$

This pressure is transmitted equally throughout the whole liquid and, in particular, is exerted upwards on the piston in the large cylinder. If the area of the large piston is 100 cm^2 then the total upward force or thrust on it would be

(Pressure × Area) = 40 × 100 kgf
= 4000 kgf (= 4 tonne f)

A force of 4000 kgf is therefore obtained simply by exerting a force of only 10 kgf.

Hare's Apparatus

In chapter 27 we saw how the relative density of a liquid can be found by using a relative density bottle. An entirely different method for measuring the relative density of a liquid was devised by Hare and is based on the pressure exerted by a liquid column.

The apparatus consists of two vertical, wide-bore glass tubes, connected at the top by a glass T-piece. The two tubes dip into beakers, one containing the liquid whose relative density is required and the other water (Fig. 270).

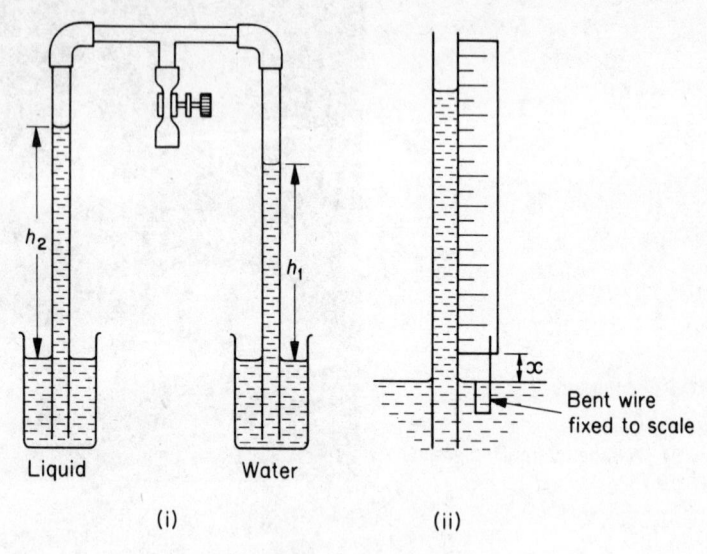

Fig. 270. Hare's apparatus.

Some air is sucked out of the tubes through the centre limb of the T-piece and the clip closed. Removal of some of the air causes a reduction of air pressure inside, with the result that atmospheric pressure forces the liquids up the tubes. The two liquids rise in the tubes until the pressures exerted at the base of each liquid column are both equal to atmospheric pressure.

Now the pressure at the base of a column is made up of two parts,

(a) the pressure p of the air in the tube above the liquid and
(b) the pressure of the liquid column itself.

The pressure of a column of liquid = height × density

Thus if
d_2 = density of liquid, h_2 = height of liquid column
and d_1 = density of water, h_1 = height of water column

then
$$p + h_2 d_2 = p + h_1 d_1$$
Therefore
$$h_2 d_2 = h_1 d_1$$
or
$$\frac{d_2}{d_1} = \frac{h_1}{h_2}$$

But $\qquad \dfrac{d_2}{d_1}$ = R.D. of liquid

Therefore $\qquad \dfrac{h_1}{h_2}$ = R.D. of liquid

One of the difficulties in this experiment is to measure the height of the liquid columns, on account of the meniscus which forms when a boxwood scale touches the surface of the liquid. This may be overcome by the use of a bent wire attached to the lower end of the scale, as shown in Fig. 270(ii). The scale is adjusted until the tip of the wire is just level with the liquid surface. The scale reading of the liquid level in the tube is then taken, and added to the distance x between the tip of the wire and the lower end of the scale.

Several pairs of values of h_2 and h_1 are taken, entered in a suitable table, and the mean value of the relative density of the liquid calculated.

Summary

1. The *common pump* is a device by means of which water is pushed up to a limiting theoretical height of about 10 m by atmospheric pressure.

2. The *force pump* not only utilises atmospheric pressure for lifting water, but also raises the water to a height greater than 10 m by means of a mechanical force exerted on its plunger.

3. *Atmospheric pressure* produces the force which (*a*) holds the cap on a preserving jar and (*b*) holds a suction pad firmly to a flat surface.

4. The *principle of transmission of pressure* in fluids states that any pressure applied to the surface of a fluid is transmitted equally throughout the whole of the fluid.

5. The *hydraulic press* and *hydraulic brakes* are applications of the principle of transmission of pressure in a liquid.

6. *Hare's apparatus* enables the densities of two liquids to be compared by measuring the heights of two liquid columns which exert the same pressure.

EXERCISES

1. Describe the construction of the common pump. Give diagrams to show its two main working strokes and explain its action.

2. Why does the common pump fail to lift water to a height of more than approximately 9 m? Give a diagram of a pump capable of raising water to a height of 20 m and explain its action.

3. Describe how fruit may be preserved in a vacuum jar and explain the principles involved.

4. A force pump lifts water to an average height of 15 m above the pump. Find the average pressure which the pump has to withstand. If the diameter of the barrel of the pump is 70 mm calculate the force which must be exerted on the plunger.

5. State the principle of transmission of pressure in liquids and describe an experiment to illustrate it in the case of water.

6. Give a labelled diagram to show the essential parts of a hydraulic press, and explain its action.

7. The ram of a hydraulic press has an area of cross-section of 80 cm^2; that of the pump is 0·8 cm^2. Find the force which must be applied to the pump piston in order that a load of 2 tonne f may be overcome by the ram.

8. Describe a method of measuring the relative density of a liquid by a method which depends on the pressure exerted by a column of liquid.

CHAPTER THIRTY

The Principle of Archimedes

Upthrust of Liquid

The sight of a boat floating in water, or of a cork bobbing up and down in water, makes us realise that liquids exert an upward force on objects immersed in them. The weight of the boat pulls it downwards, but the water exerts an upward force, called the *upthrust,* which keeps the boat floating. If it were not for the upthrust of the water we should not be able to swim, and ships would sink.

Apparent Loss in Weight

A simple but striking experiment to illustrate the upthrust of a liquid can be shown by tying a length of cotton to a brick. Any attempt to lift the brick by the cotton fails through breakage of the cotton, but if the

Plate *52*. The loss of weight of these large boulders in a flooded river caused them to be carried downstream, uprooting trees and demolishing buildings

brick is immersed in some water in a large trough or sink, it may be lifted quite easily. The water exerts an upthrust on the brick, and the upward force helps the person pulling the cotton to overcome the weight of the brick.

In popular (but not strictly accurate) terms, it is often said that an object appears to "lose weight" when immersed in a liquid. Thus if the upthrust on the brick in water was 2 kgf the "apparent loss" in weight was 2 kgf. If the brick weighed 5 kgf, the upward force required to lift it while totally immersed in the water was only 3 kgf.

Stone boulders immersed in water have an upthrust on them of about four-tenths of their weight. This being so, the ease with which large boulders are moved by water in time of flood becomes less surprising. Much heavy debris was transported by flood water at Lynmouth in the summer of 1952. Some of these boulders weighed 20 tonne, and thus were more easily transported by the force of moving water. Totally immersed they have an apparent weight of about 12 tonne-force.

Archimedes' Principle

Experiments to measure the upthrust of a liquid on an object were first carried out by the Greek scientist Archimedes, who lived in the third century B.C. The result of his work was a most important discovery which is now called Archimedes' Principle. In its most general form, this states:

When a body is wholly or partially immersed in a fluid it experiences an upthrust equal to the weight of the fluid displaced.

It should be noticed that the word "fluid" is used in the above statement. This word means either a liquid or a gas. Its application to gases will be discussed later.

Experiment to verify Archimedes' Principle for a Body in Liquid

A eureka (or displacement) can is placed on the bench with a beaker under its spout (Fig. 271). Water is poured in until it runs from the spout. When the water has ceased dripping the beaker is removed, and replaced by another beaker which has been previously dried and weighed.

Any suitable solid body, e.g. a piece of metal or stone, is suspended by thin thread from the hook of a spring balance and the weight of the body in air is recorded. The body, still attached to the balance, is then carefully lowered into the displacement can, and its new weight noted when it is completely immersed.

When no more water drips from the spout, the beaker containing the displaced water is weighed.

THE PRINCIPLE OF ARCHIMEDES · 319

The results should be set down as follows:

Weight of body in air	=	gf
Weight of body in water	=	gf
Weight of empty beaker	=	gf
Weight of beaker plus displaced water	=	gf
Apparent loss in weight of body	=	gf
Weight of water displaced	=	gf

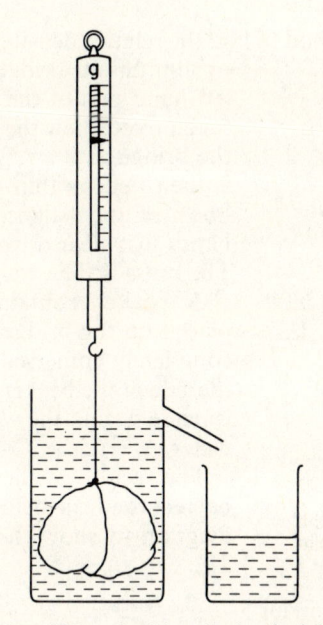

Fig. 271. Archimedes' principle

The apparent loss in weight of the body, or the upthrust on it, should be equal to the weight of the water displaced, thus verifying Archimedes' Principle in the case of water. Similar results are obtained if any other liquid is used.

Relative Density of a Solid using Archimedes' Principle

We have already seen in Chapter 27 that
Relative density of a substance

$$= \frac{\text{Mass of any given volume of substance}}{\text{Mass of an equal volume of water}}$$

Archimedes' Principle gives us a simple and accurate method for finding the relative density of a solid. If we take a sample of the solid and weigh it first in air and then in water, the apparent loss in weight, obtained by subtraction, is equal to the weight of a volume of water equal to that of the sample.

We may therefore write, since weight is proportional to mass

R.D. of substance

$$= \frac{\text{Weight of a sample of the substance}}{\text{Apparent } loss \text{ in weight of the sample in water}}$$

Let us use this method to find the relative density of brass. A wooden or aluminium bridge is placed over the left-hand pan of the balance, care being taken to see that the pan does not touch the bridge as it swings. A piece of brass is then tied by thin thread to the lower hook of the balance stirrup so that it hangs just clear of the top of the bridge. The brass is then weighed.

A beaker containing water is then placed on the bridge so that the brass is completely immersed and does not touch the side of the beaker. A second weighing is made to find the weight of the brass in water.

The results of the experiment should be recorded as below, together with a diagram to show the method as in Fig. 272.

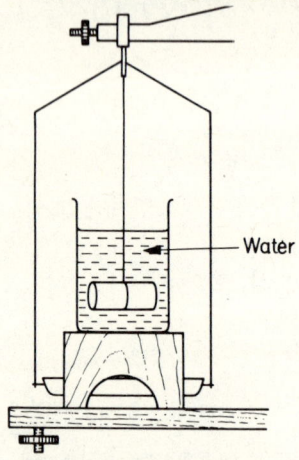

Fig. 272. Measuring the relative density of a solid object

Weight of brass in air = gf

Weight of brass in water = gf

Apparent loss in weight of brass = gf

$$\text{R.D. of brass} = \frac{\text{Weight in air}}{\text{Apparent loss in weight in water}} = \frac{\text{gf}}{\text{gf}}$$

=

Relative Density of a Liquid using Archimedes' Principle

Using the same procedure as in the previous experiment, a sinker is weighed first in air, then in alcohol and finally in water. The sinker is any convenient solid body, e.g. a piece of metal or a glass stopper.

Since the same sinker is used in both liquids, the two apparent losses in weight will be the weights of equal volumes of alcohol and water respectively.

THE PRINCIPLE OF ARCHIMEDES · 321

The results should be recorded as follows:

Weight of sinker in air = gf
Weight of sinker in alcohol = gf
Weight of sinker in water = gf
Apparent loss in weight of sinker in alcohol = gf
Apparent loss in weight of sinker in water = gf

R.D. of alcohol

$= \dfrac{\text{Weight of any given volume of alcohol}}{\text{Weight of an equal volume of water}}$

$= \dfrac{\text{Apparent loss in weight of sinker in alcohol}}{\text{Apparent loss in weight of sinker in water}}$

$= \dfrac{\text{gf}}{\text{gf}}$

$=$

Relative Density of a Solid which Floats

The relative density of a substance which floats in water, such as cork, may be determined if a sinker is used in conjunction with it. A

Sinker in water
x gf

Sinker in water
cork in air y gf

Sinker in water
cork in water z gf

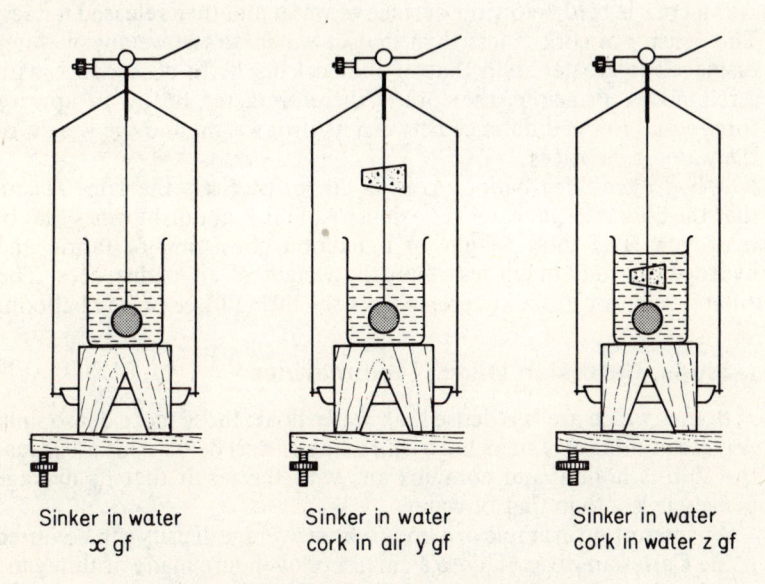

Fig. 273. Measuring the relative density of a cork

piece of lead will serve for this purpose, but any small heavy body will also prove suitable provided it is unaffected by water and is heavy enough to sink the cork when attached to it.

The manner in which the experiment is carried out is illustrated in Fig. 273. The sinker is weighed in water whilst suspended by cotton from the lower hook of the balance. Next, the cork is attached to the cotton *above* the water so that a second weighing may be carried out to find the weight of the cork in air. A third weighing is taken with the cork attached to the cotton so that both cork and sinker are totally immersed in the water. The method of attaching the cork to the cotton, so that the same piece of cotton only is used in each weighing, is left to the reader's own ingenuity.

If the three weighings are called x, y and z gf respectively, we have
$$\text{Weight of cork in air} = (y-x) \text{ gf}$$
$$\text{Upthrust on cork in water}$$
$$= \text{Weight of water displaced} = (y-z) \text{ gf}$$
Hence,
$$\text{Relative density of cork} = \frac{\text{Weight of cork in air}}{\text{Weight of an equal volume of water}}$$
$$= \frac{y-x}{y-z}$$

Corks and Balloons

If a cork is held below the surface of water and then released it rises. The density of cork is less than that of water, so the weight of water displaced is greater than that of the cork itself. In accordance with Archimedes' Principle, the cork is therefore acted on by an upward force equal to the difference between its own weight and the weight of the water it displaces.

A hydrogen-filled balloon rises in air for precisely the same reason that the cork rises in water. The density of air is about 14 times that of hydrogen. The total weight of a balloon consisting of fabric and hydrogen is thus much less than the weight of air it displaces. The difference between the two represents the lifting force on the balloon.

Ships, Cartesian Diver. Submarines

Bodies which are less dense than water float; those more dense sink. A piece of solid steel sinks but a ship made of steel floats. This is because the ship is hollow and contains air, with the result that its average density is less than that of water.

An interesting example of a body whose average density can be varied is the Cartesian diver. This is a small hollow figure made of thin glass and having a hollow, open-ended tail. Normally, being full of air it

Plate 53. A balloon race in 1909. The bags of sand in the foreground were released from the balloon until the weight of the balloon and its load was equal to the weight of air displaced by its volume

floats on water. If, however, the diver is put inside a bottle full of water with a nicely fitting cork, it can be made to sink by pressing in the cork. Pressure on the cork increases the pressure inside the bottle with the result that water is forced into the body of the figure through the hollow tail. The diver thus consists of a mixture of glass, water and air. It will sink, remain stationary or rise in the bottle according as its total weight is greater than, equal to or less than the weight of the water it displaces.

In a similar manner, the buoyancy of a submarine depends on the quantity of water in its ballast tanks. When it is required to dive, water is admitted to special tanks. When the water is ejected from the tanks by means of compressed air, the submarine rises to the surface and floats just like any other ship.

The Law of Flotation

When a piece of wood or other material of density less than that of water is placed in water, it sinks until the weight of water displaced is just equal to its own weight. It then floats.

This fact is sometimes stated as the *Law of Flotation*:

It must be remembered, however, that this is in no sense a new law, but is merely a statement of Archimedes' Principle applied to a special case.

A floating body displaces its own weight of the fluid in which it floats.

An Experiment to Verify the Law of Flotation

A measuring cylinder is about half filled with water and the reading noted. An ordinary test-tube with a cotton loop attached is then placed in the measuring cylinder, and lead shot added to the tube a little at a time until the tube floats upright (Fig. 274).

The new water level reading in the measuring cylinder is taken. The difference between this and the previous reading gives the volume of water displaced by the test-tube. Since the density of water is equal to 1 g per cm^3, we are justified in assuming that the weight of water displaced in gf is numerically equal to its volume in cm^3.

The test-tube is removed from the cylinder, dried, and then weighed, using the cotton loop to attach it to the balance hook.

The experiment is repeated several times, each time adding a little extra lead shot, and a table of results made out as shown.

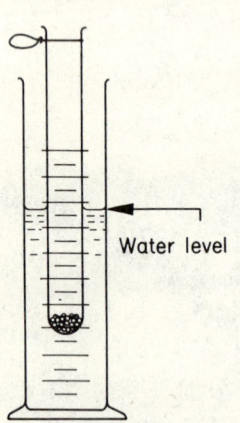

Fig. 274. Testing the law of flotation

Corresponding figures in the first and last columns of this table should be found to agree, thus verifying the Law of Flotation.

Wt. of lead shot and test-tube gf	Measuring cylinder readings in cm^3		Volume of water displaced in cm^3	Wt. of water displaced in gf
	(1)	(2)		

Hydrometers

If we had performed the experiment with the test-tube and lead shot just described with several liquids of differing densities, we should have found that the tube sank to a different level in each of the liquids. In every case, however, the total weight of liquid displaced (numerically equal to volume × density) would have been equal to the weight of the tube and shot, which is constant.

This is the principle of an instrument called a *hydrometer,* used for rapid and easy measurement of the density of liquids.

The modern form of hydrometer shown in Fig. 275 differs scarcely at all from those made by Robert Boyle in the seventeenth century. The lower bulb is weighted with mercury or lead shot to keep it upright, and the upper stem, graduated to read the density of the liquid, is made thin to give the instrument a greater sensitivity. Such hydrometers are usually made in sets of four or more, each covering a certain range of density.

In addition, others are obtainable for special purposes. One, called a lactometer, has a range of relative density from 1·015 to 1·045 and is used for testing milk. Another, enclosed in a glass tube fitted with a rubber bulb, is used for measuring the relative density of accumulator acid. The rubber bulb is squeezed and the short rubber tube dipped below the surface of the acid. On releasing the bulb it expands, causing the air pressure inside to decrease. The greater atmospheric pressure outside pushes acid up into the glass tube, and the density can then be read on the floating hydrometer. The acid in a fully charged cell should have a relative density of 1·25 to 1·30. A reading of less than 1·18 indicates that re-charging is necessary.

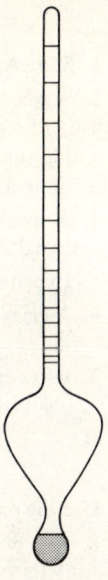

Fig. 275.
A hydrometer

Summary

1. *Archimedes' Principle* states that when a body is wholly or partially immersed in a fluid it receives an upthrust equal to the weight of the fluid displaced.

2. The *Law of Flotation* (Archimedes' Principle applied to floating bodies) states that a floating body displaces its own weight of the fluid in which it floats.

3. The *relative density of a solid* may be determined, using Archimedes' Principle, by weighing a sample of the solid first in air and then in water. The relative density is given by dividing the weight in air by the apparent loss in weight in water.

4. The *relative density of a liquid* may be determined by weighing a sinker, first in air, then in the liquid, and finally in water. The relative density of the liquid is obtained by dividing the apparent loss in weight of the sinker in the liquid by its apparent loss in weight in water.

EXERCISES

1. State Archimedes' Principle, and describe an experiment to verify it.

2. A piece of marble weighs 57·2 gf in air and 35·3 gf in water. Find the relative density of marble.

3. Find the upthrust on a piece of brass of relative density 8·9 and mass 150 g when immersed (*a*) in water, (*b*) in alcohol of relative density 0·79.

4. A wooden cube of side 12 cm floats on water. What volume is immersed? (Relative density of wood = 0·8.)

5. Explain why a ship made of steel floats while a steel bar sinks.

6. A glass stopper weighs 37·5 gf in air, 22·5 in water and 24·0 gf in lubricating oil. Find the relative density of (*a*) glass, (*b*) lubricating oil.

7. In an experiment to determine the relative density of paraffin wax (cf. Fig. 273) the following results were obtained:
   Weight of sinker in water = 63·2 gf
   Weight of sinker in water + wax in air = 78·9 gf
   Weight of sinker in water + wax in water = 61·5 gf
Use the results to find the relative density of paraffin wax.

8. A rubber balloon weighs 5 gf when empty. When filled with hydrogen of density 0·090 kg per m^3; it has a volume of 5 litre. What is the smallest weight which, attached to the ballon, will prevent it from rising in the air? (Density of air = 1·3 kg per m^3, 1 m^3 = 1000 litre.)

9. State the Law of Flotation and describe an experiment to verify it using a test-tube weighted with lead shot.

10. Describe a hydrometer and explain the principle underlying it.

Assume that the force of gravity on a mass of 1 kg is 10 N.

CHAPTER THIRTY-ONE

Parallelogram and Triangle of Forces

Forces and their Resultant

In Chapter 22. we saw that a *force* is measured in newton (N), or sometimes in gf, kgf, or tonne f, and that it can be represented in magnitude and direction by a straight line drawn to scale in the direction of the force. We have now to see how forces can be added together.

Suppose two ropes are attached to a sledge S and pulled in the same direction by two boys with forces of 14 and 20 N respectively (Fig. 276(i)). The total or resultant force is then $14+20$, or 34 N. If one of the ropes is taken off, tied to the other end of S, and pulled with a force of 20 N in the opposite direction, the resultant force is then $20-14$, or 6 N (Fig. 276(ii)).

Plate *54*. 1/18 scale model trawlers being tested in storm conditions in the ship tank at the National Physical Laboratory. The models are guided by forces in the three ropes attached to each one

Resultant force to right = 34 N

[S] → 14 N
    → 20 N

(i)

Resultant force to left = 6 N

20 N ← [S] → 14 N

(ii)

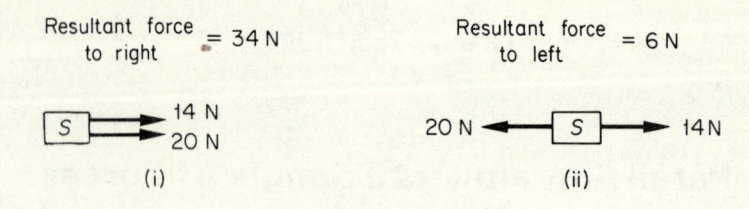

Fig. 276. Resultant forces

Parallelogram of Forces

When two tugs are pulling on a grounded steamer O in different directions OA, OB, with forces of 4000 and 2000 N respectively, their resultant is *not* 6000 N (Fig. 277). In this case, the resultant can be found (1) by drawing a line OA to represent 4000 N in magnitude and direction, and a line OB to represent 2000 N in magnitude and direction, (2) then drawing the parallelogram OBCA by drawing BC

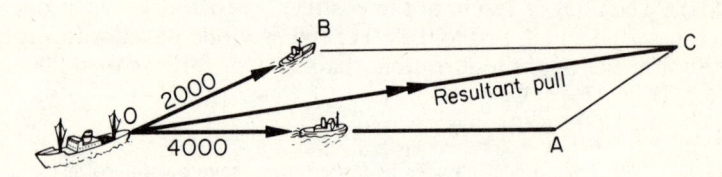

Fig. 277. Resultant of inclined forces

parallel to OA and AC parallel to OB. *The resultant is given in magnitude and direction by the diagonal OC.* Thus, for example, if the scale chosen for OA was 40 mm = 4000 N, and OC, by measurement, was 46 mm long, then

$$\text{Resultant} = 4600 \text{ N}$$

The diagonal OC gives not only the magnitude (size) of the resultant force but also its direction. Thus the steamer at O would tend to move along the direction OC. The parallelogram OBCA is called the "Parallelogram of Forces", because OB, OA represent the two forces.

Experiment to verify Parallelogram of Forces Principle

An experiment to verify the principle of the parallelogram of forces is shown in Fig. 278(i). Spring balances A, B are suspended from two

PARALLELOGRAM AND TRIANGLE OF FORCES · 329

points, and their respective hooks are tied to two strings OH, OL. A knot is made in the strings at O, and a weight W, of 200 gf for example, is suspended from O by a third string OE. The forces P, Q in the strings OH, OL are balanced by the weight W (otherwise the knot O would move). Hence the resultant of P, Q is equal in magnitude to W, the 200 gf and acts in the opposite direction, i.e. vertically upwards.

A sheet of paper (not shown) is now placed behind the strings, and two lines parallel to OH, OL are copied on the paper in pencil. This can also be done by marking the positions of the shadows of the strings

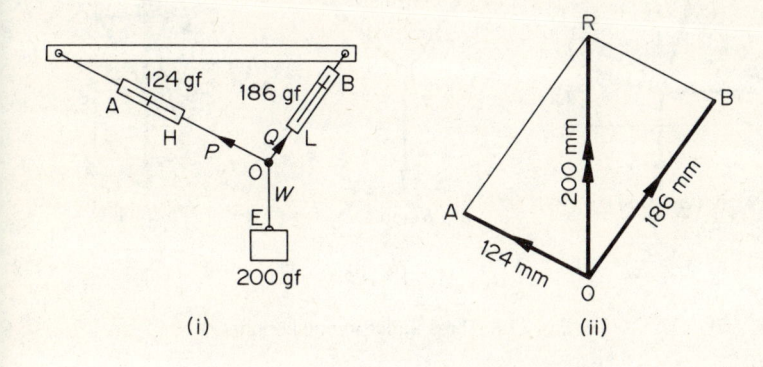

Fig. 278. Testing the parallelogram of forces

formed by light from a distant lamp or window. The readings on the spring balances are observed,* suppose they are 124 and 186 gf respectively, and OA, OB are then drawn along the two lines to represent the two forces on a scale of 1 mm to represent 1 gf (Fig. 278 (ii)). The parallelogram OARB is now completed, and the diagonal OR measured. It will be found to represent very nearly 200 gf. Further, the direction of OR at O in Fig. 278 (i) will be found to be nearly vertical, which is the direction of the resultant of P, Q. Thus the diagonal of the parallelogram represents the resultant.

Three Forces in Equilibrium

There are many cases in which three forces act on an object and keep it in equilibrium. In Fig. 279 (i) an object O is kept on a smooth plane by a horizontal force P. The other forces on O are its weight W, which acts vertically downwards, and the force R due to the plane on the

* Unless used in a vertical position, spring balance readings have slight errors; more accurately, the strings can be passed round pulleys and a weight attached at each end.

object, called the *reaction* of the plane, which acts *at right angles* to the surface if the surface is smooth.

In Fig. 279 (ii) an object A is supported by two strings. The forces on A are its weight W, and the tensions P, Q in the respective strings.

In Fig. 279 (iii) a ladder CD rests against a smooth wall, with the foot C on rough ground. The forces on the ladder are its weight W,

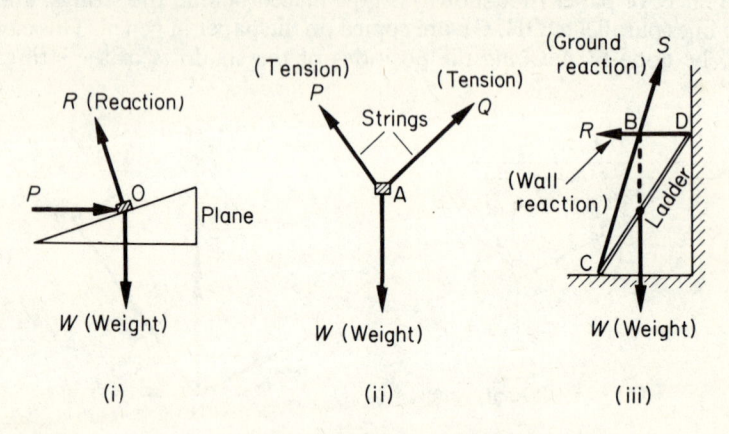

Fig. 279. Three forces in equilibrium

acting at the middle of CD if the weight is distributed evenly, the reaction R at the wall, which acts at right angles to the wall since it is smooth, and the reaction S at the ground, which passes through the point of intersection B of the weight W and R as shown.

Triangle of Forces

Consider an object of weight W, 30 kgf, supported by two strings whose tensions are P, Q kgf respectively (Fig. 280 (i)). If OA, OC

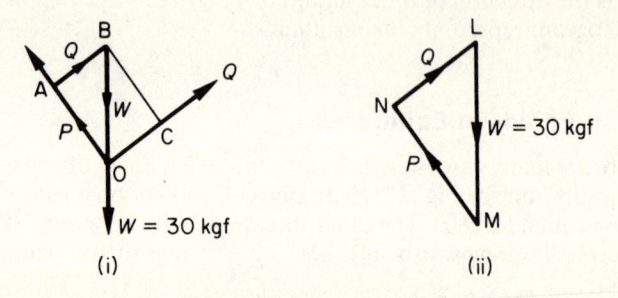

Fig. 280. Triangle of forces

represent P, Q respectively in magnitude and direction, and OABC is the completed parallelogram of forces, then OB represents the resultant of P, Q. Since the object is in equilibrium the resultant of P, Q is equal to W. It therefore follows that OB also represents W.

The side OA of triangle OAB thus represents P, the side AB represents Q since AB = OC, and the side BO represents W. Triangle OAB is therefore called the *triangle of forces* for P, Q, W. The *triangle of forces principle* states: *If three forces acting at a point can be represented in magnitude and direction by the sides of a triangle taken in order, they will be in equilibrium.* This principle is used to find the magnitude of unknown forces, as we now illustrate for the case of Fig. 280 (i).

Firstly, draw the known force W, 30 kgf to scale and in the correct direction; suppose it is represented by LM (Fig. 280 (ii)). Then from L draw a line parallel to one of the two remaining forces, Q say, and from M draw a line parallel to the third force P. If the two lines intersect at N, LNM is a triangle of forces. The line LN is measured, converted to kgf from the scale chosen, and this gives the magnitude of Q. Similarly, MN represents P, and this force can therefore be found.

Summary

1. A *force* is represented in magnitude and direction by a straight line drawn to scale.

2. The Principle of the *Parallelogram of Forces*: If two forces are represented by the sides of a parallelogram drawn to scale, their resultant is represented by the diagonal of the parallelogram passing through their point of intersection.

3. Principle of the *Triangle of Forces*: If three forces acting at a point can be represented in magnitude and direction by the sides of a triangle taken in order, they will be in equilibrium.

4. When *three forces are in equilibrium,* and one force is known the other two forces can be found by first drawing the known force to scale, and then completing the triangle of forces by lines parallel to the others.

EXERCISES

1. A force P of 8 N is inclined at an angle of 30° to a force Q of 10 N, and at an angle of 90° to a force R of 6 N, on the opposite side of it to Q. Draw a diagram of the three forces, stating the scale you use.

2. Find the resultant, by drawing, of the following forces P and Q:
   (i) $P = 32$ N acting at an angle of $60°$ to $Q = 24$ N
   (ii) $P = 150$ gf acting at $90°$ to $Q = 200$ gf
   (iii) $P = 8$ kgf acting at $120°$ to $Q = 5$ kgf.

In each case state the scale used, and also measure the angle which the resultant makes with P.

3. Three ropes pull on an object with forces X (15 N), Y (20 N) and Z (25 N), in this order. The angle between X and Y is $30°$ and between Y and Z it is $90°$. Find the resultant, by drawing, of the three forces. [Begin by adding two of the forces by the parallelogram method, and then add the resultant to the third force by the parallelogram method.]

4. Find the resultant of the following three forces, P, Q, R, in this order, acting on an object:
$$P = 80 \text{ N}, \quad Q = 100 \text{ N}, \quad R = 150 \text{ N}.$$
Angle between P and $Q = 45°$, angle between Q and $R = 60°$.

5. The resultant R of two forces X, Y is 20 N. If $X = 12$ N, and the angle between X and Y is $90°$, find Y by drawing.

6. The resultant R of two forces X, Y is 50 N and acts at $60°$ to X. If $X = 80$ N, find the value of Y.

7. State the *Principle of the Parallelogram of Forces*. Describe an experiment to verify the Principle.

8. A weight of 40 kgf is supported by two strings inclined at $30°$ and $60°$ respectively to the vertical. By drawing the triangle of forces, calculate the tensions (forces) P, Q in the strings.

9. Repeat question 8 if the weight is 100 kgf and the two strings are inclined to the vertical at $45°$ and $60°$ respectively.

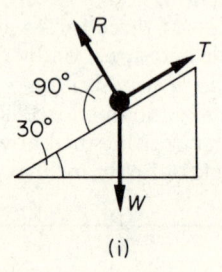

Fig. 281

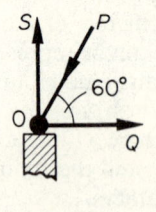

10. In Fig. 281 (i) an object of weight W rests on a smooth plane inclined at $30°$ to the horizontal, and is kept up by a string whose tension is T. R is the reaction (force) of the plane.
   (a) Find R and T if $W = 40$ kgf.
   (b) Find W and R if $T = 60$ kgf.
   (c) If $R = 30$ kgf, find W and T.

11. In Fig. 281 (ii) two girders, with forces P, Q respectively in them, are jointed at O. They rest on a support which exerts a vertical reaction (force S).
  (*a*) Calculate P and Q if $S = 4000$ N.
  (*b*) Find P and S if $Q = 100$ N.
  (*c*) If $P = 80$ N, calculate S and Q.
    Assume that the force of gravity on a mass of 1 kg is 10 N.

Answers

CHAPTER 10
5. 300 mm

CHAPTER 11
11. 1·0 m; 0·9 m

CHAPTER 12
7. Real, inverted, 100 cm from mirror, 4 cm tall
8. Virtual, erect, 2·5 cm from mirror, 0·2 cm tall
9. Virtual, erect, 19 mm from mirror, 5·6 mm high
12. (i) 15 cm; 1·5   (ii) 12 cm; 3·0
13. 6·7 cm; 0·6   **14.** 3·2 cm; 5·0
15. 6 cm   **16.** 36 cm; 2
17. 20 cm; 0·5   **18.** 11·8 cm

CHAPTER 13
4. (i) 22·1°   (ii) 35·2°
5. (i) 19·5°   (ii) 48·6°
7. 48·8°

CHAPTER 14
7. Real, inverted, 84 mm from lens, 28 mm high
8. 31·1 mm; 93·3 mm
9. Virtual, erect, 78·5 mm from lens, 17·3 mm tall
10. Virtual, erect, 45·4 mm from lens, 11·8 mm tall
14. (i) 600 mm; 5·0   (ii) 150 mm; 2·5
15. 40 mm; 5·0
16. (i) 68·6 mm; 0·57   (ii) 30 mm; 0·75

CHAPTER 17
3. 15° C

CHAPTER 18
8. 10·8 mm
9. (a) 5·7 mm   (b) 1·8 mm   (c) 1·2 mm
10. 515° C   **11.** 0·63 m

15. 0·000 125 per K; 0·000 100 per K
16. 0·001 09 per K   17. 23·4 cm

CHAPTER 21
9. 37·0 gf; 11·1 gf

CHAPTER 22
1. 4 N m   2. 0·14 N m anticlockwise; 0·117 N m clockwise
3. (i) 30 cm   (ii) 300 g   4. 4·2 N
5. (i) 51 N   (ii) 18 mm   (iii) 48 N
6. (i) 19·2 N   (ii) 2200 N   (iii) 17 m

CHAPTER 23
4. (a) 180 J   (b) 40 J   (c) 100 000 J
5. 7800 J
6. (a) 400 000 J   (b) 10 000 J per s   (c) 10 kW
7. (a) 1800 J   (b) 300 W
9. (a) Potential energy = 1500 J; kinetic energy = 1500 J
   (b) Potential energy = zero; kinetic energy = 3000 J

CHAPTER 24
1. (a) 355·3 J   (b) 483·6 J   (c) 1040·6 J   (d) 552·5 J
3. (a) 35·1 J per K   (b) 27·75 J per K
4. (d) (b) (a) (c)
5. (a) 38·6° C   (b) 27·0° C   (c) 42·0° C   (d) 21·0° C
6. Water (2940 J)
10. 463° C   11. 2·60 J per g K
13. 35·2 g   14. 0·127 J per g K; lead

CHAPTER 25
2. (a) 1650 J   (b) 7912·8 J   (c) 13 560 J   (d) 39 444 J
3. (a) 2310 J   (b) 2509·2 J   (c) 18 080 J   (d) 23 250·6 J
6. 45 150 J   7. 34·9 g
8. 9·67 g   9. (a) 66 s   (b) 3282 s
11. 198·6 J per g   12. 62·0° C
15. 107·6 g   16. 26·2° C

CHAPTER 26
6. 3·9; 256 N   7. 75%
8. 1200 tonne f   9. 833 N; 863 N
10. 5024 N   11. 33·3 N
12. 51·3 N

ANSWERS · 337

CHAPTER 27
2. (a) 2·5 g per cm³ (b) 19·3 g per cm³ (c) 11·8 g per cm³
   (d) 1·05 g per cm³
3. (a) 200 cm³ (b) 300 cm³ (c) 1266 cm³ (d) 1·25 m³
4. 36 kg
5. 405 g
6. 42·6 g
8. 0·87
9. 750 kg
10. 9·23 m

CHAPTER 28
1. 200 000 kN per m²
3. 392·9 N
6. 103 632 N per m²
8. (i) 4 kN (ii) 25 kN on each face
11. 2667 cm³
12. 2·4 m³
13. 1·5 cm³
14. 1·8 cm³

CHAPTER 29
4. 150 kN per m²
7. 200 N

CHAPTER 30
2. 2·61
3. (a) 0·169 N (b) 0·133 N
4. 1382 cm³
6. (a) 2·5 (b) 0·9
7. 0·90
8. 1·05 g

CHAPTER 31
2. (i) 49 N at 25° to P (ii) 250 gf at 53° to P
   (iii) 7 kgf at 38° to P
3. 37 N at 58° to X
4. 243 N at 63° to P
5. 16 N
6. 70 N at 142° to X
8. 346 N; 200 N
9. 896 N; 732 N
10. (a) 34·6 kgf; 20·0 kgf (b) 120 kgf; 104 kgf
    (c) 34·6 kgf; 17·3 kgf
11. (a) 4619 N; 2310 N (b) 200 N; 173 N
    (c) 69·3 N; 40·0 N

Tables

LOGARITHMS

	0	1	2	3	4	5	6	7	8	9	1	2	3	4	5	6	7	8	9
10	0000	0043	0086	0128	0170	0212	0253	0294	0334	0374	4	8	12	17	21	25	29	33	37
11	0414	0453	0492	0531	0569	0607	0645	0682	0719	0755	4	8	11	15	19	23	26	30	34
12	0792	0828	0864	0899	0934	0969	1004	1038	1072	1106	3	7	10	14	17	21	24	28	31
13	1139	1173	1206	1239	1271	1303	1335	1367	1399	1430	3	6	10	13	16	19	23	26	29
14	1461	1492	1523	1553	1584	1614	1644	1673	1703	1732	3	6	9	12	15	18	21	24	27
15	1761	1790	1818	1847	1875	1903	1931	1959	1987	2014	3	6	8	11	14	17	20	22	25
16	2041	2068	2095	2122	2148	2175	2201	2227	2253	2279	3	5	8	11	13	16	18	21	24
17	2304	2330	2355	2380	2405	2430	2455	2480	2504	2529	2	5	7	10	12	15	17	20	22
18	2553	2577	2601	2625	2648	2672	2695	2718	2742	2765	2	5	7	9	12	14	16	19	21
19	2788	2810	2833	2856	2878	2900	2923	2945	2967	2989	2	4	7	9	11	13	16	18	20
20	3010	3032	3054	3075	3096	3118	3139	3160	3181	3201	2	4	6	8	11	13	15	17	19
21	3222	3243	3263	3284	3304	3324	3345	3365	3385	3404	2	4	6	8	10	12	14	16	18
22	3424	3444	3464	3483	3502	3522	3541	3560	3579	3598	2	4	6	8	10	12	14	15	17
23	3617	3636	3655	3674	3692	3711	3729	3747	3766	3784	2	4	6	7	9	11	13	15	17
24	3802	3820	3838	3856	3874	3892	3909	3927	3945	3962	2	4	5	7	9	11	12	14	16
25	3979	3997	4014	4031	4048	4065	4082	4099	4116	4133	2	3	5	7	9	10	12	14	15
26	4150	4166	4183	4200	4216	4232	4249	4265	4281	4298	2	3	5	7	8	10	11	13	15
27	4314	4330	4346	4362	4378	4393	4409	4425	4440	4456	2	3	5	6	8	9	11	13	14
28	4472	4487	4502	4518	4533	4548	4564	4579	4594	4609	2	3	5	6	8	9	11	12	14
29	4624	4639	4654	4669	4683	4698	4713	4728	4742	4757	1	3	4	6	7	9	10	12	13
30	4771	4786	4800	4814	4829	4843	4857	4871	4886	4900	1	3	4	6	7	9	10	11	13
31	4914	4928	4942	4955	4969	4983	4997	5011	5024	5038	1	3	4	6	7	8	10	11	12
32	5051	5065	5079	5092	5105	5119	5132	5145	5159	5172	1	3	4	5	7	8	9	11	12
33	5185	5198	5211	5224	5237	5250	5263	5276	5289	5302	1	3	4	5	6	8	9	10	12
34	5315	5328	5340	5353	5366	5378	5391	5403	5416	5428	1	3	4	5	6	8	9	10	11
35	5441	5453	5465	5478	5490	5502	5514	5527	5539	5551	1	2	4	5	6	7	9	10	11
36	5563	5575	5587	5599	5611	5623	5635	5647	5658	5670	1	2	4	5	6	7	8	10	11
37	5682	5694	5705	5717	5729	5740	5752	5763	5775	5786	1	2	3	5	6	7	8	9	10
38	5798	5809	5821	5832	5843	5855	5866	5877	5888	5899	1	2	3	5	6	7	8	9	10
39	5911	5922	5933	5944	5955	5966	5977	5988	5999	6010	1	2	3	4	5	7	8	9	10
40	6021	6031	6042	6053	6064	6075	6085	6096	6107	6117	1	2	3	4	5	6	8	9	10
41	6128	6138	6149	6160	6170	6180	6191	6201	6212	6222	1	2	3	4	5	6	7	8	9
42	6232	6243	6253	6263	6274	6284	6294	6304	6314	6325	1	2	3	4	5	6	7	8	9
43	6335	6345	6355	6365	6375	6385	6395	6405	6415	6425	1	2	3	4	5	6	7	8	9
44	6435	6444	6454	6464	6474	6484	6493	6503	6513	6522	1	2	3	4	5	6	7	8	9
45	6532	6542	6551	6561	6571	6580	6590	6599	6609	6618	1	2	3	4	5	6	7	8	9
46	6628	6637	6646	6656	6665	6675	6684	6693	6702	6712	1	2	3	4	5	6	7	7	8
47	6721	6730	6739	6749	6758	6767	6776	6785	6794	6803	1	2	3	4	5	5	6	7	8
48	6812	6821	6830	6839	6848	6857	6866	6875	6884	6893	1	2	3	4	4	5	6	7	8
49	6902	6911	6920	6928	6937	6946	6955	6964	6972	6981	1	2	3	4	4	5	6	7	8
50	6990	6998	7007	7016	7024	7033	7042	7050	7059	7067	1	2	3	3	4	5	6	7	8
51	7076	7084	7093	7101	7110	7118	7126	7135	7143	7152	1	2	3	3	4	5	6	7	8
52	7160	7168	7177	7185	7193	7202	7210	7218	7226	7235	1	2	2	3	4	5	6	7	7
53	7243	7251	7259	7267	7275	7284	7292	7300	7308	7316	1	2	2	3	4	5	6	6	7
54	7324	7332	7340	7348	7356	7364	7372	7380	7388	7396	1	2	2	3	4	5	6	6	7
	0	1	2	3	4	5	6	7	8	9	1	2	3	4	5	6	7	8	9

LOGARITHMS

	0	1	2	3	4	5	6	7	8	9	1	2	3	4	5	6	7	8	9
55	7404	7412	7419	7427	7435	7443	7451	7459	7466	7474	1	2	2	3	4	5	5	6	7
56	7482	7490	7497	7505	7513	7520	7528	7536	7543	7551	1	2	2	3	4	5	5	6	7
57	7559	7566	7574	7582	7589	7597	7604	7612	7619	7627	1	2	2	3	4	5	5	6	7
58	7634	7642	7649	7657	7664	7672	7679	7686	7694	7701	1	1	2	3	4	4	5	6	7
59	7709	7716	7723	7731	7738	7745	7752	7760	7767	7774	1	1	2	3	4	4	5	6	7
60	7782	7789	7796	7803	7810	7818	7825	7832	7839	7846	1	1	2	3	4	4	5	6	6
61	7853	7860	7868	7875	7882	7889	7896	7903	7910	7917	1	1	2	3	4	4	5	6	6
62	7924	7931	7938	7945	7952	7959	7966	7973	7980	7987	1	1	2	3	3	4	5	6	6
63	7993	8000	8007	8014	8021	8028	8035	8041	8048	8055	1	1	2	3	3	4	5	5	6
64	8062	8069	8075	8082	8089	8096	8102	8109	8116	8122	1	1	2	3	3	4	5	5	6
65	8129	8136	8142	8149	8156	8162	8169	8176	8182	8189	1	1	2	3	3	4	5	5	6
66	8195	8202	8209	8215	8222	8228	8235	8241	8248	8254	1	1	2	3	3	4	5	5	6
67	8261	8267	8274	8280	8287	8293	8299	8306	8312	8319	1	1	2	3	3	4	5	5	6
68	8325	8331	8338	8344	8351	8357	8363	8370	8376	8382	1	1	2	3	3	4	4	5	6
69	8388	8395	8401	8407	8414	8420	8426	8432	8439	8445	1	1	2	2	3	4	4	5	6
70	8451	8457	8463	8470	8476	8482	8488	8494	8500	8506	1	1	2	2	3	4	4	5	6
71	8513	8519	8525	8531	8537	8543	8549	8555	8561	8567	1	1	2	2	3	4	4	5	5
72	8573	8579	8585	8591	8597	8603	8609	8615	8621	8627	1	1	2	2	3	4	4	5	5
73	8633	8639	8645	8651	8657	8663	8669	8675	8681	8686	1	1	2	2	3	4	4	5	5
74	8692	8698	8704	8710	8716	8722	8727	8733	8739	8745	1	1	2	2	3	4	4	5	5
75	8751	8756	8762	8768	8774	8779	8785	8791	8797	8802	1	1	2	2	3	3	4	5	5
76	8808	8814	8820	8825	8831	8837	8842	8848	8854	8859	1	1	2	2	3	3	4	5	5
77	8865	8871	8876	8882	8887	8893	8899	8904	8910	8915	1	1	2	2	3	3	4	4	5
78	8921	8927	8932	8938	8943	8949	8954	8960	8965	8971	1	1	2	2	3	3	4	4	5
79	8976	8982	8987	8993	8998	9004	9009	9015	9020	9025	1	1	2	2	3	3	4	4	5
80	9031	9036	9042	9047	9053	9058	9063	9069	9074	9079	1	1	2	2	3	3	4	4	5
81	9085	9090	9096	9101	9106	9112	9117	9122	9128	9133	1	1	2	2	3	3	4	4	5
82	9138	9143	9149	9154	9159	9165	9170	9175	9180	9186	1	1	2	2	3	3	4	4	5
83	9191	9196	9201	9206	9212	9217	9222	9227	9232	9238	1	1	2	2	3	3	4	4	5
84	9243	9248	9253	9258	9263	9269	9274	9279	9284	9289	1	1	2	2	3	3	4	4	5
85	9294	9299	9304	9309	9315	9320	9325	9330	9335	9340	1	1	2	2	3	3	4	4	5
86	9345	9350	9355	9360	9365	9370	9375	9380	9385	9390	1	1	2	2	3	3	4	4	5
87	9395	9400	9405	9410	9415	9420	9425	9430	9435	9440	0	1	1	2	2	3	3	4	4
88	9445	9450	9455	9460	9465	9469	9474	9479	9484	9489	0	1	1	2	2	3	3	4	4
89	9494	9499	9504	9509	9513	9518	9523	9528	9533	9538	0	1	1	2	2	3	3	4	4
90	9542	9547	9552	9557	9562	9566	9571	9576	9581	9586	0	1	1	2	2	3	3	4	4
91	9590	9595	9600	9605	9609	9614	9619	9624	9628	9633	0	1	1	2	2	3	3	4	4
92	9638	9643	9647	9652	9657	9661	9666	9671	9675	9680	0	1	1	2	2	3	3	4	4
93	9685	9689	9694	9699	9703	9708	9713	9717	9722	9727	0	1	1	2	2	3	3	4	4
94	9731	9736	9741	9745	9750	9754	9759	9763	9768	9773	0	1	1	2	2	3	3	4	4
95	9777	9782	9786	9791	9795	9800	9805	9809	9814	9818	0	1	1	2	2	3	3	4	4
96	9823	9827	9832	9836	9841	9845	9850	9854	9859	9863	0	1	1	2	2	3	3	4	4
97	9868	9872	9877	9881	9886	9890	9894	9899	9903	9908	0	1	1	2	2	3	3	4	4
98	9912	9917	9921	9926	9930	9934	9939	9943	9948	9952	0	1	1	2	2	3	3	4	4
99	9956	9961	9965	9969	9974	9978	9983	9987	9991	9996	0	1	1	2	2	3	3	3	4
	0	1	2	3	4	5	6	7	8	9	1	2	3	4	5	6	7	8	9

NATURAL SINES (left-hand column and top)

Differences (ADD)

	0′	6′	12′	18′	24′	30′	36′	42′	48′	54′	—	1′	2′	3′	4′	5′	
0°	·0000	0017	0035	0052	0070	0087	0105	0122	0140	0157	·0175	3	6	9	12	15	89°
1	·0175	0192	0209	0227	0244	0262	0279	0297	0314	0332	·0349	3	6	9	12	15	88
2	·0349	0366	0384	0401	0419	0436	0454	0471	0488	0506	·0523	3	6	9	12	15	87
3	·0523	0541	0558	0576	0593	0610	0628	0645	0663	0680	·0698	3	6	9	12	15	86
4	·0698	0715	0732	0750	0767	0785	0802	0819	0837	0854	·0872	3	6	9	12	14	85
5	·0872	0889	0906	0924	0941	0958	0976	0993	1011	1028	·1045	3	6	9	12	14	84
6	·1045	1063	1080	1097	1115	1132	1149	1167	1184	1201	·1219	3	6	9	12	14	83
7	·1219	1236	1253	1271	1288	1305	1323	1340	1357	1374	·1392	3	6	9	12	14	82
8	·1392	1409	1426	1444	1461	1478	1495	1513	1530	1547	·1564	3	6	9	12	14	81
9	·1564	1582	1599	1616	1633	1650	1668	1685	1702	1719	·1736	3	6	9	11	14	80
10	·1736	1754	1771	1788	1805	1822	1840	1857	1874	1891	·1908	3	6	9	11	14	79
11	·1908	1925	1942	1959	1977	1994	2011	2028	2045	2062	·2079	3	6	9	11	14	78
12	·2079	2096	2113	2130	2147	2164	2181	2198	2215	2233	·2250	3	6	9	11	14	77
13	·2250	2267	2284	2300	2317	2334	2351	2368	2385	2402	·2419	3	6	8	11	14	76
14	·2419	2436	2453	2470	2487	2504	2521	2538	2554	2571	·2588	3	6	8	11	14	75
15	·2588	2605	2622	2639	2656	2672	2689	2706	2723	2740	·2756	3	6	8	11	14	74
16	·2756	2773	2790	2807	2823	2840	2857	2874	2890	2907	·2924	3	6	8	11	14	73
17	·2924	2940	2957	2974	2990	3007	3024	3040	3057	3074	·3090	3	6	8	11	14	72
18	·3090	3107	3123	3140	3156	3173	3190	3206	3223	3239	·3256	3	6	8	11	14	71
19	·3256	3272	3289	3305	3322	3338	3355	3371	3387	3404	·3420	3	5	8	11	14	70
20	·3420	3437	3453	3469	3486	3502	3518	3535	3551	3567	·3584	3	5	8	11	14	69
21	·3584	3600	3616	3633	3649	3665	3681	3697	3714	3730	·3746	3	5	8	11	14	68
22	·3746	3762	3778	3795	3811	3827	3843	3859	3875	3891	·3907	3	5	8	11	13	67
23	·3907	3923	3939	3955	3971	3987	4003	4019	4035	4051	·4067	3	5	8	11	13	66
24	·4067	4083	4099	4115	4131	4147	4163	4179	4195	4210	·4226	3	5	8	11	13	65
25	·4226	4242	4258	4274	4289	4305	4321	4337	4352	4368	·4384	3	5	8	11	13	64
26	·4384	4399	4415	4431	4446	4462	4478	4493	4509	4524	·4540	3	5	8	10	13	63
27	·4540	4555	4571	4586	4602	4617	4633	4648	4664	4679	·4695	3	5	8	10	13	62
28	·4695	4710	4726	4741	4756	4772	4787	4802	4818	4833	·4848	3	5	8	10	13	61
29	·4848	4863	4879	4894	4909	4924	4939	4955	4970	4985	·5000	3	5	8	10	13	60
30	·5000	5015	5030	5045	5060	5075	5090	5105	5120	5135	·5150	3	5	8	10	13	59
31	·5150	5165	5180	5195	5210	5225	5240	5255	5270	5284	·5299	2	5	7	10	12	58
32	·5299	5314	5329	5344	5358	5373	5388	5402	5417	5432	·5446	2	5	7	10	12	57
33	·5446	5461	5476	5490	5505	5519	5534	5548	5563	5577	·5592	2	5	7	10	12	56
34	·5592	5606	5621	5635	5650	5664	5678	5693	5707	5721	·5736	2	5	7	10	12	55
35	·5736	5750	5764	5779	5793	5807	5821	5835	5850	5864	·5878	2	5	7	9	12	54
36	·5878	5892	5906	5920	5934	5948	5962	5976	5990	6004	·6018	2	5	7	9	12	53
37	·6018	6032	6046	6060	6074	6088	6101	6115	6129	6143	·6157	2	5	7	9	12	52
38	·6157	6170	6184	6198	6211	6225	6239	6252	6266	6280	·6293	2	5	7	9	11	51
39	·6293	6307	6320	6334	6347	6361	6374	6388	6401	6414	·6428	2	4	7	9	11	50
40	·6428	6441	6455	6468	6481	6494	6508	6521	6534	6547	·6561	2	4	7	9	11	49
41	·6561	6574	6587	6600	6613	6626	6639	6652	6665	6678	·6691	2	4	7	9	11	48
42	·6691	6704	6717	6730	6743	6756	6769	6782	6794	6807	·6820	2	4	6	9	11	47
43	·6820	6833	6845	6858	6871	6884	6896	6909	6921	6934	·6947	2	4	6	8	11	46
44	·6947	6959	6972	6984	6997	7009	7022	7034	7046	7059	·7071	2	4	6	8	10	45
	—	54′	48′	42′	36′	30′	24′	18′	12′	6′	0′	1′	2′	3′	4′	5′	

Differences (SUBTRACT)

NATURAL SINES (left-hand column and top)

Differences (ADD)

	0'	6'	12'	18'	24'	30'	36'	42'	48'	54'	—	1'	2'	3'	4'	5'	
45°	·7071	7083	7096	7108	7120	7133	7145	7157	7169	7181	·7193	2	4	6	8	10	44°
46	·7193	7206	7218	7230	7242	7254	7266	7278	7290	7302	·7314	2	4	6	8	10	43
47	·7314	7325	7337	7349	7361	7373	7385	7396	7408	7420	·7431	2	4	6	8	10	42
48	·7431	7443	7455	7466	7478	7490	7501	7513	7524	7536	·7547	2	4	6	8	10	41
49	·7547	7559	7570	7581	7593	7604	7615	7627	7638	7649	·7660	2	4	6	8	9	40
50	·7660	7672	7683	7694	7705	7716	7727	7738	7749	7760	·7771	2	4	6	7	9	39
51	·7771	7782	7793	7804	7815	7826	7837	7848	7859	7869	·7880	2	4	5	7	9	38
52	·7880	7891	7902	7912	7923	7934	7944	7955	7965	7976	·7986	2	4	5	7	9	37
53	·7986	7997	8007	8018	8028	8039	8049	8059	8070	8080	·8090	2	3	5	7	9	36
54	·8090	8100	8111	8121	8131	8141	8151	8161	8171	8181	·8192	2	3	5	7	8	35
55	·8192	8202	8211	8221	8231	8241	8251	8261	8271	8281	·8290	2	3	5	7	8	34
56	·8290	8300	8310	8320	8329	8339	8348	8358	8368	8377	·8387	2	3	5	6	8	33
57	·8387	8396	8406	8415	8425	8434	8443	8453	8462	8471	·8480	2	3	5	6	8	32
58	·8480	8490	8499	8508	8517	8526	8536	8545	8554	8563	·8572	2	3	5	6	8	31
59	·8572	8581	8590	8599	8607	8616	8625	8634	8643	8652	·8660	1	3	4	6	7	30
60	·8660	8669	8678	8686	8695	8704	8712	8721	8729	8738	·8746	1	3	4	6	7	29
61	·8746	8755	8763	8771	8780	8788	8796	8805	8813	8821	·8829	1	3	4	6	7	28
62	·8829	8838	8846	8854	8862	8870	8878	8886	8894	8902	·8910	1	3	4	5	7	27
63	·8910	8918	8926	8934	8942	8949	8957	8965	8973	8980	·8988	1	3	4	5	6	26
64	·8988	8996	9003	9011	9018	9026	9033	9041	9048	9056	·9063	1	3	4	5	6	25
65	·9063	9070	9078	9085	9092	9100	9107	9114	9121	9128	·9135	1	2	4	5	6	24
66	·9135	9143	9150	9157	9164	9171	9178	9184	9191	9198	·9205	1	2	3	5	6	23
67	·9205	9212	9219	9225	9232	9239	9245	9252	9259	9265	·9272	1	2	3	4	6	22
68	·9272	9278	9285	9291	9298	9304	9311	9317	9323	9330	·9336	1	2	3	4	5	21
69	·9336	9342	9348	9354	9361	9367	9373	9379	9385	9391	·9397	1	2	3	4	5	20
70	·9397	9403	9409	9415	9421	9426	9432	9438	9444	9449	·9455	1	2	3	4	5	19
71	·9455	9461	9466	9472	9478	9483	9489	9494	9500	9505	·9511	1	2	3	4	5	18
72	·9511	9516	9521	9527	9532	9537	9542	9548	9553	9558	·9563	1	2	3	4	4	17
73	·9563	9568	9573	9578	9583	9588	9593	9598	9603	9608	·9613	1	2	2	3	4	16
74	·9613	9617	9622	9627	9632	9636	9641	9646	9650	9655	·9659	1	2	2	3	4	15
75	·9659	9664	9668	9673	9677	9681	9686	9690	9694	9699	·9703	1	1	2	3	4	14
76	·9703	9707	9711	9715	9720	9724	9728	9732	9736	9740	·9744	1	1	2	3	3	13
77	·9744	9748	9751	9755	9759	9763	9767	9770	9774	9778	·9781	1	1	2	3	3	12
78	·9781	9785	9789	9792	9796	9799	9803	9806	9810	9813	·9816	1	1	2	2	3	11
79	·9816	9820	9823	9826	9829	9833	9836	9839	9842	9845	·9848	1	1	2	2	3	10
80	·9848	9851	9854	9857	9860	9863	9866	9869	9871	9874	·9877	0	1	1	2	2	9
81	·9877	9880	9882	9885	9888	9890	9893	9895	9898	9900	·9903	0	1	1	2	2	8
82	·9903	9905	9907	9910	9912	9914	9917	9919	9921	9923	·9925	0	1	1	2	2	7
83	·9925	9928	9930	9932	9934	9936	9938	9940	9942	9943	·9945	0	1	1	1	2	6
84	·9945	9947	9949	9951	9952	9954	9956	9957	9959	9960	·9962	0	1	1	1	1	5
85	·9962	9963	9965	9966	9968	9969	9971	9972	9973	9974	·9976	0	0	1	1	1	4
86	·9976	9977	9978	9979	9980	9981	9982	9983	9984	9985	·9986	0	0	1	1	1	3
87	·9986	9987	9988	9989	9990	9990	9991	9992	9993	9993	·9994						2
88	·9994	9995	9995	9996	9996	9997	9997	9997	9998	9998	·9998						1
89	·9998	9999	9999	9999	9999	1·000	1·000	1·000	1·000	1·000	1·0000						0
	—	54'	48'	42'	36'	30'	24'	18'	12'	6'	0'	1'	2'	3'	4'	5'	

Differences (SUBTRACT)

The bold type indicates that the integer changes.

Index

Accumulator 1, 2, 4, 52–53
Acoustics 78–94
Air
  as insulator 4
  vibration of column 88–89
Alcohol
  density of 284
  in thermometers 179
Alloys 5
  see also Mumetal, Nichrome, Fuse
Alternator 60
Altimeter 298–299
Altitude 290–291, 300
Ammeter 54, 55–56
Ampere 3
Amplitude 83–84, 90
Aneroid barometer 298–299
Angle of
  declination 28–29
  deviation 141–142
  dip 28
  incidence 102–103, 130–131
  inclination 28
  reflection 102–103
  refraction 130–131
  variation 28–29
Archimedes' principle
  application of 324–325
  and floating bodies 321–324
  to determine relative density 319–322
  verification of 318–319
Armature 56
Atmospheric pressure 289–292, 296–300
  and altitude 290–291, 300
  application in
    preserving jar 310
    pumps 307–310
    suction pad 306
  and barometric pressure 297
  demonstration of 289
Atom, electric charge in 63–64
  see also electron, neutron, proton
Atomic energy 75–76

Balance
  chemical 218–221
  spring 221–223

Balance wheel 193
Balloons 322
Barometers
  aneroid 298–299
  Fortin 298
  Pascal's experiments 297
  simple 296
  water 300
Battery 1, 3–4
  dry cell 51–52
Beam
  electron 74
  light 96
  see also ray, ray box
Bicycle
  mechanical advantage of 270
  torque in 229–230
Bimetal strip 190–192
Binoculars 155–156
Boyle's Law 300–304
Breeze 201–202
Bridges, forces in 226, 233

Cables 5, 43
Calibration of spring balance 221
Calipers 215
Calorimeter (Joule) 247–251, 253
Camera 152–153
Can crushing experiment 289
Car
  brakes 311
  jack 278
Carbon microphone 6–7
Cathode ray tube 73–74
Caustic curve 117–118
Cell
  electric 1–2, 49–53
  photoelectric 74
Celsius scale 174–175
Centre of gravity 234–237
Charges, electric 62–70
  in atoms 63–64
  detecting by electroscope 64–65
  from electrostatic generator 68–69
  induced 65–66
  of lightning 67

INDEX · 345

Chemical balance 218–221
Circuit, electric 4–5
Coil, *see* filament lamps, solenoid
Colour 161–166
Compass 10
Compensation for expansion
   clock pendulum 192–193
   watch balance wheel 193
Concave lens, *see* diverging lens
Concave mirrors 115–127
   focal length of 118, 122–124
   images formed by 122
   optical formulae for 125–127
   wave tank observations 116–117
Conducting wire, electric 5
Conduction, thermal 206–211
   through liquid 210–211
   through solids 206–210
   through gas 181–183
   see also expansion
Conductivity (thermal) of different solids 209–210
Conductors
   electric 4–5, 63
   lightning 67
Conservation of energy, mass and matter 242–243
Construction of ray diagrams
   lenses 149–150
   mirrors 122–124
Convection
   of air 199, 200–202
   application of 200, 202–205
   definition of 205
   explanation of 200
   of liquid 199, 202–205
Converging (convex) lens
   focal length of 151–152
   images formed by 147–149
   optical formulae of 156–158
   types of 145
   use of 152–155
Convex lens, *see* converging lens
Convex mirrors 115–127
   focal length of 118
   images formed by 122
   optical formulae for 125–127
   wave tank observations 116–117
Current, electric 1–8
   alternating 59
   conduction 5
   direct 3
   magnetic effect of 10
   measurement of 3
   potential difference 5–6
   used to make magnets 13–14
   used to demagnetise 14
Critical angle 135–138

Deniell cell 50
Davy safety lamp 208–209
Density
   of alcohol 284
   applications 283–284
   definition of 283
   determination of 284–285
   see also relative density
Demagnetising 14, 26
Depth sounding 85
Deviation of light 141–142
Declination of magnetic needle 28–29
Dip of magnetic needle 28–29
Distance, measure of 214, 215, 216–217
   units of 214
Diverging (concave) lens
   images formed by 149–151
   optical formulae of 156–158
   types of 145
Dynamo 4

Earth as magnet 26–28
Echoes 84–85
Eclipses 98–99
Edison 43
Efficiency, machine 274–276
Effort 271, 274, 278–279
Einstein, mass and energy relation 242–243
Electric
   appliances, bell 37–38
   cooker 42
   filament lamps 43–44
   fluorescent lamps 45
   heater 42
   iron 42–43
   kettle 42
   charges 62–70
   circuit 4–5
   current 1–8
      alternating 59
      conduction 5
      direct 3
      magnetic effect of 10
      measurement of 3
      potential difference 3–4
      used to make magnets 13–14
      used to demagnetise magnets 14
   energy 41–48
      effect on liquids 45–47
      heating effect of 41–45

output in appliances 42
produced by magnets 57–60
resistance 5–6
Electrolysis 45–47
Electromagnet 31–40, 56
Electrons 3, 64, 65–67, 71–75
Electroscope (golf leaf) 64–67
Electrostatic charge 62, 65
Energy
  acoustic (sound) 78–94
  and efficiency 274
  and mass conservation 242–243
  electric 41–48
  luminous (light) 95–101
  mechanical 241
  of motion (kinetic) 241
  potential 241–242, 243
  and power 243–244
  sources of 241
  thermal 247–249
  units of 243
  and work 240–241, 243
Equilibrium
  and force of gravity 235–236
  of parallel forces 233–234
  of three forces 329–330
  stable, unstable, neutral 235–236
Expansion, thermal 181–198
  allowance for 187–188
  compensation for 192–194
  disadvantage of 186–189
  force of 186
  of gases 181–182
  of liquids 181, 182–183
  of solids 185–196
  measurement of cubic 183–185
    of linear 195–196
  use of (bimetal strip) 190–192
Expansivity, thermal
  cubic 183–185
  linear 195–196
Extension of spring 222–223
Eye 153–154

Faraday 45, 57, 59
Fahrenheit scale 175
Filament lamps 43–44
Flasher unit 191
Fleming 72
Flotation law 323–324
Fluorescent lamps 45
Focal length
  of lenses 145–146, 147, 151–152
  of curved mirrors 118, 124–126

Focus
  formulae for lens 156–158
    for curved mirrors 125–127
  principal, of lens 145–146, 147
  of curved mirrors 115–118
  see also image, focal length, ray diagram
Force
  diagrams 227
  of gravity 225–226
  and levers 230–232, 269
  moment of (torque) 227–230, 232, 233–234
  moving 240–245
  parallel 233–234
  parallelogram of 328–329
  reaction 226, 234
  representation of 226–227
  resultant 327–328
  static 226
  three in equilibrium 330
  triangle of 330–331
  units of 226
Force pump 309
Fortin barometer 298
Franklin 67
Frequency of sound vibrations 80–93
  and length of air column 86–88
  and length of string 85–86
  and pitch 82
  and resonance 88
  and stationary waves 90, 91–93
Friction 242, 273
Fulcrum 227, 230
Fusion, latent heat of 257–258
Fuse 43

Galvanometer 168
Gas
  burner power 251
  ignition point 207–208
  pressure measurement 294–295, 300–304
  thermal expansion of 181–183
  thermostat 194
Generator
  electric 59–61
  electrostatic (Van de Graaff) 68–69
Glass, expansion of 190, 193–194
Gold leaf electroscope 64–67
Graph
  of extension of spring 223
  verifying Boyle's law 303–304
Gravity
  centre of 234–237
  force of 225

Hare's apparatus 313–315
Harmonics 84
Heat
  energy loss or gain 251
  form of kinetic energy 241
  latent 257–267
  specific 248–249, 251–255
  see also temperature and thermal references
Heating effect of electric current 41–45
Horsepower 244
Hot water systems 202–205
Huygen 100
Hydraulic pressure 311, 312–313
Hydrometers 324–325
Hydrostatics 292–294, 310–311, 312–313
Hypsometer 175–176

Ice and latent heat 260–261, 262–263
Images
  formed by lenses, converging 147–149
    diverging 149–151
    location of by ray diagram 149–150
  formed by curved mirrors, concave 116, 119–121
    convex 122
    location of by ray diagram 123–124
  formed by plane mirrors 103–104, 106–108, 138–139
    at angles 108–110
    in parallel 110–111
    location of 103
Incidence of light rays 102–103
Inclined plane 276–277
Induced charge 65–67
Induced current 57–60
Induced magnetism 16–18
Insulators, electric 4–5, 63
Iron as magnetic substance 14–15, 36

Joule 243
Joule calorimeter 247–251, 253

Kaleidoscope 110
Kilogramme, standard 218, 220
Kinetic energy 241

Lagging 207
Lamps, electric 4, 5, 43–44, 45
Latent heat 257–267
Lechlanché cell 50
Length, measurement of 214–217

Lenses 144–160
  see diverging and converging
Leslie's cube 169–170
Levers 230, 268–270
Light (luminous energy) 95–101
  and colour 161–167
  nature of 99–100
  reflection of 102–105
  refraction of 130–143
  transmission of 95–101
Lightning 67
Lines of flux 15, 16, 21–23, 32, 34, 35
Liquids
  conduction of heat through 210–211
  convection in 202–205
  pressure in 292–293, 294, 310–311, 312–313
  relative density of
    determined by Archimedes' principle 320–321
    by Hare's apparatus 312–315
    by weight of equal volumes 286–287
  thermal expansion of 181–185
  upthrust in 317
  volume measurement 217–218
Loudness of sound 83–84, 90
Luminous energy, *see* light

Machines 268–281
Magdeburg hemispheres 291
Magnet 9–20
  inducing electric current 56–60
  making 13–14, 35, 36
  properties of 11–12
Magnetic
  fields 15–16, 21–30
  keepers 26–27
  relays 38
  separators 18–20
  substances 12–13, 14–15, 36
Magnetism
  of earth 26–28
  induction of 16–18
  theory of 23–26
Magnification formula
  lens 151
  curved mirror 127
Magnifying glass 147–148
Manometer 294–295
Mass (weight force)
  conservation and energy 242–243
  measurement of 218–223
  units of 218

Maximum and minimum thermometer (Six's) 177, 179
Measurement 213–224
   distances 214, 215, 216–217
   liquid volume 217–218
   mass (weight force) 218–223
Mechanical advantage 231
   of bicycle 270
   of inclined plane 277
   of lever 268–270
   of pulley 271–273, 274–275
   of wheel 280
Melting point 258–259
Mercury thermometer 173–177, 179
Metre, standard 214
Micrometer gauge 216–217
Microphone (carbon) 6–7
Microscope 154
Miners' safety lamp 208–209
Mirage 140–141
Mirrors
   curved 115–129
   plane 102–114, 138, 139
   see also focal length, image, etc.
Molecules, size of 76
Moment of force, see torque
Motor, electric 56–57, 58
Moving coil
   ammeter 55–56
   galvanometer 33
   voltmeter 55–56
Moving iron instruments 54–56
Mumetal 16–17
Music notes 84, 86, 90, 93
Musical instruments 85–93

Neutral point in magnetic field 21–22
Neutrons 75
New Cartesian convention
   lens 156–158
   mirror 125–126
Newton 99, 121, 161–163
Newton (N) unit of force 226
Nichrome 5, 42
Nife cell 53
Noise 80
Notes, musical 84, 86, 90, 93
Nuclear energy 75–76

Ohm 5
Optical centre of lens 147
Optical formulae 125–126, 156–158
Optical illusions 112–113
Organ pipes 86–89, 91–93

Oscilloscope 73, 78, 82–84

Parallax 105–106
   error in measurement 214
Parallel forces 233–234
Parallel mirrors 110
Parallelogram of forces 328–329
Pascal's experiments 297
Pendulum 192–193
Pepper's ghost 112
Periscope 111, 139
Permanent magnets 35
Photoelectric cell 74
Pinhole camera 97
Pipes, vibration in 86–88, 91–93
Pitch 82, 83
Potential difference 3–4
Potential energy 241–242, 243
Power 243–244
   of electrical devices 142
   of gas burner 251
   units of 244
Preserving jar 310
Pressure
   definition of 289, 294
   electric, see potential
   expression of 290
   and volume of gas (Boyle's law) 300–304
   see also atmospheric, gas, liquid
Principal focus
   lens 145–146, 147
   curved mirror 115–118
Principle of work 277, 278
Prism 139–140, 141–142
   comparison with lens 146
   light dispersion through 161–163
Protons 64, 75
Pulleys 271–273, 274–276
Pumps 307–310
Pyrex glass 190, 193

Quantum theory of light 100

Radar 73–74
Radiation
   nature of 168, 172
   thermal, absorption by different surfaces 170
   detection of 168–169
   detection of from different surfaces 169–170
   uses of 171–172
Radio valve 71–73

Railway lines, expansion of 187
Ray 95
  box 96, 134
  diagrams, lens 149–150
    mirrors 122–124
  incident 102–103, 141–142
  for locating images 118–119
  reflected 102–103
Reaction of force 226, 234
Real images 116, 120–121, 122–123
"Real is positive" convention
  lens 156–158
  mirrors 125–126
Reflecting telescope 121–122
Reflection of light 102–103
  diffuse 105
  law of 103
  total internal, in prism 139–140
  see also image, wave tank observations
Refraction of light 130–143
  experiments 132–134
  law of 134
Refractive index 134–135, 137–138, 157
Refrigerator 260–261
Relative density 286–287
  determination of by Archimedes' principle 319–320
    by Hare's apparatus 312–315
    by weight of equal volumes 286–287
Relays (magnetic) 38
Resistance wire 5, 6
Resonance 88
Reversibility of light 135
Rheostat 5, 6

Screw as machine 278
Seebeck's disc 82
Shadows 98
Snell's law (refraction) 134
Solenoid 14, 34–35
Solids
  density of 284
    relative density of 287
  measurement of dimensions of 215
    of mass of 215–223
  thermal conduction through 206–210
    expansion of 185–196
      disadvantage of 186–187
      force of 185
      measurement of 195–196
      use of (bimetal strip) 190–192
Sonometer 85
Sound 78–94
  nature of 78–81
  track 74

  transmission of 79
  vibrations 78–79
    of strings 85–86
    in pipes 87–88
  wave tank observations 79–80
  see also frequency, pitch, wavelength
Specific heat capacity 248–249, 251–255
  of copper 252–253
  of other metals 253–254, 255
  of liquids 254
  rule of 249
Specific latent heat 257–258, 263–265
Spectrum 161–163
Speed ratio, see velocity ratio
Spring balance 221–223
  rule of extension 222
Standard metre 214
  kilogramme 218
Stationary waves 89–93
Stationary forces 225–239
Steam, specific latent heat of 263–265
Stringed instruments 84, 85, 89, 90–91
Surfaces and thermal radiation 169–170
Swann 43
Symbols in electric circuit 5

Telegraph system, early 33–34
  magnetic relay 38
Telephone 6–7, 36–37
Telescope, reflecting 121–122
  refracting 155
Television 6, 73–74, 75
Temporary magnets 36–38
Temperature 173–180
  Celsius scale 174–175
  definition of 180
  Fahrenheit scale 175
  fixed points 174, 175, 176
Theories of light behaviour 100
  of magnetism 23–26
Thermal
  capacity 248, 249–251, 253
    rule 249
  conduction, see conduction
  energy measurement 246–256
  expansion, see expansion
  radiation, see radiation
Thermionic emission 72–75
Thermocouples 168–169
Thermometers 173–189
  bimetal 192
  maximum and minimum 177, 179
  mercury
    making 173
    clinical 177
      advantages over alcohol 179

Thermopile 169
Thermostat, electric 191
    gas 194
Timbre 83–84
Tonne 218
Torch cell 1–2, 4, 5, 51–52
Torricelli's experiment 296
Torque 227–232
    calculation of 227–228
    clockwise, anticlockwise 228, 233–234
    demonstration of 229
    example of 229–230, 232
    rule of 228
Transistor 73
Transmission of light 95–101
    of sound 79
Triangle of forces 330–331
Tuning fork 78, 80–81, 86
Turning moment, *see* torque

Vacuum flask 171–172
Vacuum pump 291–292
Vaporisation, latent heat of 257
Variable resistance 5, 6
Variation of magnetic needle 28–29
Velocity ratio
    and efficiency 247
    of inclined plane 277
    of pulley 273
    of wheel and axle 279
Vernier scale 215–216
Vibration, sound 78–93
    nature of 78–81
    in pipes 86–88, 91–93
    of strings 85–86, 90–91
    see also frequency
Virtual images 107, 116, 119, 120

Vision, persistence of 163
Volatility 259–260
Volt 3
Volta 1, 49
Voltameters 45–46
Voltmeter 55
Volume
    measurement of, liquid 217–218
    and pressure of gas (Boyle's law) 300–304
    units of 218

Water barometer 300
Watt, definition of 244
    unit of power 42, 43
Wave, sound 78–94
    stationary 89–93
    see also frequency
Wave theory of light behaviour (Huygen) 100
Wave tank observations
    light reflection, curved mirrors 116
    plane mirrors 104–105
    light refraction 131
    sound 79–80
Wavelength 80–83
Weight
    definition of 225
    apparent loss in 317–318
    see also mass
Wheel and axle as machine 279
Work
    and energy 240–241, 243
    of machine (efficiency) 274
    and power 243–244
    principle of 277, 278